of related interest

Promoting the Emotional Well Being of Children and Adolescents and Preventing Their Mental Ill Health
A Handbook
Edited by Kedar Nath Dwivedi and Peter Brinley Harper
ISBN 1 84310 153 X

Disorganised Children
Edited by Uttom Chowdhury and Samuel Stein
ISBN 1 84310 148 3

Mental Health Aspects of Autism and Asperger Syndrome
Mohammad Ghaziuddin
ISBN 1 84310 733 3 hardback
ISBN 1 84310 727 9 paperback

Kids in the Syndrome Mix of ADHD, LD, Asperger's, Tourette's, Bipolar, and More!
The one stop guide for parents, teachers, and other professionals
Martin L. Kutscher MD, with contributions from Tony Attwood PhD and Robert R. Wolff MD
ISBN 1 84310 810 0 hardback
ISBN 1 84310 811 9 paperback

Raising a Child with Autism
A Guide to Applied Behavior Analysis for Parents
Shira Richman
ISBN 1 85302 910 6

Conduct Disorder
and Behavioural Parent Training

Research and Practice

Dermot O'Reilly

Foreword by Brian Sheldon

Jessica Kingsley Publishers
London and Philadelphia

First published in 2005
by Jessica Kingsley Publishers
116 Pentonville Road
London N1 9JB, UK
and
400 Market Street, Suite 400
Philadelphia, PA 19106, USA

www.jkp.com

Library of Congress Cataloging in Publication Data
O'Reilly, Dermot, 1956-
    Conduct disorder and behavioural parent training : research and practice / Dermot
O'Reilly ; foreword by Brian Sheldon.
        p. cm.
    Includes bibliographical references (p.   ) and indexes.
    ISBN-13: 978-1-84310-163-5 (pbk. : alk. paper)
    ISBN-10: 1-84310-163-7 (pbk. : alk. paper) 1. Conduct disorders in children--Treat-
ment. 2. Child psychotherapy--Parent participation. 3. Behavior therapy for children. 4.
Behavior modification. 5. Child rearing. 6. Parenting. I. Title.
    RJ506.C65O74 2005
    618.92'89--dc22
                                        2005010915

British Library Cataloguing in Publication Data
A CIP catalogue record for this book is available from the British Library

ISBN-13: 978 1 84310 163 5
ISBN-10: 1 84310 163 7

Printed and Bound in Great Britain by
Athenaeum Press, Gateshead, Tyne and Wear

To Suzanne, as ever,
and to Dan, Evin, Adam and Nathan

Acknowledgements

This book is based on research which was conducted for a postgraduate degree at the School of Social Work, Queen's University Belfast. I am indebted to Dr Karola Dillenburger who, as my academic supervisor, introduced me to the discipline of applied behaviour analysis in 1994, and who guided me through fogs of incomprehension and self-doubt during the course of the next seven years.

I owe an immense debt of gratitude to a range of people who provided assistance to me in conducting the research: to the 11 families who participated in the studies and who so readily welcomed me into their homes; to Dr Judy Hutchings of the Child Behaviour Project, Bangor, North Wales (now Incredible Years Wales) for her generous advice on high-intensity behavioural parent training; to Professor Dorota Iwaniec, School of Social Work, Queen's University Belfast, who acted as my second supervisor, for her advice and encouragement; to the Dr Diane Jones Bursary, for financial support which prompted me to convert the thesis into book form; to Patricia Byrne (MSW), Jenny Casey (MSW), Deirdre McCabe (MSW), Nora McCafferty and Ruth Byrne (MSW) who collected data; to Dr Joan Michael and my colleagues at Lucena Clinic, Bray, Co. Wicklow for their goodwill and support; to Dr Peter Reid, whose commitment to evidence-based practice has been an inspiration; to the management team at Lucena Clinic who helped me to balance the demands of research activities with clinical responsibilities; and to my employers, the Hospitaller Order of St John of God, whose commitment and support to research activities made the whole daunting task possible.

Chapter 1 was first published in the *Irish Journal of Social Work Research*, and is reprinted with kind permission. Study 1 was first published in 1997 in *Advances in Behaviour Analysis* by University College Dublin Press, and is reprinted with kind permission. Studies 2 and 3 were published in *Research on Social Work Practice*, and are reprinted with kind permission.

Finally, I am responsible for all the views expressed in this book.

Contents

Part 2 Implementing Behavioural Parent Training

List of figures

List of tables

Foreword

A very curious thing happened in the field of applied behavioural analysis (ABA) recently: the academic editor of the premier US journal appeared to call for less research(!) Thus, breaking all the rules of membership, since academics have to make a solemn promise always to call for *more*. Eccentrically, he suggested that we really have little further need for large, randomised controlled trials on the effectiveness of these procedures; the work has been done and its effectiveness well established. The editor went on to say that the biggest challenge now facing us is to establish these techniques in standard, routine practice, not just with psychotherapy clients who can afford to pay, or with those who can't but can survive the long waiting times for help, but in ordinary, and sometimes up-against-it communities. Spot on, as far as Dermot O'Reilly and I are concerned. But what are the impediments to this worthy aim? Dr O'Reilly addresses these throughout his lucid volume and I have some experience myself of this rough trade. Now for the obstacles:

1. There is an unnatural, but nonetheless well-entrenched separation between academic research (we fence with each other after the manner of the georgic poets – clever stuff, but often a bit off the point) and evaluations of clinical practice. Yet the appliance of science is our raison d'être. To switch analogies, it is the difference between steeplechasing and dressage.

2. Dr O'Reilly makes a compelling case – one of the best I have seen – for making behavioural approaches readily available to troubled families, and then rigorously evaluating what happens when you do. The content of these discussions of hands-on work in unpropitious circumstances is inspiring. They represent just what we are for. But there is also a paradox confronting us because training courses in these techniques have been around for years.

There is also a massive research literature testifying to their effectiveness, where most other approaches make either no, or only marginal differences. Yet, perversely, these are the techniques least likely to be taught on a social work training course, either at qualifying level or afterwards. When they are (e.g. as part of the Centre for Evidence-Based Social Services project, or by the excellent group of staff at Queens University Belfast) the courses and supervision arrangements are highly valued, but the level of practical application remains disappointingly low at about 30–40 per cent. Were we to apply the principles of applied behavioural analysis to this problem we would quickly conclude that the reinforcement contingencies in the workplace are rather adverse. That is, staff spend 70–80 per cent of their time, not in face to face contact with clients, but on target-chasing administrative tasks aimed at preventing loss of face by the organisation: 'virtual reality social work' I call it. So, the clients themselves are encouraged to make behavioural changes to their lives by groups of professionals who feel they have little or no control over their own. This is perverse, and we must address this problem. At present our best hope of re-establishing a therapeutic role for social care staff (very few problems are simply practical in nature) is through learning the lessons from specialist projects like the one described in this volume – which offers not only a thorough grounding in effective practice, but a guide to how to get to be allowed to do it in the first place.

The strengths of this book are as follows:

- It gives a thorough grounding in the theory and research which gave rise to the approach – everything here is accurate and cogently explained and exemplified.

- The case studies are detailed and 'warts and all' descriptions, in contrast to some texts which give the impression that all this is pretty straightforward – it isn't.

- Just about everything being argued for is backed by research of good quality – a tenet of the broader evidence-based practice movement, at last becoming established.

- Nevertheless, with all this work done, there is no neglect of issues regarding the process of helping or of ethical concerns.

- The book is written in an accessible style, which should appeal to social work, nursing, and medical personnel, but is not written in the 'Janet and John' language of many recent publications: 'engage and support', 'enable and promote'.

If there is something practitioners need to know, even if it is a bit complicated, then Dr O'Reilly has a sympathetic go, and regularly reminds readers that the application of 'current best evidence' is an ethical as well as a technical obligation.

This volume will be on my shelf, and, if my powers of persuasion have not waned too much, on the shelves of staff and students who come across me. An excellent, scholarly, but essentially practical book. Saluté. One to keep at your elbow.

Professor Brian Sheldon
University of Exeter

Introduction

The impulse to discover an effective method of intervention for conduct disorder arose through my own practice experience. As a social worker, based in a special school for children with severe emotional and behavioural problems between 1986 and 1995, I had responsibility for working with the child in the family context. My clinical impression was that behavioural gains in the school setting were not transferred to the home setting, where parents of conduct-problem children reported that they continued to find the child's behaviour unmanageable. This was confirmed by Fitzgerald, Butler and Kinsella (1990) who found that parents having a child who was placed in a special school reported with frustration that they were not taught how to manage their child in the home setting. I shared their frustration, because it was evident that these children were usually manageable in the school setting. Generic social work training and post-qualifying training in family therapy did not, however, provide the means to intervene effectively with the child's behaviour in the home setting.

The research which is presented in this book was conducted in the course of the development of a high-intensity behavioural parent-training programme for children with significant conduct problems. This client group has not responded well to traditional methods of social work intervention. The programme is based on applied behavioural analysis, an approach which is not widely used in therapeutic social work practice. This book is intended to contribute to the treatment of child conduct problems, as well as to the expansion of social work practice methods which is now occurring within the context of a renewed emphasis on evidence-based therapeutic practice in general (Carr 1999). It is also intended to exemplify the positive contribution which behavioural methods in general, and applied behaviour analysis in particular, can make to social work practice.

During the last 25 years, the treatment of conduct disorder has moved from occupying a marginal position, where it was regarded as unproductive and resistant to the best efforts of health and social service personnel, to its current position as the focus of health, social service and political strategies. Conduct disorder is no longer viewed as resulting from intractable individual pathology, but as resulting from the coincidence of individual, familial and social factors, and, most important, as being amenable to intervention. Painstaking research on conduct disorder and on behavioural parent training during this period of time has transformed the landscape and provides the basis of the current optimism in the field.

This book aims to provide a comprehensive introduction to the field of conduct disorder and behavioural parent training (BPT). It is designed to complement a number of outstanding texts in the area; Forehand and McMahon (1981), Sanders and Dadds (1993) and Webster-Stratton and Herbert (1994). It is also designed as an introduction to the principles and practice of applied behaviour analysis. It is beyond the scope of this book to provide a comprehensive overview of applied behaviour analysis. For an exhaustive account of procedures and issues relating to applied behaviour analysis in general, the reader is referred to Cooper, Heron and Heward (1987). For an equally thorough and highly engaging account of the principles of applied behaviour analysis, the reader is referred to Grant and Evans (1994).

Part 1, 'Conceptual Framework and Empirical Background', provides an introduction to the methodology (applied behavioural analysis), the client group (conduct-problem children) and the intervention strategy (behavioural parent training) which together are the focus of this book. One of the basic tenets of applied behaviour analysis is that studies should include explicit and comprehensive descriptions of all procedures which are used, to the extent that it should be possible to replicate them. Part 2 provides a detailed account of a sequence of studies and also includes an overview of the assessment protocol which was used (Chapter 4), and the observational coding scheme which was used for data collection (Appendices II and IV).

Chapter 1 provides an overview of applied behaviour analysis, issues relating to social work and scientific practice, and ethical issues relating to practice-based research.

Chapter 2 examines childhood conduct disorder in terms of the methods by which it is classified, its prevalence, and its course and outcome. A range of factors which are associated with conduct disorder, including child-specific, ecological and family factors, are examined. These factors are reviewed in terms of their implications for parent–child interactions.

Finally, the role of parent–child interactions in the development and maintenance of child conduct disorder is discussed.

Chapter 3 examines BPT as a method of treatment for conduct disorder. It examines the triadic model, alternative training formats and the expansion of the treatment paradigm.

Part 2, 'Implementing Behavioural Parent Training', focuses initially on the assessment of child conduct problems. Chapter 4 focuses on the assessment procedure and describes the initial assessment interview in terms of content and process, parent records, behavioural checklists and behavioural observations.

Chapter 5 reviews the use of compliance training within BPT and Study 1 examines the effectiveness of a compliance training strategy for the treatment of moderate/severe child conduct problems. Chapter 6 reviews punishment techniques and the controversies which have arisen over their use in the context of BPT, and Study 2 examines the effectiveness of high-intensity training in time out. Chapter 7 reviews positive parenting practices and Study 3 examines the effects of teaching parents a broad range of attentional skills. Chapter 8 reviews the generalisation of treatment effects. Study 4 examines the generalisation of treatment effects to an untreated sibling, and Study 5 examines the generalisation of treatment effects from the home to the school setting.

Chapter 9 presents an overview of the studies presented in Chapters 5 to 8 and examines the following topics: compliance training, effective discipline, positive parenting practices, generalisation of treatment effects and ethical issues. It also considers practice issues and areas for future research.

While a broad range of terms has been used to describe child problem behaviour this book adopts the term *conduct disorder*. It is used as a generic term rather than connoting a formal medical diagnosis, as proposed by Gardner (1992), on the basis that it has practical utility and empirical support:

> Children with CD exhibit a wide range of behaviours that can be classified as antisocial to some degree, such as aggression, temper tantrums, disobedience, destructiveness, rudeness, defiance, lying, restlessness, and disruptiveness at school. To be considered as conduct-disordered, children need to show several of these behaviours, persisting for at least six months, and occurring more frequently than in most children of the same age. (p.136)

The description *conduct-problem* is used in preference to *conduct-disordered* on the basis that it is less suggestive of an underlying disorder and does not constitute a label to the same extent. The term *therapist* is used, although I wish to emphasise that the relationship with clients was collaborative rather than instrumental. The terms *client* and *parent* are interchanged throughout. As the majority of children with conduct problems are boys, and as children in the studies described in Chapters 5 to 8 were exclusively male, I plead immunity from gender bias for having referred to conduct-problem children as male.

Part 1

Conceptual Framework and Empirical Background

Chapter 1

Integrating applied behaviour analysis into social work practice

Paradigms of social work theory

Before proceeding to examine what constitute behavioural methods, it is important to locate behavioural social work practice within the broad spectrum of activities which social work accommodates. Behavioural social work has been defined as:

> the informed use, by professional social workers, of intervention techniques based upon empirically-derived learning theories that include but are not limited to, operant conditioning, respondent conditioning, and observational learning. Behavioural social workers may, or may not subscribe to the philosophy of behaviourism. (Thyer and Hudson 1987, p.1, cited in Gambrill 1995, p.469)

The use of intervention techniques which are based on the philosophy of behaviourism clearly identifies the position which behavioural social work occupies within social work theory. Howe (1987) adopted a system of classifying sociological theories which was devised by Burrell and Morgan (1979) and generated four paradigms into which social work theories could be accommodated, according to whether they involved social change or social regulation, and according to whether they viewed people and society in 'subjective' or 'objective' terms:

1. the *functionalists* (termed 'fixers' by Howe), whose activities involve individual adjustment rather than social change. Functionalists examine regularities in human relationships and view individuals from the standpoint of an objective observer. Behavioural and psychoanalytic social work are located within this paradigm.

2.   the *interpretivists* (termed 'seekers after meaning' by Howe), whose activities involve individual adjustment rather than social change, and who consider that subjective experience holds the key to understanding human relations. Client-centred approaches are located within this paradigm.

3.   the *radical humanists* (termed 'raisers of consciousness' by Howe), whose activities are designed to lead to social change fuelled by the subjective experience of inequality and oppression. Radical social work and feminist theory are located within this paradigm.

4.   the *radical structuralists* (termed 'revolutionaries'), whose activities pose a direct challenge to mainstream social work practice. Marxist social work is located within this paradigm, although Howe acknowledges that, as Marxist theory has also influenced the radical humanists, the distinction between both paradigms in terms of subjectivity and objectivity is somewhat tenuous.

Howe (1987) proposes that theories that are located within the functionalist paradigm are, in political terms, reformist:

> Of course, some changes in social organisation are necessary if equilibrium is to be held. For example, if the poorest members of society are too hard done by, they become restive. This would threaten social stability. Functionalists, therefore…are quite prepared to go in for modest social engineering. (p.52)

Behavioural social work therefore belongs to the functionalist paradigm of social work theories and is concerned with individual rather than social change. It is a form of therapeutic social work practice whose principles and priorities are different from, and not necessarily applicable to, other activities in which social workers engage (Sheldon 1995). These principles and priorities are now examined.

Applied behaviour analysis

The term *behaviourism* originated in a paper which was published by J.B. Watson in 1913, entitled 'Psychology as the behaviourist views it', in which he drew upon the objective tradition of psychology which had emerged in the nineteenth century (Baum 1994). Watson expressed the uneasiness psychologists who espoused the objective tradition felt with introspection as a method of enquiry because it relied too much on the individual (Watson 1913). The term behaviourism refers to the set of ideas upon which the science of behaviour is based, and it has been described as a philosophy of science, rather than the science of behaviour itself (Baum 1994). Behaviourism is based upon the central premise that 'there can be a science of behaviour' (Baum 1994, p.3). *Behaviour modification* refers to the assessment, evaluation and alteration of behaviour according to behavioural principles, and is conducted within a broad range of social, educational and therapeutic settings; 'The approach focuses on the treatment of clinical problems and on the development of adaptive functioning in everyday life' (Kazdin 1994, p.1). Kazdin identifies applied behaviour analysis as a form of behaviour modification and proposes that, rather than being a single entity, behaviour modification is a collective term for a range of practices that share the following major characteristics:

- they regard behaviour as the primary focus of interest
- they assert that behaviour can be changed through the provision of new learning experiences
- they rely on direct and active treatments
- they are committed to the assessment and evaluation of treatment methods
- they recruit key personnel from the learning environment, such as teachers, parents and institutional staff, to participate in the delivery of treatment.

While Kazdin contends that applied behaviour analysis is a form of behaviour modification, Walshe (1997) argues that behaviour modification is outmoded, and that it needs to be replaced by an approach which is based more directly on behavioural principles.

Mediational and *non-mediational* concepts of learning have given rise to two distinct traditions within the field of behaviour therapy (Kazdin 1994). Mediational concepts of learning recognise the role of subjective states and cognitions (such as perceptions, plans, attributions and expectations) in processing or mediating environmental events. Mediational concepts emerged in the context of the *cognitive revolution* which took place in the 1970s, when behavioural therapists began to designate their activities as *cognitive-behavioural* (Sheldon 1995). Kazdin (1994) identifies social learning theory, which belongs to the mediational tradition, as the dominant view within contemporary behaviour therapy because:

it recognizes the importance of both cognitive and environmental influences and their interaction. A broad social learning view is a useful way of considering multiple influences on behaviour and of incorporating research from different areas. (p.24)

Radical behaviourism is based on non-mediational concepts of learning and provides the philosophical basis for *behaviour analysis*, a discipline which focuses exclusively on observable behaviour and environmental variables (Skinner 1953). Mattaini and Thyer (1996) identify a number of distinct but interrelated activities within behaviour analysis which include:

- the *experimental analysis of behaviour*, which involves laboratory research with humans and animals and of which Skinner's own experimental work with pigeons and rats is an example

- the *conceptual analysis of behaviour*, which involves theoretical and historical explorations (for example, Baum 1994)

- *cultural analysis and design*, which seeks to understand and design social systems (for example, Thyer 1996)

- *applied behaviour analysis*, of which the research which is presented in this book is an example.

Applied behaviour analysis has a more narrow focus than forms of behaviour therapy that are based on mediational concepts of learning and that attempt to generate broad theories of behaviour (Kazdin 1994).

In 1968, Baer, Wolf and Risley published 'Current dimensions of applied behaviour analysis', which represents a milestone in the emergence of applied behaviour analysis as a distinct discipline and which identified seven criteria for assessing research which is based on this method:

1.   *Applied.* This term distinguishes applied behaviour analysis from the experimental analysis of behaviour, which is usually conducted in laboratory settings and involves the examination of functional relations. These may not be directly related to human problems. This criterion requires that research should focus upon behaviour which is directly relevant to the client or to society. Applied behaviour analysis has been applied to virtually all socially significant human behaviour including (to cite but a few examples which illustrate its broad range of application) smoking, littering, speeding, child-rearing, marital conflict, academic skills and child-rearing practices (Cooper *et al.* 1987).

2.   *Behavioural.* Behaviour analytic research focuses on behaviours which have a specific *topography*, or physical shape, which is distinct from the verbal report of that behaviour (Cooper *et al.*

1987). The specific topography of a behaviour allows it to be measured in terms of one or a number of dimensions of behaviour which include frequency, duration, latency (which refers to the length of time, or the delay, between the stimulus and the behaviour), and percentage correct or incorrect (Grant and Evans 1994). Baer *et al.* (1968) emphasise that, while the client's target behaviour must be measured, so too must the behaviour of all people involved in a study in order to ensure that what appears to be a change in the client's behaviour is not due to change in the behaviour of the experimenters.

3. *Analytic.* Behaviour analytic studies are designed to demonstrate a causal relationship between a manipulated event (the independent variable) and the target behaviour (the dependent variable). In a laboratory setting, the experimenter can demonstrate a causal relationship between the independent and dependent variables by controlling the occurrence or non-occurrence of the independent variable. In applied settings, however, ethical considerations often prevent the removal of the independent variable (e.g., the cessation of a form of therapeutic intervention) and behaviour analysts have adopted a pragmatic approach to the demonstration of experimental control (Cooper *et al.* 1987).

4. *Technological.* Behaviour analytic studies must include explicit and comprehensive descriptions of all procedures which are used, to the extent that it should be possible to replicate them.

5. *Conceptually systematic.* The procedures which are used in behaviour analytic studies must be conceptually systematic, to the extent that the procedures which are applied are derived from behavioural concepts (Cooper *et al.* 1987).

6. *Effective.* In order to be judged effective, an applied behavioural study must demonstrate behavioural change which is socially, rather than theoretically or statistically, significant (Skinner 1953).

7. *Concerned with generalisation.* Generalisation has been defined as the 'occurrence of relevant behaviour under different, non-training conditions (i.e., across subjects, settings, people, behaviours and/or time without the scheduling of the same events in those conditions as had been scheduled in the training conditions)' (Stokes and Baer 1977, p.350). This definition of generalisation has been characterised as being both pragmatic and relative: generality of

behaviour change is accepted as having occurred if the trained behaviour occurs at other times or in other places without being re-taught completely, or if training results in the occurrence of other, related behaviours which do not require complete training (Cooper *et al.* 1987). Stokes and Baer (1977) contend that even if additional training is provided in order to produce change of behaviour in non-training conditions, generalisation can be deemed to have occurred as long as the cost or the extent is less than the initial intervention. The emphasis which applied behaviour analysis places on generalisation is consistent with its emphasis upon socially (rather than theoretically) significant behaviour change. Generalisation of treatment effects is an important issue because treatment is successful only when the desired change is achieved in relevant settings or in the presence of relevant persons: 'If the application of behavioural techniques does not produce large enough effects for practical value, then the application has failed' (Baer *et al.* 1968, p.7). For example, if behavioural change is achieved in the clinic setting but does not generalise to the home setting, treatment cannot be considered complete or successful. Without due consideration of the generalisation of treatment effects, treatment becomes unnecessarily prolonged and relapse is much more likely.

These criteria for the assessment of behaviour analytic research indicate that evaluation is an integral dimension of intervention and that the criteria for research apply equally to intervention.

The exclusive focus on observable behaviour which characterises applied behaviour analysis has led to the popular misconception that the discipline dispenses with subjective experience from its analysis, and is therefore at odds with other contemporary theoretical and philosophical approaches to human behaviour (Taylor and O'Reilly 1997). Applied behaviour analysis is, however, distinguished from *methodological behaviourism* (a version of behaviourism which pre-dated it) which relies exclusively on objective definitions of behaviour (Baum 1994). Methodological behaviourism involves the definition of behaviour in purely objective terms (Skinner 1989). Baum (1994) identifies the distinction between methodological and applied behaviour analysis in terms of their different philosophical foundations. Methodological behaviourism reflects a philosophical outlook termed *realism*. Realism, when applied to the study of behaviour, contends that knowledge of behaviour which is based on sensory data is imperfect and that scientific knowledge provides a means of studying an objective reality, to which behaviour belongs. Methodological behaviourism therefore accepts the distinction between objective data obtained through scientific method and subjective data. Subjective data such as an individual's verbal explanation of why he or she is behaving in a particular fashion is not of interest to methodological behaviourism, which focuses exclusively on the mechanics of that action. Applied behaviour analysis and radical behaviourism, however, reflect a philosophical outlook termed *pragmatism*, which is not as concerned with the question of what constitutes real behaviour as much as it is concerned with providing a useful explanation of behaviour. A useful explanation of behaviour from a radical behaviourist perspective may include an individual's verbal explanation of why he or she is behaving in a particular fashion, but it will also include an examination of immediate and historical environmental events which influence the behaviour. The environmental events which influence behaviour do not, however, exist exclusively outside the individual, because the environment is not conceived as an objective reality (Skinner 1953).

Private events, such as a toothache, are accessible to and can only be reported on by one individual. Public events, such as a storm, are accessible to and can be reported on by a range of individuals. Apart from accessibility, the distinction between public and private events is of little importance to radical behaviourism, which asserts that both are governed by the same laws of behaviour (Skinner 1953). From the perspective of radical behaviourism, private events such as thoughts and feelings are governed by the same laws of behaviour as public events, and are therefore not the sole cause of behaviour. This approach to private events is a distinguishing characteristic of applied behaviour analysis (Baer 1997).

While radical behaviourism is distinct from methodological behaviourism, which dispenses altogether with private events, it is also distinct from a range of orientations within the behavioural sciences which focus primarily on private events in the search for the causes of behaviour (e.g. Rogers 1975). The application of science to human behaviour stands in direct contrast to these orientations, involving as it does description, prediction and, ultimately, control (Skinner 1953). Prediction and control of human behaviour involve determinism, which is a fundamental characteristic of science. When science is applied to human affairs it runs counter to long-standing cultural traditions which explain human behaviour in terms of free will, choice and individual responsibility (Baum 1994).

From the perspective of radical behaviourism, the explanation of behaviour in terms of inner causes constitutes *mentalism* (Baum 1994).

Mentalism involves the explanation of behaviour by reference to inner states and feelings such as, for example, interpretations, perceptions, attitudes, thoughts, beliefs, wants and desires (Taylor and O'Reilly 1997). From a mentalist perspective, behaviour is not a focus of primary interest, but is indicative of an hypothesised inner entity (Skinner 1971). Baum (1994) identifies two characteristics of mental fictions that limit their usefulness in providing explanations of behaviour:

1. *Mental fictions obstruct enquiry.* When behaviour is attributed to an hypothesised inner entity (e.g. 'Paul's aggressive behaviour and other symptoms indicate that he is conduct-disordered'), further enquiry is deflected because it is not possible to study the entity (Skinner 1974).

2. *Mental fictions lead to circular reasoning.* The use of mental fictions to explain behaviour involves inferring a fictional entity from behaviour and then using the inferred entity as the explanation. For example, a statement such as 'Paul's aggressive behaviour and other symptoms indicate that he is conduct-disordered', usually leads to a statement such as 'Paul is conduct-disordered, and this causes him to be aggressive'. According to this explanation the behaviour is considered to be evidence of an hypothesised inner entity which in turn is offered as an explanation of behaviour.

The explanation of behaviour by reference to hypothesised inner entities is facilitated by the use of *summary labels* (Grant and Evans 1994). Summary labels refer to a number of different categories of behaviour which share a common quality, and they can lead to explanations of behaviour which are based on mental fictions. They differ from behavioural descriptions referring to behaviour which is observable, whether privately or publicly. While acknowledging that summary labels can quickly provide useful information about an individual's behavioural repertoire, Grant and Evans (1994) identify three other disadvantages which are associated with their use: first, they can lead to a person, rather than the behaviours which he or she performs, being labelled; second, they obstruct the quantification of discrete behaviours and, third, they can distract from an accurate perception of an individual's behaviour and lead to stereotyping.

From the pragmatic perspective of applied behaviour analysis, both mentalism and realism are restrictive because they inhibit enquiry (Cooper *et al.* 1987). In order to pursue the study of behaviour as a primary subject of interest, applied behaviour analysis has developed a 'consistent, systematic, comprehensive, natural science of behaviour' (Taylor and O'Reilly

1997, p.41). Applied behaviour analysis therefore resembles other natural sciences, such as physics, biology and chemistry, in its focus on a physical (as opposed to a non-physical or mental) subject matter:

> Natural scientists are consistent in attending only to physical phenomena – events that are known or at least strongly suspected to exist. Furthermore, they attempt to explain physical phenomena only in terms of other physical phenomena. (Johnston and Pennypacker 1993, p.4)

Johnston and Pennypacker (1993) identify two fundamental differences between the study of behaviour from a natural science and from a social science perspective:

1. *The generation of theory.* The natural sciences generate theories which are based on empirical evidence derived from their physical subject matter. By contrast, the social sciences are freed from the constraints of physical subject matter: 'in the social sciences, a style of theorising seems to have evolved in which theories are also free to ignore facts that are inconvenient. It is almost as if the theories are more important than the facts' (p.5).

2. *Techniques of measurement.* The natural sciences use an *idemnotic* method of measurement which is based on absolute units 'whose existence is established independently of variability in the phenomena being measured' (p.35). The use of absolute standards of measurement (such as duration, latency or percentage correct) is appropriate to a science which has a physical subject matter and which seeks to explain variability between and within phenomena. This form of measurement is employed in both experimental analysis and applied behaviour analysis, where the focus of interest is on variation in the dependent variable in response to manipulation of the independent variable, in order to investigate functional relationships. The social sciences, in contrast to this practice, have adopted a *vagonitic* method of measurement, which is suited to the description of non-physical subject matter, such as the variability of static characteristics in a population or the variability between groups in a population. Vagonitic measurement involves describing variability in natural phenomena 'with the aid of the calculus of probability and, from these descriptions, not only are new phenomena defined, but units for scaling them are created' (p.29). For example, the *null hypothesis*, which forms the basis of

between-group experimental designs, contends that the differences between an experimental and a control group are not caused by the independent variable, but by the variability which is inherent in the population to which both groups belong. The probability of obtaining the observed differences among the means of each group is calculated and, if it is sufficiently small, one can conclude that the between-group differences are caused by the independent variable, rather than being a reflection of variability which is inherent in the population. The vagonitic measurement strategy of the social sciences approaches variability as an inherent quality of its non-physical subject matter. The statistical methods of the vagonitic strategy are therefore designed to take into account the potentially disruptive influence of the variability which is inherent in the population which is being studied. This approach to variability is fundamentally different from the idemnotic strategy, where variability in the dependent variable, as the result of manipulation of the independent variable, is the focus of interest; 'We argue that the measurement strategy adopted influences the resulting tactics of subject matter definition, experimental design, reduction and analysis of data, and interpretation' (p.35).

These fundamental differences between a natural science and a social science perspective in the study of behaviour are apparent in the field of child development. For example, Schlinger (1995) notes that the reliance on *normative* or *correlational* (vagonitic) methods has led developmental psychology to focus on the *structure* rather than the *function* of behaviour. The structure of behaviour refers to its topography, or form. The function of behaviour refers to its relationship to environmental antecedents and consequences which elicit and maintain behaviour. The focus on the structure rather than the function of behaviour in developmental psychology often leads to the introduction of explanatory fictions which inhibit enquiry, such as, for example, *maturational effects* (Richman, Stevenson and Graham 1982); 'the purpose of much of the correlational, normative research in developmental psychology seems to be to demonstrate whether a behaviour is present or not at a particular age, but not how the behaviour came to be' (Schlinger 1995, p.22).

Nevertheless, Schlinger (1995) also acknowledges that normative data is not useless because it provides 'clues about environmental changes rather than about underlying genetic or biological changes, as many developmental psychologists believe' (p.42). Behaviour analysis advocates that, rather than concentrate on the structure of behaviour that reflects hypothesised inner entities, the study of child development should 'concentrate on changes in the environmental contingencies and analyse how they affect human behaviour' (Dillenburger and Keenan 1997, p.15).

Learning theories and the complexity of human behaviour

Applied behaviour analysis, in common with behaviour therapy in general, is characterised by an emphasis on learning experiences as the basis of behaviour change, whether this occurs in a therapeutic, educational or social domain. Three types of learning are fundamental to the development and alteration of behaviour and form the basis of behaviour therapy; *classical (or respondent) conditioning, operant conditioning,* and *observational learning.* (An examination of learning theories is beyond the scope of this book. For an exhaustive account, see Grant and Evans (1994) and Cooper *et al.* (1987).)

The *principles of behaviour* refer to the four types of relationship between behaviour and its controlling variables which can be described in terms of the three-term contingency: *positive reinforcement, negative reinforcement, type 1 punishment* and *type 2 punishment.* The principles of behaviour were developed in laboratory settings with non-human subjects and, while they have been demonstrated repeatedly in applied behavioural studies, it is acknowledged that their successful application to human subjects in non-laboratory settings represents a significantly more complex task: 'Human behaviour is perhaps the most difficult subject to which the methods of science have ever been applied, and it is only natural that substantial progress should be slow' (Skinner 1953, p.41).

Cooper *et al.* (1987) identify three sources of complexity in human behaviour:

1. *The complexity of the human repertoire.* In any given setting, a number of contingencies may vie simultaneously for control of different behaviours, so that a single event often has multiple effects. For example, when an individual trims a hedge, the positive reinforcement provided by having a brighter garden may compete with the negative reinforcement of being more visible to neighbours. Furthermore, verbal behaviour adds an extra layer of complexity to the study of humans which is not present in the study of animals. Behaviour analysis has developed a series of procedures termed *functional assessment* which is designed to unravel the complexities of the antecedent and consequent variables which elicit and maintain operant responding (O'Neill *et al.* 1997; O'Reilly 1997; Taylor 1999).

2.   *The complexity of controlling variables.* The environment which
     controls human behaviour is also more complex, as several
     contingencies can combine to increase the probability that a
     behaviour will recur in a similar situation. Wahler and Fox (1981)
     propose that applied behaviour analysis should expand its focus
     beyond immediate antecedents and consequences in order to
     accommodate complex controlling stimuli called *setting events.* The
     proposal that the focus is broadened beyond the immediate
     determinants of behaviour has potentially far-reaching
     consequences for applied behaviour analysis, which is primarily
     concerned with establishing functional relationships between
     independent and dependent variables. Wahler and Fox (1981),
     while advocating that the analysis of behaviour should include
     setting events, acknowledge that it may not be possible to control
     them as one would in a laboratory setting. Wahler and Fox (1981)
     anticipate that the inclusion of setting events within the analysis of
     behaviour will lead to a period of 'theoretical confusion' for the
     discipline because setting events may not be comprehensible in
     terms of operant and respondent concepts (p.334).

3.   *Individual differences.* The concept of individual difference is cited as
     an explanation for the observation that people often respond
     differently to the same set of environmental circumstances.
     Behaviour analysis has adapted evolutionary theory in order to
     explain such differences in individual behaviour in terms of the
     history of reinforcement and punishment, rather than in terms of
     'nonscientific accounts that refer to a hidden intelligent agent
     directing evolutionary or behavioural change' (Baum 1994, p.69).
     While a history of reinforcement and punishment operates on an
     individual within his or her life-span and determines how he or
     she responds to a particular situation, natural selection operates on
     a species over generations.

Social work and scientific practice

While, as noted above, there are different views as to whether applied behaviour analysis is a sub-category of behaviour modification or whether
behaviour modification is an outmoded form of behavioural practice, both
are fundamentally scientific activities: they involve the selection of intervention methods based on what research suggests is effective, and the on-

going evaluation of progress (Gambrill 1995). A concern with evaluation is a central distinction between scientific and non-scientific activity:

> Measurement is the cornerstone of all scientific activity. The history of science is coextensive with the history of measurement of natural phenomena because without measurement, science is indistinguishable from natural philosophy. (Johnston and Pennypacker 1993, p.21)

Much of the controversy which has greeted the introduction of behavioural methods to social work practice relates to the essentially scientific character of these activities. The position of social work in relation to applied behaviour analysis can therefore be viewed within the broader context of the difficult introduction and accommodation of behaviour therapy (including behaviour modification) within social work theory and practice, because many of the objections which apply to behaviour therapy relate to the scientific status which it shares with applied behaviour analysis.

The introduction of behaviour modification to social work practice derived its imperative from two important areas of controversy (Payne 1997). First, behaviourism emerged as a credible alternative to psychodynamic theory, on which much social work practice was based. From the perspective of the newly emerging *empirical practice movement* (EPM), traditional social work practice was characterised as 'vague, unvalidated and haphazardly-derived' (Fischer 1993, p.19). From the perspective of the behavioural practitioner, it was 'lacking clarity and purpose, possessing a vagueness of method and showing a wishy-washiness that is altogether indefensible' (Howe 1987, p.82). Furthermore, social work practice resembled a client beset by 'lack of stable identity…chronic self doubt…depression punctuated by bouts of mania and self-destructiveness' (Sheldon 1995, p.2). Second, empirical studies of social work practice indicated that they were not effective (Fischer 1978). While later reviews have suggested that this is not the case, they also suggest that if there are grounds for optimism about the effectiveness of social work intervention, they rest squarely on the shoulders of behavioural methods (Macdonald, Sheldon and Gillespie 1992; Reid and Hanrahan 1981; Rubin 1985).

It is not surprising that the implicit and explicit criticism of non-scientific social work practice which has attended the introduction of behavioural methods has provoked a generally hostile response within the discipline. Social work's resistance to scientific method in general and to behaviour therapy in particular has been expressed from a range of perspectives including gender (Davis 1985), politics (Trinder 1996) and history (Lorenz 1994). Philosophical objections to the application of scientific methods to social work practice and research were raised within the context of an epistemological debate which took place within the discipline in the 1980s, and which was conducted in terms of *logical positivism* (or *logical empiricism*) versus other philosophies (Fischer 1993).

Prominent among the views which oppose logical positivism is that of *social constructionism*. Social constructionism provides an analysis of the social and cultural context within which theoretical knowledge (including scientific knowledge) is developed (Barber 1996; Slife and Williams 1995; Witkin and Gottschalk 1988). Fischer (1993) notes that, while there is some variation in the specific philosophical standpoints of those who oppose logical positivism as it applies to social work practice and research, they share a number of common priorities: an emphasis on the value of subjective experience and the social context within which research is conducted; a recognition of the biases which are inherent in all methods of data collection and support of the use of the insights and involvement of researchers, practitioners and clients.

The philosophical debate between proponents and opponents of logical positivism has also been conducted in terms of the relative merits of *quantitative* versus *qualitative* methods in social work research (Barber 1996; Epstein 1986). Quantitative (or experimental) designs, such as those described in Chapters 5 to 8, test and validate hypotheses about cause-and-effect relationships, whereas qualitative (or exploratory) designs are used either to arrive at descriptions of social phenomena as primary sources of interest or to assist in generating hypotheses for further investigation (Fischer 1993). Quantitative studies obtain data by means of surveys, correlational and experimental designs, and standardised observational methods (Fischer 1993). Quantitative research methods are designed to measure specific aspects of client behaviour (for example, changes in the behaviour of a client or group of clients in response to intervention). In direct contrast to these methods, qualitative studies use participant observation and investigative interviews, in order to understand the meaning of the client's world and actions (Kvale 1996). Qualitative research methods therefore reflect the influence of postmodernism, which contends that an understanding of social behaviour is achieved, not through measurement, but through active engagement with the participants (Slife and Williams 1995).

The debate about the application of scientific methods to the evaluation of social work practice has been distinguished by exchanges which are polarised (for example, Nagel 1988; Thyer 1987, 1988) and, at times, personalised (for example, Harrison, Hudson and Thyer 1992; Witkin 1991,

1992). The polarity of the debate has been characterised by the use of rhet-oric rather than discourse (Piele 1988).

The polarised debate has been characterised as a 'divisive and destruc-tive paradigm war' which has split the evaluation community as a whole, and which has been reproduced within social work (Worthen 2000, p.6).

A number of solutions to the unproductive polarity of the debate have been proposed. For example, Piele (1988) suggests that a solution lies in the development of an all-inclusive *new paradigm research* approach which avoids absolutism, which includes both empirical and non-empirical research methods and in which 'neither is seen as better than the other' (p.12). Similarly, Sells, Smith and Sprenkle (1995) suggest a *multi-method* or an *integrated multi-methodological* approach which includes both qualitative and quantitative methods within individual studies. Furthermore, Gibbs (2001) advocates the integration of research methods which examine pro-cess issues and those which examine outcome issues (p.700). These solu-tions, however, appear to resemble 'methodological relativism...in which all propositions and findings are created equal, which in turn implies that all investigators have won, and all must have prizes' (Sheldon 1998, p.4). It seems unlikely that methodological relativism, which is in itself reminis-cent of eclecticism, can withstand scrutiny from a scientific perspective which expects that the choice of social work practice methods should be based on evidence, rather than blind affiliation (Barber 1996; Sheldon 1995). Worthen (2000) therefore concludes that no convincing resolution to the debate is apparent:

> Unless some way is found to re-channel the dialogue about these 'opposing' paradigms and methodologies into more productive avenues, the field of evaluation will still be hampered conceptually and opera-tionally as it moves into the next century. (p.7)

Ethical issues relating to practice-based research

The clarification and resolution of ethical issues that arise in the course of practice-based social work research is by no means straightforward. First, the emergence of new specialisms and the enactment of new legislation which defines the social work role in the areas of community care, child protection and criminal justice has led to the fragmentation of social work (Banks 1998; Powell 1998). The emergence of different models of social work, such as professionalism, consumerism and radicalism, suggest 'the end of a universal professional ethics and of social work as a unitary enter-prise' (Banks 1998, p.229). Second, social research activities (which includes research based on the methods of both natural science and social science) can be distinguished from practice evaluation in terms of purpose, doctrine, theoretical basis, intended audiences, methodology and dissemination. It has therefore been suggested that the ethical guidelines which pertain to social science research are not appropriate to practice evaluation, which is adequately covered by codes of ethics pertaining to social work practice (Holosko and Thyer 2000).

In addition to these complications, there may be no explicit professional ethical guidelines for social workers who wish to conduct research (as is the case in Ireland, where the research which is described below was conducted). The current code of ethics of the Irish Association of Social Workers consists of a definition of social work, a statement of values and an enunciation of seven principles of social work practice (Irish Association of Social Workers 1995). The seven principles of social work practice endorse the highest standards of practice in the following areas:

- client need as the primary focus of interest
- objectivity in professional practice
- empowerment of individuals, groups, communities and societies
- involvement of other professionals and agencies
- the effects of social policy and service delivery on clients
- the provision of information to clients, including access to records
- a duty of respect and confidentiality.

The second principle, which relates to objectivity in professional practice, states that 'Constant development of self-awareness will continuously build upon knowledge and skills to maintain and enhance standards of professionalism' (p.2). Introspection is therefore the only source of knowledge which is explicitly cited, and no mention is made of the development of knowledge through research. By contrast, the code of ethics of the Australian Association of Social Workers specifies 14 ethical responsibilities of social workers who engage in research, in addition to the general provisions of the code of ethics (Australian Association of Social Workers 2000). These responsibilities are compatible with the primary and explicit commitment of applied behaviour analysis to achieve change in behaviour which is directly relevant to the client, and to use methods which are demonstrably effective.

To those who advocate an empirical approach to practice, there is an ethical imperative to choose social work practices on the basis of proven effectiveness, rather than on the basis of unsubstantiated preference, affiliation or habit. Sheldon (1995) advises that social workers should choose practice methods in a rational manner, much as doctors, dentists, plumbers and garage mechanics choose the most effective method of intervention in their different fields, rather than by relying on *reflexive practice*, which refers to practice which is chosen on the basis of habit. Macdonald and Macdonald (1995) emphasise the ethical dimension to the choice of practice methods (p.48). Similarly, Barber (1996) identifies the choice of social work practice methods on the basis of proven effectiveness as an ethical responsibility for the profession. However, Myers and Thyer (1997) note that while the code of ethics of the National Association of Social Workers stipulates that social workers should 'critically examine and keep current with emerging knowledge relevant to social work' (National Association of Social Workers 1996, p.289), there are no direct requirements to provide effective treatment. Similarly, while the code of ethics of the Australian Association of Social Workers (2000) stipulates that social workers 'will inform their practice from a recognised social work knowledge base' (4.6a) there are no direct requirements to provide effective treatment. In contrast, the Association for Behaviour Analysis' Task Force on the Right to Effective Treatment has formulated a statement which asserts that the client has the right to the most effective treatment available (Myers and Thyer 1997).

In addition to the general ethical issues that pertain to practice-based research, a number of ethical issues that arise in child behavioural assessment and intervention and which are directly relevant to the research which is described below have been identified (Rekers 1984):

1. *Children's rights.* The minority legal status of children complicates the ethical responsibilities towards them as consumers of behavioural assessment and intervention. For example, the guarantee of a child's rights against excessive intrusion may conflict with the potential benefits of intervention.

2. *Proper and legal consent.* The three legal criteria which apply to consent to intervention with adults involve a consideration of the *competence* of the person to give consent, whether consent was given on a *voluntary* basis and whether consent was *informed*. In the case of a child, it is necessary to obtain consent from a legal surrogate, such as parent(s) or guardian(s).

3. *Professional judgement.* The professional who is involved in behavioural assessment and intervention must make judgements in a number of areas such as the most appropriate intervention, the definition of deviant behaviour, the prognosis and treatment goals.

All professional decisions pertaining to assessment and treatment have ethical ramifications.

4.   *Social values.* Parents in collaboration with professionals are appropriate agents to make value judgements about what constitutes acceptable and unacceptable social behaviour in children.

Summary

Applied behaviour analysis views itself, not as a specialism within behaviour modification, but as a discipline which is more closely based on the principles of behaviour. Applied behaviour analysis is based on the methods of natural science and on non-mediational concepts of learning. Applied behavioural research (and intervention) can be assessed in terms of whether it is applied, behavioural, analytic, technological, conceptually systematic, effective and achieves generalised behaviour change. Private events are recognised in applied behaviour analysis, but they are distinguished from public events only in terms of their accessibility. Radical behaviourism offers a critique of mentalism, a tendency in the social and behavioural sciences and in western European culture in general to attribute behaviour to an hypothesised inner entity.

Applied behaviour analysis involves classical conditioning, operant conditioning and modelling. It is acknowledged that the application of the principles of behaviour to humans in applied settings is difficult because of the complexity of the human behavioural repertoire, the complexity of controlling variables and the reinforcement histories of individuals.

Social work's objections to behaviour therapy relate to its essentially scientific character, which emphasises the importance of evaluation. Applied behaviour analysis shares this characteristic with behaviour therapy in general, and it is therefore possible to consider the position of applied behaviour analysis in relation to social work in terms of social work's objections to behaviour therapy in general. These objections have been expressed in terms of gender, politics, history and philosophy. The introduction of behavioural methods into social work practice has generated intense debate during the last 30 years. The debate, whether conducted in terms of positivism versus postmodernism, or quantitative versus qualitative methods, has been polarised and ideological. This debate within social work has replicated the terms of a debate which has been conducted in the broader evaluation community. As no convincing resolution to this debate is yet apparent, persuasion through demonstration rather than debate has been advised.

It has been suggested that there is an ethical imperative to choose social work practice methods on the basis of empirical evidence, rather than on the basis of preference, affiliation or reflexive practice. Specific ethical issues arise in the course of behavioural assessment and intervention with children which relate to children's rights, consent, professional judgement and social values.

Chapter 2

Childhood conduct disorder

Introduction

All children, at one time or another during the course of childhood, behave in ways that can be termed antisocial. This is because all children, as part of the learning and socialisation process, break family or community values, expectations or rules. Although rule-breaking behaviour in children is very common, it varies greatly according to the age of the child and must therefore be seen in the context of overall development (Achenbach 1991). Antisocial behaviours such as hitting, cheating, stealing, truancy or lying are usually transient and do not attract clinical attention. However, children and adolescents in whom these behaviours persist and become more serious usually come to the attention of professionals in the health and social care, educational or juvenile justice systems. The term *conduct disorder* has been applied to children who break family or societal rules to this extent (Kazdin 1987).

Although the terms *antisocial behaviour*, as applied to problem behaviour which occurs in the course of normal development, and *conduct disorder*, as applied to problem behaviour which is of clinical significance, suggest two distinct patterns of behaviour, the definition and classification of child behaviour problems is by no means straightforward. Wolff (1977) queried whether childhood conduct problems can be classified with the same degree of rigour as other clinical syndromes. Usually clinical syndromes are categorised either by the occurrence of clusters of common symptoms or by a single conspicuous symptom. The definition of conduct disorder differs from other clinical syndromes because it involves the consideration both of specific instances of antisocial behaviour by the child and of the effect of these behaviours on others (Earls 1994). In an attempt to draw some kind of diagnostic distinction, Wolff (1977) looked at the boundary between delinquent and non-delinquent disturbances of conduct. This distinction is difficult to sustain, however, owing to the occurrence of broad and overlapping patterns of behaviour.

The term conduct disorder, then, does not refer to a clinical syndrome in the traditional sense. It is a diagnostic category which has limitations, both in terms of the identification of individuals with the disorder, and because 'the correlates of such behaviour are likely to be less valuable in the management of individual cases than if we were dealing with a more specific clinical syndrome' (Wolff 1977, p.490).

Classification

Three distinct methods of classifying child behaviour disturbance have been identified, all of which are relevant to research and clinical intervention (Sanders and Dadds 1993). These are the *diagnostic taxonomy*, the *dimensions of dysfunction* approach, and the *behavioural* approach.

The diagnostic taxonomy

The diagnostic taxonomy is a classification of symptoms upon which the diagnosis of a disorder by a medical practitioner is based. Diagnostic taxonomies summarise symptom clusters by giving them a common label, and the diagnosis is made on the basis of explicit criteria for inclusion or exclusion such as, for example, the number or the duration of symptoms. There are currently two main systems of classification: the *Diagnostic and Statistical Manual of Mental Disorders* (DSM-IV) (American Psychiatric Association 1994) and the ICD-10 *Classification of Mental and Behavioural Disorders* (World Health Organisation 1992). The two systems of classification were developed independently until recently, when an increasing level of interaction between them has led to a convergence of definitions (Earls 1994). Both systems of classification distinguish between behavioural problems which occur in early childhood and which are classified as *oppositional defiant disorder* (ODD), and those which occur in late childhood and adolescence, which are classified as conduct disorder (CD). CD is rarely diagnosed in children who are less than six years of age.

Both ODD and CD involve a pattern of behaviour which leads to impaired functioning in the social, the academic or (in the case of adolescents) the occupational spheres. In order for a diagnosis of ODD to be made, a pattern of negativistic, hostile and defiant behaviour lasting at least six months must be present, as well as at least four of the following eight symptoms:

- throwing tantrums

- arguing with adults

- defiance and refusal to comply with adult rules

- blaming others

- annoying behaviour

- touchy behaviour

- angry behaviour

- resentful behaviour.

The ICD-10 elaborates on the distinction between ODD and CD; ODD is defined

> by the *presence* of markedly defiant, disobedient, provocative behaviour and by the *absence* of more severe dissocial or aggressive acts that violate the law or the rights of others. (World Health Organisation 1992, p.270)

A diagnosis of CD therefore requires the presence of a pattern of behaviour which is repetitive and persistent and which involves the violation either of the rights of others or of social rules, as well as impaired social, academic or occupational functioning. Fifteen symptoms of CD are categorised in terms of aggression to other people and animals, destruction of property, deceitfulness or theft and serious violations of rules. A diagnosis of CD requires the presence of at least three symptoms in the previous twelve months, and the presence of at least one symptom in the previous six months. Both systems of classification distinguish between *childhood onset* CD, where the disorder occurs before the age of ten, and *adolescent onset* CD, where the disorder does not occur before the age of ten. The severity of the disorder is also rated as mild, moderate or severe.

The integrity of ODD as a discrete clinical syndrome has been challenged on a number of grounds. First, it has been suggested that the symptoms of ODD are not serious enough to amount to a handicapping condition and therefore do not constitute a psychiatric disorder (Rutter and Shaffer 1980). Second, empirical evidence suggests that ODD is not a distinct clinical syndrome (Schachar and Wachsmuth 1990). Third, as well as the apparent overlap between CD and ODD, both syndromes also overlap with the syndromes of overactivity and attention deficit.

It has been suggested that the overlap between CD, ODD and the syndromes of overactivity and attention deficit reflects diagnostic ambiguity as well as true comorbidity (Webster-Stratton and Herbert 1994). Diagnostic ambiguity arises because, in contrast to CD and ODD, the definitions of syndromes of overactivity and attention deficit in the ICD and the DSM classification systems have not converged. Comorbidity between attention deficit hyperactivity disorder (ADHD) and ODD is evident among children who are referred for help due to disruptive behaviour, many of whom display hyperactivity as well as defiant and oppositional behaviour (Szatmari, Offord and Boyle 1989). Nevertheless, ADHD is associated with developmental delays in cognitive, language and motor skills which are not associated with either CD or ODD (Schachar 1991). The symptoms of ADHD and CD among children with both disorders tend to be more extreme and more resistant to treatment than those of children with either disorder (Taylor 1994). The differentiation between ADHD and CD or ODD is therefore important in terms of research and clinical intervention (Taylor 1994).

The adoption of common criterion symptoms by both the ICD-10 and the DSM-IV represents a move towards a more standard classification of child conduct problems. Nevertheless, the classification of child conduct problems in terms of these two major diagnostic taxonomies has been criticised on a number of grounds. First, it has been argued that the criteria for reaching a diagnosis in terms of a specified number and a specified duration of symptoms are quite arbitrary (Kazdin 1995). Second, the symptoms which have been included in the most recent editions of the DSM and the ICD include symptoms which are more likely to be displayed by males, and therefore display a gender bias (Robins 1991). Third, it has been suggested that symptoms of CD should not be applied in fixed terms throughout childhood and adolescence, but should vary with age, as some of these symptoms do not occur in younger children (Kazdin 1995).

The dimensions of dysfunction approach

The dimensions of dysfunction approach to the classification of child conduct problems identifies the degree to which a child's behaviour varies from that of a normative comparison group. The approach is characterised by the use of behavioural checklists, such as the Child Behaviour Checklist (CBCL) (Achenbach 1991), the Conners' Rating Scales (CRS) (Conners 1997) and the Eyberg Child Behaviour Inventory (ECBI) (Eyberg and Ross 1978). These checklists contain lists of specific behaviours which are deemed to be constituents of categories of behaviour, termed *dimensions of dysfunction*. The dimensions of dysfunction and the specific items of behaviour are empirically derived from studies of problem behaviour among populations of children and adolescents, and take into account the child's age and sex (Eyberg and Robinson 1983). Behavioural checklists provide a means of comparing a child's behaviour with that of a normative comparison group which is matched to the child in terms of age, sex and nationality. Behavioural checklists are designed to be completed by parents and teachers and provide information about the child from the perspective of adults who see the child in very different circumstances.

The classification of childhood disorders according to dimensions of dysfunction assumes that disorders can be distinguished on the basis of the number and intensity of problems which children experience. However, the dimensions of dysfunction which are associated with CD vary considerably, and range from delinquent to non-delinquent behaviour. It is also difficult to establish concrete normative data of antisocial or conduct-disordered behaviours as family and cultural norms and values differ considerably and what is considered antisocial in one family or culture may well be acceptable in another.

The behavioural approach

The behavioural approach to the classification of child behaviour problems relies on a clear description of the individual's repertoire and focuses on excesses and deficits of behaviour within the context in which the behaviour is performed (Sanders and Dadds 1993). A behavioural approach to child conduct problems focuses on the actual behaviour of the child. A clear description of the child's behaviour is obtained by observing the child in the natural setting, such as the home or the classroom. It identifies how the child's behaviour is influenced by aspects of the environment (such as home, school or community). The influence of the environment upon the child's behaviour is described in terms of the laws of behaviour. The behavioural approach is characterised by its focus upon specific behaviours as primary sources of interest. The approach does not involve the process of inferring that specific behaviours are symptomatic of another underlying entity, such as a disorder or dimension of dysfunction. It also advocates the use of behavioural descriptions which are precise and which facilitate measurement in terms of frequency, duration and latency. The precise measurement of target behaviours is the first step towards effective intervention (Grant and Evans 1994).

The classification of child behaviour disturbance according to diagnostic taxonomies and dimensions of dysfunction is attended by the disadvantages which are associated with the use of summary labels (see the section 'Applied behaviour analysis' in Chapter 1). Nevertheless, both methods of classification provide a common international language of child psychopathology to clinicians and researchers (Sanders and Dadds 1993). The internationally accepted terminology has in turn provided a basis for epidemiological studies (e.g. Robins 1991). However, diagnosis and classification do not necessarily assist in the management of specific cases of child behaviour disturbance (Wolff 1977). The behavioural approach to classification is based on precise descriptions of behaviour which facilitate effective intervention, rather than on summary labels. Each of the approaches to the classification of child conduct problems has advantages and disadvantages in terms of research and practice, and the incorporation of all three methods into the assessment and treatment process has been advocated (Ollendick and Hersen 1984; Sanders and Dadds 1993).

Prevalence

The prevalence of childhood CD has been examined in a number of epidemiological studies. These studies differ in terms of the measures of behavioural deviance, the criteria for inclusion, the age of the child and the geographical location. Not surprisingly, different rates of prevalence are reported.

The prevalence of behavioural problems in children of preschool age who lived in the London Borough of Waltham Forest was examined in the first phase of a prospective study of children aged between three and seven years and their families, which found that 78 per cent of children did not demonstrate clinical disturbance; 15 per cent demonstrated mild clinical disturbance; 6 per cent demonstrated moderate clinical disturbance and 1 per cent demonstrated severe clinical disturbance (Richman et al. 1982). The prevalence of behaviour problems in seven-year-old children was examined in a longitudinal study of child health and development from birth to seven years of age in Dunedin, New Zealand (McGee, Silva and Williams 1984). This study found that a high level of problem behaviour was identified in 17 per cent of children by parents, in 9 per cent by teachers, and in 6 per cent by both parents and teachers. The prevalence of conduct problems among 10–11-year-old children living on the Isle of Wight was examined in an epidemiological study of childhood disorder which found that the prevalence rate for conduct disorder was 4 per cent and for neurotic disorder (the second most common condition) was 2.5 per cent (Rutter, Tizard and Whitmore 1970). A study of psychiatric disorder in a sample of ten-year-old Norwegian children, which used a screening and individual assessment procedure similar to that of the Isle of Wight study, found a prevalence rate of 5 per cent for unspecified psychiatric disorder (Vikan 1985).

These studies suggest that the prevalence of childhood disorders varies according to geographical location. A systematic comparison of the rates prevalence of childhood psychiatric disorder in an urban and a rural setting was conducted by Rutter *et al.* (1975). The prevalence of psychiatric disorder in ten-year-old children from a typical inner London borough (ILB) was compared with those from the Isle of Wight (IOW). Of the ILB children, 19 per cent were rated as deviant on teacher questionnaires, in comparison with 11 per cent of IOW children. When these children were assessed individually, 25 per cent of ILB children received a psychiatric diagnosis in comparison to 12 per cent of IOW children. The increased prevalence of disorder in ILB children applied to both conduct and emotional disorders. A similar comparison between the prevalence of childhood disturbance among children aged between seven and ten years in an urban and a rural setting in an Irish context found that among urban children, 35 per cent were rated as behaviourally deviant in comparison with 11 per cent of the rural children (Fitzgerald and Kinsella 1989).

Course and outcome

Childhood conduct problems have traditionally been seen either as transient milestones which occur in the course of normal development or as being no more than the reflection of disapproval of what constitutes normal behaviour among working-class children by middle-class teachers (Robins 1981).

The course and continuity of conduct problems

Children of preschool age manifest problem behaviours most frequently in the general areas of feeding, sleeping, manageability, and bowel and bladder control (Jenkins, Bax and Hart 1980; Richman *et al.* 1982). Child problem behaviours do not necessarily indicate the presence of behavioural disturbance, but can also reflect developmental immaturity in a specific domain, which usually resolves in the course of normal development (Richman *et al.* 1982; Rutter *et al.* 1970). Behavioural disturbance is indicated by the presence of problem behaviours across a range of domains, such as sleeping, feeding and manageability, rather than by the presence of circumscribed problems within one domain (Richman *et al.* 1982). Behavioural disturbance which is manifest in preschool-age children often persists into childhood (Campbell *et al.* 1986).

The study of the persistence of CD from childhood to adolescence is complicated by the reliance upon police and court statistics in adolescent studies, whereas childhood studies usually rely upon parents as sources of information (Loeber 1991). Despite the apparent discontinuity between child CD and juvenile delinquency, a review of longitudinal studies of conduct problems in childhood and adolescence concluded that:

> between 10 and 15 years, and probably between 8 and 15 years, it is likely that there is little change in the overall proportion of children showing disturbances of conduct, although patterns of behaviour and the administrative recognition of delinquent activities change during these years. (Rutter and Giller 1983, p.51)

It has also been suggested that the dramatic increase in the rate of criminal conviction of children over 13 years of age can be attributed to the use of police cautioning of younger children as an alternative to conviction, rather than to the sudden onset of antisocial behaviour at the age of 13 and over (West 1982).

Early childhood conduct problems have been strongly implicated in the persistence of antisocial behaviour in adolescence (Farrington 1985; Farrington, Loeber and Van Kammen 1990). Official arrest statistics indicate that the rate of first-time criminal convictions peaks during adolescence before declining in early adulthood (West 1982). The decline in the overall rate of offences in late adolescence, as well as the decrease in the rate of first-time offences during these years, suggest that the acquisition of a criminal conviction in adolescence does not necessarily indicate the beginning of a long criminal career, as a large number of adolescents acquire only one or two convictions (West 1982). Adolescents who acquire a high number of convictions are distinguished by early initial conviction (Farrington 1985; West 1982).

Although the continuity of antisocial behaviour in adolescence has been established for some individuals, it is equally evident that many individuals desist from antisocial behaviour. A number of pathways have been proposed to account for patterns of continuity and discontinuity of antisocial behaviour in adolescence (Loeber 1991; Moffitt 1993; Robins 1981).

In view of the persistence of conduct problems from childhood to adolescence in some children, it is not surprising that a high degree of continuity has been found between child conduct problems and serious adjustment problems in adult life (Robins 1966). Furthermore, a high degree of continuity between child conduct problems and adult criminality has been established in a number of longitudinal studies (Huesmann, Eron and Lefkowitz 1984; McGee *et al.* 1992; Mitchell and Rosa 1981; Quinton, Rutter and Gulliver 1990; Robins 1966; Robins and McEvoy 1990). Despite the high degree of continuity between childhood antisocial behaviour and adult maladjustment, antisocial behaviour does not persist into adulthood in the majority of cases (Mitchell and Rosa 1981; Robins 1966, 1978).

Child-specific factors

The study of childhood behaviour problems differs from the study of personality structures in the emphasis which it places on the role of the environment in the development and maintenance of behaviour problems. This contrasts with the earlier constitutionalist trend, which focused upon heredity and constitution as the basis for personality structure (e.g. Freud 1936; Klein 1932). Despite the emphasis upon environmental factors in the field, Webster-Stratton and Herbert (1994) refer to the emergence of a *child deficit hypothesis* which proposes that elements of the child's internal organisation at a physiological and neuropsychological level make a partial contribution to the development of behaviour problems. This hypothesis has led to a number of child-specific factors being implicated in the development of childhood behaviour problems, including gender, temperament, neuropsychological impairment, social skills deficits and academic deficits.

Gender

Childhood conduct problems are more prevalent among boys. Richman *et al.* (1982) found that the male:female gender ratio for the prevalence of conduct problems at three years of age was 1.5:1, which had increased to 1.7:1 at eight years of age. Rutter *et al.* (1970) found that the male:female gender ratio for CD among a population of 10- and 11-year-old children was 3.7:1. There is some evidence to suggest that the course and outcome of conduct problems among boys and girls differ, and that conduct problems are associated with restlessness, overactivity and developmental immaturity in boys but not in girls (Richman *et al.* 1982). During adolescence, however, a reversal is evident in the prevalence of psychiatric disorder among boys and girls. While psychiatric disorders are more prevalent among boys during childhood, most disorders become more prevalent among girls during adolescence (McGee *et al.* 1990). The reversal in the prevalence of general disorders among boys and girls between 11 and 15 years is also evident in relation to non-aggressive CD (McGee *et al.* 1992). Explanations for the gender differences in the prevalence and persistence of conduct problems in childhood and adolescence tend to incorporate both biological and environmental influences (Earls 1994; Maccoby and Martin 1983; Richman *et al.* 1982).

Neuropsychological deficits

Child conduct problems are often accompanied by deficits across a range of domains which include concentration, motor coordination, emotional regulation, verbal functioning and language comprehension. Although these deficits are not as pronounced as they are among children with specific developmental delays, the consistently poor scores achieved by children with conduct problems on tests of language, self-control and cognitive ability suggest that there may be an organic or neuropsychological basis to these deficits among children with conduct problems. Neuropsychological deficits have been defined as 'the extent to which anatomical structures and physiological processes within the nervous system influence psychological characteristics such as temperament, behavioural development, cognitive abilities, or all three' (Moffitt 1993, p.681). A number of studies have identified specific neuropsychological deficits among conduct-problem children, to an extent which suggests that children with conduct problems have specific neuropsychological deficits (Coble *et al.* 1984; Schmidt, Solant and Bridger 1985). Goodman (1994), however, distinguishes between these 'soft' neurological signs which reflect immature motor development, and frank signs of brain injury such as a history of seizures, spasticity or an abnormal electroencephalogram profile. Goodman (1994, p.173) also notes that the adjustment problems of individuals who have distinguishing physical characteristics are associated with social prejudice rather than genetic endowment in itself, and cautions against the attribution of childhood disorders to 'underlying hardware defects in the child's brain' without consideration of environmental factors.

Similarly, although the developmental immaturity which is associated with child conduct problems and which is usually present at a sub-clinical level may have a neurophysiological basis, it is not a sufficient explanation for the development of child conduct problems, but may serve as a setting event for environmental influences such as punitive parenting, peer rejection and academic failure. Other environmental factors also suggest themselves as possible explanations for the indicators of developmental immaturity which frequently accompany CD, especially in boys. These include poor diet, food allergies and an impoverished play environment.

Temperament

The study of temperament emerged in reaction to what was perceived as an exclusive concentration upon the role of environment in the development of child conduct problems (Thomas, Chess and Birch 1968). Temperament is defined as 'the behavioural style' of an individual, which is distinguished from motivation and ability (Thomas *et al.* 1968, p.4). It is considered to be an aspect of the individual's constitution rather than a response to the immediate environment, and is consistent across time and circumstance. From a behaviour analytic perspective, the concept of temperament, like that of CD, is a summary label (see the section 'Applied behaviour analysis' in Chapter 1). From this perspective, temperament is an unhelpful concept because it deflects attention away from variables which control behaviour and because its ambiguity leads to inconsistent findings. Nevertheless it has been studied extensively in relation to CD. Earls (1994) identifies two distinct orientations in the study of temperament. First, temperament is viewed as a stable organismic phenomenon which determines behaviour (Reitsma-Street, Offord and Finch 1985; Scholom, Zucker and Stollak 1979; Thomas *et al.* 1968). Second, temperament is viewed as an interactive concept, which provides a measure of how parents perceive and interact with the child (Barron and Earls 1984; Simpson and Stevenson-Hinde 1985).

Academic deficits

The concept of intelligence and its measurement have given rise to much controversy. A central controversy relates to whether IQ tests are free from cultural influences and provide a measure of innate intelligence (which can be used as the basis for claims of superiority by one social class or racial group over another) or whether an IQ test measures a sample of behaviour which is susceptible to cultural influence (Rutter and Madge 1976). Unlike IQ tests, which provide a measure of performance across a wide variety of tasks, reading tests assess performance on a task which is directly attributable to schooling. Reading tests therefore provide an important measure of academic functioning. CD is strongly associated with both low IQ and reading delay (Rutter *et al.* 1970; Sturge 1982; West 1982). Rutter *et al.* (1970) found some evidence that conduct problems are secondary to educational failure. This was, however, only partially confirmed by Sturge (1982).

The studies which have been reviewed suggest that the association between childhood conduct problems and academic deficits is complex, and that no single explanation suffices. Nevertheless, it seems reasonable to conclude that the restlessness, poor concentration and developmental immaturity which have been strongly associated with conduct problems serve as obstacles to school adjustment and the development of reading skills.

Social skills deficits

Children with CD exhibit a range of aversive behaviours more frequently than other children. The behavioural excesses of children with CD are accompanied by social skill deficits, such as an inability to initiate social interaction appropriately, to share, to take turns and to solve problems (Freedman et al. 1978; Shinn et al. 1987). The social skills deficits of children with conduct problems are accompanied by cognitive distortions and poor problem-solving ability (Asarnow and Callan 1985; Dodge and Newman 1981; Richard and Dodge 1982).

The social skills deficit model proposes that the aversive behaviour of children with conduct problems that leads to peer rejection can be remedied by teaching children specific skills such as turn-taking, sharing, listening and anger management (Webster-Stratton 1991). There is some evidence to challenge the hypothesis that children with conduct problems want the same social experiences as popular children, but lack the necessary skills (Asarnow and Callan 1985). Patterson, Reid and Dishion (1992) contend that antisocial boys fail to use the social skills which they possess, and conclude that social skills deficits are secondary to coercive behaviour which develops and is maintained in response to coercive interactions within the home.

Intra-familial and extra-familial factors

While the early research on child conduct problems focused upon dyadic interactions between mother and child, the focus of more recent research has broadened to include an ecological perspective which focuses upon hierarchical levels of interacting systems inside and outside the family (Dadds 1987). These systems are thought to operate at a *molecular* or *micro level* within the family, in terms of patterns of interaction, and at a *molar* or *macro level* outside the family, in terms of broad social processes such as social class, employment, poverty, ethnic status and cultural beliefs and attitudes. Patterson *et al.* (1992) identifies a concern with the relationship between context, or social structure, and family interaction patterns as characteristic of a social interactional perspective, and notes that the focus of research on child conduct problems has broadened to include molar as well as molecular events. Webster-Stratton (1990) distinguishes between intra-familial and extra-familial stressors which disrupt family functioning and notes that research on families of conduct-problem children has focused upon parent-and-child variables, to the exclusion both of intra-familial stressors (such as marital discord, maternal depression and parental criminality) and extra-familial stressors (such as poverty, unemployment and overcrowding). This section therefore reviews the role which a number of intra-familial and extra-familial factors play in the development and maintenance of CD. Parental antisocial behaviour, maternal depression and family discord are reviewed initially. These are among the most well-researched intra-familial variables, and they illustrate some of the processes through which conduct problems develop and are maintained within the family. Finally, the role of socio-economic disadvantage in the development and maintenance of CD is considered.

Parental antisocial behaviour

A history of parental antisocial behaviour has been strongly associated with a range of measures of child and adolescent disturbance, all of which are indicative of childhood CD (Robins 1966; Robins, West and Herjanic 1975; Rutter *et al.* 1974; West 1982). While these studies all indicate an association between parental and child antisocial behaviour, Huesman *et al.* (1984) found a stronger association between aggression in children and the level of aggression which their parents displayed when they themselves were children, than with the contemporary level of aggression which their parents displayed.

The studies which have been reviewed indicate that a history of parental antisocial behaviour, and paternal antisocial behaviour in particular, places children and adolescents at risk for behavioural disturbance, according to various measures of parental and child antisocial behaviour. A number of mechanisms have been suggested whereby the continuity between parental and child antisocial behaviour is established, including the presence of a physically abusive father (Robins 1966) and stigmatisation of the child on the basis of the father's reputation (West 1982). Lytton (1990) concluded that while there is some evidence that antisocial behaviour is transmitted not only from parents but from grandparents (which gives some support for the argument that transmission is based on genetic inheritance), it is also likely that a parent whose antisocial behaviour leads to criminal conviction acts as a reinforcer and as a model for antisocial behaviour in the child.

Maternal depression

All studies of the prevalence of depression have found that the condition is twice as common among women as among men, both in the general population and in patient populations (Kendell 1993). The gender difference in the prevalence of depression is greatest in early adulthood, as the prevalence of depression among women increases considerably during the reproductive years (Kendell 1993). Three distinct forms of depression have been identified among women: *postnatal depression* (or *baby blues*), *puerperal psychosis* and *maternal depression* (Puckering 1989). Postnatal depression is experienced by 50 per cent of mothers and refers to a transitory disturbance of mood during the first ten days after childbirth which involves crying, irritability, depression and emotional lability. Puerperal psychosis involves confusion, perplexity and lability of mood in the absence of a definite physical cause (Cox 1993). Although puerperal psychosis is rare, occurring in only 0.02 per cent of women, this figure represents a 20-fold increase in the prevalence of psychosis among women in general populations (Kendell 1993).

Maternal depression refers to depression which may or may not arise after the birth of a child but which is associated with child-rearing (Puckering 1989). Maternal depression involves depressed mood, low self-esteem, a lack of hope for the future and an inability to cope with the demands of everyday life. There is also an accompanying loss of energy, poor sleep, poor appetite and general irritability (Kendell 1993). The condition is less severe than endogenous depression or melancholia, and many mothers who fulfil the criteria for a major depressive episode never seek professional help (Kendell 1993). Environmental factors have been found to play a significant role in the aetiology and maintenance of maternal depression. These include recurrent daily stressors, social class, housing, having young children, marital problems, the lack of full-time or part-time work outside the home; the loss of one's mother before adolescence and a negative relationship with one's mother in childhood were also associated with depression.

Maternal depression has been strongly associated with the parental role. Women with young children are particularly vulnerable to depression (Browne and Harris 1978, 1989; Jeffers and Fitzgerald 1991; Leader, Fitzgerald and Kinsella 1985; Richman *et al.* 1982). There is evidence to suggest that the high rate of depression among mothers of young children is caused by the numerous daily stressors which the parental role involves (Patterson and Forgatch 1990). Patterson *et al.* (1992) suggest that the higher prevalence of depression among mothers than among fathers of young children is associated with the burdensome nature of the caretaking role which falls primarily to mothers.

Maternal depression appears to be more prevalent among mothers of young children whose caretaking needs are greater (Browne and Harris 1978), and mothers of children who exhibit behaviour problems are more likely to suffer from depression (Leader *et al.* 1985; Richman *et al.* 1982; Rutter *et al.* 1974;). There is some evidence that the experience of depression in mothers influences their perception of their child's behaviour (Webster-Stratton and Hammond 1988), that specific child characteristics influence the perception of mothers who are depressed (Brody and Forehand 1986) and that maternal ratings of child maladjustment vary according to the level of maternal depression and the gender of the child (Friedlander, Weiss and Traylor 1986).

The experience of depression in mothers appears to influence directly the manner in which they interact with their child (Conrad and Hammen 1989; Cox *et al.* 1987; Webster-Stratton and Hammond 1988). Rutter (1966) distinguishes between direct effects of psychiatric disturbance in a parent, where exposure to adult symptoms such as delusional and bizarre thinking is distressing to the child, and indirect effects, where the child's distress is caused by the parent's inability to parent adequately. Puckering (1989) suggests that the distinction between direct and indirect effects is not helpful because 'all parent behaviours to which a child is exposed can be seen as a component of child-rearing' (p.918). There is also evidence that the adverse effect of maternal depression on parenting behaviour varies according to the severity of depression (Webster-Stratton and Hammond 1988).

Maternal depression has been strongly associated with child emotional and behavioural disturbance (Cox *et al.* 1987; Dumas, Gibson and Albin 1989). In contrast, however, Hops *et al.* (1987) found that unhappy affect in depressed mothers served to suppress aggressive behaviour in family members. Dumas *et al.* (1989) found partial support for each of these apparently contradictory findings, and Dumas and Gibson (1990) proposed that conduct-disordered children of depressed mothers are selectively disturbed: they behave less aversively towards their mothers but behave more aversively towards siblings and fathers.

These studies on the environmental determinants of maternal depression and the implications of maternal depression for child disturbance suggest that aversive parenting is the pathway through which ecological factors lead to child CD. Wahler (1980) proposed the term *insular* to describe mothers who perceive their social interactions, relatives and helping agencies negatively, and who experience little support from friends. Maternal insularity leads to aversive parenting practices which in turn lead to child CD.

Family discord

Attachment theory proposes that a stable family background is vital to healthy child development and that family disruption leads to child disturbance (Bowlby 1969). Rutter *et al.* (1970) lent some support to this view. Nevertheless, a broad range of evidence suggests that the level of conflict and disharmony between parents, rather than the alteration in family structure or the separation from one or both parents which attends marital difficulties and divorce, contributes to the development and maintenance of child conduct problems (Farrington 1978; Quinton *et al.* 1990; Richman *et al.* 1982; Robins 1966; Rutter *et al.* 1974; Schachar and Wachsmuth 1990).

A number of studies have found that the association between marital discord and child behaviour problems is both direct, through the exposure of children to displays of anger between parents, and indirect, with aversive parenting behaviour as a mediating factor (Dadds and Powell 1991; Jenkins and Smith 1991; Johnson and Lobitz 1974; Webster-Stratton and Hammond 1999). Webster-Stratton and Hammond (1999) conclude:

> negative parenting and negative marital conflict management are highly intertwined…and even if parents do maintain positive parenting relations with their children despite high levels of marital conflict, children will still be affected directly by the negative conflict management style of the marriage. (p.925)

Socio-economic disadvantage

Socio-economic disadvantage refers to the accumulated effects of a broad range of social adversities which include poverty, unemployment, dependence upon social welfare, overcrowding and poor housing. It has been identified as a risk factor for the development of child conduct problems and juvenile delinquency. Rutter *et al.* 1974 found that single stressors, even if chronic, are surprisingly unimportant, and concluded that 'the damage comes from multiple stress and disadvantage, with different adversities interacting and potentiating each other's influence' (p.111). Similarly, West (1982) found that low family income was associated not only with overcrowding but with inadequate parenting and particularly with poor supervision, and concluded:

> It is easy to see how the social alienation imposed by poverty may lead to identification with a subculture of low social standards and to the abandonment of middle-class ideals of conformity and respectability. Parents in overcrowded accommodation in poor tenements cannot protect and supervise their young children as they might wish. They have to let them out to roam the streets and fight their own battles among a similarly disadvantaged peer group. (p.37)

Farrington (1985) found that a number of measures of family adversity were consistently implicated in CD at different ages in late childhood and adolescence. Farrington *et al.* (1990) found that the families of children who had both hyperactivity-impulsivity-attentional problems (HIA) and CD were characterised by low income, large family size and poor housing.

Rutter and Giller (1983) suggested that it is difficult to establish a direct association between socio-economic adversity and juvenile delinquency because socio-economic disadvantage is so strongly associated with other family variables, such as maternal depression and parental anti-social behaviour. Rutter and Giller (1983) concluded:

> it seems likely, that at least in part, poverty and poor living conditions predispose to delinquency, not through any direct effects on the child, but rather because serious socio-economic disadvantage has an adverse effect on the *parents*, such that parental disorders and difficulties are more likely to develop and that good parenting is impeded. (p.185)

Parent–child interactions

The examination of parenting practices represents one method of studying parent–child interactions. This approach assumes that the parent influences the child in a unidirectional fashion, and is characteristic of early research on social interaction in general (Lytton 1990; Parke 1979). The assumption that parents exhibit a range of aversive behaviours towards their children as a result of parenting skills deficits is based on the *parenting skills deficit hypothesis* (Webster-Stratton and Herbert 1994). The parenting skills deficit hypothesis is supported by a number of studies of child-rearing practices which indicate that parents of children with conduct problems are significantly more negative in their behaviour and attitudes towards their children (Dowdney *et al.* 1985; Farrington 1978; Forehand *et al.* 1975; Richman *et al.* 1982).

Between 1960 and 1970 investigators of social interaction began to study interaction in natural settings and adopted a reciprocal rather than unidirectional model of interaction (Parke 1979): 'The current zeitgeist...has clearly shifted to a study of the reciprocity of interaction and the ways that individuals mutually regulate each other during the course of interaction' (p.17).

From a behaviour analytic perspective, mutual reinforcement is an essential feature of social interaction, whether this is verbal or non-verbal, cooperative or conflictual:

> We call verbal episodes and coercive episodes *social* because each person's behaviour provides reinforcement for the other's... For an episode to be called a social interaction and to count as the basis for a relationship, reinforcement must be mutual. (Baum 1994, p.176)

The examination of reciprocal reinforcement in parent–child interactions has revealed a higher rate of coercive exchanges in families of children with behaviour problems (Pettit and Bates 1989). Coercive relationships involve interaction between a *controller* and a *controllee* whose behaviour is mutually reinforcing; the controller's aversive behaviour is positively reinforced by the submission of the controllee, and the submissive behaviour of the controllee is negatively reinforced by the cessation of the controller's aversive behaviour (Baum 1994). Coercive relationships are a pervasive feature of social interaction among humans and mammals, whose hierarchical social groups include relationships which are based upon dominance and submission (Sidman 1989). Coercive relationships are pervasive because they are effective:

> All...coercive relationships can be replaced by noncoercive ones... Why do people so often resort to coercion?... The main reason is that coercion usually works. Those who suggest that coercion is ineffective are mistaken, for, trained properly, human beings are exquisitely sensitive to potential aversive consequences, particularly disapproval and social isolation. (Baum 1994, p.154)

The coercive exchanges of children with conduct problems and their parents have been studied extensively by two research programmes, each of which has generated highly influential theories which attempt to explain how antisocial child behaviour (and by extension, child conduct problems) are maintained by specific patterns of family interaction. *Coercion theory* was developed by Gerald Patterson and colleagues at the Oregon Center for Social Learning (OCSL) (Patterson 1976, 1982, 1986; Patterson *et al.* 1992), and *predictability theory* was developed by Robert Wahler and colleagues at the University of Tenessee (Dumas and Wahler 1984; Wahler and Dumas 1986).

Coercion theory was developed through the direct observation and analysis of patterns of interaction among families referred to OCSL for treatment of antisocial child behaviour. Although OCSL data indicated that coercive exchanges constituted only 12 per cent of family interaction among clinic-referred families (Patterson 1982), these coercive exchanges appeared to determine the development and maintenance of antisocial behaviour. The sequential analysis of coercive parent–child exchanges indicated that child aversive behaviour is maintained by parental responses which provide both positive and negative reinforcement. Positive reinforcement is evident when coercive child behaviour functions to maintain parental attention. However, although OCSL data indicated that 54 per cent of coercive child behaviour occurred in the context of positive parent–child interactions and was positively reinforced by parental attention, only 39 per cent of coercive child behaviour in clinic-referred families occurred during positive exchanges. These findings do not support the hypothesis that positive reinforcement plays a significant role in the maintenance of coercive child behaviour. Patterson (1982) also suggests that, in addition to being positively reinforced by parent attention, child coercive behaviour is positively reinforced by the victim's pain reaction, but acknowledges that 'the notion of victim pain reaction as a reinforcer for aggression remains plausible but unproven' (p.107).

While coercion theory has continued to acknowledge the role of positive reinforcement in maintaining coercive child behaviour, it has focused primarily upon the role of negative reinforcement in maintaining coercive child behaviour (Patterson *et al.* 1992). Negative reinforcement arrangements form the basis of the *compliance hypothesis*, according to which coercive child behaviour functions in task avoidance and immediate gratification:

Problem children use aversive behaviour to maximise immediate gratification and to deflect or neutralise requests and demands made by others... These are the ultimate 'here and now' children: They are not concerned about long-term consequences or the feelings of others who get in their way. (Patterson *et al.* 1992, p.23)

The compliance hypothesis contends that when an aversive approach by a family member (such as an instruction that a child tidy his room) is terminated by coercive child behaviour (such as whingeing and non-compliance), the behaviour of both parties serves to reduce the aversive events which impinge upon them. The negative reinforcement arrangements which characterise such coercive exchanges involve a discrepancy between short-term goals and long-term outcomes which is called a *reinforcement trap* (Baum 1994; Patterson 1982). Reinforcement traps are evident in situations where individuals sacrifice long-term welfare to short-term gains, for example by smoking cigarettes despite overwhelming evidence that the practice leads to lung cancer (Baum 1994). When a parent gives in to a child's demands or fails to follow through with an instruction, the short-term solution leads to problems in the long-term: the child is more likely to whinge and to be non-compliant in the future, the parent is more likely to give in and the task is less likely to be completed. Even if the parent does not yield to the child's counterattack, but counterattacks in turn, the short-term victory has deleterious long-term consequences because the parental counterattack serves as a model of coercive behaviour for the child (Forehand and McMahon 1981).

There is evidence to suggest that negative reinforcement arrangements maintain coercive child behaviour, in accordance with the compliance hypothesis. OCSL data indicated that although a high proportion of coercive child behaviours occurred in response to aversive approaches by other family members, the proportion among clinic-referred families (32%) was not significantly higher than that among non-clinic families (25%) (Patterson 1982). Nevertheless, clinic-referred children experienced twice as many aversive approaches by their mothers as non-clinic children, four times as many by their fathers and three times as many by their siblings (Patterson 1982). Although clinic-referred children were less likely to attack than either parent, they were four times more likely to attack their mothers than non-clinic children and twice as likely to attack a sibling (Patterson 1982). These findings suggest that coercive child behaviour serves to ward off aversive approaches by other family members. While child coercive behaviour has also been found to deter parents from following through on instructions (Gardner 1989), it does not appear to lead parents to capitulate to aversive child demands (Gardner 1989; Wahler and Dumas 1986).

Negative reinforcement arrangements, in which coercive child behaviour deters aversive parental approaches, also account for the *punishment paradox*, whereby parental reprimands lead to the persistence of aggressive child behaviours (Patterson 1976). Patterson (1976) found that once clinic-referred children emitted an aversive response, they were more likely than non-clinic children to persist in this response than non-clinic children. Specific responses by other family members were associated with the persistence of coercive child behaviour, and these were five times more prevalent among clinic-referred families. Parental punishment functioned as a maintaining stimulus for clinic-referred children, who were twice as likely to persist in aggressive behaviour as non-clinic children (Patterson 1976). Patterson (1982) referred to the ineffectual parental reprimands of clinic-referred families as *nattering*:

> Nattering is an expression of parental displeasure. It signifies irritation with no intention of following through... Parents of antisocial children...do not really try to stop coercive behaviour; they only ineptly meddle in it. The effect of their nattering is to produce extensions of the behaviours which elicit their displeasure. (Patterson 1982, p.112)

The potentially serious outcome of extended coercive chains is suggested by OCSL data that over 30 per cent of clinic-referred children had been physically abused by their parents (Patterson 1982) and by the finding that many children are physically abused by their parents during extended disciplinary confrontations (Milner and Chilamkurti 1991).

While the compliance hypothesis contends that the dual function of coercive child behaviour is task avoidance and immediate gratification, the *predictability* (or *uncertainty*) *hypothesis* contends that aggressive child behaviour serves to reduce the unpredictability of parental responses (Wahler and Dumas 1986). The predictability hypothesis is based upon the observations that clinic-referred children received higher rates of maternal aversive responses, regardless of whether they behaved prosocially or aversively (Patterson 1976), and that the probability of receiving a positive, neutral or aversive consequence from parents was independent of child behaviour. The predictability hypothesis contends that these inconsistent, indiscriminate parental responses are experienced as aversive by the child, who engages in aversive behaviour in order to elicit a more predictable maternal response, regardless of whether this response is aversive (Wahler and

Dumas 1986). Dumas and Wahler (1985) found that, while non-insular mothers became increasingly aversive in response to aversive child behaviour, insular mothers became aversive in response to both aversive and non-aversive child behaviour. They concluded that:

> These results provided evidence to indiscriminate mothering in insular families by suggesting that the aversive behaviour of insular mothers was under the stimulus control of child antecedents, almost irrespective of the valence of these antecedents. In other words, aversive and nonaversive child behaviours acted as if they were discriminative for aversive maternal responding (p.10).

Wahler and Dumas (1986) found further support for the predictability hypothesis: maternal indiscriminate attention was positively associated with child aversive behaviour but decreased during extended aversive exchanges, when mothers became more discriminating and consistent but more aversive. The measures of maternal insularity in both these studies suggest that while intervention with the mother–child dyad is effective with non-insular mothers, it is not effective with insular mothers who, while they report that they respond to the cues provided by their children 'may in fact often attend and respond to a broader pattern of cues that includes cues provided by other social agents in other settings' (Wahler and Dumas 1986, p.15)

Coercion theory has been criticised for its almost exclusive concentration on conflictual family interactions and its consequent failure to examine the role of non-conflictual parent–child interactions in the development of CD (Gardner 1992, 1998). A number of studies have suggested that, while coercive exchanges play a significant role in the development of CD, the quality of non-conflicted parent–child interactions also makes a contribution (Gardner 1987, 1994; Pettit and Bates 1989).

Summary

This review identified three methods of classifying child problem behaviours, all of which make distinctive contributions to treatment and research: the diagnostic taxonomy, the dimensions of dysfunction approach and the behavioural approach, which involves a focus on specific behaviours.

Considerable variation in the prevalence of CD between countries and between urban and rural settings has been found. While variation in prevalence may be an artefact of the different definitions and measures, it also suggests that the prevalence of CD is influenced by ecological factors. CD emerges in some children at preschool age, and persists throughout childhood. Evidence suggests that persistent antisocial behaviour in adolescence is preceded by CD in childhood. Similarly, various measures of adult maladjustment indicate that childhood CD is an important precursor.

The child deficit hypothesis proposes that a range of factors within the child which include gender, temperament, neuropsychological, academic and social skills deficits give rise to CD. These child-specific factors are manifested as clumsiness, awkwardness, overactivity, inattentiveness, irritability, impulsiveness, delays in both reading and in reaching developmental milestones, and difficulties in comprehension, in expression, in staying on task and in adapting to new learning situations. It is suggested that this broad range of behavioural excesses and deficits gives rise to peer rejection, academic failure and, perhaps crucially, to differential parenting. The child deficit model is useful in highlighting the partial role which child-specific factors, which may originate in genetic inheritance, play in the development and maintenance of CD.

Intra-familial and extra-familial factors occupy a central position in the development and maintenance of CD. These include parental antisocial behaviour, maternal depression and interparental discord. Aversive parenting practices gave rise to the parenting skills deficit hypothesis which is based on a unidirectional model of influence. Coercion theory and predictability theory are based on models of reciprocal influence and provide coherent accounts of the pain-inflicting and apparently self-defeating patterns of interaction which are found in families of children with conduct problems. CD arises from the coincidence of child-specific factors that place the child at risk of aversive parenting, with intra-familial and extra-familial stressors, which also increase the likelihood of aversive parenting practices.

Chapter 3

Behavioural parent training

Introduction

The vast majority of children in modern western society are reared within the context of the nuclear family. While the nuclear family has endowed its members with greater privacy and independence than was available to the traditional family in pre-industrial society, it has also isolated them from sources of extra-familial and communal support (Shorter 1975). This isolation has implications for parents who are reliant on familial, social and cultural contexts as sources of advice and information on child-rearing methods (Callias 1994). In the absence of traditional sources of advice on child-rearing from kinship and community groups, parents in modern society have become increasingly reliant on professionals for this information. Professional advice on infant and child care, which is based upon research on child development and clinical experience, is now available through books and increasingly through parent training. Parent training refers to 'educative interventions with parents that aim to help them cope better with the problems they experience with their children' (Callias 1994, p.918). Many parent training programmes are designed to help parents to cope with problems which arise within the normal course of childhood and adolescence. For example, Quinn and Quinn (1997, 2000) provide advice to parents on how to understand their child's behaviour in motivational terms and include training in reflective listening and problem solving. These programmes emphasise the importance of improved communication and relationships between parents and children, and are based upon Rogerian and Adlerian concepts (Callias 1994).

Behavioural parent training (BPT) refers to a form of clinical intervention with children who present with a range of problems which are more persistent and/or more serious than those which occur within the course of normal development, and for which their parents have sought help. BPT has been described as a set of 'treatment procedures in which parents are trained to alter their child's behaviour at home' (Kazdin 1997a, p.1349). Kazdin (1997a) identifies two main influences in the development of BPT:

1.   The emergence of *operant theory* (Skinner 1953, 1971), which is based on laboratory research settings with animals and on applied research with a range of populations which include clinical samples.

2.   Research upon the role of parental disciplinary practices in the development of aggression in children.

BPT is based upon both operant and social learning concepts, and in common with behaviour therapy in general, it represents a convergence of a range of theories and influences into a heterogeneous movement (see the section 'Applied behaviour analysis' in Chapter 1). The influence of operant theory on BPT is indicated by the prominent position which the three-term contingency occupies in BPT. Parents who undergo BPT are taught to identify, record and modify a range of events and stimuli which occur prior to the child's behaviour. Typical antecedents include the parent's own behaviour, such as unclear or aversive instructions which can elicit non-compliance, or the immediate environment, such as a disorganised household at mealtime or upon departure for school, which can elicit aggression. Typical child behaviours which are the focus of interest in BPT include prosocial behaviours such as compliance to instruction, engaging in positive social interaction with the parent or other family members, independent or cooperative play; and aversive behaviours such as non-compliance to instruction, tantrums and physical aggression. Consequences which act as positive reinforcers for prosocial or positive behaviours are provided by parents and include social reinforcers, such as praise or positive attention, and material reinforcers, such as treats or tokens which can earn treats. Consequences which decrease aversive child behaviour include time out and the loss of tokens or privileges. Modelling plays a key role both in the manner in which child management skills are taught to parents and as a means whereby parents demonstrate prosocial (and aversive) behaviour to the child (Forehand and McMahon 1981).

BPT has been used as method of intervention for a broad range of problem behaviours which children present. These include circumscribed problem behaviours such as thumb-sucking (Ross 1975), hyperactivity (Erhardt and Baker 1990; Frazier and Schneider 1975), stealing (Stumphauzer 1976), enuresis (Houts and Mellon 1989), sleep problems (Douglas 1989), tics and stuttering (Levine and Ramirez 1989), headaches (Beames, Sanders and Bor 1992), food refusal (Werle, Murphy and Budd

1993) and chronic hair-pulling (Gray 1979). BPT has been used as a method of intervention for children with learning disabilities, with whom an emphasis is placed upon the acquisition of self-help skills (Carr 1995), and with children who have developmental disabilities, with whom an emphasis is placed upon the acquisition of communication skills (Koegal *et al.* 1984) as well as upon behaviour problems (Breiner and Beck 1984). BPT has also been used as a method of intervention with parents who have physically abused their children (Urquiza and McNeil 1996). Among the broad range of presenting problems to which BPT has been applied, however, conduct disorder (CD) occupies a prominent position because of the reciprocal influence which is evident between research on parent training and research on CD, and because the factors which promote the emergence of CD also inhibit the effectiveness of BPT (Rutter 1985). A review of four methods of intervention for CD which comprised BPT (also termed parent management training or PMT), functional family therapy, cognitive problem-solving skills training and community-based interventions concluded that: 'On balance, PMT is one of the most promising treatment modalities. No other intervention for antisocial children has been investigated as thoroughly and shown as favourable results' (Kazdin 1987, p.192). While BPT continues to occupy the central position in the treatment of CD, concerns have been raised about the demands which it makes on families and about the extent to which the child-management techniques which it promotes are culturally specific to the United States (Fonagy *et al.* 2002).

The triadic model

The emergence of parent training as an intervention strategy represents a change from the traditional dyadic model of service delivery, in which the therapist intervenes directly with the child, to a triadic model in which the clinician trains a caretaker to intervene with the child. The recruitment of teachers and institutional staff as behaviour change agents has been a distinguishing feature of behavioural therapy since its inception (Kazdin 1994). The recruitment of parents as behaviour change agents was a logical step when children became the focus of intervention (Sanders and Dadds 1993). Early studies demonstrated that parents and caretakers could be reliably trained to participate actively in behaviour modification programmes (Adubato, Adams and Budd 1981; Hall *et al.* 1970; Hall *et al.* 1972; Herbert and Baer 1972; Zeilberger, Sampen and Sloane 1968).

The active involvement of parents in programmes which are designed to alter their children's behaviour has implications for parent–professional relationships. Callias (1994) distinguishes between the *expert model*, where the professional is in charge of treatment and decisions, the *transplant model* in which parents are trained to use specific skills under the supervision of the professional, and the consumer model, where the parents choose and decide what they believe is most appropriate for their child. Callias (1994) concludes that parent training is largely based upon the transplant and consumer models which emphasise collaboration and partnership. Webster-Stratton and Herbert (1994) advocate a collaborative model for working with parents of children with conduct problems, which is characterised by equality and joint problem solving:

> The therapists' role as collaborator, then, is to understand the parents' perspectives, to clarify issues, to summarise important ideas and themes raised by the parents, to teach and interpret in a way which is culturally sensitive, and finally, to teach and suggest possible alternative approaches or choices when parents request assistance and when misunderstandings occur. (p.108)

The collaborative model also involves empowering parents, and helping them to develop support systems (Webster-Stratton and Herbert 1994).

Similarly, Sanders and Dadds (1993) emphasise the importance of actively involving parents in behavioural intervention and suggest four strategies to achieve this:

1.   the development of a shared definition of the problem

2.   the careful explanation of the rationale upon which the intervention is based

3.   the sharing of inferences and hypotheses by the clinician with the parents

4.   the reinforcement of parent behaviour change.

Alternative training formats

A number of different training formats have been adopted in the application of BPT to the treatment of CD. These include clinic-based programmes, using an individual- or group-training format, and home-based programmes. Forehand and McMahon (1981) is an example of a clinic-based programme which uses an individual-training format. The programme content is standardised and parents are taught individually in the clinic setting during twice-weekly training sessions in order to prevent 'performance decay' (p.49). The programme has also been adapted for self-administration in book format (Forehand and Long 1996). Five specific skills are taught in two phases. In the first phase the parent is taught to be a more effective reinforcing agent through the use of differential attention to the target child. Differential attention is taught before disciplinary practices in order to reduce the risk of drop-out before the acquisition of skills for promoting and maintaining prosocial child behaviour. The skills that are taught during this phase include positive attending, giving rewards and ignoring. In the second phase of the programme, the parent is trained to decrease child non-compliant behaviour through the use of clear instructions and time out. The duration of the programme depends on the speed with which the parent reaches a specified treatment criterion for each skill and varies between 5 and 12 sessions. The skills are taught in a prescribed sequence and the parent does not proceed to the next skill until the criterion for each skill has been reached. The programme is practice-based, and each phase is taught through rehearsal in the clinic setting. Differential attention is rehearsed by means of an unstructured play activity which is termed the *child's game*, during which the parent practises each of the three skills while the child is engaged in free play. The clinician observes parent and child behaviours and provides the parent with feedback on how each skill was implemented, as well as prompts by means of a bug-in-the-ear device. The parent is encouraged to practise and self-record implementation of the specific skills in the home setting by engaging in the child's game at home between clinic-based sessions. Compliance training is rehearsed by means of a structured activity, which is termed the *parent's game*, during which the parent gives instructions and provides consequences for compliance and non-compliance. Parents are not encouraged to practise the parent's game in the home setting until they have reached the criterion for clear instructions and time out in the clinic setting, as it is in the context of the parent's game that conflict between parent and child is most likely to arise. Clinic-based BPT, which uses an individual training format, has been found to lead to significant changes in both parent and child behaviours (Peed, Roberts and Forehand 1977), improvement in maternal perceptions of the target child (Forehand and King 1977) and the maintenance of treatment gains after 14 years (Long *et al.* 1994).

The Incredible Years series (IY) (Webster-Stratton 1992a) is an example of BPT which is based on a group training format. It is designed for presentation to groups of 8 to 12 parents during 12 weekly two-hour sessions, but it can also be self-administered or presented in a lecture format to large groups. The programme is presented through a multimedia teaching format involving the use of video-cassettes and a manual for leaders. The programme content is also available in book form, and is provided to participants (1992b). The small group format encourages discussion and the exchange of experiences, information and support among participants. The IY series includes basic and school-age curricula. The basic curriculum is designed for parents of pre- and early-school-age children, and emphasises the importance of play by devoting the first three sessions to promoting the child's self-esteem, creativity and imagination, cooperation and problem-solving skills through play. The curriculum also includes material on praise and encouragement, tangible rewards, limit-setting and ignoring, and time out and other consequences. The school-age curriculum focuses on how parents can enhance the child's school adjustment by promoting self-confidence and good learning habits, responding to discouragement and working collaboratively with teachers. The curriculum is designed for parents of children aged between five and ten years. Both curricula can be presented in a range of settings which include health centres, mental health centres, community colleges, high schools and hospitals or medical settings. They can also be used as an educational tool to illustrate child development with teenagers and child management principles with a range of health professionals. The curricula can be administered by a wide range of people including teachers, psychologists, nurses, social workers, doctors and parents. IY parent training has been found to lead to significant treatment effects among self-referred families, which include increased positive affect and decreased lead-taking, non-accepting and dominant behaviours among mothers (Webster-Stratton 1981) and significant reductions in negative, non-compliant and aggressive child behaviours (Webster-Stratton 1982a). Changes in mothers' and children's behaviour post-treatment were either maintained or improved at one-year follow-up (Webster-Stratton 1982b). The basic programme has been evaluated extensively as a treatment programme for children with conduct problems and has been found to lead to improved parental attitudes and parent–child interactions, reduced coercive disciplinary practices and reduced child conduct problems (Webster-Stratton 1984, 1989, 1994; Webster-Stratton, Hollinsworth and Kolpacoff 1989). The programme has also been evaluated as a universal prevention programme with children at risk of CD and found to lead to improved parenting skills (Gross, Fogg and Tucker 1995; Webster-Stratton 1998). Spanish and English language versions of the IY curricula have been developed to make them accessible to different ethnic groups, and for use in different settings (Gross et al. 1999; Reid, Webster-Stratton and Beauchaine 2001; Scott et al. 2001). The original videotape vignettes have been dubbed in order to ensure fidelity with the original programme. In the Irish context, the Parenting Plus Programme (Behan *et al.* 2001) uses the same videotape modelling and group training format as IY. The videotape vignettes use actors with Irish accents and idioms. It is not clear whether the programme is a localised variant of the IY formula, and whether it represents a substantive contribution to the field, or not.

Child management training (CMT) is an example of BPT which is based on behaviour analytic methods. CMT uses a home-based individual training format which involves direct observations of parent and child behaviours in the home setting as an integral part of the treatment process (Dadds, Sanders and James 1987; Sanders and Dadds 1982; Sanders and Glynn 1981). The clinician observes parent and child interactions in the home setting before, during and after treatment and provides feedback to the parent on programme implementation and on changes in the behaviour of the target child. The parent receives initial instruction during two clinic-based training sessions by means of didactic instruction, role-play, modelling and the provision of printed material. The programme content includes descriptive praise and rewards to increase prosocial child behaviour, and a behaviour correction procedure to reduce aversive child behaviour. The behaviour correction procedure involves verbal correction, followed by response cost or time out if the aversive child behaviour persists. Subsequent training is provided in the home setting during feedback sessions, when a clinician calls to the home twice weekly to observe parent–child interactions for 30 minutes and provides feedback to the parent on how the behaviour management techniques have been implemented. The clinician also encourages the parent to discuss any problems that have arisen in implementing the techniques in the home setting at other times. CMT has been implemented by clinical psychologists who are practising in the area of child behaviour (Dadds *et al.* 1987).

Comparisons of group- and individual-training formats suggest that there is little to choose between them in terms of effectiveness. Pevsner (1982) found a lower rate of treatment drop-out, a higher rate of resolution of the primary problem behaviour during the course of treatment and better knowledge of behaviour principles as applied to children among parents who received BPT in a group-training format in comparison to parents who received BPT in an individual-training format. Brightman *et al.* (1982) concluded that a group-training format was more effective than an individual-training format because, although parents achieved similar treatment gains in terms of knowledge of behaviour modification acquired and improvements in child self-help skills and behaviour, the group-training format required half the amount of therapist time. Webster-Stratton (1984) found no significant differences in either attitudinal or behavioural measures between BPT based on an individual-training format and a video-modelling group-training format among a clinic population, but noted that the video-modelling group-training format was more cost-effective in terms of therapists' time. Sutton (1992) found that parents could be successfully trained to implement behavioural principles in the management of child conduct problems, whether they had been trained in groups or individually through home visits or through telephone contact.

Expansion of the treatment paradigm

The parenting skills deficit hypothesis has played a significant role in the application of behavioural parent training to the treatment of CD (see the section 'Parent–child interactions' in Chapter 2). The parenting skills deficit hypothesis contends that parent training provides a means of offsetting deficits in those parenting skills that lead to the development and maintenance of child conduct problems which include the absence of positive parenting behaviours and supervision of the child's behaviour and whereabouts, the use of excessively punitive discipline, the inadvertent reinforcement of aversive child behaviours and the extinction of prosocial child behaviours through ignoring (Webster-Stratton and Herbert 1994). The parenting skills deficit hypothesis led to an initial focus upon parent–child interactions in the treatment of CD without examining the influence of parent and family variables on treatment outcome. For example, Forehand and King (1977) examined the effectiveness of a standardised parent training programme with a group of families whose economic status ranged from upper-middle-class business executives and university professors to welfare recipients. Similarly, Peed et al. (1977) examined the generalisation from the clinic to the home setting of the treatment gains of a standardised treatment programme among a group of families whose socio-economic status ranged from upper middle class (social class I) to welfare recipients (social class V).

It has become apparent that a range of contextual factors outside the parent–child dyad can influence the outcome of BPT in the treatment of CD (Dumas and Wahler 1983; Furey and Basili 1988; McMahon, Forehand, Griest and Wells 1981; Prinz and Miller 1994; Webster-Stratton 1985a; Webster-Stratton and Hammond 1990). As the influence of contextual factors upon treatment outcome has become apparent, a number of reviews have recommended an expansion of the parent training model as it is applied to the treatment of CD. McAuley (1982) noted that some researchers have begun to look beyond parent–child interactions and to examine different levels of parental functioning and family interaction which influence treatment outcome. Griest and Wells (1983) suggested that *multi-modal family therapy* may be more effective than circumscribed parent training, which focuses upon parent–child interactions. Multi-modal family therapy addresses a range of parent and family variables, which include parent cognitive variables (such as parental perception of the child), parent adjustment variables (such as parental depression), marital adjustment variables (such as marital discord) and social variables (such as extra-familial social contacts) and which have been linked to the aetiology and mainte-nance of conduct problems, as well as with a poor response to BPT. McMahon (1987) recommends that the conceptual model of assessment is broadened from a focus on the parent–child dyad to a multi-method, multi-informant and multi-setting assessment of conduct-disordered chil-dren and families, in order to address the multiple family factors which are associated with CD.

Variations in the strength and in the continuity of intervention have also emerged as potential areas for expansion in the application of behav-ioural parent training to the treatment of CD. Kazdin (1987) suggests that increasing the strength of treatment is a potential option, but expresses a number of reservations, including the difficulty in defining this dimension of psychosocial treatments, the acceptability to consumers, the presence of side effects and the expense in terms of therapist time and training. Kazdin (1997b) notes that child psychotherapy research in general rarely considers the influence of treatment variables such as dose, strength and duration on treatment outcome and recommends that high-strength treatment should be considered as a viable treatment and research option:

> For severe or recalcitrant clinical problems in particular, it may be valuable to test the strongest feasible version of treatment to see if the problem *can* be altered and, if so, to what extent. The high-strength model is not only an effort to maximise clinical change, but also to test the current limits of our knowledge. (p.122)

Dumas (1989) challenges the expectation that brief, time-limited interven-tions such as parent training intervention can 'cure' a multi-faceted, chronic and stable problem such as CD and suggests that regular, periodic interven-tion over years may be more appropriate. Similarly, Kazdin (1997b) sug-gests that it might be more helpful to consider CD as a protracted condition, comparable to mental disability or to pervasive developmental disorders in terms of the need for continued intervention rather than one-off intervention.

The expansion in the models of treatment and assessment of CD has also been accompanied by an expansion in conceptual models of child deviance. Wahler and Dumas (1984) propose a *multiple coercion hypothesis* as an explanation for the failure of some families to respond to behavioural parent training. This hypothesis is related to the concept of maternal insularity which identified causal links between aversive exchanges with the broader social system and aversive maternal parenting behaviour (Dumas and Wahler 1985; Wahler and Dumas 1986) (see the section 'Parent–child interactions' in Chapter 2). The multiple coercion hypothesis proposes that the presence of constant sources of aversive stimulation prevents some parents from responding to parent training. Wahler and Dumas (1984) challenge the parenting skills deficit hypothesis and suggest that multiple coercion involves both behavioural and attentional consequences for the mother:

> The behavioural consequences centre on the dual increase in parental aversiveness and inconsistency…while the attentional consequences result from the fact that troubled mothers commonly fail to monitor accurately the many environmental events which repeatedly set them up to act toward their children in ways likely to maintain their deviance. (p.389)

Similarly, Dumas (1989) challenged the competence-based hypotheses that CD is caused by deficits of skills among children or parents in the social, cognitive, educational or interpersonal domains, and proposed a performance model which focuses upon the examination of patterns of interaction rather than offsetting skills deficits.

The expansion of models of treatment, assessment and conceptualisation of child deviance has been reflected in the increasing tendency to combine BPT with *adjunctive treatments*, which are designed to offset the influence of contextual variables upon parent–child interactions and to enhance the generalisation of treatment effects. Kelly, Embry and Baer (1979) found that a combination of training in *marital conflict management* and *spouse support*, which was considered the most valuable aspect of training by the clients, led to the maintenance of treatment effects after six months. Wells, Griest and Forehand (1980) found significantly greater treatment gains among children whose parents had received parent training combined with *self-control training* than among children whose parents had received parent training only, although there was no difference between the two groups in terms of changes in parental behaviour. Self-control training consisted of self-monitoring and positively reinforcing the implementation of the parent management techniques. Griest *et al.* (1982) found significantly greater treatment gains among parents who received parent training and *parent enhancement therapy*, which focused upon parental perception of the child's behaviour, parental personal adjustment, parental marital adjustment and extra-familial relationships, than among parents who received parent training only. The combined treatment package led to a higher level of maintenance of changes in both parent and child behaviours at two months' follow-up. Kazdin *et al.* (1987) compared the effectiveness of a treatment programme which combined parent training with cognitive-behavioural problem-solving skills training, with parent training alone. Children whose parents underwent the combined treatment programme showed significantly less aversive behaviour and more prosocial behaviour one year after treatment than children whose parents had received parent training only. Wahler *et al.* (1992) compared the effectiveness of parent training with a treatment programme which combined parent training with *synthesis teaching.* Synthesis teaching involved training parents to discriminate between stressful stimuli which originate with the target child and those which originate either within or without the family domain. Although neither the parent training alone nor the combined treatment group manifested treatment gains in the clinic setting, the combined treatment group manifested delayed but progressive improvements in both parent and child behaviours in the home setting six months and one year after treatment.

Webster-Stratton (1994) found that, in families who received supplemental *advance training*, which comprised communication and problem-solving skills training, children showed significant increases in the number of prosocial solutions generated during problem-solving discussions, and parents were observed to have improved communication and problem-solving skills.

The contribution of adjunctive treatments to the generalisation of treatment effects of CMT has been extensively investigated. Sanders and Glynn (1981) examined the generalisation of treatment effects upon parent and child behaviours across settings during CMT followed by *self-management training.* During the self-management training phase of treatment, parents were trained in goal setting, self-monitoring and planning or arranging the stimulus environment. Self-management training led to increased changes in parent and child behaviours which generalised to non-training home and community settings and which were maintained three months after treatment. Sanders and Dadds (1982) examined setting generalisation during CMT followed by *planned activities training*. Planned activities training comprised skills in advance planning which were designed to be implemented in situations where parents had competing demands on their attention, for example during preparation of meals, during telephone calls or during shopping trips. Planned activities training led to increased changes in parent and child behaviour in both home and community settings in 60 per cent of families. Sanders and Christensen (1985) found, however, that planned activities training did *not* lead to increased changes in parent and child behaviour in a range of settings within the home and concluded that planned activities may produce greater effects in community settings. Sanders and Christensen (1985) also suggested that while some parents can employ management skills in all circumstances, other parents require setting-specific training for situations where either the child is especially difficult to manage or the parent engages in high rates of coercive behaviour. Dadds, Sanders and James (1987) examined setting generalisation among a group of multi-distressed families who received CMT and *generalisation training*, which comprised planned activities and social-marital support training. Generalisation training led to increased improvements in both parent and child behaviours in non-training home and community settings which were maintained at three months' follow-up. Dadds, Schwartz and Sanders (1987) compared changes in parent and child behaviour in response to CMT only and in response to CMT combined with *partner support training* (PST) among two groups of families who were distinguished by the presence and absence of marital discord. PST focused upon the marital relationship as a source of support in order to reduce sources of coercion and to increase parental supportive and problem-solving skills. While PST made little contribution to changes in parent and child behaviour in the non-discordant group, it led to significant changes in parent and child behaviour among the discordant group, although the rate of marital satisfaction continued to be lower among this group after treatment. Dadds and McHugh (1992) compared the treatment outcome of a group of single parents who received CMT only with that of a similar group who received CMT combined with *ally support training* (AST). AST consisted of training a nominated ally (such as a friend, neighbour or relative) of the single parent to respond to problems when needed, to share in casual discussions and to participate in problem-solving discussions. Although the combined treatment group did not differ from the CMT-only group on measures of parent and child behaviour either post-treatment or at six-month follow-up, a high rate of social support from friends was associated with responsiveness to treatment in both groups. Dadds and McHugh (1992) concluded that the results indicate both the importance of social support for positive treatment outcome and the difficulty in incorporating this variable into treatment programmes.

In an important development, in addition to addressing a range of contextual factors, BPT is increasingly implemented as a form of early intervention on a preventive basis. For example, the IY curriculum includes teacher and child training as part of an early intervention strategy for the prevention of child CD and attendant drug addiction and criminality. The children's curriculum (Dina Dinosaur School) (Webster-Stratton 1991) is a social skills programme which is designed to offset social skills deficits in conduct-problem children. The curriculum uses multiple media, including life-size puppets. It can be delivered in a small group format during 18 to 20 two-hour sessions and covers the following topics: making new friends and learning school rules, understanding feelings, problem-solving, how to be friendly and how to talk to friends. The curriculum can also be presented in a classroom format. The Teacher's Videotape series (Webster-Stratton 1992a, 1999) is designed to promote effective teacher responses to child conduct problems in the classroom setting. The curriculum covers the following topics: the importance of attention, encouragement and praise; motivating children through incentives; preventing problems; decreasing inappropriate behaviour and building positive relationships with students. A number of studies have examined the relative effectiveness of providing these curricula separately or in combination. Webster-Stratton and Hammond (1997) found that the combination of parent and child training was more effective than parent training alone. Webster-Stratton, Reid and Hammond (2004a) found that teacher training in conjunction with parent training led to greater improvements in classroom and social behaviour. Webster-Stratton, Reid and Hammond (2004b) suggested that the combination of parent training with either teacher training or child training might be the most effective means of intervention for children with severe conduct problems.

The preventive treatment model has also been expanded to include whole populations. The Triple P-Positive Parenting Programme (Sanders 1999) comprises five levels of intervention which vary in strength and comprise:

- Level 1, a universal parent information strategy based on a coordinated media campaign
- Level 2, a brief one- to two-session primary health care intervention

- Level 3, a four-session intervention which targets children with mild conduct problems
- Level 4, an intensive eight- to ten-session individual or group parent training programme for children with moderate conduct problems
- Level 5, a high-strength behavioural family intervention programme using the CMT home-based format and adjunctive treatment such as partner support skills.

The Triple-P programme is aimed at whole populations and has therefore not been evaluated as a complete entity to date. A number of its components have been evaluated, however. Sanders, Montgomery and Brechman-Toussaint (2000) found that high- and low-strength levels of intervention were equally effective in reducing child behaviour problems, but that parents in therapist-assisted levels of intervention were more satisfied in their parenting roles than parents who participated in self-directed training. The authors concluded, however, that 'more is not always better than less' (p.12) and advised that high-strength intervention should only be offered to those families where lower level intervention has not been effective. Connell, Sanders and Markie-Dadds (1997) found that parents who were provided with self-directed behavioural family intervention reported higher levels of competence and lower levels of dysfunctional parenting practices. Sanders *et al.* (2000) found that parents who had watched a 12–episode television series on disruptive behaviour and family adjustment reported lower levels of disruptive child behaviour and higher levels of perceived parental competence.

Summary

BPT is a form of therapeutic intervention in which parents are trained to alter their child's behaviour. While BPT has been implemented in connection with a wide range of problems in children, it is closely identified with CD because ecological factors which promote CD have been found to inhibit the effectiveness of BPT. The triadic model which applies in BPT has led to the recruitment of parents as cotherapists with whom the therapist works in a collaborative relationship. BPT has been delivered in a number of different formats which include individual clinic-based programmes, group-training programmes which are community-based or clinic-based, and home-based programmes. While there appears to be little to choose between the different formats in terms of overall effectiveness, the group format appears to be the least expensive to implement.

The models of assessment, treatment and conceptualisation of child deviance on which BPT is based have expanded as research has revealed the role which ecological variables play in the development and maintenance of CD. This expansion has led to the development of a range of adjunctive treatments designed to offset the influence of factors outside the parent–child dyad. Generalisation of treatment has been assessed across settings, across behaviours, to siblings and over defined periods of time. The expansion of the treatment model has also led to the provision of child and teacher training in conjunction with parent training and to the provision of BPT on a preventive and universal basis.

Part 2

Implementing Behavioural Parent Training

Chapter 4

Assessment

Introduction

During the discussion of the classification of child conduct problems in Chapter 2, it was noted that the incorporation of all three methods of classification into the assessment process has been advocated. This chapter therefore describes an assessment procedure which includes a comprehensive initial assessment interview which facilitates formal diagnosis, a brief review of behavioural checklists, which are relevant to the assessment of child conduct problems, and a scheme for conducting observations of parent–child interactions.

The initial assessment interview: Content

Child conduct problems which lead parents to seek professional intervention usually involve a broad range of problem behaviours which occur in a number of settings. Careful assessment of particular problem behaviours can inform the focus of intervention because conduct problems which occur in a number of settings tend to be more severe and resistant to intervention (Richman *et al.* 1982). Furthermore, it is important to assess the different settings in which conduct problems occur, as parents find child management tasks more difficult to perform in different settings (Sanders and Christensen 1985).

Presenting concerns (home settings)

Detailed information about problem behaviours in the home setting can be obtained by asking specific questions about discrete behaviours. A parental report that the child is 'very difficult at home' can be explored to yield detailed information about types and instances of behaviour. These may include the following: non-compliance (the refusal to follow adult instructions), defiance (verbal protests in response to adult instructions), oppositional behaviour (the refusal to follow adult instruction before the instruction has been issued), verbal aggression (curses, insults, screams), physical aggression (hitting, kicking, punching), damage to belongings (the child's own and others') and tantrums. The ABC contingency provides a useful tool for the analysis of each behaviour. For example, when a detailed account of the frequency, intensity and duration of tantrums has been obtained, it is useful to ask about what leads to tantrums and what follows them. Parents often report extreme responses by the child to innocuous events or minor frustrations that occur in the course of the normal daily routine and which the child experiences as 'noxious intrusions' (Patterson 1982).

Problem behaviours are more likely to occur in certain settings in the home such as at morning time, mealtime and bedtime (Sanders and Christensen 1985). Problem behaviours in these settings, which comprise behavioural excesses, often mask behavioural deficits in terms of self-help skills (e.g. getting dressed, using cutlery and sitting at the table, brushing teeth and settling self in bed).

Presenting concerns (community settings)

Community settings (such as supermarkets, shopping malls, households of extended family and friends, as well as while travelling by car and by public transport) can serve as setting events for child conduct problems. This is because parents who resort to coercive methods of discipline in the home are often inhibited from using them in public. Furthermore, community settings often expose children to preferred items (such as sweets) which elicit demanding behaviour. Settings which involve crowds and traffic raise considerations of safety and therefore require a high degree of cooperation between parent and child. Children's behaviour often deteriorates in the households of extended family (particularly grandparents) and friends in response to interference by adults other than parents. Parents often report that they avoid bringing the child to community settings (such as the supermarket) where they experience the child as unmanageable. Although parents often present the management of difficult behaviour in community settings as a primary source of concern, and although behavioural parent training (BPT) programmes have been devised for specific problem settings such as, for example, the supermarket (Barnard, Christopherson and Wolf 1977; Clark *et al.* 1977), child conduct problems which occur in community settings are generally also evident in the home setting. Parents are often overwhelmed by the apparent impossibility of negotiating the extra complications of child management in community settings successfully. It is therefore advisable to assure them that the initial focus of intervention will be on child management in the security of the home setting. Behavioural excesses in community settings usually involve tantrums and going missing. Frequently reported skill deficits in community settings include the inability to sit in a supermarket trolley or buggy, to stand or walk beside the parent, to hold the parent's hand or to use a seatbelt.

Presenting concerns (school settings)

The occurrence of child conduct problems in more than one setting is an important indicator of severity (Richman et al. 1982). It is therefore important to obtain information about the child's adjustment in the school setting by seeking the following information:

- the number of schools which the child has attended, reasons for leaving any previous school (if applicable), status of current school
- the role played by the school in the referral for professional help
- a parental verbal report of any current school-based difficulties, which should also include the current and past parent/school relationship in terms of collaboration and joint problem solving
- copies of school reports including, if available, educational psychological reports
- indicators of learning difficulties and/or difficulties in the areas of concentration and activity in written school work
- a parent's (and, if possible, a teacher's) verbal report of school adjustment in terms of engagement in individual and group activities and transitions, and behaviour in the schoolyard and on school transport.

Developmental history

A comprehensive history of the child's development yields important information about the child's development, as well as information about the parent–child relationship and how it developed, and about the child's reinforcement history. Specific questions about the following topics yield detailed and relevant information:

- *Conception*: whether planned or unplanned, although this sensitive topic should not be discussed in the child's presence.

- *Pregnancy*: mother's health during pregnancy.

- *Birth*: whether premature, at the expected time, or delayed; whether the delivery was normal or required intervention; whether the baby was stressed and required special care or not; if the baby required special care, what it comprised and the parental concerns and anxieties associated with it; the length of hospital stay and the circumstances of departure.

- *Early infancy (to three months)*: whether the parent(s) could establish a feeding and sleep routine; when the baby first slept through the night; illnesses and/or hospitalisations; how parent(s) experienced baby care.

- *Year 1*: developmental milestones, including sitting up, standing and (perhaps) walking; illnesses and/or hospitalisations; how the parent(s) experienced the child's increasing mobility and levels of activity.

- *Years 2 and 3*: speech and language development; the course and outcome of toilet training.

- *Preschool experience*: whether the child attended preschool and if not, why; the experience of the child and parent(s) of separation; information which the parent(s) received about the child's adjustment and functioning in the preschool setting.

- *School*: further experience of separation by parent(s) and child; initial adjustment to classroom and yard settings; school reports on learning, behaviour and social relationships; level of cooperation between parent(s) and school.

- *Social relationships*: joint play and the development of relationships with siblings and with neighbouring children.

- *Involvement in community activities*: such as sports and recreational clubs; ability to participate in group or team activities; responses to supervising adults and peers; parental support for child's involvement in community activities.

Parental background

Parents can experience direct questions about their own background as intrusive. In order to facilitate the development of a cooperative relationship with the parent(s), it important to explain the rationale for such questions. (See the following section for a discussion of the interview process.) It is also important to emphasise that only personal information which is relevant to their role and functioning as a parent is being sought. Questions can be asked about the following topics:

- Ordinal position in family of origin; whether the ordinal position affected the parents' childhood experiences.

- Child care practices in family of origin; what degree of priority was given to child care.

- Parenting practices in the family of origin: whether parents lived together; whether parenting roles were joint or discrete; whether parenting style was authoritarian or *laissez faire*; whether discipline was harsh and/or fair; whether the family of origin's parenting practices provide a constructive model of parenting; whether the parents experienced particular challenges; how they would have dealt with the current difficulties.

- Family functioning, whether stable or disrupted; specific stressors, such as financial or health problems.

- School experience: whether parental experience of school was positive or negative; whether particular difficulties arose and, if so, how teachers and parents dealt with them.

- Experience of adolescence; whether parenting style changed to accommodate the onset of adolescence.

- Circumstances of leaving home: what they were and whether it was with agreement and support of parents.

- Current level of contact with the extended family; whether they are aware of the current difficulties and, if so, what their views on them are; whether family of origin members are available as a source of practical and emotional support; other sources of stress and support within the social and community network; involvement with other services.

Family history

As noted above, it is important to assure parents that information about their background, adjustment and functioning is being sought inasmuch as it is relevant to the parenting role. Questions about the history of the nuclear family (as distinct from that of the family of origin, which is covered when obtaining information about the parent's history) distinguish between lone- and two-parent families. With lone-parent families, it is important to ascertain whether the other parent is or has been involved in the family and whether or not he or she is involved in parenting. With two-parent families, it is important to ascertain the course and history of the parent relationship in terms of continuities and discontinuities.

Parenting

- Parental response to current difficulties: areas of success and failure to date.
- Parenting style: whether the parent(s) characterise their own parenting practices as strict or easygoing; areas of similarity and difference between parents; areas of conflict and cooperation.
- Disciplinary practices: whether disciplinary practices are harsh; whether they involve loss of self-control on the part of the parent; what sanctions are resorted to and whether they are implemented consistently.
- Current experience of parenting: areas of stress and fulfilment.

Parental adjustment

- Intra-familial stressors: sources of intra-familial stress other than the specific child, whether the partner or other children.
- Extra-familial stressors: sources of extra-familial stress, such as employment or relations with neighbours, friends and extended family.
- Parental adjustment: physical health and emotional well-being.
- Coping mechanisms and sources of support: parental coping mechanisms with sources of intra-familial and extra-familial stress; sources of intra-familial and extra-familial support.
- Parental expectations of intervention: whether the parent(s) expect(s) the service to intervene directly with the child or whether they expect to be involved in the intervention plan.

The initial assessment interview: Process

Pre-interview process issues

The decision as to whom to invite to the initial assessment interview is influenced by family circumstances. Both parents should be expected to attend. If parents are living separately, divorced or legally separated, joint attendance should be expected, unless there is a history of acrimony to the extent that they would be unable to tolerate a joint assessment interview. While it is important to be flexible in order to accommodate parental work schedules and other commitments, it is also important to convey the expectation that both parents should attend, on the basis that both parents are engaged in child care. As with all the therapist's expectations that are communicated to the client, it is important to attend to the client's response and to make adjustments that are sensitive to the circumstances of the family through discussion. The decision as to whether to invite the specified child only or all children in the family will be influenced by agency policy and practice.

Parent–therapist interactions

The initial assessment interview may provide the first face-to-face contact between the therapist and parent. As has been noted, the quality of engagement with the parent and the manner in which the parent–therapist relationship is structured have been identified as a central issue in BPT, with an increasing emphasis upon a collaborative, rather than an expert, model of service delivery (see the section 'The triadic model' in Chapter 3). The initial assessment interview therefore presents an opportunity to establish a collaborative alliance with the parent. The therapist can establish a collaborative alliance with the parent by implementing the following practices:

1. *Involving the parent in decision making.* While decisions regarding the establishment of the initial assessment interview will be largely determined by agency policy and practice, parents can be involved directly in decision making once face-to-face contact has been established. This includes decisions about how to accommodate the needs of the child during the interview, the structure and duration of the interview and further assessment measures, such as the completion of behavioural checklists and parental record-keeping (if these are indicated).

2. *Explaining the rationale for the therapist's activity.* The provision of a clear and explicit rationale for one's professional behaviour, particularly in a setting such as that of an interview, which can so easily support the expert role, can serve to demystify the expertise of the therapist and to enhance the engagement between therapist and client.

3. *Recognising and emphasising parental expertise.* While the therapist can acknowledge professional expertise about child problem behaviour and its influences in general, it is helpful to emphasise parental expertise about the specific child's unique personality, strengths, likes and dislikes. It is also helpful to note parental assets and areas in which the parent has been successful in managing the child's behaviour, rather than to assume that the parenting history is uniformly negative.

Throughout the assessment and intervention phases, the therapist provides an important role model to the parent of appropriate adult- and child-oriented behaviour.

1. *Modelling appropriate behaviour towards adults.* During the assessment phase, the therapist's behaviour towards the parent should be consistent with the overall goal of establishing a collaborative working relationship and include active listening, accurate empathy, constructive problem solving, humour which does not distract from the assessment process, and expressions of optimism.

2. *Modelling appropriate behaviour towards children.* The therapist can model child-management skills such as positive attention for appropriate behaviour and issuing clear instructions. Most importantly, in the event of a temper tantrum arising during the course of the interview, the therapist can model ignoring by persisting with, and engaging the parent in, the interview process.

Parent–child interactions

While the initial assessment interview is designed to obtain detailed information about the specific child and about aspects of the family context within which problem behaviour occurs, it also provides an opportunity to observe parent–child interactions. The interview requires the parents to engage actively in discussion with the therapist, thereby providing a setting in which the parent's attention is diverted from the child. The situation is therefore analogous to home situations in which child problem behaviours frequently occur, such as when parents are speaking on the phone or engaged in discussion with visitors. It is important to note parent behaviours towards the child that arise in the interview setting. This can be facilitated by a brief initial discussion about respective roles for the duration of the interview, with the therapist being responsible for the collection of information and the parent being responsible for child management. When respective roles have been agreed upon, the therapist can note the following parent and child behaviours, and how each is responded to.

1. *Settling the child.* During discussion, the parent will have been introduced to the setting and to the play materials which are available, such as toys and drawing materials, and encouraged to respond to the child as if talking to a visitor at home. Does the parent introduce the child to the relevant materials, attend to the child's initial response and positively reinforce appropriate play skills?

2. *Monitoring the child's behaviour.* Does the parent maintain an awareness of the child's activity and whereabouts by scanning at intervals, anticipating the child's frustration and providing guidance, support and reassurance?

3. *Reinforcing appropriate child behaviour.* Does the parent attend to and positively reinforce appropriate child behaviour such as independent play?

4. *Ignoring inappropriate child behaviour.* Does the parent ignore inappropriate child behaviour such as whining and demanding?

5. *Setting limits.* Does the parent give clear or unclear instructions during the interview?

The interview setting also provides an opportunity to observe a range of child behaviours. It is important to consider these in terms of the child's development and behavioural repertoire.

1. *Separation.* Does the child separate from the parent in order to engage in play activities or cling to the parent by, for example, sitting on the parent's knee?

2. *Play.* Is the child's play constructive or destructive? Does the child engage in imaginative play or is play repetitive?

3. *Appropriate behaviour.* Does the child seek parental attention at regular intervals during the assessment interview?

4. *Inappropriate behaviour.* It is likely that the parent will have to set some limits on the child owing to the restricted setting of the interview room and the duration of the interview. How does the child respond to limits?

Child–therapist interactions

If direct observations of parent–child interaction are planned as part of the overall assessment strategy, it may not be necessary to include the child in the initial assessment interview – in fact it may be counterproductive to do so. The initial assessment interview, in which the therapist actively engages with the parent, also constitutes an opportunity to engage with the child. Direct engagement with the child will, however, increase the child's awareness of the therapist, so that the *reactor effect* (where the behaviour of participants is influenced by the presence of the observer) is more likely to come into play. If another therapist is due to conduct direct observations, this does not arise as an issue. The therapist can provide a model of appropriate adult–child behaviour, being responsive to cues from the child and positive in demeanour, and (if necessary) setting firm limits.

Parent records

It is important to check the parent's level of literacy and the level of detail with which the parent is comfortable, and to keep the recording task simple and practicable. (For sample record sheets, see Appendix I.) The request of parents to keep a record of their child's behaviour serves a number of functions.

1. *Active engagement in assessment process.* First, the act of keeping records at the request of the therapist actively engages the parent in the assessment process and enhances the collaborative relationship between therapist and parent. Parent record-keeping is a joint effort between the two parties: the therapist provides the record sheets and expertise about their use (including, if possible, sample sheets already completed), encouragement and practical support (such as stamped addressed envelopes) and the parent provides the data. This task therefore initiates a productive working relationship between therapist and parent, and it also serves as a useful indicator of the extent to which the parent is in agreement with and committed to the intervention process.

2. *Challenge global perceptions of child.* Parent records can challenge global parental perceptions, which are usually negative, of the child's behaviour by providing detailed information on its frequency, duration or intensity. A review of the record with the parent can provide a basis for exploring the parent's role in the maintenance of child problem behaviour in a non-threatening

manner. ABC charts are particularly useful in this regard (see Appendix I for a sample ABC chart). ABC charts are also useful in helping to select target behaviours.

3. *Data collection.* As primary caregivers, parents are in a unique position to collect data on a range of child behaviours in a broad range of settings. The identification of target behaviours will determine the choice of observational strategy. An event recording strategy is both practicable and informative for recording frequently occurring behaviours, whereas duration is a useful dimension for recording infrequent behaviours (see Appendix I for sample event and duration recording sheets). A time-sampling strategy, which was used in the studies described below, is also useful for recording frequently occurring behaviours.

Behavioural checklists

It is important to explain to parents why they are being asked to complete checklists and how they function. It is also important to be sensitive towards parents with low levels of literacy. Achenbach and Rescorla (2000) recommend that, when parents have literacy problems, they should be provided with a copy of the checklist to review while the therapist reads out the specific items. This procedure allows respondents who can read well enough to read the items themselves, and avoids inaccuracies and embarrassment for those who cannot read. Below is a brief description of some checklists which are relevant to the assessment of child conduct problems.

Child Behavior Checklist for ages 4–18 (CBCL) (Achenbach 1991)

The CBCL comprises 118 items. It measures parental perceptions of child behaviour problems. Each item contributes to eight specific dimensions of dysfunction which comprise anxious, somatic, depressed, social problems, thought problems, attentional problems, delinquent and aggressive behaviour. Five of the sub-scales are aggregated into two global dimensions of disturbance termed *internalising behaviour* and *externalising behaviour,* and yield a *total problems score.* The CBCL is of proven reliability and validity.

Child Behavior Checklist for ages 1.5–5 (CBCL) (Achenbach and Rescorla 2000)

The CBCL (1.5–5) is designed to be completed by parents and others who see children in the home setting. The manual also describes an accompanying Language Development Survey or LDS for ages 18–35 months and a Caregiver/Teacher Report (1.5–5). The CBCL (1.5–5) comprises 100 items about specific problems, and includes open-ended questions about the greatest concerns and the best things about the child. The individual items contribute to seven specific dimensions of behaviour which comprise emotionally reactive, anxious/depressed, somatic complaints, withdrawn, sleep problems, attention problems and aggressive behaviour. The first four dimensions are aggregated as internalising behaviour, and the last two as externalising behaviour, yielding a total problems score.

Eyberg Child Behavior Inventory (ECBI and Sutter-Eyberg Student Behaviour Inventory–Revised) (SESBI-R) (Eyberg and Pincus 1999)

The ECBI and the SESBI-R assess the severity of conduct problems and the extent to which parents and teachers find the behaviour difficult to manage in children of 2–16 years of age. The ECBI contains 36 items, each of which is rated on two scales: a seven-point Intensity which gives an indication of the frequency of the behaviour and a Yes/No Problem Scale which indicates whether or not the behaviour is a problem. The measure takes approximately ten minutes to complete. The psychometric properties of both the ECBI and the SESBI-R are well established.

Conners' Rating Scales – Revised (CRS-R) (Conners 1997)

The CRS-R includes parent, teacher and self-report scales, has long and short versions for teachers and parents and is used primarily in the assessment of ADHD. Parents are asked to rate the child's behaviour during the past month. The long version for parents (which the authors recommend for use where possible as it yields more information) includes 80 items which are aggregated into 14 sub-scales: oppositional, cognitive problems, hyperactivity, anxious-shy, perfectionism, social problems, psychosomatic, Conners' global index, restless-impulsive, emotional lability, attention deficit hyperactivity disorder (ADHD) index, DSM-IV symptoms sub-scale, DSM-IV inattentive and DSM-IV hyperactive-impulsive. The CRS-R is of proven reliability and validity.

Parenting Stress Index (PSI) (Abidin 1990)

The PSI is designed to measure the relative components of stress in the parent–child dyad and has a long and short version. The long version has 101 items and has been tested for reliability and validity. The child domain includes items on adaptability, acceptability, demandingness, mood and distractibility-hyperactivity. The parent domain includes items on depression, attachment, restriction of role, sense of competence, social isolation, relationship with spouse and parental health.

The General Health Questionnaire (GHQ) (Goldberg and Williams 1988)

The GHQ is a self-administered screening test designed to detect psychiatric disorders which may affect the current functioning of the respondent. Its focus is therefore on the psychological components of ill health and it examines two classes of phenomena: the inability to continue to carry out one's normal functions and the appearance of new, distressing phenomena. The questionnaire contains 93 items which yield four sub-scales: depression, anxiety, objectively observable behaviour and hypochondriasis. It is of proven reliability and validity.

Observations of parent–child interactions

Consent

It is necessary to seek written consent from parents when conducting direct observations of parent–child interactions, whether these are conducted in the home or the agency setting. The consent form should specify the time, the duration and the primary therapeutic purpose of observations. It should also specify whether a written or a videotaped record of the observation will be kept, and the measures which will be taken to ensure secure storage of the record. If it is intended to use the data that is obtained for other purposes, such as teaching or research, these should be stated explicitly. (See Appendix III for a sample consent form.)

Defining the field of observation

It is interesting to note that the strategic dilemmas which arise for the therapist in conducting observations of parent–child interactions are not dissimilar to those of the naturalist engaged, for example, in observing ant colonies in the natural setting (Parke 1979). The task of conducting direct observations in the natural setting requires the observer to compromise between environmental conditions and the needs of the observer. In order to observe parent and child interactions in the home setting the observer must accommodate him- or herself to the vagaries of the setting. The observer must, however, also impose some degree of structure on the setting, in order to increase the likelihood that behaviours of interest, such as defiance, non-compliance and giving instructions arise during the period of observation. Clinic-based observations ensure that each family is observed in the same setting (e.g. Forehand and McMahon 1981), whereas home-based observations ensure that parent–child observations are observed in the natural setting. The Parent and Child's Game (Forehand and McMahon 1981) provides a very useful means of structuring home observations (see the section 'Alternative training formats' in Chapter 3). This format requires the parent to engage the child initially in a preferred activity, such as a game of his or her choice. When 10–15 minutes have elapsed, the parent instructs the child to tidy up, and then instructs the child to perform an age-appropriate chore. Parents generally report that the three-stage sequence of a preferred activity followed by a transition to a non-preferred activity, resembles many situations that arise naturally in the home setting. Sanders and Dadds (1993) includes an extra phase, termed *parent preoccupied*, in which the parent's attention is devoted to a task such as washing dishes or conversing on the telephone, on the basis of research which found that this situation frequently elicits problem child behaviour (Sanders and Christensen 1985). Gardner (1994) introduced a similar variation to the format by requiring the parent to complete checklists and to interact with the researcher during some portion of the observation period, and provided a set of play materials in order to ensure some degree of standardisation between home settings.

It is helpful to provide the parent with a set of printed guidelines for structuring 30-minute observation sessions:

1. Family members to remain in the living area of the house within view of the observer.

2. The television set to be switched off.

3. Visitors and phone calls to be kept to a minimum.

4. Other family members to be present.

5. The observation session should include 15 minutes of play activity chosen by the child followed by 15 minutes of goal-directed activity chosen by the parent.

These guidelines are discussed with the parent prior to the observation session. This discussion addresses the following issues:

1. *Location in the home.* Parents identify the area of the home (rather than a reception room, if the house includes one) where the family generally congregates as the most appropriate setting for the observation.

2. *Distractions.* While the requirement to turn off the television and computer game consoles is often greeted with surprise, and at times bewilderment, parents readily accept the rationale that these media greatly reduce the level of parent–child interactions because they engage children's attention very effectively.

3. *Interruptions.* Parents are assured that, while they are requested to keep interruptions to a minimum, they can terminate the observation session should a situation arise which requires their urgent attention.

4. *Other family members.* The observational coding scheme which was used in the studies described in Chapters 5 to 8 focuses on the interaction between the specific child and one parent and therefore does not require the presence of both parents (see Appendix II). Siblings who are older than ten years of age generally object to being included in home observations, are reactive to an observer and therefore can be excluded. Siblings who are younger than ten years should be present and can be actively included in observation sessions, as their presence can often lead to the minor frustrations which elicit child problem behaviour. Furthermore, the presence of these siblings can provide an opportunity to assess to what extent generalisation of child management techniques to siblings is being achieved.

Observational procedures

Observation sessions should be arranged for a time which is convenient for the family and feasible for the therapist. Observation sessions are limited to 30 minutes as there is a large body of evidence that *observer drift*, which refers to the lapse of the observer's attention and consequent loss of data reliability, increases when the observation period exceeds 30 minutes (Cooper *et al.* 1987). The observation schedule which was used for data collection in the studies described in Chapters 5 to 8 is provided in Appendix II. The coding sheets for the schedule are included in Appendix IV.

Behaviour categories

This observational coding schedule is based on the Family Observation Schedule – V (FOS-5) (Dadds and Sanders 1996). The FOS-5 was modified to include an instructional sequence (Table 4.1), categories for specific parent behaviours (Table 4.2) and categories for specific child behaviours

(Table 4.3). (For a comprehensive description of these behaviours, see Appendix II.) The coding schedule was modified during Studies 1 and 2 (see Chapters 5 and 6). The schedule which is printed in Appendix II is the final version, which was used in Studies 3, 4 and 5 (see Chapters 7 and 8).

Table 4.1 Instructional sequence categories

Category	Symbol	Definition
Alpha instruction	Ia	An order, suggestion, rule or question to which a motor response is feasible and which is presented in a non-aversive manner
Aversive alpha instruction	Ia-	An alpha instruction which is presented aversively
Beta instruction	Ib	A command with which the child has no opportunity to comply owing to vagueness or to lack of opportunity to respond
Aversive beta instruction	Ib-	A beta instruction which is delivered in an aversive manner
Compliance	c	Compliance or attempt to comply with parental instruction within five seconds
Non-compliance	nc	Non-compliance with parental instruction within five seconds

Table 4.2 Parent behaviour categories

Category	Symbol	Definition
Parent contingent attention		
Praise	Pr	Praise, approval or acknowledgement, in response to compliance or prosocial child behaviour
Response cost	RC	Warning or withdrawal of privilege in response to non-compliance
Time out	TO	Warning or implementation of time out in response to noncompliance or aversive child behaviour
Contingent attend positive	cA+	Parent attends to child behaviour with verbal or non-verbal positive affect
Contingent attend negative	cA-	Parent attends to child behaviour with verbal or non-verbal negative affect
Contingent attend neutral	cAo	Parent attends to child behaviour with verbal or non-verbal neutral affect
Parent non-contingent attention		
Non-contingent attend positive	A+	Parent verbal or non-verbal positive attention which is not contingent on the child's behaviour
Non-contingent attend negative	A-	Parent verbal or non-verbal negative attention which is not contingent on the child's behaviour
Non-contingent attend neutral	Ao	Parent verbal or non-verbal neutral attention which is not contingent on the child's behaviour
Non-attend	Na	Parent does not attend to the target child

Table 4.3 Child behaviour categories

Category	Symbol	Definition
Child aversive		
Physical negative	p-	Actual or threatened motor movement in relation to another person that involves inflicting physical pain. Also destruction of objects
Complaint	ct	Whining, crying, protesting, temper tantrums
Demand	d	An instruction or command which is aversive due to tone and/or content
Oppositional	o	Inappropriate child behaviour that cannot be included readily into any other categories
Child prosocial		
Appropriate	apr	Constructive, self-directed behaviour
Social attention	s+	Prosocial, verbal or non-verbal child attention to other family members
Off task	ot	Child stops performing task

Chapter 5

Compliance training

Introduction

Compliance training refers to a set of procedures where the child is reinforced for responding appropriately to parental instructions. Ducharme and Popynick (1993) describe compliance as a keystone behaviour, because an increase in compliant responding has been associated with an increase in non-targeted prosocial behaviours, a phenomenon which is termed *behavioural co-variation*. The inverse co-variation between compliance and aversive responding has been examined in a number of studies (Parrish *et al.* 1986; Russo, Cataldo and Cushing 1981). Cataldo *et al.* (1986) concluded that there was 'strong support for a clinical treatment strategy based on reinforcing children for complying with instructions in order to also modify a variety of problem behaviours in addition to non-compliance' (Cataldo *et al.* 1986, p.279).

The therapeutic potential of compliance training to modify non-compliance as well as untreated aversive behaviour has been illustrated in a number of studies. Mace *et al.* (1988) found a *behavioural momentum* effect whereby compliance to high-probability commands led to an increase in compliance to low-probability commands. Ducharme and Popynick (1993) also distinguished between high- and low-probability commands in order to teach compliant responding to four developmentally disabled children. This distinction formed the basis of an *errorless learning* approach to compliance training, whereby compliance to high-probability instructions was reinforced before the presentation of low-probability instructions. The positive reinforcement of compliance to high-probability instructions led to less non-compliance to low-probability instructions. The treatment potential of compliance training has also been discussed in terms of the generalisation of treatment effects:

> Since almost any behaviour problem can be identified as a compliance problem, an immediate solution is provided for the target or referred problem… Generalisation is inherent in the procedure instead of a process that parents must extrapolate from successive behaviour programmes or from being taught principles. (Cataldo 1984, p.340)

Although all these studies suggest that compliance training is an indirect means of reducing both aversive behaviour and non-compliance, a number of ethical considerations arises. First, it is important to establish that compliance to instruction is not a terminal goal and that compliance training takes place within the context of a programme which includes other elements which promote prosocial responding (LaVigna and Donnellan 1986). Second, some compliance training programmes have advocated the use of *forced responding*, which refers to the physical management of the subject in order to ensure compliance (Englemann and Colvin 1983). The physical management of severely oppositional and aggressive children within the context of a compliance training programme can lead to confrontational parent–child interactions (Ducharme and Popynick 1993). There are risks associated with the physical management of conduct-disordered children. First, abusive parents have been found to engage in more physical discipline strategies than non-abusive parents (Urquiza and McNeil 1996). Second, the physical abuse of children often takes place within the context of disciplinary confrontations (Bourne 1993). Third, a higher rate of physical abuse has been found among aggressive clinic-referred children (Patterson 1982).

Study 1 was designed to examine the inverse co-variation between compliance and aversive behaviour in a child with conduct problems. It was anticipated that if only one instance of child behaviour was recorded in each interval, the reduction in the overall rate of aversive child behaviour during sessions could be explained by *physical incompatibility* between aversive and compliant responding (Cataldo *et al.* 1986). According to this explanation, the rate of aversive responding decreases because there is less time available to the client to respond aversively due to the increase in the rate of compliance, rather than because of a functional relationship between these two classes of behaviour. The strategy which was suggested by Cataldo *et al.* (1986) as a solution to this problem was therefore adopted: during intervals when child compliance was observed, a further measure of child behaviour during the same interval was also recorded. It was hypothesised that this strategy would facilitate the examination of the functional relationship between compliant and aversive responding.

Study 1

Background

The behavioural parent training (BPT) programme which is described in Study 1 adopts the home-based training format of child management training (CMT) (Sanders and Dadds 1982, 1993), but it is based upon a different treatment strategy. CMT is based primarily upon a behaviour reduction strategy, according to which parents are trained to apply a behaviour correction procedure to specified problem behaviours such as demands, aggression, temper tantrums, interrupting and non-compliance. A compliance training strategy was adopted as an alternative to a behaviour reduction strategy for four reasons. First, compliance occupies a central position in the socialisation of children (Patterson *et al.* 1992). Second, the inverse co-variation between compliance and aversive responding endows compliance training with the potential to reduce aversive child behaviour indirectly by increasing compliant responding (Cataldo 1984). Third, the reduction of child conduct problems by indirect methods is consistent with a growing trend in behaviour analysis to adopt constructive interventions which increase prosocial responding as an alternative to punishment (Donnellan *et al.* 1988; LaVigna and Donnellan 1986; Sidman 1989). Fourth, it has been argued that a wide range of aversive child behaviours can be construed as non-compliance and responded to appropriately by an instructional procedure (Cataldo 1984).

The choice of the programme's constituent elements was determined by the adoption of a compliance training strategy. First, compliance training comprised instruction-giving and positive reinforcement of compliance. Second, planned activities training was chosen in order to enable parents to issue instructions in a positive context (Sanders and Dadds 1982). This procedure enables the parent to plan activities in advance. It therefore establishes the stimulus context within which positive instructions, with which the child is likely to comply, can be issued. It also offers opportunities for positive reinforcement of compliance. Third, a mild correction procedure (response cost) was chosen in order to reduce non-compliance. Response cost was chosen as an alternative to planned non-reinforcement (extinction) (Little and Kelly 1989). The decision not to employ an extinction procedure in response to non-compliance was based upon the observation by Patterson (1982) that when parents ignored aggressive behaviour they appeared to reinforce it. It was hypothesised that compliance training, in combination with planned activities training and response cost, would increase prosocial parent and child behaviours. The aim of the study was to examine the inverse co-variation of compliant responding and aggressive behaviour in a child with conduct problems.

Method

Client

The client was a six-year-old boy, an only child who had been referred due to behaviour problems. His mother reported physical aggression, non-compliance and oppositional behaviour during an initial assessment interview. Child problem behaviours had developed while she and her son lived with her parents, who were over-indulgent and inconsistent in child management. The father was not involved at any stage in the client's upbringing and was not involved in treatment. Mother and son were housed by the local authority when the subject was five years old, when child management difficulties became more pronounced. The mother had attended a community-based parent training group which had improved her ability to manage problem behaviour. She sought further assistance when problem behaviours re-emerged. The mother's verbal report of problem behaviour was confirmed during baseline home observations.

Screening

The following criteria were set for inclusion in the study:

1. The subject was between three and seven years of age and not suffering from an organic condition which was directly associated with behaviour problems.

2. During a pre-baseline assessment interview, parents reported child behaviour problems including non-compliance.

3. The child scored within the clinically significant range for externalising behaviour on the Child Behaviour Checklist (CBCL) (Achenbach 1991).

4. A score was recorded within the clinically significant range on the child domain of the Parenting Stress Index (PSI) (Abidin 1990).

5. A rate of compliance to instructions of 40 per cent or less was noted during baseline home observations (Forehand and McMahon 1981).

Consent

Written consent was obtained from the mother to conduct home observations and to use the data for treatment and research. (See Appendix III.)

Settings

Observation/feedback sessions were conducted twice-weekly in a training setting within the home during all phases of the study. The mother was issued with written guidelines on how to structure the observation session. (See Chapter 4.)

Design

The design in this study included baseline, two training phases, post-training and follow-up.

Observational procedures, behaviour categories

Observational procedures and behaviour categories which were adopted in Study 1 are described in Chapter 4.

Baseline

Three observations were conducted during the baseline phase.

Intervention Phase 1

The author acted as therapist and conducted observations in the training setting. The mother was instructed in the use of activity planning, instruction-giving and response cost during an initial clinic-based training session which was of two hours' duration. Didactic methods included printed handouts, role-play and discussion. Further instruction took place during twice-weekly observation/feedback sessions, which consisted of 30 minutes' observation and 30 minutes' feedback and discussion, during which the mother was provided with verbal and written feedback on her implementation of procedures.

Intervention Phase 2

The mother was taught to apply the planned activities procedure to the test setting and to devise specific strategies for the reduction of aggressive behaviour (e.g., to give her son advance warning of time to come in from play).

Post-training phase

Written feedback was discontinued and the mother was encouraged to make her own evaluation of her implementation of procedures during observation sessions.

Follow-up

One observation was conducted after an interval of six weeks.

Results

Child compliance and aversive child behaviour

The inverse co-variation between child compliance and aversive child behaviour was examined by comparing the percentage of intervals in which these behaviours occurred across observation sessions. The average incidence of child compliance and of aversive child behaviour during baseline were respectively 14 per cent and 24 per cent (Figure 5.1). The introduction of Phase 1 of treatment was associated with an inverse co-variation between compliance, which increased to an average of 29 per cent, and aversive behaviour, which decreased to an average of 6 per cent of intervals. The incidence of compliance during Phase 2 of treatment did not alter significantly and averaged 32 per cent of intervals. The incidence of aversive behaviour during Phase 2 averaged 8 per cent of intervals. The incidence of compliance and of aversive behaviour during post-training were 27 per cent and 17 per cent respectively. At follow-up, compliance and aversive behaviour were 35 per cent and 3 per cent respectively.

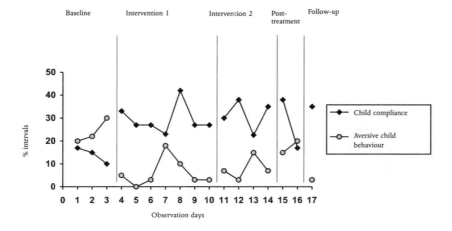

Figure 5.1 Percentage intervals compliance and aversive child behaviour across sessions

Rate of effective instructions

The rate of effective instructions was calculated by taking alpha instructions as a percentage of total instructions across sessions. The average rate of effective instructions was 50 per cent during baseline (Figure 5.2). This increased significantly to an average rate of 82 per cent during Phase 1 of treatment, which was maintained at 89 per cent during Phase 2 and at 86 per cent during post-training. The rate of effective instructions at follow-up was 80 per cent.

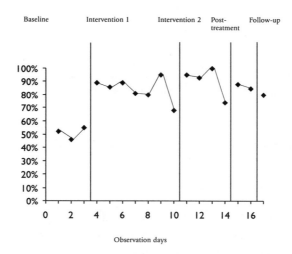

Figure 5.2 Rate of effective instructions across sessions

Rate of behaviour reduction procedure

The rate of the implementation of the behaviour reduction procedure in response to non-compliance was calculated by taking response cost as a percentage of child compliance across sessions. The average rate of parental use of the behaviour reduction procedure in response to child non-compliance during baseline was zero (Figure 5.3). The average rate of child non-compliance during baseline was 62 per cent. The rate of behaviour reduction in response to non-compliance increased significantly to an average of 52 per cent during Phase 1 of treatment. The rate of behaviour reduction on observation days eight and ten was zero, as child non-compliance was not observed on either day. The average rate of behaviour reduction during Phase 2 of treatment was 70 per cent, which decreased to 50 per cent during post-training. The rate of parental use of the behaviour reduction procedure in response to child non-compliance at follow-up was zero, as child non-compliance was not observed.

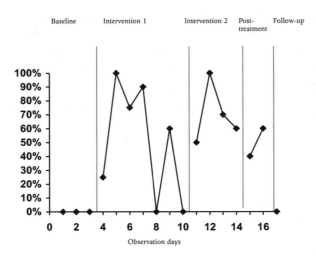

Figure 5.3 Rate of behaviour reduction procedure in response to child non-compliance across sessions

Discussion

BPT was implemented with a lone parent and her six-year-old son. The programme was based on a compliance training strategy and included three procedures: planned activities, instruction-giving and response cost. The inverse co-variation between compliance and child aversive behaviour was demonstrated. The results of this study show that parent and child behaviours changed in response to BPT. The changes in parent and child behaviour were significant and were maintained at six weeks' follow-up. The results of the study must be treated with some caution due to the lack of independent reliability assessments for observational data in the training setting, the reliance on self-report data in the test setting and the relatively short length of time between treatment and follow-up observations. The results do suggest, however, that the procedures were effective in increasing child compliance and in reducing aversive child behaviour. They also suggest that parent instructional skills improved in response to BPT.

Chapter 6

Non-coercive discipline

Introduction

While the inverse co-variation effect associated with compliance training represents an indirect means of reducing aversive child behaviour, the reduction of aversive behaviour by direct means has been strongly advocated in behavioural parent training (BPT):

> If I were allowed to select only one concept to use in training parents of antisocial children, I would teach them how to punish more effectively. It is the key to understanding familial aggression. (Patterson 1982, p.111)

This emphasis on the use of punishment techniques with children whose families are characterised by a high rate of coercive interactions initially appears to be self-contradictory. However, Patterson (1982) also emphasised the distinction between parental punishments such as spanking, beating and 'nattering', which function as maintaining stimuli for aggressive child behaviour, and effective punishment. Effective punishment is defined, not by its inherent aversiveness, but by its function in reducing target behaviours: 'Specifically, a decrease in the future probability of the occurrence of the behaviour must be observed before a procedure can be called punishment' (Cooper *et al.* 1987, p.411).

Type 2 punishment techniques, such as response cost and time out, which involve the removal of a positive reinforcer subsequent to a behaviour, have been widely implemented within the context of BPT. (Type 1 punishment, which involves the presentation of an aversive stimulus or event subsequent to a behaviour, is not used for reasons discussed below.)

Response cost

Response cost has been defined as 'a form of punishment in which the loss of a specific amount of reinforcement occurs, contingent upon the performance of an inappropriate behaviour, and results in the decreased probability of future occurrence of the behaviour' (Cooper *et al.* 1987). The loss of reinforcement is generally in the form of conditioned reinforcers such as points, tokens or stars. The reinforcers can be given non-contingently at the beginning of the day, contingently in response to appropriate behaviour as part of a token economy, and as part of an individual or group contingency programme (Pazulinec, Meyerrose and Sajwaj 1983). Cooper *et al.* (1987) emphasise that, while the procedure may be implemented correctly, it does not constitute response cost unless it functions to reduce target behaviours. Response cost has been implemented by teachers and residential staff to reduce inappropriate child behaviour in classroom and institutional settings (Pazulinec *et al.* 1983). Response cost has also been implemented successfully by parents in home and community settings (Hall *et al.* 1970). Response cost has also been used in conjunction with token reinforcement to increase appropriate behaviour in the supermarket (Barnard *et al.* 1977; Clark *et al.* 1977). Little and Kelly (1989) found that a response cost procedure, in which the child was awarded free points at the beginning of three or four intervals during the course of an entire day, was effective in decreasing non-compliance and aversive parent and child behaviour, and concluded: 'response cost may be a new procedure to add to current behaviour management techniques offered to parents. Response cost was relatively easy, effective and acceptable to parents' (p.533).

Time out

Time out has been defined as:

> the withdrawal of the opportunity to earn positive reinforcement or the loss of access to positive reinforcers for a specified period of time, contingent upon the occurrence of a behaviour; the effect is to reduce the future probability of that behaviour. (Cooper *et al.* 1987, p.440)

Whereas response cost involves the withdrawal of a positive stimulus, such as a token, contingent upon the occurrence of the target behaviour, both time out and extinction involve the withholding of a reinforcing consequence, such as being included in conversation, following a response (Pazulinec *et al.* 1983). Time out can be either *exclusionary* or *non-exclusionary*. Exclusionary time out involves the physical removal of the individual from the immediate environment for a specified period of time, contingent upon a target behaviour. Within the home setting, exclusionary time out typically involves sending the child to a bedroom or the hallway. Non-exclusionary time out does not involve the physical removal of the child from the immediate environment and is implemented in the home setting by having the child sit in a chair that has been designated beforehand.

Both exclusionary and non-exclusionary time out have been widely implemented within BPT (Olmi, Sevier and Nastasi 1997; Parke 1977). Forehand and McMahon (1981) advocate placing the child on a chair facing the corner of the room for three minutes in response to non-compliance. Webster-Stratton (1992a) advocates placing the child on a chair within view of the parent or in a hallway, bathroom or bedroom in response to inappropriate behaviour which cannot be ignored, with the age of the child determining the length of time out in minutes. Webster-Stratton (1992b) also recommends that time out should not be used for every instance of inappropriate behaviour, but advocates the use of ignoring for non-aggressive, irritating behaviours such as whining. Sanders and Dadds (1993) advocate exclusionary time out as a back-up for non-exclusionary time out and *logical consequences* in response to a broad range of inappropriate child behaviours which range in seriousness from fighting, teasing or irritating siblings to minor whining and interrupting parents' conversations or telephone calls.

Although time out has been widely advocated within BPT, its acceptability as a treatment method for aversive child behaviour has been questioned (Kazdin 1980). Webster-Stratton (1992a) makes advance explanation an integral part of the time-out procedure. Resistance to time out, whether by refusal to go to the designated place (*time-out refusal*), or by refusal to stay there (*time-out escape*), must be managed successfully if time out is to be established as an effective punishment practice within the home. Forehand and McMahon (1981) advocate the threat and use of a mild spank as a back-up means of enforcing compliance to time out, while acknowledging that the use of spanking is not appropriate for parents with a history of child abuse. Alternatives to spanking include loss of privileges for older children, or the use of a time-out room, physical restraint or logical consequences with younger children. Webster-Stratton (1992a) advocates increasing the duration of time out up to a maximum of ten minutes, followed by back-up consequences in response to time-out refusal and the use of a time-out room in response to time-out escape. McNeil *et al.* (1994) devised a *two-chair hold* technique as an alternative to spanking for the management of time-out escape. The two-chair hold technique involves the physical restraint of the child in a designated holding chair by a parent who sits on a second chair. The child is held on a chair rather than on the parent's lap in order to provide minimal reinforcement. McNeil *et al.* (1994) acknowledge that the technique is not therapeutic: 'It is used only as an aversive consequence for children who test the limits of time-out' (p.34). Furthermore, the technique is not suitable for children over six years of age. Reitman and Drabman (1996) developed the *read my fingertips* technique for the management of verbal resistance to time out. The technique involves the parent signalling to the child by hand that the duration of time out will be increased by one minute for each word of protest uttered after a warning to stop talking.

The effective management of time-out refusal and time-out escape is essential to the successful establishment of time out, which is itself a non-coercive form of discipline. Nevertheless, the use of mild spanking, which constitutes Type 1 punishment, or physical restraint in order to establish time out has generated intense controversy. While it can be argued that physical restraint is a Type 1 punishment, the rationale for its use is preventive: it is implemented when the child not only refuses or escapes from time out but also engages in destructive or assaultive behaviour which cannot be ignored because it is dangerous to himself or others. Properly administered, physical restraint involves a neutral holding technique rather than the active infliction of pain and is therefore not coercive (Hughes *et al.* 2001). Nevertheless, Lutzker (1994) strongly criticised the two-chair hold technique as being both morally and scientifically unacceptable and characterised McNeil *et al.* (1994) as 'appalling' (p.35). Kemp (1996) placed Lutzker's reservations about the two-chair hold technique in the context of the more general trend against the use of aversive methods in behaviour therapy (for example, LaVigna and Donnellan 1986), but concluded that McNeil *et al.*, (1994) represents an important contribution to the treatment of children with serious conduct problems:

> While the procedure can be described as aversive, most would agree that a brief period of timeout and a brief period of physical restraint is certainly in the category of *mild* aversiveness, with little or no likelihood of pain, tissue damage, injury, dehumanisation, or humiliation... No one wants to use aversives, any more than anyone wants to use surgery or radiation or amputation or powerful medications. But there are extremes in the world and there are extremes of severe behaviour problems that cry out for treatment (p.22).

Study 2 was designed to examine a means of reducing child aversive behaviour directly rather than indirectly, as was the case in Study 1. Furthermore, generalisation probes and a more rigorous experimental design were adopted.

Study 2
Method
Screening

Screening procedures were used as in Study 1. The fifth criterion for inclusion (an observed rate of compliance of 40 per cent or less) was broadened to include the observation of aversive child behaviour during 20 per cent of intervals of the initial baseline observation.

Clients: Family 1

The client was a seven-year-old boy who was referred due to verbal and physical aggression towards his mother and two sisters aged four and 11 years. Both parents attended an initial assessment interview and the mother reported that her son's behaviour became excessively dominant in the home when his father, who worked in construction, was away from home. She reported that her son was oppositional and defiant. He frequently kicked and punched her and his sisters, particularly when he did not get his own way. She acknowledged that she frequently lost her temper and was concerned that she or her husband would injure him during a confrontation. His father left home each morning before the children rose and returned when they were in bed, six days each week. The parents reported that their marriage was harmonious.

The rate of compliance during the initial baseline observation was 61 per cent (above the criterion of 40%) and aversive child behaviour was observed in only 10 per cent of intervals. Further baseline observations indicated a criterion level of compliance and of aversive child behaviour. BPT was therefore recommended. The father undertook to attend clinic-based training sessions but was unavailable for home observations due to work commitments.

Clients: Family 2

The client was a seven-year-old boy who was referred due to non-compliance and oppositional behaviour at home. He lived at home with his parents and his twin sister. His father was in full-time employment as a factory worker and his mother was the primary caretaker. Both parents reported that their son had been difficult to manage since infancy in comparison to their daughter, who presented no management problems. The parents described wilful, oppositional behaviour which escalated to verbal and physical aggression during disciplinary confrontations. They attributed child management difficulties to the burden of caring for twins. They reported that their marriage was harmonious, and reported no major stressors on the family. A criterion level of compliance (41%) and of aversive child behaviour (20%) was observed during the initial baseline observation, and the client met all the criteria for inclusion in the study. BPT was therefore recommended. The father undertook to attend clinic-based training sessions but was unavailable for home observations due to work commitments.

Consent

Written consent was obtained as in previous studies.

Observation procedures

Observations of mother–child interactions were conducted in two different settings within the home:

1. Training setting (twice weekly). Observation was carried out by the author, who also acted as therapist.

2. Generalisation setting (once weekly). This setting differed from the training setting across a number of dimensions: it took place on a different day, at a different time, and involved an activity that was not included in the training settings and that parents had identified as being associated with problem behaviour. Both families chose homework as the generalisation setting activity. The observer in this setting was a social work trainee (Master's level) who had received eight hours of training in the use of the coding schedule. Video sequences were reviewed during training and decisions about coding were discussed. Re-calibration sessions were conducted weekly during the course of the study, during which video sequences were reviewed and dilemmas about coding were discussed.

Behaviour categories

Data were obtained on child aversive behaviour and parental use of time out in response to child aversive behaviour. Time out was defined as 'Warning or implementation of time out in response to noncompliance or aversive child behaviour.'

Design

A multiple-baseline-across-clients design was used during Study 2.

Baseline

Three baseline points were collected from Family 1 and four from Family 2 on parent and child behaviour specified above.

Intervention Phase 1

Treatment was identical to Intervention Phase 1 in Study 1.

Intervention Phase 2

A high-intensity training format was used in order to instruct parents in the use of an exclusionary time-out procedure. Parents were encouraged to use time out in response to non-compliance and aversive child behaviour. Training in the use of time out took place during the course of the day. Both parents and all children attended a self-contained annex in a residential unit which was arranged to resemble a family home. It comprised a kitchen and a living-room which were joined by a short corridor, in which was placed a time-out chair. The child was sent to time out for two minutes in response to non-compliance and aversive child behaviours. The duration of time out was extended by means of an electronic kitchen timer for refusal to go to time out. A maximum duration of ten minutes was specified. Time out was re-initiated for refusal to remain on the chair and for refusal to sit quietly. Parents were encouraged to use the procedure consistently with all their children. The parent was instructed in the use of active ignoring for refusal to go to time out. A restraint procedure was also devised in the event of the target child becoming assaultive in the home setting. When the restraint procedure was implemented an adult who could physically restrain the child (the maternal grandfather in the case of Family 1 and the father in Family 2) was contacted by telephone. The child was held until he undertook to go to time out.

The therapist initially intervened directly by training the child to accept time out. When the procedure had been established in the clinic setting, the mother was encouraged to take responsibility for its implementation, initially with the clinician present. The therapist and the father then observed the mother implementing the procedure by means of a video link-up, following which both parents and therapist reviewed a video recording of the mother implementing the procedure. The family returned home for the final stage of training in the time-out procedure. The therapist called to the family home and conducted an observation and feedback session. Parents were encouraged to explain the consequences of refusal to go to time out in the home setting to their children. Two hours after the observation and feedback session, the therapist telephoned the parents in order to review any difficulties which had arisen during the interim.

Post-training phase

Treatment was identical to post-training in Study 1.

Follow-up

One observation session was conducted with each family in the training setting three months after post-training.

Results

Child aversive behaviour

An overall measure of child aversive behaviour was calculated by taking the total incidence of physical negatives, complaints, demands, oppositional child behaviour and non-compliance across sessions. Child aversive behaviour was observed in an average of 20 per cent of intervals in Family 1 and 17 per cent of intervals in Family 2 during baseline (see Figure 6.1). The introduction of Phase 1 of treatment led to an increase in the average incidence of aversive child behaviour to 35 per cent (Family 1) and 37 per cent (Family 2). The introduction of Phase 2 of treatment led to a significant decrease in aversive child behaviour in Family 1 and an average of four per cent was recorded. The introduction of Phase 2 of treatment led to an initial increase in aversive child behaviour in Family 2, but this quickly decreased and an average of 6.7 per cent was recorded. During post-treatment the average incidence of aversive child behaviour was two per cent in Family 1 and seven per cent in Family 2. At follow-up, the average incidence of aversive child behaviour was two per cent in Family 1 and three per cent in Family 2.

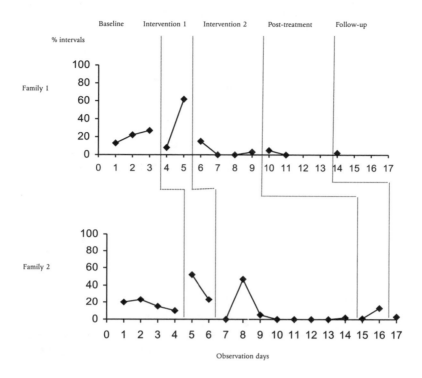

Figure 6.1 Percentage intervals of child aversive behaviour across sessions

Use of behaviour reduction procedures

The rate of behaviour reduction procedures was calculated by taking response cost and time out as a percentage of target child behaviours (non-compliance and aversive child behaviour). The average rate of parental use of behaviour reduction procedures in response to target child behaviour during baseline was zero in Family 1 and Family 2 (Figure 6.2). The introduction of Phase 1 of treatment led to an increase in the rate of behaviour reduction to 18 per cent in Family 1 on Observation Day 5. The introduction of Phase 1 of treatment led to an increase in the average rate of behaviour reduction to 16 per cent in Family 2. The introduction of Phase 2 of treatment led to an increase in the rate of behaviour reduction to 67 per cent in Family 1 on Observation Day 6. The introduction of Phase 2 of treatment led to an increase in the rate of behaviour reduction in Family 2 to 96 per cent on Observation Day 7 and 100 per cent on Observation Days 9, 11 and 14. A high rate of behaviour reduction was observed during post-treatment in Family 1 (75% on Observation Day 10) and in Family 2 (89% on Observation Day 16).

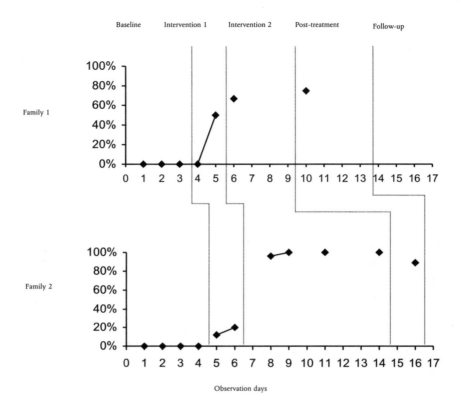

Figure 6.2 Use of behaviour reduction procedures in response to non-compliance and aversive child behaviour across sessions

Generalisation probes

Five observations in the generalisation setting were conducted with Family 1. One observation was conducted during baseline, one during Phase 1 and three during Phase 2 of treatment. No observations were conducted in the generalisation setting during post-training or at follow-up. The percentage of intervals of aversive child behaviour reduced from 21 per cent (baseline) to 13 per cent (Phase 1) and to an average of 2 per cent (Phase 2) (Table 6.1). The rate of use of the behaviour reduction procedure in response to non-compliance and aversive child behaviour decreased from 33 per cent (baseline) to 46 per cent (Phase 1) to zero (Phase 2).

Table 6.1 Generalisation probes, Family 1

	Baseline	Intervention 1	Intervention 2
% intervals aversive child behaviour	21	13	2
Use of behaviour reduction procedures	33	46	0

Ten observations in the generalisation setting were conducted with Family 2. One observation was conducted during baseline, one during Phase 1, five during Phase 2 of treatment and three during post-training. The percentage of intervals of aversive child behaviour decreased from 22 per cent (baseline) to 8 per cent (Phase 1) (Table 6.2). The average percentage of intervals of aversive child behaviour during the first two observations in Phase 2 was 68 per cent, which reduced to an average of 5 per cent of intervals during the last three observations in Phase 2. This low average rate was maintained at 5 per cent during post-training. The rate of use of behaviour reduction procedures in response to non-compliance and aversive child behaviour increased from zero per cent (baseline) to 25 per cent (Phase 1). This increased during the first two observations in Phase 2 to 88 per cent, which reduced to an average of 53.6 per cent of intervals during the last three observations in Phase 2. This reduced again to an average of 17.3 per cent of intervals during post-training.

Table 6.2 Generalisation probes, Family 2

	Baseline	Intervention 1	Intervention 2	Post-training
% intervals aversive child behaviour	22	8	30	5
Use of behaviour reduction procedures	0	17	67	40

Discussion

BPT, which included home-based training and high-intensity clinic-based training was implemented with two families. The results of this study show that parent and child behaviours changed in both families in response to

BPT. The rate at which parents implemented behaviour reduction procedures increased significantly following the high-intensity training in the implementation of a time-out procedure. The rate of aversive child behaviour increased significantly in Family 1 during Phase 1 of intervention, when a response-cost procedure was used, and decreased significantly with the introduction of time out. The rate of aversive child behaviour decreased in Family 2 during Phase 1, increased initially with the introduction of time out and decreased significantly as time out was used consistently. The significant reduction in the rate of aversive child behaviour during Phase 2 of treatment led to zero rates of implementation of the behaviour reduction procedures during Phase 2, during post-treatment and at follow-up in both Family 1 and Family 2. The changes in parent and child behaviours were significant and all were maintained at three months' follow-up.

Setting generalisation was assessed by means of generalisation probes which were conducted with both families in a non-training setting during baseline and intervention phases. Generalisation probes indicate that the rate of treatment generalisation on measures of parent behaviour differed between families. A high rate of use of behaviour reduction procedures was observed in Family 1 in the generalisation setting during baseline and Phase 1 of treatment. This was also observed during Phase 1 in the training setting (data point 5, Figure 6.2), and was attributed to the mother's use of logical consequences. (She reported that she learned this parenting skill at a parent education course which she had attended in a community setting one year previously.) Generalisation probes indicate a higher level of treatment generalisation on the measure of parent behaviour in Family 2. The data on setting generalisation must be interpreted with some caution, however, as inter-observer reliability was not assessed in this study, due to scheduling difficulties. The setting generalisation data suggest that the parent in Family 1 did not implement the techniques as consistently as the parent in Family 2.

In both families parents reported that the target child become more manageable, that intense aggression no longer occurred and that they had a more positive relationship with the target child.

Chapter 7

Positive parenting practices

Introduction

While the use of time out has generated some controversy (as discussed in Chapter 6), behavioural parent training (BPT) also places a great emphasis upon the promotion of prosocial child behaviour through positive reinforcement. This emphasis is also consistent with behaviour analysis' abiding concern with the application of positive reinforcement procedures as an alternative, or as an antidote to punishment (Grant and Evans 1994; Sidman 1989).

A range of positive reinforcement practices has been applied in BPT. Forehand and McMahon (1981) include training in *positive attending* and *rewards* within Phase 1 of the programme, which focuses upon differential attention. Phase 1 also provides instruction in ignoring. Positive attending and rewards are used to increase desirable child behaviour, while ignoring is used to decrease undesirable child behaviour. Positive attending refers to monitoring and enthusiastically describing the child's play activity. Positive attending is distinguished from issuing instructions, asking questions and teaching, all of which involve the parent imposing structure upon the child's activity. Rewards refer to the provision of social reinforcement through labelled praise (which contains a verbal description of the behaviour being praised) and unlabelled praise (which contains a positive statement about the child, but which does not describe a specific child behaviour) and through physical affection. The main thrust of Phase 1 is to alter parent–child interactions from a negative to a positive focus, and the parent is instructed to implement the positive reinforcement practices by adopting the motto 'Catch your child being good' (Becker 1971, p.89). The constructive focus of the programme is emphasised by introducing positive reinforcement practices in Phase 1, whereas compliance training, which includes time out, is introduced in Phase 2. The rationale for this arrangement is clearly outlined:

> We have found that parents who are first taught a disciplinary procedure such as TO [time out] (which is a type of punishment) will frequently reduce their children's problem behaviours and terminate therapy. Unfortunately, these parents have not learned any positive skills for interacting with their children or for maintaining their child's positive behaviour. Therefore, for both ethical reasons and overall therapeutic effectiveness, it is important to teach punishment procedures to parents last in the therapy process. (Forehand and McMahon 1981, pp.50–51)

Webster-Stratton (1992a, b) emphasises the important role which play occupies in child development and specifies skills which enable parents to play more effectively with children. Four types of play are described:

- physical play
- manipulative and exploratory play
- games
- symbolic or make-believe play.

These play activities enable children to learn conflict resolution and problem-solving skills and to develop their vocabulary and values as well as their creativity, imagination and self-esteem. Parents are taught a range of positive reinforcement practices in order to promote play activities and desirable behaviour in general:

> One of the most important tasks of parents is to teach their children appropriate behaviours. One of the best ways to do this is for parents to give their children attention and encouragement whenever they observe them doing something positive. Those moments of positive behaviours are opportunities for teaching appropriate behaviour by focusing on it and praising it. (Webster-Stratton 1992a, Programme 9, Part 1, p.7)

Specific positive reinforcement skills include showing interest, following the child's lead, self-praise, labelled and unlabelled praise, physical affection and tangible rewards such as tokens and stickers.

Child management training (CMT) (Sanders and Dadds 1993) teaches parents to use eight positive reinforcement strategies which are designed to encourage positive interactions between parent and child and to promote socially appropriate behaviours and skills in self-care and independence.

Positive reinforcement strategies comprise:

- spending quality time with children
- tuning in to desirable behaviour
- giving plenty of physical affection
- conversing with children
- using incidental teaching
- setting a good example through modelling
- encouraging independence through the provision of verbal, gestural and manual prompts
- providing engaging activities for children.

All these programmes emphasise the importance of using positive reinforcement practices contingent upon desirable behaviour and anticipate parental reservations that the practices constitute bribery.

While a broad range of positive reinforcement practices have been applied in BPT, there have been remarkably few evaluations of what contribution, if any, these practices make to the overall effectiveness of BPT with conduct problem children (Gardner 1994). Bernhardt and Forehand (1975) found that labelled praise was more effective at changing the behaviour of young children than unlabelled praise, and that this effect was not influenced by social class. Nevertheless, two strands of research suggest that praise does not serve positively to reinforce appropriate child behaviour. First, no difference has been found in the rate at which mothers of clinic-referred and non-clinic children provide praise in response to compliance (Griest et al. 1980) and provide positive attention in response to appropriate child behaviour (Forehand et al. 1975). Second, a number of studies have shown that differential attention, which consisted of praise in response to compliance and ignoring in response to non-compliance, was ineffective in influencing child behaviour until it was used in combination with time out (Budd, Green and Baer 1976; Wahler 1969). Wahler (1969) suggested that parental praise influenced child behaviour only when it was implemented in combination with time out because the overall treatment package increased child responsiveness to parental positive reinforcement practices. Roberts (1985), however, found that child responsiveness to parental praise did not increase following successful treatment of child non-compliance. Roberts (1985) also found that child compliance was maintained for reasons other than immediate praise and concluded 'praising child compliance did not appear to serve a reinforcement function.

Given overt compliance as the independent variable, the practice appeared to be a socially acceptable, widely used ritual' (p.627). Wahler and Meginnis (1997) examined whether praise and mirroring (the description of appropriate child behaviour with neutral affect) were components of a broader construct, which is termed *responsiveness* and which derives from social attachment theory, and advised those who question the nature of positive parenting practices:

> Clearly, their search for answers will be most fruitful if they focus on a means of attaining interactional synchrony instead of pursuing a more narrow focus on refining their selective use of any particular practice. (p.439)

Study 3 was undertaken to examine whether teaching parents a broad range of attentional skills would provide an enduring source of positive reinforcement for prosocial child behaviour.

Study 3
Method
Family 1
The client was a six-year-old boy who lived with his parents, his eight-year-old brother and his four-year-old sister. His father was employed on a full-time basis and his mother on a part-time basis. His parents reported no major financial stressors. His father acknowledged that he was rarely at home due to work commitments and his mother denied that this was a source of disagreement between them, as she was committed to the role of primary caregiver. She reported that her son was non-compliant, oppositional and generally heedless of her authority. She acknowledged that she frequently lost her temper with him and resorted to restricting him to his bedroom for long periods of time. She reported that she felt demoralised by her inability to manage her son. She also expressed concern about intense conflict which arose with his older brother, which she largely attributed to the target child's domineering behaviour. She noted that she did not have similar difficulties managing the other two children, who responded less extremely than the target child to minor frustrations. A previous teacher had reported disruptive behaviour in class, although this was not a concern with his current teacher. She attributed her son's problem behaviour to his fiery temperament, which resembled his father's. His father agreed with this opinion and acknowledged that he was more comfortable in his role as a breadwinner than as a parent. A criterion level of compliance

was observed (40%) and the client met all other criteria for inclusion in the study. The father undertook to attend clinic-based training sessions but was unavailable for home observations due to work commitments.

Family 2

The client was a five-year-old boy who lived with his parents and six-month-old brother. His father was in full-time employment and the family enjoyed middle-income status with no major financial stressors. The parents reported a harmonious marriage and both parents reported difficulty in managing persistent oppositional and non-compliant behaviour in the home setting and in a variety of community settings. His mother, who was the primary caregiver, acknowledged that her inability to manage her son effectively was a source of demoralisation for her. She reported with bewilderment that she engaged in extended disputes with her son over minor matters. Behaviour management difficulties had become a source of concern two years previously, while she was in full-time employment, and a succession of child-minders had reported that they found her son unmanageable. She attributed her difficulties to both her tendency to be overindulgent and to her son's stubborn temperament (which resembled her own). The father expressed bewilderment at his son's difficult behaviour and found that serious punishment, such as spanking and sending his son to bed early, seemed to have no effect other than to leave both parents feeling demoralised. The referral was precipitated by complaints from the client's class teacher that he was uncooperative in class and domineering with his peers in the schoolyard. The observed level of aversive child behaviour was three times higher than the criterion (60% of intervals) and the client met all other criteria for inclusion in the study. The father undertook to attend clinic-based training sessions but was unavailable for home observations due to work commitments.

Consent

Written consent was obtained as in previous studies.

Observation procedures

Observations of mother–child interactions were conducted in the training setting twice-weekly by the author, who also acted as therapist.

Behaviour categories

A number of changes were made in the categories of parent and child behaviour which were recorded in Study 3, although the instructional sequence was recorded as in previous studies. In previous studies, the first parent behaviour which was observed in each interval was recorded, and aversive behaviour took precedence over prosocial behaviour. Parent behaviour in Study 3 was recorded not on the basis of the first parent behaviour which was observed in each interval, but on the basis of whether the parent responded contingently or non-contingently to the child behaviour which was recorded in that interval (see Table 4.2 and Appendix II). These changes were designed to facilitate the examination of parental contingent attention to prosocial child behaviour. Both *contingent* and *non-contingent attends* were coded as positive, negative or neutral. The category *non-attend* was retained.

Child prosocial referred to prosocial behaviour in response to either the parent or other family members (see Table 4.3 and Appendix II).

Design

A multiple-baseline-across-subjects design was used during Study 3.

Baseline

Two baseline points were collected from Family 1 and four from Family 2.

Intervention Phase 1

Intervention Phase 1 was conducted as in Study 2.

Intervention Phase 2

During Intervention Phase 2, parents were instructed in the use of time out as in Study 2. They were also instructed in positive reinforcement practices (PRP) in response to prosocial child behaviour. PRP comprised the following reinforcement skills:

1.   *Praise.* Labelled praise consists of a positive statement which describes what the child has done, for example 'I really like the picture of the house that you've drawn'. It provides more information to the child and is more specific than unlabelled praise which consists of a general statement about the child, for example 'Good man!'

2.   *Positive attending* is a method of positively reinforcing constructive and imaginative play. It consists of observing and describing the child's play activity. For example, when the child places a figure in the toy garage, the parent says, 'Now the man has gone into the garage'. Positive attending does not include asking questions or

providing information because both of these activities place the parent in charge of the play activity.

3. *Active listening* is designed to encourage the child to seek attention and assistance from the parent appropriately. First, it involves the parent displaying interest in response to the child's approach. Second, the parent listens to what the child is saying. Third, the parent states his/her understanding of what the child is saying and checks this out with the child. For example, 'Do you mean you don't want to visit Granny?'

Training in PRP also emphasised observational skills, the importance of timing in the delivery of positive reinforcement, and the frank expression of a range of positive emotional responses such as pleasure, pride and amusement. The emotional valence of each form of positive reinforcement was emphasised. A variety of didactic methods, comprising role-play, discussion, modelling and provision of printed material, were used to instruct parents in the use of PRP.

Post-training and Follow-up 1

Post-training and follow-up were conducted as in previous studies.

Booster

A one-day home-based booster session which focused on the consistent implementation of time out was provided to Family 2. The booster session involved the same instructional techniques that were employed in Intervention Phase 2 and the use of the 'Read my fingertips' technique, which is designed to reduce resistance to time out through argument (Reitman and Drabman 1996). The parent was instructed to devise an explicit set of house rules that the child assisted in formulating. The list of house rules was placed in a prominent position in the kitchen and the client was reminded of them on a daily basis. Rule-breaking led to automatic time out. The parent was also advised that new rules could be devised for a range of settings, such as visits to the supermarket or to relatives.

Follow-up 2

A follow-up observation was conducted in the home setting three months after the booster session.

Results

Rate of child compliance

The rate of child compliance during baseline averaged 48 per cent in Family 1 and 31 per cent in Family 2 (Figure 7.1). The introduction of Phase 1 of treatment led to an increase in the average rate of compliance to 61 per cent in Family 1 and to 34 per cent in Family 2. This increase was maintained during Phase 2 of treatment, and an average rate of 83 per cent compliance was recorded in Family 1 and of 72 143per cent in Family 2. The average rate of compliance during post-treatment was 90 per cent in Family 1 and 70 per cent in Family 2. At Follow-up 1, the average rate of compliance in Family 1 was 100 per cent, and in Family 2 was 67 per cent. During the booster phase in Family 2, the average rate of compliance was 77 per cent, and 96 per cent at Follow-up 2.

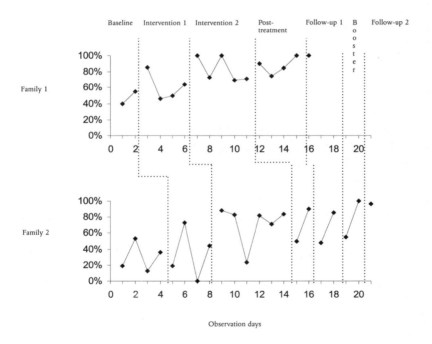

Figure 7.1 Rate of child compliance across sessions

Rate of positive reinforcement of compliance

The average rate of positive reinforcement of compliance during baseline was 6 per cent in Family 1 and 5 per cent in Family 2 (Figure 7.2). The introduction of Phase 1 of treatment led to a slight increase in the average rate of this behaviour to 8 per cent in Family 1 and to a significant increase in Family 2 to 54 per cent. The introduction of Phase 2 of treatment led to a slight increase in the average rate of positive reinforcement of compliance to 9 per cent in Family 1 and to a decrease to 36 per cent in Family 2. During post-training the average rate of positive reinforcement of compliance in Family 1 increased to 18 per cent, and decreased to 11 per cent in Family 2. At Follow-up 1, the average rate of positive reinforcement of compliance in Family 1 was 20 per cent, and in Family 2 was 53 per cent. The average rate of this behaviour during the booster treatment in Family 2 was 47 per cent, which decreased to 33 per cent at Follow-up 2.

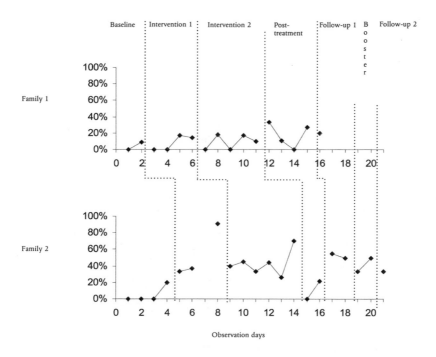

Figure 7.2 Rate of positive reinforcement of compliance across sessions

Contingent positive attention

The average rate of contingent positive attention during baseline was 2 per cent in Family 1 and 24 per cent in Family 2 (Figure 7.3). The average rate of contingent positive attention during Phase 1 of treatment in Family 1 was 2 per cent, and in Family 2 was 22 per cent. The introduction of Phase 2 of treatment led to a slight increase in the average rate of contingent positive attention in Family 1 to 8 per cent, and in Family 2 to 33 per cent. During post-training the average rate of contingent positive attention increased to 22 per cent in Family 1 and to 45 per cent in Family 2. At Follow-up 1, the average rate of contingent positive attention in Family 1 was 30 per cent, and in Family 2 was 27 per cent. The average rate of contingent positive attention during the booster treatment in Family 2 was 42 per cent, which decreased to 19 per cent at Follow-up 2.

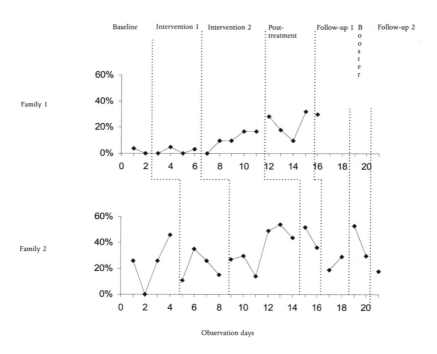

Figure 7.3 Rate of positive reinforcement practices (PRP) across sessions

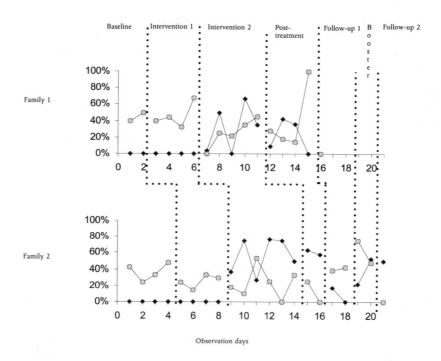

Figure 7.4 Parent aversive attention and time out across sessions

Parent contingent negative attention and time out

The average rate of time out during baseline in Family 1 was 0, and of contingent negative attention was 45 per cent (Figure 7.4). In Family 2, the average rate of time out during baseline was 0 and of contingent negative attention was 37 per cent. A zero rate of time out was observed in Family 1 during Phase 1 of treatment, when the average rate of contingent negative attention was 46 per cent. In Family 2, a zero rate of time out was observed during Phase 1 of treatment, when the average rate of contingent negative attention was 25 per cent. The introduction of Phase 2 of treatment led to an increase in the average rate of time out in Family 1 to 33 per cent, and to a decrease in the average rate of contingent negative attention to 25 per cent. In Family 2, the introduction of Phase 2 of treatment led to an increase in the average rate of time out to 57 per cent, and to a decrease in the average rate of contingent negative attention to 21 per cent. The average rate of time out during post-training in Family 1 was 27 per cent, and of contingent negative attention was 40 per cent. In Family 2, the average rate of time out during post-training was 61 per cent, and the average rate of contingent negative attention was 13 per cent. At Follow-up 1, the rate of time out in Family 1 was 0, as was the rate of contingent negative attention. In Family 2, the average rate of time out during Follow-up 1 increased to 9 per cent, and the average rate of contingent negative attention increased to 46 per cent. The average rate of time out in Family 2 during the booster treatment was 36 per cent, and the average rate of contingent negative attention was 63 per cent. At Follow-up 2, the rate of time out in Family 2 was 50 per cent, and the rate of contingent negative attention was 0.

Discussion

The results of Study 3 show that both parent and child behaviours changed in both families in response to BPT. There was an increase in the rate of compliance in both families. Study 3 was designed to examine whether teaching parents a broad range of attentional skills would lead to an enduring source of positive reinforcement of prosocial child behaviour. The results indicate that the rate of contingent positive attention increased in response to treatment, but that the overall increase in Family 1 was small, and the increase in Family 2 was not maintained either at Follow-up 1 or at Follow-up 2. These disappointing results suggest that the treatment programme did not lead to changes in parental use of positive reinforcement practices.

In an interesting corolary, the modifications to the coding scheme, which were introduced to facilitate the analysis of parent positive reinforcement practices, facilitated a useful analysis of the inverse co-variation between non-aversive discipline and contingent negative attention. The results indicated that the techniques were not implemented as consistently in Family 2 as in Family 1. A low rate of child compliance and a moderate rate of aversive child behaviour were observed at Follow-up 1 and confirmed during a second observation. These observations indicated that the mother responded to these behaviours with contingent negative attention rather than with time out, and that the target child became argumentative when his mother issued a warning that she would implement it. A home-based booster treatment was recommended on the basis of these observations. Booster treatment led to a significant decrease in the incidence of child aversive behaviour. Booster treatment also led to higher rates of effective instructions and use of time out. The mother reported that she found it easier to implement time out and to avoid getting drawn into argument by not issuing a warning. This technique appeared to be an effective means of dealing with resistance to time out, and it was decided to adopt it in further studies.

Chapter 8

Generalisation at home and at school

Introduction

While the generalisation of treatment effects is a central concern in applied behaviour analysis, it is treated as a peripheral concern in early studies of behavioural parent training (BPT). In the early 1980s, Moreland *et al.* (1982) reviewed the presentation of data on the generality of treatment effects in parent management training studies which were published between 1975 and 1981 and concluded that the question of treatment generalisation had not received sufficient attention:

> Since there now appears to be substantial evidence that parent training procedures do reduce targeted children's behaviour problems, future studies should focus upon evaluating factors which may facilitate the generalisation of parent training effects. (p.268)

It would appear that researchers of BPT have heeded their recommendations, as data on the generalisation of treatment effects is now produced more often in this area than it is among behavioural studies in general. For example, a review of 146 studies in three behavioural journals found that only 12 per cent presented data on temporal generality, 10 per cent on setting generality and 9 per cent on behavioural generality (Keeley, Shemberg and Carbonell 1976). By comparison, a review of 148 parent training studies found that, between 1975 and 1984, 51 per cent of studies included a consideration of generalisation, which increased to 63 per cent between 1984 and 1990 (Wiese 1992). Edelstein (1989), however, noted 'the continued meagre attention' which is paid to the topics of generalisation and maintenance in the behaviour therapy outcome literature (p.309).

Within the field of BPT, four types of generality of treatment effects have been identified as therapeutic goals (Forehand and Atkeson 1977):

1. *Temporal generality*, which refers to the maintenance of treatment effects following termination of treatment. The maintenance of treatment effects has been demonstrated after varying periods of time which include two months (Griest *et al.* 1982), three months (Dadds, Sanders and James 1987; Sanders and Christensen 1985), five months (Oltmanns, Broderick and O'Leary 1977) and one year (Kazdin *et al.* 1987; Webster-Stratton *et al.* 1989).

2. *Setting generality*, which refers to the occurrence of treatment effects in non-training settings. Setting generality has been assessed in terms of a number of different dimensions which include clinic-to-home generalisation (Peed *et al.* 1977), generalisation to a range of settings within the home, such as breakfast time, departure for school, play time, bath time and bedtime (Sanders and Christensen 1985), and home–community generalisation (Sanders and Dadds 1982). These studies suggest that setting generality is enhanced by teaching parents antecedent skills in addition to contingency management skills. Antecedent skills such as planned activities training (Sanders and Dadds 1993) help the parent to influence the child's behaviour by re-arranging the immediate environment. The assessment of home–school generalisation has found that, while both home-based (Wahler 1969) and clinic-based BPT (Breiner and Forehand 1981; Forehand *et al.* 1979) led to a decrease in aversive child behaviour in the home setting, neither form of BPT led to behavioural gains in the school setting. Wahler (1975) found some evidence of a *contrast effect* whereby BPT led to both a decrease in child aversive behaviour in the home setting and an increase in child aversive behaviour in the school setting. In contrast, McNeil *et al.* (1991) found that a group of children whose parents were provided with clinic-based BPT (parent–child interaction therapy – PCIT) showed significant decreases in aversive behaviour in the school setting, in comparison with a normal classroom control group and an untreated deviant classroom control group. McNeil *et al.* (1991) speculate that the emphasis in PCIT, which is on compliance training and on the promotion of prosocial child behaviour, enhanced the generalisation of these behaviours from the clinic to the school setting. Overall, these findings suggest that BPT may not lead to spontaneous improvements in child behaviour in the school setting, and both Webster-Stratton (1992a) and Sanders and Dadds (1993) advocate training parents in school liaison skills as a

means of promoting behavioural gains which have occurred in the home setting in response to BPT.

3. *Behavioural generality*, which refers to changes in behaviours that were not the focus of treatment. Sanders and Dadds (1993) note that the generalisation of parent behaviour change is important because parents must apply child management techniques in a range of settings, often with more than one child, and that changes in parent and child behaviour must be maintained over time if interventions are to be considered effective. Sanders and Dadds (1993) also note that most BPT programmes teach parents all component skills rather than only a sub-set of these skills:

> It is probably better to provide direct instruction for parents in the range of skills they require to deal with specific problems…than to train only a subset of these skills. Such training makes it unnecessary to demonstrate behaviour generalisation. (p.144)

Patterson (1974), however, found minimal support for the hypothesis that parents would apply behaviour management techniques to child behaviours other than those to which they had been specifically trained to respond.

4. *Sibling generality*, which refers to changes in the behaviours of the specific child's siblings. There is some evidence that BPT leads to sibling generality (Patterson and Fleischman 1979), although Forehand and Atkeson (1977) noted that observational data were obtained in few studies. Forehand and Atkeson (1977) suggest that sibling generality can occur because of parents' use of behavioural techniques with siblings, because of siblings' observational learning and because of reduced sibling reinforcement for deviant behaviour. The inclusion of siblings in the training process has been recommended as a means of enhancing sibling generality (Forehand and Atkeson 1977).

Cooper *et al.* (1987) proposed six general strategies for producing behaviour changes with generality, all of which have been applied in BPT:

1. *Aim for natural contingencies of reinforcement.* The rationale behind this strategy is that behaviours which are not reinforced are less likely to be maintained. When parents are trained in settings where child management problems occur, they are more likely to continue to use child management techniques. While BPT is conducted largely

in clinic or community settings, home-based training has also been adopted (Herbert and Iwaniec 1981; Sanders and Dadds 1993), and some programmes have been conducted in specific problem settings such as the supermarket (Barnard *et al.* 1977; Clark *et al.* 1977).

2.   *Teach enough examples.* BPT involves teaching parents to increase the behavioural deficits and to decrease the behavioural excesses which children with conduct disorder (CD) display in a range of settings. Parents are therefore taught a number of different skills to be used with a range of behaviours. For example, the Incredible Years programme (Webster-Stratton 1992a) provides parents with an opportunity to view up to 18 vignettes of the effective and ineffective use of praise and encouragement. Similarly, child management training teaches parents eight strategies for increasing desired behaviour or teaching a new skill: spending quality time with children, tuning in to desirable behaviours, giving physical affection, conversing with children, using incidental teaching, modelling desirable behaviour and encouraging independence (Sanders and Dadds 1993).

3.   *Programme common stimuli.* The rationale behind this strategy is that a target response is likely to be emitted in the presence of stimuli which resemble the stimulus conditions under which it was previously reinforced. One example of the application of this strategy in BPT is the involvement of both parents in treatment. While parent training has been criticised for its almost exclusive concentration upon training mothers (Strauss and Atkeson 1984), the role of fathers in BPT has also received some consideration (Adubato *et al.* 1981). Although Martin (1977) found that treatment outcome was not enhanced by the inclusion of fathers in treatment, Patterson (1974) and Webster-Stratton (1985b) found a higher level of maintenance of treatment effects among families where the father had been involved in BPT.

4.   *Train loosely.* Generality is enhanced by varying as many dimensions of the antecedent stimuli as possible during instruction, such as the teaching format, and reinforcing a wide range of responses. Baer (1981) suggests a wide range of variation in the teaching procedures which can enhance generality, including:

- the use of two or more teachers
- the presence or absence of other people
- the variation of aspects of the training setting in terms of furniture, brightness, temperature and level of noise
- even alterations in the teacher's appearance.

The application of this strategy within the field of BPT is evident in the wide range of didactic methods which are utilised including direct instruction, discussion, role-play, the provision of printed material, video-modelling and feedback. The provision of training in social learning principles has been found to enhance generalisation of treatment effects (McMahon, Forehand and Griest 1981). It has been suggested, however, that the provision of training, which includes direct observation and feedback rather than education in social learning principles, is more effective with parents who experience literacy problems (Sanders and Dadds 1993).

5. *Use indiscriminable contingencies.* This strategy is designed to address the vulnerability to extinction of behaviours which are developed and maintained under continuous schedules of reinforcement. In BPT this refers to the tendency of parents to revert to pre-intervention levels of coercive behaviour towards the target child when the programme has ended. In order to counteract this tendency, Sanders and Dadds (1993) include a post-training phase, during which the clinician continues to conduct observations but, rather than provide feedback, encourages the parent to assess his/her implementation of the child management techniques. Webster-Stratton (1992a) includes a *buddy system* according to which group participants provide support to one another between weekly training sessions. The buddy system establishes an informal support network of which participants can avail themselves when training sessions have ended. Patterson (1974) advocates regular monitoring of child behaviour during the first year after treatment and the use of booster sessions to retrain parents when necessary. Kendall (1989) questions the expectation that clinical intervention can cure those forms of psychopathology which are particularly resistant to treatment, and advocates the concept of continuing care, such as the provision of short-term booster treatments on a long-term basis, as a realistic means of achieving generalisation and maintenance of treatment effects.

6.   *Teach self-management techniques.* The rationale behind this strategy is
     that, if parents can be taught to prompt and reinforce themselves
     for changing their behaviour in different settings, at different times
     and in relevant forms, then the likelihood of the generalisation of
     treatment effects is ensured. In an early study, Herbert and Baer
     (1972) found some evidence that self-recording helped parents to
     increase their rate of attention to appropriate child behaviour.
     Self-management skills have been used widely as an adjunctive
     treatment to BPT (see the section 'Expansion of the treatment
     paradigm' in Chapter 3).

Cataldo (1984) identified two main strategies that have been adopted in
BPT for the enhancement of generalisation. On one hand, specific procedures are applied to the target problem behaviours in a range of settings.
This approach can, however, present certain problems, especially when 'the
consequence is that parents then seek additional behavioural programmes
for each succeeding problem' (Cataldo 1984, p.340). The other approach
to enhancing generalisation effects in BPT is not to deal with the target
problem immediately, but instead to teach parents general behavioural
principles first. This approach is based on the assumption that if parents are
'well versed in the principles, generalisation of techniques to successive behaviour problems is supposed to be enhanced' (Cataldo 1984, p.340). In
most studies this assumption is not explicitly tested. In fact, this approach is
so unpredictable that Stokes and Baer (1977) refer to it as the *train and hope
strategy* for promoting generalisation.

     Study 4 was designed to examine whether BPT would lead to imple-
mentation of the child management techniques with a sibling and to
changes in sibling behaviour.

Study 4

Method

Family 1

The client was a seven-year-old boy who lived with his mother and
five-year-old brother. His father had left the family home three years previously following a period of intense acrimony and maintained minimal contact with his sons. He was not involved in the intervention programme. The
mother reported that she experienced difficulty managing her older son,
whom she described as generally uncooperative and not accepting of correction since his father had left the home. She reported that his class teacher
had begun to express concern about uncooperative and disruptive behav-

iour at school. She reported non-compliance, verbal aggression and destruction of belongings (both his own and hers) following disciplinary confrontations. She was also concerned at the level of conflict between her sons, which she attributed to the older boy's domineering behaviour. She attributed her current level of difficulties to the level of conflict which had prevailed in the home and which had been witnessed by the boys. She acknowledged that her older son reminded her of his father in both appearance and temperament and that consequently she was less patient with him than with her younger son, whom she found more easy to manage. The mother was negative in her descriptions of her older son's behaviour and acknowledged that she felt angry with him constantly. She reported that she had significant family and social supports. A criterion level of aversive child behaviour was observed (28%) and, as the client met all the criteria for inclusion in the study, BPT was recommended.

Family 2

The client was a six-year-old boy who lived with his mother and his four-year-old brother. His parents were not married and had separated three years previously by mutual agreement. The boys visited their father, who lived with his family of origin some distance away, at weekends. The father gave his consent to treatment, but was unable to participate because of transport difficulties. The family was dependent on social welfare provision, and the mother reported that she experienced stress due to financial difficulties. She also experienced stress due to the dilapidated state of their accommodation and had applied to the local authority to be re-housed, but was not hopeful that this would happen in the foreseeable future. She reported that the boys were non-compliant and difficult to manage in a range of a settings both in the home (such as mealtime and bedtime) and in the community (such as in the supermarket). The mother reported that she had experienced difficulty in managing her sons since she moved to her current accommodation two years previously. She reported that she had few social supports, and that family contacts tended to be acrimonious. She impressed as being socially isolated and depressed, but was reluctant to avail of either individual casework or psychiatric intervention, and strongly requested that intervention would focus on child management. A criterion level of aversive child behaviour was observed (40% of intervals) and, as the client met all criteria for inclusion in the study, BPT was recommended.

Consent

Written consent was obtained as in previous studies.

Observation procedures

The observational procedures adopted in Study 4 were identical to those adopted in Study 3 (see Chapter 7). The behaviour of the target child was observed in the training setting, and that of the sibling was observed in the test setting.

Behaviour categories

Sibling generalisation was assessed in terms of child compliance and effective parent instructions. The behavioural definitions were identical to those which were used in Study 3.

Inter-observer reliability

Inter-observer reliability was assessed on 3 of the 21 observations (14%) that were conducted in the test setting, with the author acting as the second observer. Inter-observer reliability was calculated on an interval-by-interval basis, using the following formula:

$$\frac{\text{agreement intervals}}{\text{agreement} + \text{disagreement intervals}} \times 100 = \% \text{ agreement}$$

(Cooper *et al.* 1987, p.94)

The average levels of overall agreement were 96 per cent for compliance and 96 per cent for effective instructions.

Design

A multiple-baseline-across-subjects design was used during Study 4.

Baseline

Two baseline points were collected from Family 1 and seven from Family 2 on parent and child behaviours.

Intervention Phases 1 and 2, post-training and follow-up

Intervention Phases 1 and 2, post-training and follow-up were conducted as in Study 3.

Results

Rate of child compliance

The rate of child compliance during baseline averaged 50 per cent in Family 1 and 53 per cent in Family 2 (Figure 8.1). The introduction of Phase 1 of treatment led to an increase in the average rate of compliance to 58 per cent in Family 1 and to 72 per cent in Family 2. The average rate of child compliance increased further during Phase 2 of treatment to 90 per cent in Family 1, but decreased to 61 per cent in Family 2. The average rate of compliance during post-treatment was maintained at 90 per cent in Family 1 and increased slightly to 68 per cent in Family 2. At follow-up, the average rate of compliance in Family 1 was 100 per cent. No follow-up data was available for Family 2.

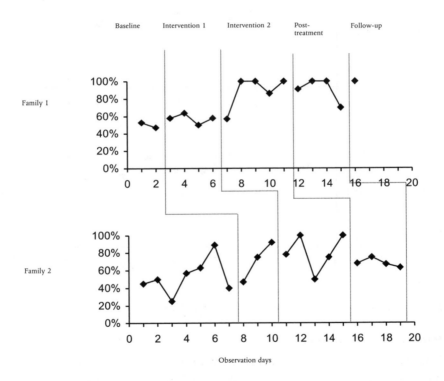

Figure 8.1 Rate of child compliance across sessions (target child)

Sibling generalisation: Rate of child compliance

The rate of child compliance during baseline averaged 82 per cent in Family 1 and 78 per cent in Family 2 (Figure 8.2). The average rate of compliance in Family 1 during Phase 1 of treatment was maintained at 81 per cent, and increased to 91 per cent in Family 2. The average rate of child compliance decreased during Phase 2 of treatment to 67 per cent in Family 1 but was maintained at 89 per cent in Family 2. The average rate of compliance during post-treatment increased to 93 per cent in Family 1 and decreased slightly to 80 per cent in Family 2.

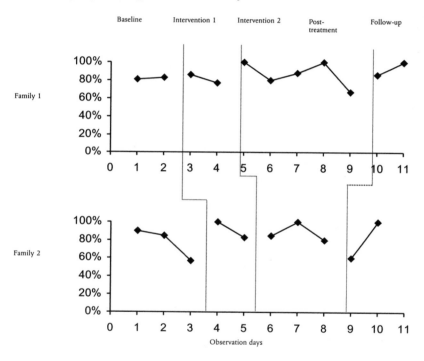

Figure 8.2 Sibling generalisation: Rate of compliance across sessions

Rate of effective instructions

The average rate of effective instructions during baseline in Family 1 was 51 per cent, and in Family 2 was 54 per cent (Figure 8.3). The introduction of Phase 1 of treatment led to an increase in the average rate of effective instructions to 63 per cent in Family 1 and 57 per cent in Family 2. The introduction of Phase 2 of treatment led to an increase in the average rate of effective instructions to 83 per cent in Family 1 and 70 per cent in Family 2. During post-treatment the average rate of effective instructions in Family

1 decreased to 73 per cent in Family 1 and increased to 79 per cent in Family 2. At follow-up, the rate of effective instructions in Family 1 was 73 per cent. No follow-up data was available for Family 2.

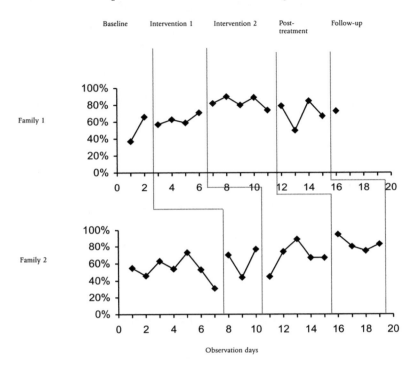

Figure 8.3 Rate of effective instructions across sessions (target child)

Sibling generalisation: Rate of effective instructions

The average rate of effective instructions during baseline in Family 1 was 85 per cent, and in Family 2 was 65 per cent (Figure 8.4). The average rate of effective instructions during Phase 1 of treatment was maintained at 87 per cent of intervals in Family 1 but increased to 100 per cent in Family 2. The introduction of Phase 2 of treatment led to a decrease in the average rate of effective instructions in Family 1 to 76 per cent, and to 67 per cent in Family 2. During post-treatment the average rate of effective instructions in Family 1 was maintained at 72 per cent in Family 1 but decreased to 41 per cent in Family 2.

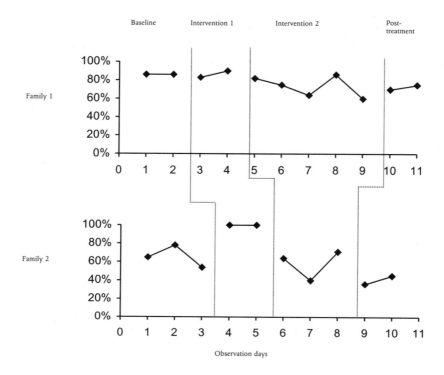

Figure 8.4 Sibling generalisation: Rate of effective instructions across sessions

Discussion

BPT was implemented with two families and the generalisation of treatment effects to untreated siblings was examined in terms of compliant responding and effective instructions. While the results of this study show that BPT led to changes in both parental and target child behaviour, there was only moderate evidence of treatment generalisation on the measure of child behaviour which was adopted in this study. The average rate of compliance among both target children increased in response to treatment, but that of the siblings increased only slightly.

The measure of parent behaviour also provided moderate evidence of treatment generalisation. The rate of effective instructions with the target child increased in response to treatment in both Family 1 and Family 2, but did not increase with the sibling in Family 1. The rate of effective instructions with the sibling increased in response to treatment in Family 2, but this increase was not maintained.

A comparison of the behaviour of the target child with that of the sibling at baseline indicates a lower rate of compliance in the target child than in the sibling in both families. In neither sibling was a criterion level of compliance observed. These differences confirmed the mother's opinion in Family 1 that the target child was more difficult to manage than the sibling.

BPT led to a reduction in the differences between measures of the behaviour of the target child and of the sibling in both Family 1 and Family 2. The rate of target child compliance in both families increased while the rate of sibling compliance remained constant. Similarly, BPT led to a reduction in the differences between parenting behaviours towards the target child and the sibling, which were evident at baseline.

These figures indicate that in both families the target child presented more management difficulties than the sibling and that, while parenting skill deficits which are associated with CD were observed in relation to the target child, they were not observed in relation to the sibling.

Study 5

Method

Study 5 was designed to examine whether behavioural parent training would lead to increased compliance and reduced aversive child behaviour in the school setting. It was also designed to examine whether a home–school contract (Sanders and Dadds 1993) would lead to improvement in classroom functioning.

Family 1

The client was a seven-year-old boy whose parents sought assistance owing to complaints about his behaviour in school. He had been referred previously as a five-year-old due to behaviour problems in the home setting. His parents had attended briefly and had been offered general management guidelines. The client lived with his parents and three-year-old sister. His father was absent from the home due to long working hours, and his mother was the primary caretaker. She reported that, despite her son's and her previous clinic attendance, she continued to find her son stubborn, uncooperative, moody and non-compliant. While there was little joint parenting owing to the father's general unavailability, parents reported that their marriage was currently harmonious. They acknowledged, however, the impact of a major extra-familial stressor during the previous year which had led to marital disharmony and general irritability. They reported that they were currently attempting to contain the impact of this stressor on family functioning and on parenting. The mother presented as demoralised by her continuing inability to manage her son's behaviour at home, and the father acknowledged that he had become increasingly punitive in an attempt to influence his son's behaviour when he himself was not at home. This in turn had led to increasing disagreements between the parents over child management issues. The client's class teacher reported that he presented as uncooperative, attention-seeking and frequently off-task in the classroom setting, but that there were no concerns about learning difficulties. He had been referred frequently to the school principal due to disruptive behaviour and rule-breaking in the school yard. The principal reported that the client's behaviour had been a significant source of concern for the previous two years. Both parents and school reported that home–school relations were constructive and cooperative. A criterion level of aversive child behaviour (30%) was observed in the home setting, and the client met all criteria for inclusion in the study. BPT was therefore recommended. The father undertook to attend clinic-based training sessions but was unavailable for home observations due to work commitments.

Family 2

The client was a five-year-old boy whose mother sought assistance owing to complaints about his behaviour in the school setting. His mother had attended nine months previously due to management difficulties in the home setting, when she had reported that her son's problem behaviour had responded to general management guidelines. The client's family circumstances were anomalous; his mother had lived with the maternal grandparents until recently, when she and her son moved to live with her long-term partner. His mother worked on a full-time basis, but changed to part-time work in order to avail of clinic intervention. The mother denied continuing management difficulties in the home setting. The class teacher reported that the client was disruptive and uncooperative in the classroom setting, where he refused to participate in written tasks unless he was closely supervised. Concern was expressed about the client's poor level of attention, although a psychiatric assessment at the time of the client's previous attendance had ruled out attention deficit hyperactivity disorder (ADHD). The client was reported to be highly aggressive with peers and with older children in the schoolyard, where his behaviour frequently brought him to the attention of the school principal. It was evident from verbal reports that home–school relations were conflicted; the mother considered that the school was focusing unduly on her son's misdemeanours and school personnel considered that the mother was minimising management difficulties in the home setting. A criterion level of aversive child be-haviour was observed (28% of intervals) and the client met all criteria for inclusion in the study. His mother undertook to participate in a BPT programme as a precursor to possible school-based intervention.

Consent

Written consent was obtained as in previous studies.

Observation procedures

Observations were conducted within both home and school settings using the partial-interval time-sampling strategy which was used in previous studies.

1. *Home observations.* Observations were conducted by the author, who also acted as therapist, in a training setting within the home on a twice-weekly basis, during all phases of the study.

2. *School observations.* Observations of Client 1 were conducted in the classroom setting on a weekly basis during baseline and during Intervention Phases 1, 2, and 3. Observations of Client 2 were conducted in the classroom setting twice-weekly during baseline, Intervention Phases 1 and 2, and post-training (Intervention 3). School observations were conducted at a pre-arranged time and included a representative range of classroom activities that included individual and group activities. The school observations were conducted by a social work trainee (Master's level). Observational training and recalibration procedures were identical to those adopted in Study 4.

Behaviour categories

The behaviour categories which were used during observations in the home setting were identical to those which were used in Study 4. The be-haviour categories which were used in school observations comprised:

1. *Individualised instructions* that referred to instructions that addressed directly to the target child only. These were coded as alpha, alpha negative, beta or beta negative instructions.

2. *General instructions* that referred to instructions addressed to the whole class. These were coded as alpha, alpha negative, beta or beta negative instructions.

3. *Compliance and non-compliance,* coded as in home observations.

4. *Child aversive behaviour,* coded as in home observations and including the following categories: physical negative, complaint, demand and oppositional.

5. *Child prosocial behaviour,* coded as in home observations and including social attention and constructive behaviour.

Inter-observer reliability

Inter-observer reliability was assessed on 2 of the 14 (14%) school observations of Client 1, with the author acting as the second observer. Inter-observer reliability was calculated on an interval-by-interval basis, as in Study 3. Inter-observer reliability of the following categories of behaviour was assessed: individualised instructions and compliance, general instructions and compliance, and aversive child behaviour. The average levels of overall agreement are shown in Table 8.1.

Table 8.1 Average levels of overall agreement between observers (Client 1, school setting)

Behaviour categories	Average level of overall agreement (%)
Individualised instructions	98
Compliance to individualised instructions	98
General instructions	95
Compliance to general instructions	88
Aversive child behaviour	87

Design

A multiple-baseline-across-subjects design was used during Study 5.

Baseline

Two baseline points were collected from Family 1 and six from Family 2 on parent and child behaviours in the home setting. One baseline point was collected on Client 1 and four baseline points were collected on Client 2 in the classroom setting.

Intervention Phases 1, 2, 3 and follow-up (Family 1)

Intervention Phases 1 and 2 were conducted with Family 1 as in Study 4. During Intervention Phase 3, post-training was conducted in the home setting, as in Study 4, and a daily report card system was introduced. Five classroom goals were established at a joint meeting with both the mother and the class teacher which comprised:

- beginning assigned work promptly
- obeying teacher's instructions
- attempting all assigned work
- cooperating in group work
- completing set homework.

The teacher rated each of these behaviours on a scale from 1 (very poor) to 7 (excellent). Points were allocated at the end of three two-hour periods during the school day on the basis of Client 1's performance in the classroom setting, and the total number of points earned was recorded on the daily report card. The mother provided a reward in the home setting (access to a new computer game for a period of time which was determined by the number of points earned during the day).

Intervention Phases 1 and 2, post-training and follow-up (Family 2)

Intervention Phases 1 and 2, post-training and follow-up were conducted with Family 2 as in Study 4.

Results

All measures of behaviour were calculated as in previous studies.

Rate of child compliance

The rate of child compliance during baseline averaged 58 per cent in Family 1 and 59 per cent in Family 2 (Figure 8.5). The introduction of Phase 1 of treatment led to an increase in the average rate of compliance to 84 per cent in Family 1 and to 70 per cent in Family 2. The average rate of child compliance increased further during Phase 2 of treatment to 91 per cent in Family 1 and to 96 per cent in Family 2. The average rate of compliance during post-treatment was maintained at 95 per cent in Family 1 and at 92 per cent in Family 2. At Follow-up, the average rate of compliance in Family 1 was 100 per cent, and in Family 2 was 100 per cent.

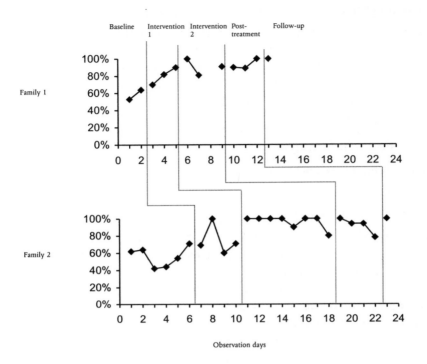

Figure 8.5 Rate of child compliance across sessions

Child aversive behaviour

Child aversive behaviour was observed in an average of 35 per cent of intervals during baseline in Family 1 and in an average of 27 per cent of intervals in Family 2 (Figure 8.6). During Phase 1 of treatment, child aversive behaviour was observed in 39 per cent of intervals in Family 1 and in 23 per cent of intervals in Family 2. The introduction of Phase 2 of treatment led to a decrease in child aversive behaviour to an average of 7 per cent of intervals in Family 1 and 6 per cent of intervals in Family 2. The decrease in child aversive behaviour was maintained during post-training, when it was observed in an average of 3 per cent of intervals in Family 1 but increased to an average of 11 per cent of intervals in Family 2. At follow-up, child aversive behaviour was observed in 7 per cent of intervals in Family 1 and in 7 per cent of intervals in Family 2.

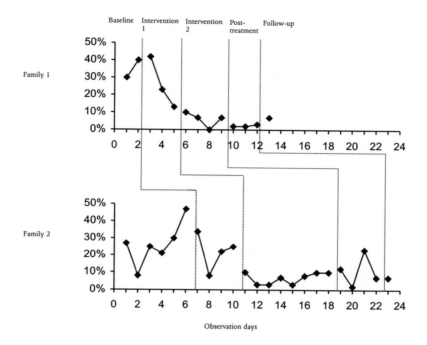

Figure 8.6 Percentage intervals of non-compliance and aversive child behaviour across sessions

Home–school generalisation: Rate of compliance to general classroom instructions

The rate of compliance to general classroom instructions (compliance-g) that was observed during baseline in Client 1 was 63 per cent (Figure 8.7). The average rate of compliance-g in Client 2 during baseline was 58 per cent. The rate of compliance-g during Phase 1 of treatment increased to 77 per cent in Client 1 and to 70 per cent in Client 2. The average rate of compliance-g during Phase 2 of treatment was 100 per cent in Client 1 and 92 per cent in Client 2. The introduction of Phase 3 of treatment led to an average rate of 100 per cent compliance-g being maintained in Client 1. The average rate of compliance-g decreased to 73 per cent in Client 2 during the post-treatment-only phase.

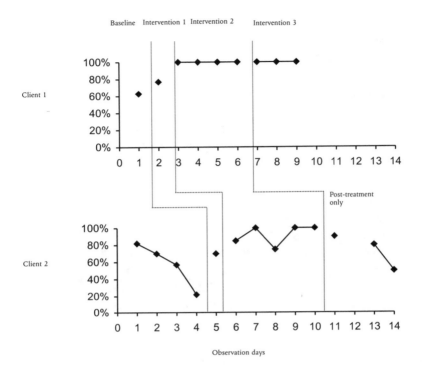

Figure 8.7 Home–school generalisation: Rate of compliance to general instructions in classroom setting across sessions

Home–school generalisation: Rate of compliance to individualised classroom instructions

The rate of compliance to individualised classroom instructions (compliance-i) which was observed during baseline in Client 1 was 100 per cent (Figure 8.8). The average rate of compliance-i in Client 2 during baseline was 67 per cent. The rate of compliance-i during Phase 1 of treatment decreased to 67 per cent in Client 1 and increased to 75 per cent in Client 2. The average rate of compliance-i during Phase 2 of treatment decreased to 34 per cent in Client 1 and to 66 per cent in Client 2. The introduction of Phase 3 of treatment led to an average rate of 95 per cent compliance-g in Client 1. The average rate of compliance-g increased to 83 per cent in Client 2 during the post-treatment-only phase.

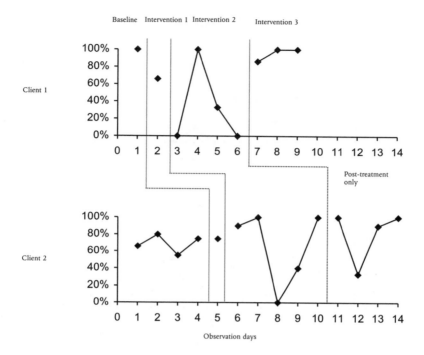

Figure 8.8 Home–school generalisation: Rate of compliance to individualised instructions in classroom setting across sessions

Home–school generalisation: Percentage intervals of aversive child behaviour in classroom setting

Aversive child behaviour was observed in 10 per cent of intervals in Client 1 and in an average of 28 per cent of intervals in Client 2 during baseline (Figure 8.9). During Phase 1 of treatment, aversive child behaviour was observed in 3 per cent of intervals in Client 1 and 13 per cent of intervals in Client 2. Aversive child behaviour was observed in 22 per cent of intervals in Client 1 and in 18 per cent of intervals in Client 2 during Phase 2 of treatment. The introduction of Phase 3 of treatment led to a reduction in the average number of intervals in which aversive child behaviour was observed to 2 per cent in Client 1. Aversive child behaviour was observed in an average of 11 per cent of intervals in Client 2.

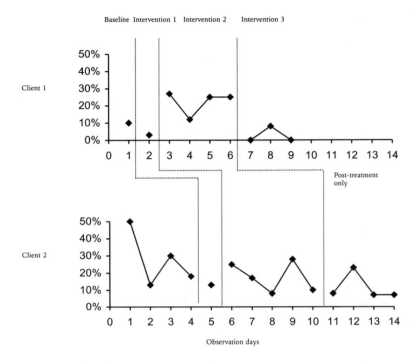

Figure 8.9 Home–school generalisation: Percentage intervals of child aversive behaviour across sessions in classroom setting

Discussion

Home-based BPT was implemented with two families in Study 5 and the generalisation of treatment effects to the school setting was examined. The results of this study show, first, that BPT led to changes in child behaviours in the home setting. An increase in the rate of child compliance and a decrease in the incidence of aversive child behaviour in response to treatment were observed, and these changes in child behaviour were maintained at three-month follow-up observations. Second, the implementation of home-based BPT was reflected in measures of child behaviour in the classroom setting. The rate of compliance to general instructions in the classroom setting (compliance-g) increased with both clients in response to BPT in the home setting. The level of inter-observer agreement for this category of behaviour (88%) indicates that these changes in child behaviour were not a function of observer behaviour. The rate of compliance to individual classroom instructions (compliance-i) decreased in both cases in response to BPT in the home setting. The high level of inter-observer agreement for this category of behaviour (98%) indicates that these changes in child behaviour were not a function of observer behaviour. The incidence of aversive child behaviour in the classroom setting increased in Client 1, but not in Client 2, in response to BPT in the home setting. The level of inter-observer agreement for this category of behaviour (87%) indicates that these changes in child behaviour were not a function of observer behaviour.

Chapter 9

Emerging issues

Introduction

Chapters 5–8 describe a series of five studies which was conducted in the course of developing a high-intensity behavioural parent training (BPT) programme. The programme adopts an individual training format and included extensive home-based training. Study 1 examined the effectiveness of a compliance training strategy for the treatment of moderate/severe conduct problems. While the programme which is described in Study 1 was based primarily on a single compliance-training strategy, Studies 2 and 3 describe the inclusion of additional components. Study 2 sought to increase the effectiveness of the programme by including high-intensity training in time out in response to non-compliance and aversive child behaviour. Study 3 examined the effectiveness of training parents positively to reinforce prosocial child behaviour by means of positive parenting practices which comprised praise, positive attending and active listening. No additional components were included in the programme after Study 3. Study 4 examined the generalisation of treatment effects to untreated siblings. Study 5 examined the generalisation of treatment effects from the home to the school setting. The multi-component programme which was implemented in Studies 4 and 5 therefore provided parents with training in a range of skills which included effective instruction-giving, time out and positive parenting practices in response to both compliance and prosocial child behaviour.

Each of the five studies which were conducted in the course of developing the programme has been discussed separately. The overall programme of research is now discussed under the following headings:

- compliance training
- effective discipline
- positive parenting practices

- generalisation of treatment effects
- ethical issues
- practice issues.

Finally, areas for future research which are suggested by these studies are discussed.

Compliance training

Study 1 demonstrated the inverse co-variation between compliance and aversive behaviour in a six-year-old boy with conduct disorder (CD) in the home setting with the mother as therapist. Previous studies had demonstrated the inverse co-variation effect in developmentally delayed children and adults in institutional settings with trained personnel as therapists (Parrish *et al.* 1986; Russo *et al.* 1981). Study 2 confirmed that compliance training can be used as an indirect method of reducing aversive behaviour outside institutional settings with non-delayed clients (Cataldo *et al.* 1986). The mother's report of persistent aggression in a range of non-training settings, however, confirmed the author's clinical impression and the evidence of research (Dumas 1989; Kazdin 1997b) that, while a single-strategy approach may be helpful in the treatment of circumscribed behaviours, it is too narrow to treat the broad range of behavioural excesses and deficits which comprise CD. Study 2 therefore indicated that a home-based training format does not obviate the need for a multi-component strategy in the treatment of CD.

The modification to the observational coding scheme which was introduced after Study 1, whereby a measure of both compliance and child behaviour was recorded in each interval, was designed to facilitate the analysis of the inverse co-variation effect. This modification was reversed in Study 3 and in subsequent studies, because aversive child behaviour was reduced directly by means of time out. The inverse co-variation effect was therefore not examined in these studies. The decrease in the average levels of child aversive behaviour which was observed in Phase 1 of Studies 2–5, in which compliance training was introduced with no accompanying behaviour reduction procedure, is, however, suggestive of the inverse co-variation effect.

While some concern has been expressed about the early inclusion of compliance training in BPT curricula due to the risk that parents will drop out of treatment once they have learned more effective disciplinary techniques (Forehand and McMahon 1981), compliance training was the first skill which was taught to parents in Studies 1–5, and the only incidence of drop-out (Study 4, Family 2) occurred when the curriculum had been completed. Compliance training provided a useful means of training parents to monitor the antecedents and consequences of child behaviour. It also provided a useful means of demonstrating to parents that the first step to changing their child's behaviour was to change their own, and demonstrated that when they approached their child in a less aggressive and more sensitive manner, the child responded more cooperatively. It was emphasised that the goal of compliance training is not to teach obedience and submission to a set of instructions, but to promote cooperation and reciprocity within parent–child interactions (LaVigna and Donnellan 1986). Parents were able to distinguish between increasing the proportion rather than the overall level of effective instructions, and no parent had difficulty remaining below the criterion level of 20 instructions during a 30-minute observation session. The results of Study 5 provided some evidence that compliance training in the home setting led to an increased rate of compliance with generalised classroom instruction (and, by implication, to increased participation in classroom activities). This confirms the view that compliance is a key behaviour in child development, to the extent that, when the issue of compliance with instruction is resolved, children are enabled to participate in social activities and learn social skills (Patterson *et al.* 1992).

Effective discipline

Study 1 included a response cost procedure which was implemented in response to non-compliance (but not in response to child aversive behaviour, which was reduced indirectly through compliance training). While this procedure was implemented in the training setting, both parents reported that they found it cumbersome to implement in other settings and that it provoked outbursts of intense aggression. These verbal reports confirmed the extensive evidence that parental attempts to implement disciplinary techniques frequently lead to severe aggression in children with CD. This in turn either deters parents from further attempts at discipline or leads to more intense parental aggression which is associated with child physical abuse (Gardner 1989; Patterson 1982; Urquiza and McNeil 1996). On the basis of this evidence, a time-out procedure for the reduction of non-compliance and aversive child behaviour was introduced in Study 2. Parents were instructed in the procedure by means of a high-intensity training format which was designed to enable them to manage time-out refusal in a calm and non-confrontational manner. Parents were provided with a high level of advice and support in order to enable them to establish time out successfully in the home setting in a non-coercive manner. Severe aggression was exhibited by both children during Phase 2 of treatment, when time out was introduced. In each of these cases, severe aggression was precipitated by the parent withholding permission to play outside the house until time out was completed. Severe aggression consisted of assaultive behaviour towards mother and siblings, and the breaking and overturning of furniture. Severe aggression was managed successfully by the recruitment of support twice from the father (Study 2, Family 1) and once from a grandfather (Study 3, Family 2).

The introduction of time out led to a decrease in compliance and an increase in child aversive behaviour (Study 2, Family 2). These changes in child behaviour did not persist. Parents reported that they found the procedure effective in a range of settings, and that deferred time out was particularly useful in settings outside the home, such as travelling by car, visiting relatives and shopping. There was evidence that parents used time out in different settings within the home (Study 3, Family 2). Both parents reported that they rarely used time out, but that when they did, time-out refusal was not encountered. They also reported that they used a range of logical consequences for mild aversive behaviour, such as loss of access to TV or to other preferred activities, and that these practices (combined with infrequent use of time out) were effective in maintaining low levels of child aversive behaviour. All parents reported that their overall relationship with their child was more harmonious, and expressed relief that they no longer engaged in intense conflict.

Positive parenting practices

The programme content was expanded in Study 3 with the inclusion of positive parenting practices that were designed to reinforce positively prosocial child behaviour. The expansion of the programme content was accompanied by a modification of the observation coding scheme that was designed to facilitate the measurement of parental provision of contingent attention to child behaviour. The modification was based on the distinction between parent attention which was contingent and non-contingent on both aversive and prosocial child behaviours. Contingency was defined in terms of whether the parental behaviour was response, whether verbal or non-verbal, to the child behaviour that was recorded in that interval.

The distinction between contingent and non-contingent parental attention led to parent behaviours in Study 3 being recorded in a different fashion from the previous studies. In Studies 1 and 2, when the programme was based primarily on the compliance training strategy, parent contingent attention comprised praise and response cost and was coded only in the context of the instructional sequence. The instructional sequence was constructed in the Antecedent–Behaviour–Consequence (ABC) format, which facilitated the analysis of contingent attention that the parent provided to compliance and non-compliance. During intervals when the instructional sequence was not recorded, parent and child behaviours were recorded on an event basis: the first parent and child behaviour which was observed in each interval was recorded, with the exception that if aversive behaviour was observed later in the interval it took precedence over the behaviours that were observed earlier in the interval and was recorded. Aversive behaviours were prioritised in this fashion in order to provide a more stringent view of the programme's effectiveness in reducing parent and child aversive behaviours.

The introduction of the distinction between contingent and non-contingent parental attention led to a change in the rules for recording parent behaviour. While the first child behaviour in each interval (or an aversive behaviour, if it occurred later in the interval) continued to be recorded, the parent behaviour that occurred during the next five seconds was recorded on the basis of whether it was contingent or non-contingent on that behaviour.

The distinction between contingent and non-contingent attention facilitated a functional analysis of parental behaviours. For example, negative contingent attention to child aversive behaviour in Family 1 and Family 2 in Study 3, which consisted of complaints, warnings and threats, and which resembled 'nattering', as described by Patterson (1982), served to positively reinforce these behaviours. Negative contingent attention varied inversely with the use of time out, which was introduced in Phase 2 of treatment. It was not possible to conduct a functional analysis of positive parenting practices in Study 3, however, because of the broad definitions of prosocial child behaviour that were used. Child behaviour which was neither coded in the instructional sequence nor coded as aversive was recorded as either prosocial (a composite measure which comprised social attention and constructive behaviour) or off-task. The use of the composite measure of prosocial child behaviour effectively led to child behaviour being coded as either aversive or prosocial, because off-task behaviour was observed very infrequently in the home setting. It can therefore be argued that, in each observation session, increases in prosocial child behaviour occurred as the result of decreases in aversive child behaviour, rather than as a function of increased rates of positive contingent attention. Therefore, while the rate of positive contingent attention increased when the parent was trained to implement positive parenting practices in Study 3, it is not possible to define the effect of this increase in terms of prosocial child behaviour. It is noticeable that the rate of increase of positive contingent attention in Study 3 is small relative to the rates at which other parental behaviours increased in response to treatment. Furthermore, the rate of positive contingent attention at follow-up decreased to virtually baseline levels (Study 3, Family 2).

There are two possible explanations for the failure to maintain increases in the rate of positive contingent attention at follow-up in these cases. First, the definition of positive contingent attention is too narrow to detect the changes in positive parenting practices, termed responsiveness, that occur in response to BPT and that distinguish clinic from non-clinic families (Wahler and Meginnis 1997). Second, the broad measure of prosocial child behaviour that was used in these studies impaired the quality of feedback that was given to parents on their use of positive parenting practices. It has been suggested that more specific definitions of prosocial child behaviours (such as, for example, 'initiates interaction with parent', 'engages in joint play' and 'engages in individual play') facilitate the identification of parenting behaviours that act as positive reinforcers for prosocial child behaviour (Patterson et al. 1992). If parents were provided with more specific feedback on their implementation of positive parenting practices, the maintenance of these behaviours would be enhanced (Grant and Evans 1994).

The relatively small increases in the rate of positive contingent attention in response to training and the return to baseline levels at three-month follow-up reflect widespread difficulty in the definition and measurement of positive reinforcement practices which have been reported (Gardner 1994; Wahler and Meginnis 1997). In this regard Patterson et al. (1992), having failed to identify positive parenting practices that positively reinforce prosocial child behaviour in children with CD other than praise in response to compliance, concluded:

> We expected our measures of positive parenting to carry much more weight. Perhaps this is due to the fact that we put less time into developing measures of positive parenting. But it seems that we simply underestimated the importance of the parenting skills that control child compliance (p.92).

Generalisation of treatment effects

The home-based training format described in this book involves training parents in settings where child management problems occur. This training format is designed to enhance the generalisation of treatment effects by availing of natural contingencies of reinforcement. Four aspects of treatment generalisation were assessed during the course of the five studies which were conducted:

- setting generalisation within the home (Study 2)
- sibling generalisation (Study 4)
- generalisation from the home to the classroom setting (Study 5)
- temporal generalisation over three months (Studies 1–5).

The results of Study 2 indicate treatment generality on measures of child behaviour, although they must be interpreted with some caution due to the absence of reliability assessments. Measures of parent behaviour indicate treatment generality in Family 2, but not in Family 1. This finding confirmed the author's clinical impression that the parent in Family 1 did not implement the child management techniques as consistently, and that the results are attributable, perhaps, to individual differences. These findings replicate previous research on the generalisation of treatment effects of home-based BPT (Sanders and Christensen 1985; Sanders and Dadds 1982).

The results of Study 4 indicate moderate levels of sibling generalisation on measures of parent and child behaviour. The variable levels of generalisation between families may be attributed to maternal depression and insularity (Family 2), which is strongly associated with failure to implement parent management techniques and with treatment drop-out (McMahon, Forehand, Griest and Wells 1981; Prinz and Miller 1994; Wahler 1980; Webster-Stratton 1985a). The results of Study 4 also indicate differential parenting of target children and of siblings. This finding suggests that the use of aggressive strategies by parents with their conduct-problem children may not be explicable in terms of skills deficits, much as the use of aggressive strategies by coercive children may not be explicable in terms of social skills deficits, but in terms of the failure to use the skills that they actually have (Asarnow and Callan 1985; Patterson 1982).

The results of Study 5 indicate that the generalisation of treatment effects from the home to the school setting had both beneficial and adverse effects. The increase in the rate of compliance to generalised classroom instructions replicates the behavioural gains in the school setting which were found by McNeil *et al.* (1991), although this specific measure of child behaviour was not used in both studies. The increase in child aversive behaviour in the school setting (Family 1) replicates the contrast effect which was noted by Wahler (1975), whereby treatment-induced improvements in child behaviour in the home are accompanied by a deterioration in the school setting. Study 5 provided some evidence that the introduction of a daily report card system offset the contrast effect, and lends support to the inclusion of home–school liaison as an adjunct to BPT (Sanders and Dadds 1993; Webster-Stratton 1992a).

The results of Studies 1–5 indicate a high level of temporal generality over three months on measures of child behaviour, with the exception of Family 2 in Study 3. The provision of a booster treatment to Family 2 in Study 3 led to the generalisation of treatment effects on measures of child behaviour over three months (Follow-up 2). The results of Studies 1–5 indicate temporal generality on some measures of parent behaviour including effective instructions and positive reinforcement of compliance. As noted earlier, the use of time out decreased over time and, while contingent negative attention showed an increase over time, it remained below baseline levels. As also noted earlier, there was little evidence that parents persisted in using positive reinforcement practices. These results replicate previous research on the temporal generalisation of home-based BPT on measures of parent and child behaviour (Dadds, Sanders and James 1987; Sanders and Glynn 1981).

Ethical issues

In the absence of ethical guidelines for social work research from the Irish Association of Social Workers, the practice-based research which is presented in this thesis is assessed in terms of the ethical responsibilities for social workers who engage in research which are defined by the Australian Association of Social Workers (Australian Association of Social Workers 2000), and with which it fully conforms. Specifically, the interests of the clients were treated as a priority throughout the course of the seven studies. For example, the observational procedures, which were the primary method of data collection, were also an integral part of service delivery; they facilitated the provision of detailed feedback to clients on their implementation of the child management techniques. The provision of feedback also provided a means of informing the participants of the results of the research. Voluntary and informed consent was obtained in writing from each parent on their own behalf and on behalf of their child, and refusal to participate did not lead to coercion or inferred disadvantage. For example, in one case (Study 4, Family 2) the mother stopped participating in the programme, but was in evident distress. She was offered a number of follow-up appointments and eventually re-engaged with the service, which provided client-centred counselling and school liaison. The privacy and dignity of the clients were protected and all research material was stored securely. A research proposal was submitted to an ethics review body.

The provision of effective treatment is a criterion of research in applied behaviour analysis (Baer *et al.* 1968). The provision of effective treatment also constitutes an ethical imperative for those who assert that social work practice should be based on scientific methods (Barber 1996; Macdonald and Macdonald 1995), but which is not specified as an ethical responsibility in social work codes of ethics (Myers and Thyer 1997). The search for an effective method of intervention with CD provided the impetus for this programme of research. Nevertheless, while the search for an effective method of intervention was intrinsically ethical, it raised a number of important ethical issues. First, the programme that was offered to the family which participated in Study 1 was less effective than subsequent versions. In order to ensure that these clients were not disadvantaged by undergoing a less effective treatment, the family was subsequently offered, and completed, the multi-component programme. Second, although the introduction of effective disciplinary practices did not protect the conduct-problem children from distress and discomfort, effective discipline has been identified as a prerequisite to the resolution of CD (Patterson 1982). Furthermore, although ethical objections have been raised both to the use of punishment techniques in behaviour therapy (LaVigna and Donnellan 1986), and the use of time out in particular (Cooper *et al.* 1987), the use of mildly aversive practices with severely aggressive children has been justified in terms of benefits to the child (Kemp 1996). Third, although effective punishment constitutes a central component of the programme which was developed, the primary goal of the programme is the increase of prosocial parent and child behaviours, rather than the reduction of coercive parent and child behaviours. The difficulties that were encountered in defining and measuring positive parenting practices and in training parents to use them have been well documented, and remain a central concern in BPT research (Gardner 1994; Patterson *et al.* 1992).

Practice issues

The search for an effective method of intervention with CD, which has been described in this book, led to the adoption of a range of alternative methods of practice. These included training parents in the home setting, conducting observations according to an observational coding scheme, using a high-intensity training format and providing data-based feedback to parents. These practice methods conform to the principles of social work practice which are specified in the code of ethics of the Irish Association of Social Workers (Irish Association of Social Workers 1995). First, the interests of the client were treated as a priority, as has been discussed above. Furthermore, client opinion on components of the programme informed decisions about modification of programme content. Second, objectivity in professional practice is reflected in the development of the programme, although this was on the basis of client opinion and empirical findings rather than on the basis of introspection. Third, this method of intervention involves the development of a collaborative relationship between the clinician and parents which empowers parents to manage their child effectively. It must be acknowledged, however, that the parents who were empowered to manage their children more effectively were all mothers and that all the target children were boys. Fathers were not living at home in 4 of the 11 families who participated in this programme of research, and none of these fathers participated in treatment. While the seven fathers who lived at home attended clinic appointments, all were unavailable for home observations due to work or training commitments. In all seven families, however, the mother's role as primary caretaker was not a matter of contention to her, and all decided, during extensive pre-intervention discussion with both parents, to be the primary focus of intervention. Fathers were actively involved in clinic-based training and the role of fathers in child-rearing was emphasised at all times. Nevertheless, the secondary role at best which fathers played in all studies, together with the gender of all the target children, is significant in the context of increasing concern about the role of males in society in general (Clare 1998) and about the contribution of fathers to family life in particular (Featherstone 2004; McKeown Ferguson and Rooney 1998).

Future research

The series of five studies which has been described in Chapters 5–8 suggests a number of areas for further research. These relate to each of the constituent elements of the BPT programme that was developed and to the effectiveness of the programme as a whole:

1. Instructions were recorded as either alpha (clear instructions with one behavioural referent) or beta (instructions which could not be complied with). This distinction did not facilitate recording of terminating instructions ('Don't' rather than 'Do' instructions) to be recorded as a separate category. Since research indicates that parents of conduct-problem children issue more instructions than parents of non-problem children (Forehand *et al.* 1975), and since parents appeared to issue aversive terminating instructions contingent on child aversive behaviour during baseline observations, it would be useful to include terminating instructions as a separate category of parent behaviour in future studies.

2. Parents reported that they used time out less as the frequency of child aversive behaviour decreased, and this was confirmed by direct observations. They reported that the decrease in child aversive behaviour was accompanied by a decrease in time-out refusal. Parental recordings of the frequency and duration of time out would provide data on these changes in child behaviour. Parents also reported that they used logical consequences as an alternative to using the formal time out procedure. It would therefore be useful to include time out in a broader category of logical consequences in order to measure and provide feedback on this parental behaviour.

3. The measurement of prosocial child behaviour and of parental behaviours which positively reinforce them would be facilitated by more specific definitions of child prosocial behaviours. Patterson *et al.* (1992) recommend using parent-nominated child behaviours as the basis of assessment and intervention.

4. In the context of fathers not being available to participate fully in treatment, it would be useful to assess the extent to which treatment effects generalise between parents on measures of parental behaviour.

5. The cost-effectiveness of the programme could be compared with other methods of intervention, such as BPT based on a group-training format or client-centred counselling, by means of a random-controlled trial (Macdonald and Macdonald 1995). This experimental design would also allow an examination of its effectiveness with different populations, such as maritally distressed and non-maritally distressed parents or families who are at risk of child abuse.

Afterword

Behaviour parenting training (BPT) is distinguished from parent training in general because of its commitment both to behavioural principles and to evaluation. While there has been a proliferation of parent training programmes during the last 25 years, many programmes now available to practitioners lack a solid theoretical foundation and have not been thoroughly evaluated. Within the field of BPT, however, three programmes have emerged as pre-eminent, and have been dealt with extensively in this book: first, *Helping the Noncompliant Child* (Forehand and McMahon 1981), which adopts a clinic-based training format; second, the Incredible Years programme (IY), which adopts a group-training format with videotape modelling (Webster-Stratton 1992a). and third, child management training (CMT) (Sanders and Dadds 1982; Sanders and Christensen 1985), which adopts a home-based observation and feedback format. BPT has also benefited greatly from the sustained efforts of a number of eminent researchers including Gerald Patterson, Robert Wahler and Frances Gardner. These researchers have made an enormous contribution to the field, and their many and sustained studies have been referred to throughout this book. Their work reflects the close interaction between practice and research which has been a feature of BPT.

A survey of the content of the three programmes referred to above indicates that BPT has adopted the strategy of training loosely by teaching parents a broad range of skills, rather than concentrating upon a single strategy. While these three programmes differ in many aspects, such as the training format, the programme materials and the frequency of client contact, their content is broadly similar and includes the following basic elements: positive parenting practices including praise and rewards, ignoring, compliance training and non-coercive discipline. The loose training strategy of BPT provides parents with a broad range of skills with which to respond to the diversity of challenging behaviours that children with conduct problems generally display. The training strategy also facilitates the inclusion of positive parenting practices whereby parents positively reinforce prosocial child behaviour, consistent with the increasingly constructive emphasis of applied behaviour analysis and of behaviour therapy in general. Apart from teaching parents a broad range of skills, the treatment paradigm has also broadened with the inclusion of adjunctive treatments that are designed to help parents to cope with intra-familial and extra-familial stressors and which impinge on parent–child interactions.

It was against this backdrop of multiple skills and adjunctive treatments being taught within BPT that the series of studies which form the basis of this book were conducted between April 1996 and June 1999. While applied behaviour analysis, which is characterised by 'a watchmaker's attention to detail' (Baum 1994, p.xiii), has enormous heuristic value to BPT, it must be acknowledged that its narrow focus is at odds with the loose training strategy and the expanded treatment paradigm that now characterises the field. Furthermore, the functional analysis of child conduct problems, which is a hallmark of applied behaviour analysis, is largely dispensed with in BPT. Instead of conducting a functional analysis of child conduct problems, BPT practitioners have devised general intervention strategies that rely heavily on the theoretical formulations of Patterson and Wahler.

The contrast between the applied behavioural approach to BPT that is adopted in this book and trends within the field of BPT is even more pronounced when one considers the expanded curricula of two of the influential programmes noted above. The IY series (Webster-Stratton 1992a) not only includes a parent-training programme, which trains loosely and includes an adjunctive treatment component, but also includes teacher training and social skills training programmes and contains elements which are based on cognitive, humanist and attachment theories. This expanded curriculum facilitates multiple intervention, through the parents and the teacher and directly with the child. Similarly, CMT (Sanders and Dadds 1982) has expanded to become Behavioural Family Intervention (Sanders and Dadds 1993), which emphasises the inclusion of adjunctive treatments. The curriculum has further expanded to address child conduct problems of different levels of severity in whole populations (Sanders, Markie-Dadds and Turner 2003). Furthermore, high-intensity intervention with severe conduct problems is increasingly being eschewed in favour of early intervention, which is provided on a preventive basis. In the United States, IY has been provided on a preventive basis to low-income families in the context of Headstart. IY has been provided on a similar basis in Britain within the context of Surestart.

While the focus of the research in this book is somewhat different from these exciting developments in the wider field of BPT, it nevertheless provides an example of high-strength intervention, which has a distinct role to play with some families who have difficulty engaging in clinic-based BPT. It is also based firmly on behavioural principles, is evidence-based and is therefore compatible with recent developments in the field.

Sample recording sheets

1. Antecedent–Behaviour–Consequence recording sheet

Child's name:_____

Completed by:_____

Date/time	Antecedent	Behaviour	Consequence

2. Event recording sheet

Date	Behaviour	How often did it occur?	Total

3. Duration recording sheet

Date	1	2	3	4	5	6	7	8	9	10	Total

Observational coding scheme

This observational coding schedule is designed to record key aspects of child and parental behaviour: child compliance (and non-compliance) to parental instruction, as well as child aversive and prosocial behaviour, parental instruction-giving, parental contingent attention and parental non-contingent attention. It is a modified version of the Family Observation Schedule – V or FOS-5 (Dadds and Sanders unpublished).

Family Observation Schedule

Categories of parent and child behaviours are recorded on a partial-interval time-sampling basis. The observation period of 30 minutes is divided into 60 intervals of 30 seconds. Each interval consists of an *observe phase* (20 seconds) and a *record phase* (10 seconds). The observer is cued, by means of an audio-tape, to observe the parent–child dyad during the observe phase and to record one category each of parent and child behaviour during the record phase. In order to counteract observer drift, each interval is numbered. For example, at Interval 16, the observer hears the statement 'Interval number 16, observe', followed by 'Record' 20 seconds later. The FOS-5 includes seven categories of child behaviour and eight categories of parent behaviour. The child behaviour categories comprise:

- non-compliance
- complaint
- demand
- physical negative
- oppositional
- withdraw
- appropriate.

The parent behaviour categories comprise

- praise

- contact

- aversive contact

- question

- instructions

- social attention

- criticise

- (threat of) punishment.

The FOS-5 also includes affect codes for each behaviour that occurs or for an expression of affect that occurs without a category of behaviour. The affect codes comprise happy, anxious, sad, angry, neutral. A number of studies have employed this observation schedule, or variants of it, to evaluate the effectiveness of a child management programme based on a behaviour correction procedure (Dadds, Sanders and James 1987; Sanders and Dadds 1982; Sanders and Christensen 1985).

The schedule has been modified in order to focus upon two key aspects of parent–child interaction:

1.   An instructional sequence which is coded in an ABC format, with one category of Parent Instruction, Child Response and Parent Contingent Attention being scored during each interval in which the parent issues an instruction.

2.   Parental response to aversive and prosocial child behaviour.

The instructional sequence comprises a total of four categories of behaviour: Parent Instruction, child response, parent contingent attention and parent non-contingent attention. Parent instruction includes the following sub-categories: alpha, alpha negative, beta and beta negative. Child response includes the following sub-categories: compliance and non-compliance. Parent contingent attention includes the following sub-categories: praise, time out, contingent attend positive, contingent attend negative and contingent attend neutral. Parent non-contingent attention includes the following sub-categories: non-contingent attend positive, non-contingent attend negative and non-contingent attend neutral. Non-attend is a separate category.

Guidelines for recording behaviours

The field of observation

If the parent or the child leaves the field of observation the observer is advised to:

1. pause the audio cue when 'Record' sounds

2. code the behaviour of the previous 'Observe' interval

3. stop observing until both the parent and the target child returns

4. restart the audio-tape.

Recording alpha instructions

If the parent has issued an alpha instruction, the observer codes the instructional sequence in Antecedent–Behaviour–Consequence (ABC) format. The instruction is taken as the antecedent, the subsequent child compliance or non-compliance is taken as behaviour and the parental response to compliance/non-compliance is taken as consequence.

If the instructional sequence is initiated at the end of the observe phase and is interrupted by the 'Record' cue, the observer records the child behaviour and the parental response which occurred before the instruction was given.

Recording beta instructions

When a beta instruction is coded, the Behaviour–Consequence categories of the instructional sequence are not coded because there is no opportunity for the child to comply with the instruction, nor for the parent to provide a consequence (see definition of beta instruction below). The beta instruction is the only category of parent behaviour coded in the interval, with one category of child behaviour also being recorded in the usual fashion.

Recording child behaviour

At the outset of each 'observe' interval, the observer focuses upon the target child and notes one category of either aversive or child behaviour. In order to ensure that data do not exaggerate behaviour change, the coding schedule is biased towards the incidence of aversive behaviours: in the event of behaviours from more than one child behaviour category occurring in an interval, aversive behaviour takes precedence over prosocial behaviour. If the parent issues an instruction, the child's compliance or non-compliance is noted.

Recording parent behaviour

When no instruction has been issued during an interval, only two categories are scored: child behaviour (either prosocial or aversive) and parent behaviour in response to the specific child behaviour recorded in the interval. The parental response is coded as either contingent or non-contingent parent attention. If the parent attends to the target child's behaviour, contingent parent attention is recorded. If the parent does not attend to the target child's behaviour, a category of non-contingent parental attention is coded. If the parent initiates interaction with the target child, this is coded as non-contingent attention, as the parent is not reinforcing the specific child behaviour which is recorded in the interval.

Recording time out

When the parent implements the time-out procedure in response to non-compliance or in response to child aversive behaviour two possibilities arise:

1. The child goes to time out. This is coded in the same manner as when the target child leaves the room. The audio cue is paused at the end of the observe phase and is started again when the target child returns to the field of observation.

2. The child refuses to go to time out. The observer continues to record, coding subsequent parent and child behaviour for each interval.

Affect ratings

The distinctions between positive, neutral and negative affect apply to alpha instructions (Ia, Ia-), beta instructions (Ib, Ib-), contingent attention (cA+, cA-, cAo) and non-contingent attention (A+, A-, Ao).

Behavioural definitions

Definitions and some examples of each category of behaviour are provided below. The coding symbol is provided in parentheses. The coding symbols for child behaviour categories are in lower case and those for parent behaviour categories are in higher case.

Instructional sequence categories

Alpha instruction (Ia)

The explicit verbal expression of an instruction, suggestion, rule or question to which a verbal or motor response is appropriate and feasible, and which is presented in a non-aversive manner is coded as an alpha instruction. Non-verbal gestures of instruction (e.g., the parent points at something to be done) are not recorded as alpha instructions. Alpha instructions can direct the child to either initiate or terminate behaviour. The following are coded as alpha instructions:

1. *Instructions.* These are orders which specify the child behaviour to be initiated or terminated. The following are examples of instructions:

    o 'Tommy, I want you to hang up your coat.'
    o 'Hang up your coat.'
    o 'Come here.'
    o 'Tell me what happened.'
    o 'Stop that.'
    o 'Don't bang the door.'

2. *Suggestions.* The following are examples of suggestions:

    o 'You might hang up your coat now.'
    o 'Let's hang up your coat.'
    o 'See if you can hang up your coat.'
    o 'Maybe you can hang up your coat.'
    o 'You should hang up your coat.'

3. *Rules and statements of permission for the child to perform an act.* The following are examples of rules and statements of permission:

    o 'You know that you are to hang up your coat.'
    o 'You cannot go outside now.'
    o 'You can watch television now.'
    o 'It is time for you to do your homework now.'

4. *Command questions.* Command questions are distinct from questions which seek information. Command questions cue the child to respond with a particular form of behaviour. Questions which are not command questions seek information as a response. The following are examples of question commands:

    o 'Will you pick that up for me?'
    o 'Why don't you take out your book?'
    o 'Can you tell me what you have for your homework?'
    o 'Are you going to pick up your bag?' ('Where is your bag?' is not a command question.)

Aversive alpha instruction (Ia-)

An aversive alpha instruction is an alpha instruction which is presented aversively. The following are examples of aversive alpha instructions:

    o 'Tommy, hang up your coat this instant!' (Instruction)
    o 'Tommy, for God's sake, why don't you hang up your coat?' (Question)

Beta instruction (Ib)

A beta instruction is one with which the child has no opportunity to comply. Beta instructions include:

1. Instructions or rules that are vague. They do not specify the child behaviours to be initiated or terminated.

2. Alpha instructions with which the child has no opportunity to comply either because the parent performs the task herself or interrupts with verbiage before the child has an opportunity to demonstrate compliance (five seconds is allowed).

3. Instructions referring to the past or future, so that compliance cannot be assessed.

4. Multiple instructions which are presented together.

The following are examples of beta instructions:

*   'Tommy, hang up your coat, come in here and do your homework.' (This is a multiple instruction.)

*   'Tommy, I want you to be a good boy now.' (This is a vague instruction.)

*   'Come on!' (This is a vague instruction. 'Come here' is an alpha instruction.)

*   'Be careful!' (This does not specify a motor response, whereas 'Write carefully' does.)

*   'Hang on! I want you to put that in the box.' (This is a multiple instruction.)

*   'I want you to tidy your room this evening.' ('I want you to tidy your room now' is an alpha instruction.)

*   'Act your age!' (This is a vague instruction.)

Aversive beta instruction (Ib-)

Aversive beta instructions are those which are delivered in an aversive manner. The following are examples of aversive beta instructions:

*   'Tommy, hang up your coat, come in here and do your homework, now!'

*   'Tommy, grow up!'

Compliance (c)

This category refers to child compliance with parental instruction within five seconds of the instruction being given. If the child responds to the initial parental instruction with non-compliance, but complies within the interval when the instruction is repeated with a prompt, the second child response is coded; compliance takes precedence over non-compliance, being the eventual outcome. If the child has made a gesture of compliance it is coded as compliance. The following are examples of compliance:

- 'John, I want you to pick up your coat.' The child picks up his coat.
- 'John, pass me that piece beside you.' The child hands the parent the piece.
- 'John, come over here.' The child begins to move in specified direction.

Non-compliance (nc)

The child does not comply with a parental instruction after a five-second interval has elapsed. The following are examples of non-compliance:

- 'John, I want you to pick up your coat.' John ignores the instruction and continues to play with toy.
- 'John, pass me that piece beside you.' John continues to roll on the floor with his brother.
- 'John, come over here.' The child walks away from the parent.

Parent contingent attention categories

Parent contingent attention is coded if the parent attends to the specific child behaviour which is being coded in the same interval. Categories comprise praise, time out and and contingent attention positive, neutral or negative.

Praise (Pr)

This category refers to parental expressions of labelled or unlabelled praise, approval or acknowledgement, contingent upon compliance or prosocial child behaviour. An example of praise is 'John, I want you to pick up your coat'. John picks up the coat. The parent says one of the following:

- 'I'm really pleased you picked that up!' (Labelled praise)
- 'I'm really glad you did that.' (Labelled praise)
- 'Thanks for picking up your coat.' (Acknowledgement)
- 'Gosh! You picked up your coat so quickly!' (Approval)
- 'Good!' (Unlabelled praise)
- 'Well done.' (Unlabelled praise)

Time out (TO)

This category refers to the imposition of time out by the parent in response to non-compliance or in response to child aversive behaviour. It also refers to the parent issuing a warning that time out will be imposed. The following are examples of time out:

- The parent says, 'Time out' and points to the time-out chair.

- The parent says, 'If you don't do as you're asked, you'll have to go to time out.'

Contingent attend positive (cA+)

This category is coded when the parent attends to prosocial child behaviour with positive affect. This can be verbal or non-verbal. The following are examples of contingent positive attend:

- 'Look at this, Ma.' 'You've drawn a house.' (s+, cA+)

- 'This is a dog.' 'It's a very big dog.' (s+, cA+)

- 'I can't do it.' 'I'm sure I can help.' (ct, cA+)

- 'Can we go out later?' 'That sounds like a good idea.' (s+, cA+)

- Child draws a picture. Parent says, 'You've drawn a bridge.' (cv, cA+)

- Child throws dice. Parent cries 'Six!' (cv, cA+)

Contingent attend negative (cA-)

This category is coded for negative parental attention in response to child behaviour. This can be verbal (e.g., parent shouts at child) or non-verbal (e.g., parent slaps child). The following are examples of contingent attend negative:

- Child drops pencil. 'You're not trying hard enough.' (ot, cA-)

- Child makes mistake at homework. 'That is really stupid.' (cv, cA-)

- Child hits sibling. 'That's very bold.' (p-, cA-)

- Child spills food. 'You always mess up your dinner.' (ot, cA-)

Contingent attend neutral (cAo)

This category is coded for neutral parental attention in response to child behaviour. The following are examples of contingent attend neutral:

- Child says, 'What will we do later?' 'I'll see.' (Flat affect) (cv, cA-)

- The parent monitors the child doing homework. (cv, cA-)

Parent non-contingent attention categories

Parent non-contingent attention categories refer to parental attention which is not contingent upon the specific child behaviour which is coded in the interval.

Non-contingent attend positive (A+)

This category refers to prosocial verbal or non-verbal parental attention to the target child which is not contingent upon the child's behaviour. The following are examples of non-contingent attend positive (A+):

- Child draws quietly. Parent asks, 'Will we go for a walk?' (cv, A+)
- Child plays with sibling. Parent says, 'I found that toy you lost yesterday.' (cv, A+)

Non-contingent attend negative (A-)

This category refers to parent social attention to the target child that is deemed to be aversive due to overt content and/or tone of voice and which is not contingent to the child's behaviour. Aversive tone can range from relatively low-intensity complaint, nagging, grumbling or grousing to more high-intensity shouting. The following are examples of non-contingent attend negative:

- Child looks into schoolbag for books. Parent: 'Why did you not eat your lunch?' (cv, A-)
- Child begins to play with toys after a tantrum. Parent: 'I'm sick of your carrying on.' (cv, A-)
- 'Can I have a yoghurt?' 'I'm really cross that you didn't eat your dinner' (in an angry tone). (s+, A-)
- Child draws a picture. 'Where have you left the bloody rubber?' (s+, A-)

Non-contingent attend neutral (Ao)

This category refers to parent attention to the target child which is neutral in tone and content and which is not contingent upon the child's behaviour. The following are examples of non-contingent attend neutral:

- Child packs homework away. Parent says, 'Your pen is on the floor.' (cv, Ao)
- Child plays with toys. Parent says, 'Your dinner is ready now.' (cv, Ao)
- Child says, 'What are we doing later?' Parent says, 'Where is your schoolbag?' (s+, Ao)

- Parent says, 'Put the dice in the cup.' The child complies. Parent observes, takes up cup and rolls dice. (IA, c, Ao)

Non-attend (Na)

This category is coded when the parent does not attend to the child behaviour that is coded in the interval. The following are examples of non-attend:

- Child fights with sibling. Parent attends to spouse. (p-, Ao)
- Child plays with sibling. Parent performs household chore. (s+, Ao)
- Child does homework. Parent reads magazine. (cv, Ao)

Child behaviour categories

The observation schedule includes four categories of child aversive behaviour (complain, demand, physical negative and oppositional), two categories of prosocial child behaviour (constructive and social interaction) and one category of off-task behaviour.

Physical negative (p-)

This category refers to movement in relation to another person that involves or potentially involves inflicting physical pain. This category includes behaviours such as punching, pushing, kicking, biting, scratching, pinching, striking with an object, throwing an object at another person, pulling hair and poking with an object. Physical negative is also scored for any instance of destroying, damaging or attempting to damage belongings such as toys, furniture, clothing. The following are examples of physical negative:

- The child flicks a rubber band at sibling.
- The child scratches the table with his fork.
- The child chases sibling, shouting angrily 'You're dead!'

Complaint (ct)

This category is coded for instances of whining, crying, screaming, shouting, grizzling, intelligible vocal protests or displays of temper.

- The child lies on the floor kicking and screaming.
- The child whines, 'But I want to go outside.'

Demand (d)

This category is coded for an instruction, command or question, directed to another person by the child, which is judged to be aversive or unpleasant because of the content of the instruction, the voice quality of the speaker, and/or the assertive behaviour of the speaker. The following are examples of demands:

- The child says to mother, 'I want my dinner now!'

- The child shouts to brother, 'Get out of my way!'

- The child says aggressively to sibling, 'Give that to me.'

Oppositional (o)

This category is coded for instances of inappropriate child behaviours that cannot be accommodated readily into another other child aversive behaviour category. This category is scored for violations of specific family rules (e.g., no riding bikes in the house). It is also scored for instances of teasing, humiliating or embarrassing a parent or sibling. This category requires the observer to know any specific rules in a family and to judge whether the observed activity is aversive or prosocial. The following are examples of oppositional:

- The child makes a rude face at a visitor.

- The parent asks the child if she had a nice time at school and the child frowns and yawns, as though she is deliberately ignoring the mother.

- The child says repeatedly, 'Barry's a chicken.'

Social interaction (s+)

This category is coded for instances of verbal or non-verbal prosocial behaviour directed at a parent or sibling. The following are examples of social interaction:

- The child addresses a parent.

- The child addresses a sibling.

- The child plays with toys with a sibling.

Constructive (cv)

This category refers to constructive, appropriate self-directed activity. The following are examples of constructive:

- The child plays with bricks.
- The child writes in a school book.
- The child eats his lunch.

Off task (ot)

This category is coded when the child stops performing a task. The following are examples of off task:

- The child gazes out of the window during homework.
- The child stops sweeping the floor and plays with a toy.

Sample consent form

I agree to participate in a behavioural parent training programme which will be provided by [name of therapist(s)], of [name of service], which has been recommended as being appropriate to the needs of my son/daughter [name of son/daughter].

I consent to:

1. A therapist calling to my home [specify time and duration] in order to conduct observations of my child/children and myself, and to advise on the implementation of the programme.

2. A researcher calling to my home once weekly to take observations for the purposes of evaluation and research.

I have been informed that a [specify written or videotaped] record of these observations will be made, and that these will be stored securely for [specify, in accordance with agency procedures for storage of records].

I give my consent that the data which is obtained through these procedures, and through questionnaires completed by me, may be used for the purposes of evaluation and research **on the understanding that complete confidentiality will be maintained**.

Signed:_____

Date:_____

Appendix IV

Coding sheets

Mins	Int. no.	Instruction				Response				Parent contingent attention + − o	Parent non-contingent attention + − o		Child aversive				Child prosocial		Off task
	01	Ia	Ia	Ib	Ib-	c	nc	Pr	TO	cA	A	Na	p-	ct	d	o	cv	s+	ot
1:00	02																		
	03	Ia	Ia-	Ib	Ib-	c	nc	Pr	TO	cA	A	Na	p-	ct	d	o	cv	s+	ot
2:00	04																		
	05	Ia	Ia-	Ib	Ib-	c	nc	Pr	TO	cA	A	Na	p-	ct	d	o	cv	s+	ot
3:00	06																		
	07	Ia	Ia-	Ib	Ib-	c	nc	Pr	TO	cA	A	Na	p-	ct	d	o	cv	s+	ot
4:00	08																		
	09	Ia	Ia-	Ib	Ib-	c	nc	Pr	TO	cA	A	Na	p-	ct	d	o	cv	s+	ot
5:00	10																		
	11	Ia	Ia-	Ib	Ib-	c	nc	Pr	TO	cA	A	Na	p-	ct	d	o	cv	s+	ot
6:00	12																		
	13	Ia	Ia-	Ib	Ib-	c	nc	Pr	TO	cA	A	Na	p-	ct	d	o	cv	s+	ot
7:00	14																		
	15	Ia	Ia-	Ib	Ib-	c	nc	Pr	TO	cA	A	Na	p-	ct	d	o	cv	s+	ot
No. intervals																			

© Dermot O'Reilly 2005

Mins	Int no.	Instruction				Response					Parent contingent attention + − 0	Parent non-contingent attention + − 0		Child aversive				Child prosocial		Off task
8:00	16	Ia	Ia-	Ib	Ib-	c	nc	Pr	TO	cA		A	Na	p-	ct	d	o	cv	s+	ot
	17																			
9:00	18	Ia	Ia-	Ib	Ib-	c	nc	Pr	TO	cA		A	Na	p-	ct	d	o	cv	s+	ot
	19																			
10:00	20	Ia	Ia-	Ib	Ib-	c	nc	Pr	TO	cA		A	Na	p-	ct	d	o	cv	s+	ot
	21																			
11:00	22	Ia	Ia-	Ib	Ib-	c	nc	Pr	TO	cA		A	Na	p-	ct	d	o	cv	s+	ot
	23																			
12:00	24	Ia	Ia-	Ib	Ib-	c	nc	Pr	TO	cA		A	Na	p-	ct	d	o	cv	s+	ot
	25																			
13:00	26	Ia	Ia-	Ib	Ib-	c	nc	Pr	TO	cA		A	Na	p-	ct	d	o	cv	s+	ot
	27																			
14:00	28	Ia	Ia-	Ib	Ib-	c	nc	Pr	TO	cA		A	Na	p-	ct	d	o	cv	s+	ot
	29																			
15:00	30	Ia	Ia-	Ib	Ib-	c	nc	Pr	TO	cA		A	Na	p-	ct	d	o	cv	s+	ot
No. intervals																				

Mins	Int no.	Instruction				Response		Parent contingent attention			Parent non-contingent attention			Child aversive				Child prosocial		Off task
---	---	---	---	---	---	---	---	---	---	+ − 0	+ − 0	---	---	---	---	---	---	---	---	---
	31	Ia	Ia-	Ib	Ib-	c	nc	Pr	TO	cA	A	Na	p-	ct	d	o	cv	s+	ot
16:00	32																		
	33	Ia	Ia-	Ib	Ib-	c	nc	Pr	TO	cA	A	Na	p-	ct	d	o	cv	s+	ot
17:00	34																		
	35	Ia	Ia-	Ib	Ib-	c	nc	Pr	TO	cA	A	Na	p-	ct	d	o	cv	s+	ot
18:00	36																		
	37	Ia	Ia-	Ib	Ib-	c	nc	Pr	TO	cA	A	Na	p-	ct	d	o	cv	s+	ot
19:00	38																		
	39	Ia	Ia-	Ib	Ib-	c	nc	Pr	TO	cA	A	Na	p-	ct	d	o	cv	s+	ot
20:00	40																		
	41	Ia	Ia-	Ib	Ib-	c	nc	Pr	TO	cA	A	Na	p-	ct	d	o	cv	s+	ot
21:00	42																		
	43	Ia	Ia-	Ib	Ib-	c	nc	Pr	TO	cA	A	Na	p-	ct	d	o	cv	s+	ot
22:00	44																		
	45	Ia	Ia-	Ib	Ib-	c	nc	Pr	TO	cA	A	Na	p-	ct	d	o	cv	s+	ot
No. intervals																			

Mins	Int no.	Instruction				Response					Parent contingent attention		Parent non-contingent attention			Child aversive				Child prosocial		Off task
											+ − 0	+ − 0										
23:00	46	Ia	Ia-	Ib	Ib-	c	nc	Pr	TO	cA	A	Na	p-	ct	d	o	cv	s+	ot			
	47																					
24:00	48	Ia	Ia-	Ib	Ib-	c	nc	Pr	TO	cA	A	Na	p-	ct	d	o	cv	s+	ot			
	49																					
25:00	50	Ia	Ia-	Ib	Ib-	c	nc	Pr	TO	cA	A	Na	p-	ct	d	o	cv	s+	ot			
	51																					
26:00	52	Ia	Ia-	Ib	Ib-	c	nc	Pr	TO	cA	A	Na	p-	ct	d	o	cv	s+	ot			
	53																					
27:00	54	Ia	Ia-	Ib	Ib-	c	nc	Pr	TO	cA	A	Na	p-	ct	d	o	cv	s+	ot			
	55																					
28:00	56	Ia	Ia-	Ib	Ib-	c	nc	Pr	TO	cA	A	Na	p-	ct	d	o	cv	s+	ot			
	57																					
29:00	58	Ia	Ia-	Ib	Ib-	c	nc	Pr	TO	cA	A	Na	p-	ct	d	o	cv	s+	ot			
	59																					
30:00	60	Ia	Ia-	Ib	Ib-	c	nc	Pr	TO	cA	A	Na	p-	ct	d	o	cv	s+	ot			
No. intervals																						

References

Abidin, R.R. (1990) *Parenting Stress Index. Third Edition.* Charlottesville, VA: Pediatric Psychology Press.

Achenbach, T.M. (1991) *Manual for the Child Behavior Checklist/4–18 and 1991 Profile.* Burlington, VT: University of Vermont Department of Psychiatry.

Achenbach, T.M. and Rescorla, L.A. (2000) *Manual for the ASEBA Preschool Forms and Profiles.* Burlington, VT: University of Vermont, Department of Psychiatry.

Adubato, S., Adams, M. and Budd, K.S. (1981) 'Teaching a parent to train a spouse in child management techniques.' *Journal of Applied Behaviour Analysis 14*, 193–205.

American Psychiatric Association (1994) *Diagnostic and Statistical Manual of Mental Disorders* (4th edition). Washington, DC: American Psychiatric Association.

Asarnow, J.R. and Callan, J.W. (1985) 'Boys with peer adjustment problems: Social cognitive processes.' *Journal of Consulting and Clinical Psychology 53*,1, 80–7.

Australian Association of Social Workers (2000) *AASW Code of Ethics.* Kingston, South Australia: AASW.

Baer, D.M. (1981) 'How to plan for generalisation.' Austin, TX: Pro-Ed. Cited in Cooper, J.O., Heron, T.E. and Heward, W.L. (1987) *Applied Behavior Analysis.* New York: Macmillan.

Baer, D.M. (1997) 'Foreword.' In K. Dillenburger, M.F. O'Reilly and M. Keenan (eds) *Advances in Behaviour Analysis.* Dublin: University College Dublin Press.

Baer, D., Wolf, M. and Risley, T. (1968) 'Current dimensions of applied behaviour analysis.' *Journal of Applied Behaviour Analysis 1*, 91–7.

Banks, S. (1998) 'Professional ethics in social work – what future?' *British Journal of Social Work 28*, 213–31.

Barber, J.G. (1996) 'Social work and science: Are they compatible?' *Research on Social Work Practice 6*, 3, 379–88.

Barnard, J.D., Christophersen, E.R. and Wolf, M.M. (1977) 'Teaching children appropriate shopping behaviour through parent training in the supermarket setting.' *Journal of Applied Behaviour Analysis 10*, 49–59.

Barron, A.P. and Earls, F. (1984) 'The relation of temperament and social factors to behaviour problems in three-year-old children.' *Journal of Child Psychology and Psychiatry 25*, 1, 23–33.

Baum, W.M. (1994) *Understanding Behaviorism: Science, Behavior and Culture.* New York: HarperCollins.

Beames, L., Sanders, M.R. and Bor, W. (1992) 'The role of parent training in the cognitive behavioural treatment of children's headaches.' *Behavioural Psychotherapy 20*, 167–80.

Becker, W.C. (1971) *Parents Are Teachers: A Child Management Program.* Champaign, IL: Research Press.

Behan, J., Fitzpatrick, C., Sharry, J., Carr, A. and Waldron, B. (2001) 'Evaluation of the Parenting Plus Programme.' *Irish Journal of Psychology 22*, 3–4, 238–56.

Bernhardt, A.J. and Forehand, R. (1975) 'The effects of labeled and unlabeled praise upon lower and middle class children.' *Journal of Experimental Child Psychology 19*, 536–43.

Bowlby, J. (1969) *Attachment and Loss: 1 Attachment.* London: Hogarth Press.

Bourne, D.F. (1993) 'Overchastisement, child non-compliance and parenting skills: A behavioural intervention by a family centre social worker.' *British Journal of Social Work, 23,* 481–99.

Breiner, J. and Beck, S. (1984) 'Parents as change agents in the management of their developmentally delayed children's noncompliant behaviours: A critical review.' *Applied Research in Mental Retardation 5,* 259–78.

Breiner, J. and Forehand, R. (1981) 'An assessment of the effects of parent training on clinic-referred children's school behaviour.' *Behavioural Assessment 3,* 31–42.

Brightman, R.P., Baker, B.L., Clark, D.B. and Ambrose, S.A. (1982) 'Effectiveness of alternative training formats.' *Journal of Behaviour Therapy and Experimental Psychiatry 13,* 2, 113–117.

Brody, G.H. and Forehand, R. (1986) 'Maternal perceptions of child maladjustment as a function of the combined influence of child behaviour and maternal depression.' *Journal of Consulting and Clinical Psychology 54,* 237–40.

Browne, G.W. and Harris, T. (1978) *Social Origins of Depression: A Study of Psychiatric Disorder in Women.* London: Tavistock.

Browne, G.W. and Harris, T. (1989) 'Depression.' In G.W. Browne and T. Harris (eds) *Life Events and Illness.* London: Unwin.

Budd, K.S., Green, D.R. and Baer, D.M. (1976) 'An analysis of multiple misplaced parental social contingencies.' *Journal of Applied Behaviour Analysis 9,* 459–70.

Burrell, G. and Morgan, G. (1979) 'Sociological paradigms and organisational analysis.' London: Heinemann. Cited in Howe, D. (1987) *An Introduction to Social Work Theory: Making Sense in Practice.* Aldershot: Wildwood House.

Callias, M. (1994) 'Parent training.' In M. Rutter, E. Taylor and L. Hersov (eds) *Child and Adolescent Psychiatry: Modern Approaches.* Oxford: Blackwell.

Campbell, S., Ewing, L., Breaux, A. and Szumowski, E. (1986) 'Parent-referred problem three-year-olds: Follow-up at school entry.' *Journal of Child Psychology and Psychiatry 27,* 473–88.

Carr, A. (1999) *The Handbook of Child and Adolescent Clinical Psychology: A Contextual Approach.* London: Routledge.

Carr, J. (1995) *Helping Your Handicapped Child (2nd edn).* Harmondsworth: Penguin.

Cataldo, M.F. (1984) 'Clinical considerations in training parents of children with special problems.' In R.E. Dangel and R.A. Polster (eds) *Parent Training: Foundations of Research and Practice.* New York: Guilford Press.

Cataldo, M., Ward, E., Russo, D., Riordan, M. and Bennett, D. (1986) 'Compliance and correlated problem behaviour in children: Effects of contingent and noncontingent reinforcement.' *Analysis and Intervention in Developmental Disabilities 6,* 265–82.

Clare, A. (1998) *On Men: Masculinity in Crisis.* London: Random House.

Clark, H.B., Greene, B.F., Macrae, J.W., McNees, M.P., Davis, J.L. and Risley, T.R. (1977) 'A parent advice package for family shopping trips: Development and evaluation.' *Journal of Applied Behaviour Analysis 10,* 605–24.

Coble, P., Taska, L., Kupfer, D., Kazdin, A., Unis, A. and French, N. (1984) 'EEG sleep "abnormalities" in preadolescent boys with a diagnosis of conduct disorder.' *Journal of the American Academy of Child Psychiatry 23,* 4, 438–47.

Connell, S., Sanders, M.R. and Markie-Dadds (1997) 'Self-directed behavioural family intervention for parents of oppositional children in rural and remote areas.' *Behaviour Modification 21,* 4, 379–408.

Conners, C.K. (1997) *Conners' Rating Scales – Revised: User's Manual.* New York: Multi-Health Systems.

Conrad, M. and Hammen, C. (1989) 'Role of maternal depression in perceptions of child maladjustment.' *Journal of Consulting and Clinical Psychology 57*, 663–7.

Cooper, J.O., Heron, T.E. and Heward, W.L. (1987) *Applied Behaviour Analysis.* New York: Macmillan.

Cox, A.D., Puckering, C., Pound, A. and Mills, M. (1987) 'The impact of maternal depression in young children.' *Journal of Child Psychology and Psychiatry 28*, 917–28.

Cox, J.L. (1993) 'Psychiatric disorders of childbirth.' In R.E. Kendell and A.K. Zealley (eds) *Companion to Psychiatric Studies.* Edinburgh: Churchill Livingstone.

Dadds, M.R. (1987) 'Families and the origins of child behaviour problems.' *Family Process 26*, 341–57.

Dadds, M.R. and McHugh, T.A. (1992) 'Social support and treatment outcome in behavioural family therapy for child conduct problems.' *Journal of Consulting and Clinical Psychology 60*, 2, 252–9.

Dadds, M. and Powell, M.B. (1991) 'The relationship of interparental conflict and global marital adjustment to aggression, anxiety, and immaturity in aggressive and nonclinic children.' *Journal of Abnormal Child Psychology 19*, 5, 553–67.

Dadds, M.R. and Sanders, M.R. (1996) 'Family Observation Schedule-V (FOS-5).' Unpublished.

Dadds, M.R., Sanders, M.R. and James, J.E. (1987) 'The generalisation of treatment effects in parent training with multidistressed parents.' *Behavioural Psychotherapy 15*, 289–313.

Dadds, M.R., Schwartz, S. and Sanders, M.R. (1987) 'Marital discord and treatment outcome in behavioural treatment of child conduct disorders.' *Journal of Consulting and Clinical Psychology 55*, 3, 396–403.

Davis, L.V. (1985) 'Female and male voices in social work.' *Social Work 30*, 106–113.

Dillenburger, K. and Keenan, M. (1997) 'Human development: A question of structure and function.' In K. Dillenburger, M.F. O'Reilly and M. Keenan (eds) *Advances in Behaviour Analysis.* Dublin: University College Dublin Press.

Dodge, K. and Newman, J. (1981) 'Biased decision-making processes in aggressive boys.' *Journal of Abnormal Psychology 90*, 4, 375–9.

Donnellan, A.M., LaVigna, G.W., Negri-Shoultz, N. and Fassbender, L.L. (1988) *Progress Without Punishment: Effective Approaches for Learners with Behavior Problems.* New York: Teachers College Press.

Douglas, J. (1989) 'Training parents to manage their child's sleep problem.' In C. Schaeffer and J. Briemaster (eds) *Handbook of Parent Training: Parents as Co-therapists for Children's Behavior Problems.* New York: John Wiley.

Dowdney, L., Skuse, D., Rutter, M., Quinton, D. and Mrazek, D. (1985) 'The nature and qualities of parenting provided by women raised in institutions.' *Journal of Child Psychology and Psychiatry*, 599–625.

Ducharme, J.M. and Popynick, M. (1993) 'Errorless compliance to parental requests: treatment effects and generalization.' *Behaviour Therapy 24*, 209–26.

Dumas, J.E. (1989) 'Treating antisocial behaviour in children: Child and family approaches.' *Clinical Psychology Review 9*, 197–222.

Dumas, J.E. and Gibson, J.A (1990) 'Behavioural correlates of maternal depressive symptomatology in conduct-disorder children: 11 systemic effects involving fathers and siblings.' *Journal of Consulting and Clinical Psychology 58*, 877–81.

Dumas, J.E., Gibson, J.A. and Albin, J.B. (1989) 'Behavioural correlates of maternal depressive symptomatology in conduct-disorder children.' *Journal of Consulting and Clinical Psychology 57*, 516–21.

Dumas, J.E. and Wahler, R.G. (1983) 'Predictors of treatment outcome in parent training: Mother insularity and socio-economic disadvantage.' *Behavioural Assessment 5*, 301–13.

Dumas, J.E. and Wahler, R.G. (1985) 'Indiscriminate mothering as a contextual factor in aggressive-oppositional child behaviour: "Damned if you do, and damned if you don't".' *Journal of Abnormal Child Psychology 13*, 1, 1–17.

Earls, F. (1994) 'Oppositional-defiant and conduct disorders.' In M. Rutter, E. Taylor and L. Hersov (eds) *Child and Adolescent Psychiatry: Modern Approaches (3rd edn)*. London: Blackwell.

Edelstein, B.A. (1989) 'Generalisation and maintenance of behaviour change: Introduction to mini-series.' *Behaviour Therapy 20*, 309–10.

Englemann, S. and Colvin, W. (1983) *Generalized Compliance Training: A Direct-Instruction Program for Managing Severe Behavior Problems*. Eugene, OR: E-B Press. Cited in G.W. LaVigna and A.M. Donnellan (1986) *Alternatives to Punishment: Solving Behaviour Problems with Non-Aversive Strategies*. New York: Irvington.

Epstein, W.M. (1986) 'Science and social work.' *Social Service Review 60*, 144–60.

Erhardt, D. and Baker, B.L. (1990) 'The effects of behavioural parent training on families with young hyperactive children.' *Journal of Behaviour Therapy and Experimental Psychiatry 21*, 2, 121–32.

Eyberg, S. and Pincus, D. (1999) *Eyberg Child Behavior Inventory and Sutter-Eyberg Student Behavior Inventory – Revised: Professional Manual*. Odessa, FL: Psychological Assessment Resources.

Eyberg, S.M. and Robinson, E.A. (1983) 'Conduct problem behaviour: Standardisation of a behavioural rating scale with adolescents.' *Journal of Clinical Child Psychology 12*, 3, 347–54.

Eyberg, S.M. and Ross, A.W. (1978) 'Assessment of child behaviour problems: The validation of a new inventory.' *Journal of Clinical Child Psychology 7*, 113–116.

Farrington, D. (1978) 'Family backgrounds of aggressive youths.' In L. Hersov, M. Berger and D. Shaffer (eds) *Aggressive and Antisocial Behaviour in Childhood and Adolescence*. Oxford: Pergamon Press.

Farrington, D. (1985) 'Stepping stones to adult criminal careers.' In D. Olweus, J. Block and M.R. Yarrow (eds) *Development of Antisocial and Prosocial Behaviour*. New York: Academic Press.

Farrington, D.P., Loeber, R. and Van Kammen, W.B. (1990) 'Long-term criminal outcomes of hyperactivity-impulsivity-attention deficit and conduct problems in childhood.' In L.N. Robins and M. Rutter (eds) *Straight and Devious Pathways from Childhood to Adulthood*. New York: Cambridge University Press.

Featherstone, B. (2004) *Family Life and Family Support: A Feminist Analysis*. Basingstoke: Palgrave/Macmillan.

Fischer, J. (1978) 'Does anything work?' *Journal of Social Service Research 1*, 3, 215–43.

Fischer, J. (1993) 'Empirically-based practice: The end of ideology?' *Journal of Social Service Research 18*, 1/2, 19–64.

Fitzgerald, M. and Kinsella, A. (1989) 'Behavioural deviance in an Irish urban and town sample.' *Irish Journal of Medical Science 156*, 219–21.

Fitzgerald, M., Butler, B. and Kinsella, A. (1990) 'The burden on a family having a child with special needs.' *The Irish Journal of Psychological Medicine 7*, 109–13.

Fonagy, P., Target, M., Cottrell, D., Phillips, J. and Kurtz, Z. (2002) *What Works for Whom?: A Critical Review of Treatments for Children and Adolescents*. London: Guildford Press.

Forehand, R. and Atkeson, B.M. (1977) 'Generality of treatment effects with parents as therapists: A review of assessment and implementation procedures.' *Behaviour Therapy 8*, 575–93.

Forehand, R. and King, H.E. (1977) 'Noncompliant children: Effects of parent training on behaviour and attitude change.' *Behaviour Modification 1*, 1, 93–108.

Forehand, R., King, H.E., Peed, S. and Yoder, P. (1975) 'Mother–child interactions: Comparison of a non-compliant clinic group and a non-clinic group.' *Behaviour Research and Therapy 13*, 79–84.

Forehand, R. and Long, N. (1996) *Parenting the Strong-Willed Child*. Chicago: Contemporary Books.

Forehand, R. and McMahon, R.J. (1981) *Helping the Noncompliant Child: A Clinician's Guide to Parent Training*. New York: Guilford Press.

Forehand, R., Sturgis, E., McMahon, R., Aguar, D., Green, K., Wells, K. and Breiner, J. (1979) 'Parent behavioural training to modify noncompliance: Treatment generalisation across time and from home to school.' *Behaviour Modification 3*, 1, 3–25.

Frazier, J.R. and Schneider, H. (1975) 'Parental management of inappropriate hyperactivity in a young retarded child.' *Journal of Behaviour Therapy and Experimental Psychiatry 6*, 246–7.

Freedman, B., Rosenthal, L., Donahoe, C., Schlundt, D. and McFall, R. (1978) 'A social-behavioural analysis of skill deficits in delinquent and nondelinquent adolescent boys.' *Journal of Consulting and Clinical Psychology 46*, 6, 1148–462.

Freud, A. (1936) *The Ego and the Mechanisms of Defence*. London: Hogarth.

Friedlander, S., Weiss, D.S. and Traylor, J. (1986) 'Assessing the influence of maternal depression on the validity of the child behaviour checklist.' *Journal of Abnormal Child Psychology 14*, 122–33.

Furey, W.M. and Basili, L.A.(1988) 'Predicting consumer satisfaction in parent training for noncompliant children.' *Behaviour Therapy 19*, 555–64.

Gambrill, E. (1995) 'Behavioural social work: Past, present, and future.' *Research on Social Work Practice 5*, 4, 460–84.

Gardner, F.E. (1987) 'Positive interaction between mothers and conduct-problem children: Is there training for harmony as well as fighting?' *Journal of Abnormal Child Psychology 15*, 2, 283–93.

Gardner, F.E. (1989) 'Inconsistent parenting: Is there evidence for a link with children's conduct problems?' *Journal of Abnormal Psychology 17*, 2, 223–33.

Gardner, F.E. (1992) 'Parent–child interaction and conduct disorder.' *Educational Psychology Review 4*, 2, 135–55.

Gardner, F.E. (1994) 'The quality of joint activity between mothers and their children with behaviour problems.' *Journal of Child Psychology and Psychiatry 35*, 5, 935–48.

Gardner, F.E. (1998) 'Inconsistent parenting: Is there evidence for a link with children's conduct problems?' *Journal of Abnormal Child Psychology 17*, 2, 223–33.

Gibbs, A. (2001) 'The changing nature and context of social work research.' *British Journal of Social Work 31*, 687–704.

Goldberg, D. and Williams, P. (1988) *The User's Guide to the General Health Questionnaire*. Windsor: NFER-Nelson.

Goodman, R. (1994) 'Brain disorders.' In M. Rutter, E. Taylor and L. Hersov (eds) *Child and Adolescent Psychiatry: Modern Approaches (3rd edn)*. London: Blackwell.

Grant, L. and Evans, A. (1994) *Principles of Behavior Analysis*. New York: HarperCollins.

Gray, J.J. (1979) 'Positive reinforcement and punishment in the treatment of childhood trichotillomania.' *Journal of Behaviour Therapy and Experimental Psychiatry 10*, 125–9.

Griest, D.L., Forehand, R., Wells, K.C. and McMahon, R.J. (1980) 'An examination of differences between nonclinic and behaviour-problem clinic referred children and their mothers.' *Journal of Abnormal Psychology 89*, 497–500.

Griest, D.L., Forehand, R., Rogers, T., Breiner, J., Furey, W. and Williams, C.A. (1982) 'Effects of parent enhancement therapy on the treatment outcome and generalisation of a parent training programme.' *Behaviour Research and Therapy 20*, 429–36.

Griest, D.L. and Wells, K.C. (1983) 'Behavioural family therapy with conduct disorders in children.' *Behaviour Therapy 14*, 37–53.

Gross, D., Fogg, L. and Tucker, S. (1995) 'The efficacy of parent training for promoting positive parent–toddler relationships.' *Research in Nursing and Health 18*, 489–99.

Gross, D., Fogg, L., Webster-Stratton and Grady, J. (1999) 'Parent training with low-income multi-ethnic parents of toddlers.' Paper presented at the Society for Research in Child Development, Albuquerque, New Mexico.

Hall, R., Axelrod, S., Tyler, L., Grief, E., Jones, F. and Robertson, R. (1972) 'Modification of behaviour problems in the home with a parent as observer and experimenter.' *Journal of Applied Behaviour Analysis 5*, 53–64.

Hall, R., Cristler, C., Cranston, S. and Tucker, B. (1970) 'Teachers and parents as researchers using multiple baseline designs.' *Journal of Applied Behaviour Analysis 3*, 217–55.

Harrison, D.F., Hudson, W.W. and Thyer, B.A. (1992) 'On a critical analysis of empirical clinical practice: A response to Witkin's revised views.' *Social Work 37*, 461–3.

Herbert, E.W. and Baer, D.M. (1972) 'Training parents as behaviour modifiers: Self-recording of contingent attention.' *Journal of Applied Behaviour Analysis 5*, 139–49.

Herbert, M. and Iwaniec, D. (1981) 'Behavioural psychotherapy in natural homesettings: An empirical study applied to conduct disorded and incontinent children.' *Behavioural Psychotherapy 9*, 55–76.

Holosko, M.J. and Thyer, B.A. (2000) 'Ethical guidelines for designing and conducting evaluations of social work practice.' Paper presented at the International Conference on Evaluation for Practice, University of Huddersfield, UK, July.

Hops, H., Biglan, A., Sherman, L., Arthur, J., Friedman, L. and Osteen, V. (1987) 'Home observations of family interactions of depressed women.' *Journal of Consulting and Clinical Psychology 55*, 341–6.

Houts, A.C. and Mellon, M.W. (1989) 'Home-based treatment for primary enuresis.' In C. Schaeffer and J. Briemaster (eds) *Handbook of Parent Training: Parents as Co-Therapists for Children's Behavior Problems.* New York: John Wiley.

Howe, D. (1987) *An Introduction to Social Work Theory: Making Sense in Practice.* Aldershot: Wildwood House.

Huesmann, L.R., Eron, D.E. and Lefkowitz, M.M. (1984) 'The stability of aggression over time and generations.' *Developmental Psychology 20*, 6, 1120–34.

Hughes, J.C., Berry, H., Allen, D., Hutchings, J., Ingram, E. and Tulley, E.F. (2001) *A Review of Literature Relating to Safe Forms of Restraint for Children with Behaviour that is Difficult to Manage.* Welsh Office of Research and Development for Health and Social Care.

Irish Association of Social Workers (1995) *IASW Code of Ethics.* Dublin: IASW.

Jeffers, A. and Fitzgerald, M. (1991) *Irish Families Under Stress, Vol. 2.* Dublin: Eastern Health Board.

Jenkins, S., Bax, M. and Hart, H. (1980) 'Behaviour problems in pre-school children.' *Journal of Child Psychology and Psychiatry 21*, 1, 5–17.

Jenkins, J.M. and Smith, M.A. (1991) 'Marital disharmony and children's behaviour problems: Aspects of a poor marriage that affect children adversely.' *Journal of Child Psychology and Psychiatry 32*, 5, 793–810.

Johnson, S.M. and Lobitz, G. (1974) 'The personal and marital adjustment of parents as related to observed child deviance and parenting behaviours.' *Journal of Abnormal Child Psychology 2*, 3, 193–207.

Johnston, J.M. and Pennypacker, H.S. (1993) *Readings for Strategies and Tactics of Behavioural Research (2nd edn)*. London: Erlbaum.

Kazdin, A.E. (1980) 'The acceptability of time out from reinforcement procedures for disruptive child behaviours.' *Behaviour Therapy 11*, 329–44.

Kazdin, A.E. (1987) 'Treatment of antisocial behaviour in children: Current status and future directions.' *Psychological Bulletin 102*, 2, 187–203.

Kazdin, A.E. (1994) *Behavior Modification in Applied Settings (5th edn)*. Pacific Grove, CA: Brooks/Cole.

Kazdin, A.E. (1995) *Conduct Disorders in Childhood and Adolescence (2nd edn)*. London: Sage.

Kazdin, A.E. (1997a) 'Parent management training: Evidence, outcomes, and issues.' *Journal of the American Academy of Child and Adolescent Psychiatry 36*, 1349–56.

Kazdin, A.E. (1997b) 'A model for developing effective treatments: Progression and interplay of theory, research, and practice.' *Journal of Clinical Child Psychology 26*, 2, 114–29.

Kazdin, A.E., Esveldt-Dawson, K., French, N.H. and Unis, A.S. (1987) 'Effects of parent management training and problem-solving skills training combined in the treatment of antisocial child behavior.' *Journal of the American Academy of Child and Adolescent Psychiatry 26*, 3, 416–24.

Keeley, S.M., Shemberg, K.M. and Carbonell, J. (1976) 'Operant clinical intervention: Behaviour management or beyond? Where are the data?' *Behaviour Therapy 7*, 292–305. Cited in R. Forehand and B.M. Atkeson (1977) 'Generality of treatment effects with parents as therapists: A review of assessment and implementation procedures.' *Behaviour Therapy 8*, 575–93.

Kelly, M.L., Embry, L.H. and Baer, D.M. (1979) 'Skills for child management and family support: Training parents for maintenance.' *Behaviour Modification 3*, 3, 373–96.

Kemp, F. (1996) 'The ideology of aversive treatment as applied to clients and colleagues.' *Child and Family Behaviour Therapy 18*, 1, 9–25.

Kendall, P.C. (1989) 'The generalisation and maintenance of behaviour change: Comments, considerations, and the "no-cure" criticism.' *Behaviour Therapy 20*, 357–64.

Kendell, R.E. (1993) 'Mood (affective) disorders.' In R.E. Kendell and A.K. Zealley (eds) *Companion to Psychiatric Studies*. Edinburgh: Churchill Livingstone.

Klein, M. (1932) *The Psychoanalysis of Children*. London: Hogarth.

Koegel, R.L., Schreibman, L., Johnson, J., O'Neill, R.E. and Dunlap, G. (1984) 'Collateral effects of parent training on families with autistic children.' In R.E. Dangel and R.A. Polster (eds) *Parent Training: Foundations of Research and Practice*. New York: Guilford Press.

Kvale, S. (1996) *Interviews: An Introduction to Qualitative Research Interviewing*. London: Sage.

LaVigna, G.W. and Donnellan, A.M. (1986) *Alternatives to Punishment: Solving Behavior Problems with Non-Aversive Strategies*. New York: Irvington.

Leader, H., Fitzgerald, M. and Kinsella, A. (1985) 'Behaviourally deviant preschool children and depressed mothers.' *Irish Journal of Medical Science 154*, 3, 106–109.

Levine, F.M. and Ramirez, R. (1989) 'Contingent negative practice as a home-based treatment of tics and stuttering.' In C. Schaeffer and J. Briemaster (eds) *Handbook of Parent Training: Parents as Co-Therapists for Children's Behavior Problems*. New York: John Wiley.

Little, L.M. and Kelly, M.L. (1989) 'The efficacy of response cost procedures for reducing children's noncompliance to parental instructions.' *Behaviour Therapy 20*, 525–34.

Loeber, R. (1991) 'Antisocial behaviour: More enduring than changeable?' *Journal of the American Academy of Child and Adolescent Psychiatry 30*, 3, 393–7.

Long, P., Forehand, R., Wierson, M. and Morgan, A. (1994) 'Does parent training with young non-compliant children have long-term effects?' *Behaviour Research and Therapy 32*, 1, 101–7.

Lorenz, W. (1994) *Social Work in a Changing Europe.* London: Routledge.

Lutzker, J.R. (1994) 'Referee's evaluation of "Assessment of a new procedure for timeout escape in preschoolers" by McNeil *et al.*' Cited in F. Kemp (1996) 'The ideology of aversive treatment as applied to clients and colleagues.' *Child and Family Behaviour Therapy 18*, 1, 9–25.

Lytton, H. (1990) 'Child and parent effects in boys' conduct disorder: A reinterpretation.' *Developmental Psychology*, 26, 683–97.

Maccoby, E. and Martin, J. (1983) 'Socialisation in the context of the family: Parent–child interaction.' In E. Heatherington (ed) *Handbook of Child Psychology, Vol. 4: Socialization, Personality and Social Development.* New York: Wiley.

McAuley, R. (1982) 'Training parents to modify conduct problems in their children.' *Journal of Child Psychology and Psychiatry 23*, 335–42.

Macdonald, G. and Macdonald, K. (1995) 'Ethical issues in social work research.' In R. Hugman and D. Smith (eds) *Ethical Issues in Social Work Education.* London: Routledge.

Macdonald, G., Sheldon, B. and Gillespie, J. (1992) 'Contemporary studies of the effectiveness of social work.' *British Journal of Social Work 22*, 6, 615–43.

Mace, F.C., Hock, M.L., Lalli, J.S., West, B.J., Belfiore, P., Pinter, E. and Brown, D.K. (1988) 'Behavioural momentum in the treatment of noncompliance.' *Journal of Applied Behaviour Analysis 21*, 123–41.

McGee, R., Feehan, M., Williams, S., Partridge, F., Silva, P. and Kelly, J. (1990) 'DSM-III disorders in a large sample of adolescents.' *Journal of the American Academy of Child and Adolescent Psychiatry 29*, 50–9.

McGee, R., Feehan, M., Williams, S. and Anderson, J. (1992) 'DSM-III disorders from age 11 to age 15 years.' *Journal of the American Academy of Child and Adolescent Psychiatry 31*, 50–9.

McGee, R., Silva, P. and Williams, S. (1984) 'Behaviour problems in a population of seven-year-old children: Prevalence, stability and types of disorder – a research report.' *Journal of Child Psychology and Psychiatry 25*, 251–9.

McKeown, K., Ferguson, H. and Rooney, D. (1998) *Changing Fathers? Fatherhood and Family Life in Modern Ireland.* Dublin: Colins Press.

McMahon, R.J. (1987) 'Some current issues in the behavioural assessment of conduct disordered children and their families.' *Behavioural Assessment 9*, 235–52.

McMahon, R.J., Forehand, R. and Griest, D.L. (1981) 'Effects of knowledge of social learning principles on enhancing treatment outcome and generalisation in a parent training programme.' *Journal of Consulting and Clinical Psychology 49*, 4, 526–32.

McMahon, R.J., Forehand, R., Griest, D. and Wells, K. (1981) 'Who drops out of treatment during parent behavioural training?' *Behavioural Counselling Quarterly 1*, 1, 77–85.

McNeil, C.B., Clemens-Mowrer, L., Gurwitch, R.H. and Funderburk, B.W. (1994) 'Assessment of a new procedure to prevent timeout escape in preschoolers.' *Child and Family Behaviour Therapy 16*, 3, 27–35.

McNeil, C.B., Eyberg, S., Eisenstadt, T.H., Newcomb, K. and Funderburk, B. (1991) 'Parent–child interaction therapy with behaviour problem children: Generalisation of treatment effects to the school setting.' *Journal of Clinical Child Psychology 20*, 2, 140–51.

Martin, B. (1977) 'Brief family intervention: Effectiveness and the importance of including father.' *Journal of Consulting and Clinical Psychology 45*, 6, 1002–1010.

Mattaini, M.A. and Thyer, B.A. (1996) 'Introduction.' In M.A. Mattaini and B.A. Thyer (eds) *Finding Solutions to Social Problems.* Washington, DC: American Psychological Association.

Milner, J.S. and Chilamkurti, C. (1991) 'Physical child abuse perpetrator characteristics.' *Journal of Interpersonal Violence 6,* 3, 345–66.

Mitchell, S. and Rosa, P. (1981) 'Boyhood behaviour problems as precursors of criminality: A fifteen-year follow-up study.' *Journal of Child Psychology and Psychiatry 22,* 19–33.

Moffitt, T.E. (1993) 'Adolescence-limited and life-course-persistent antisocial behaviour: A developmental taxonomy.' *Psychological Review 100,* 4, 674–701.

Moreland J.R., Schwebel, A.I., Beck, S. and Wells, R. (1982) 'Parents as therapists: A review of the behaviour therapy parent training literature – 1975 to 1981.' *Behaviour Modification 6,* 250–76.

Myers, L.M. and Thyer, B.A. (1997) 'Should social work clients have the right to effective treatment?' *Social Work 42,* 288–9.

Nagel, J.J. (1988) 'Can there be a unified theory of social work practice?' *Social Work 33,* 369–70.

National Association of Social Workers (1996) *NASW Code of Ethics.* Washington DC: NASW.

Ollendick, T. and Hersen, M. (1984) 'An overview of child behavioral assessment.' In T. Ollendick and M. Herson (eds) *Child Behavioral Assessment: Principles and Procedures.* New York: Pergamon.

Olmi, D.J., Sevier, R.C. and Nastasi, D.F. (1997) 'Time-in/time-out as a response to noncompliance and inappropriate behaviour with children with developmental disabilities: Two case studies.' *Psychology in the Schools 34,* 1, 31–9.

Oltmanns, T.F., Broderick, J.E. and O'Leary, K.D. (1977) 'Marital adjustment and the efficacy of behaviour therapy with children.' *Journal of Consulting and Clinical Psychology 45,* 5, 724–9.

O'Neill, R.E., Horner, R.H., Albin, R.W., Sprague, J.R., Storey, K. and Newton, J.S. (1997) *Functional Assessment and Programme Development for Problem Behaviour: A Practical Handbook (2nd edn).* London: Brooks/Cole.

O'Reilly, M. (1997) 'Assessing challenging behaviour of persons with severe mental disabilities.' In K. Dillenburger, M. O'Reilly and M. Keenan (eds) *Advances in Behavioural Analysis.* Dublin: University College Dublin Press.

O'Reilly, D. and Dillenburger, K. (2000) 'The development of a high-intensity parent training programme for the treatment of moderate/severe child conduct problems.' *Research on Social Work Practice 10,* 6, 759–786.

Parke, R.D. (1977) 'Punishment in children: Effects, side effects, and alternative strategies.' In H. Hom and P. Robinson (eds) *Psychological Processes in Early Education.* New York: Academic Press.

Parke, R.D. (1979) 'Interactional designs.' In R.B. Cairns (ed) *The Analysis of Social Interactions: Methods, Issues, and Illustrations.* London: John Wiley.

Parrish, J.M., Cataldo, M.F., Kolko, D.J., Neef, N.A. and Egel, A.L. (1986) 'Experimental analysis of response covariation among compliant and inappropriate behaviours.' *Journal of Applied Behaviour Analysis 19,* 241–54.

Patterson, G.R. (1974) 'Intervention for boys with conduct problems: Multiple settings, treatments, criteria.' *Journal of Consulting and Clinical Psychology 42,* 471–81.

Patterson, G.R. (1976) 'The aggressive child: Victim and architect of a coercive system.' In E.S. Mash, L.A. Hamerlynch and L.C. Handy (eds) *Behavior Modification and Families.* New York: Brunel.

Patterson, G.R. (1982) *Coercive Family Process.* Eugene, OR: Castalia.

Patterson, G.R. (1986) 'Performance models for antisocial boys.' *American Psychologist 41*, 4, 432–44.

Patterson, G.R. and Fleischman, M.J. (1979) 'Maintenance of treatment effects: Some considerations concerning family systems and follow-up data.' *Behaviour Therapy 10*, 168–85.

Patterson, G.R. and Forgatch, M.S. (1990) 'Developmental growth models for depression.' Paper presented at The Fifth Annual Family Consortium Institute, Monterey, California. Cited in Patterson, G.R., Reid, J.B. and Dishion, T.J. (1992) *Antisocial Boys*. Eugene, OR: Castalia.

Patterson, G.R., Reid, J.B. and Dishion, T.J. (1992) *Antisocial Boys*. Eugene, OR: Castalia Press.

Payne, M. (1997) *Modern Social Work Theory (2nd edn)*. London: Macmillan.

Pazulinec, R., Meyerrose, M. and Sajwaj, T. (1983) 'Punishment via response cost.' In S. Axelrod and J. Apsche (eds) *The Effects of Punishment on Human Behavior*. New York: Academic Press.

Peed, S., Roberts, M. and Forehand, R. (1977) 'Evaluation of the effectiveness of a standardised parent training programme in altering the interaction of mothers and their noncompliant children.' *Behaviour Modification 1*, 323–50.

Pettit, G.S. and Bates, J.E. (1989) 'Family interaction patterns and children's behaviour problems from infancy to 4 years.' *Developmental Psychology 25*, 3, 413–20.

Pevsner, R. (1982) 'Group parent training versus individual family therapy: An outcome study.' *Journal of Behaviour Therapy and Experimental Psychiatry 13*, 2, 119–22.

Piele, C. (1988) 'Research paradigms in social work: From stalemate to creative synthesis.' *Social Service Review 62*, 1–19.

Powell, F. (1998) 'The professional challenges of reflexive modernisation: Social work in Ireland.' *British Journal of Social Work 28*, 311–28.

Prinz, R.J. and Miller, G.E. (1994) 'Family-based treatment for childhood antisocial behaviour: Experimental influences on dropout and engagement.' *Journal of Consulting and Clinical Psychology 62*, 645–50.

Puckering, C. (1989) 'Annotation: Maternal depression.' *Journal of Child Psychology and Psychiatry 30*, 807–17.

Quinn, M. and Quinn, T. (1997) *What Can a Parent Do?* Newry NI: Family Caring Trust.

Quinn, M. and Quinn, T. (2000) *What Can the Parent of a Teenager Do?* Newry NI: Family Caring Trust.

Quinton, D., Rutter, M. and Gulliver, L. (1990) 'Continuities in psychiatric disorders from childhood to adulthood in the children of psychiatric patients.' In L.N. Robins and M. Rutter (eds) *Straight and Devious Pathways from Childhood to Adulthood*. New York: Cambridge University Press.

Reid, J.W. and Hanrahan, P. (1981) 'The effectiveness of social work: Recent evidence.' In E. Goldberg and N. Connolly (eds) *Evaluative Research in Social Care*. London: Heinemann.

Reid, M.J., Webster-Stratton, C. and Beauchaine, T.P. (2001) 'Parent training in Headstart: A comparison of programme response among African American, Asian American, Caucasian, and Hispanic mothers.' *Prevention Science 2*, 4, 209–27.

Reitsma-Street, M., Offord, D. and Finch, T. (1985) 'Pairs of same-sexed siblings discordant for antisocial behaviour.' *British Journal of Psychiatry 146*, 415–23.

Reitman, D. and Drabman, R.S. (1996) 'Read my fingertips: A procedure for enhancing the effectiveness of time-out with argumentative children.' *Child and Family Behaviour Therapy 18*, 2, 35–40.

Rekers, G.A. (1984) 'Ethical issues in child behavioral assessment.' In T. Ollendick and M. Herson (eds) *Child Behavioral Assessment: Principles and Procedures*. New York: Pergamon.

Richard, B. and Dodge, K. (1982) 'Social maladjustment and problem-solving in school-aged children.' *Journal of Consulting and Clinical Psychology 50*, 226–33.

Richman, N., Stevenson, J. and Graham P. (1982) *Preschool to School: A Behavioural Study*. London: Academic Press.

Roberts, M.W. (1985) 'Praising child compliance: Reinforcement or ritual?' *Journal of Abnormal Child Psychology 13*, 4, 611–23.

Robins, L. (1966) *Deviant Children Grow Up*. Baltimore, MD: Williams and Wilkins.

Robbins, L.B. (1981) 'Epidemiological approaches to natural history research.' *Journal of the American Academy of Psychiatry 20*, 566–80.

Robins, L. (1978) 'Sturdy childhood predictors of adult antisocial behaviour: Replications from longitudinal studies.' *Psychological Medicine 8*, 611–22.

Robins, L.B. (1991) 'Conduct disorder.' *Journal of Child Psychology and Psychiatry 20*, 566–680.

Robins, L. and McEvoy, L. (1990) 'Conduct problems as predictors of substance abuse.' In L.N. Robins and M. Rutter (eds) *Straight and Devious Pathways from Childhood to Adulthood*. New York: Cambridge University Press.

Robins, L., West, P. and Herjanic, B. (1975) 'Arrests and delinquency in two generations: A study of black urban families and their children.' *Journal of Child Psychology and Psychiatry 16*, 125–40.

Rogers, C. (1975) 'The emerging person: A new revolution.' In R.I. Evans (ed) *Carl Rogers: The Man and His Ideas*. New York: Dutton.

Ross, J. (1975) 'Parents modify thumbsucking: A case study.' *Journal of Behaviour Therapy and Experimental Psychiatry 6*, 248–9.

Rubin, A. (1985) 'Practice effectiveness: More grounds for optimism.' *Social Work 30*, 469–75.

Russo, D.C., Cataldo, M.F. and Cushing, P.J. (1981) 'Compliance training and behavioural covariation in the treatment of multiple behaviour problems.' *Journal of Applied Behaviour Analysis 14*, 209–22.

Rutter, M. (1966) *Children of Sick Parents: An Environmental and Psychiatric Study*. Institute of Psychiatry, Maudsley Monographs No. 16. London: Oxford University Press. Cited in Richman, N. (1977) 'Disorders in preschool children.' In M. Rutter and L. Hersov (eds) *Child Psychiatry: Modern Approaches*. London: Blackwell.

Rutter, M. (1985) 'Family and school influence on behavioural development.' *Journal of Child Psychology and Psychiatry 26*, 349–68.

Rutter, M., Cox, A., Tupling, C., Berger, M. and Yule, W. (1975) 'Attainment and adjustment in two geographical areas: 1 – the prevalence of psychiatric disorder.' *Journal of Child Psychology and Psychiatry 126*, 493–509.

Rutter, M. and Giller, H. (1983) *Juvenile Delinquency: Trends and Perspectives*. Harmondsworth: Penguin.

Rutter, M. and Madge, N. (1976) *Cycles of Disadvantage*. London: Heinemann.

Rutter, M. and Shaffer, D. (1980) 'DSM-III: A step forward or backward in terms of the classification of child psychiatric disorders?' *Journal of the American Academy of Child Psychiatry 19*, 371–94.

Rutter, M., Tizard J. and Whitmore K. (1970) *Education, Health and Behaviour*. London: Longmans.

Rutter, M., Yule, B., Quenton, D., Rowlands, O., Yule, W. and Berger, M. (1974) 'Attainment and adjustment in two geographical areas: III – some factors accounting for area differences.' *British Journal of Psychiatry 125*, 520–33.

Sanders, M.R. (1999) 'Triple P-Positive parenting programme: Towards an empirically validated multilevel parenting and family support strategy for the prevention of behaviours and emotional problems in children.' *Clinical Child and Family Psychology Review 2*, 2, 71–90.

Sanders, M.R. and Christensen, A.P. (1985) 'A comparison of the effects of child management and planned activities training in five parenting environments.' *Journal of Abnormal Child Psychology 13*, 101–17.

Sanders, M.R. and Dadds, M.R. (1982) 'The effects of planned activities and child management procedures in parent training: An analysis of setting generality.' *Behaviour Therapy 13*, 452–61.

Sanders, M.R. and Dadds, M.R. (1993) *Behavioural Family Intervention*. London: Allyn Bacon.

Sanders, M.R. and Glynn, T. (1981) 'Training parents in behavioural self-management: An analysis of generalization and maintenance.' *Journal of Applied Behaviour Analysis 14*, 223–37.

Sanders, M.R., Markie-Dadds, C. and Turner, K.M. (2003) *Theoretical, Scientific and Clinical Foundations of the Triple P-Positive Parenting Programme: A Population Approach to the Promotion of Parenting Competence*. Parenting Research and Practice Monograph No. 1. Brisbane, Queensland: The Parenting and Family Support Centre.

Sanders, M.R., Montgomery, D.T. and Brechman-Toussaint, M.L. (2000) 'The mass media and the prevention of child behaviour problems: The evaluation of a television series to promote positive outcomes for parents and their children.' *Journal of Child Psychology and Psychiatry 41*, 7, 939–48.

Schachar, R. (1991) 'Childhood hyperactivity.' *Journal of Child Psychology and Psychiatry 32*, 1, 155–91.

Schachar, R. and Wachsmuth, R. (1990) 'Oppositional disorder in children: A validation study comparing conduct disorder, oppositional disorder and normal control children.' *Journal of Child Psychology and Psychiatry 34*, 7, 1089–1102.

Schlinger, H.D. (1995) *A Behaviour Analytic View of Child Development*. New York: Plenum.

Schmidt, K., Solant, M. and Bridger, W. (1985) 'Electrodermal activity of undersocialized aggressive children: A pilot study.' *Journal of Child Psychology and Psychiatry 26*, 4, 653–60.

Scholom, A., Zucker, R.A. and Stollak, G.E. (1979) 'Relating early child adjustment to infant and parent temperament.' *Journal of Abnormal Child Psychology 7*, 3, 297–308.

Scott, S., Spender, Q., Doolan, M., Jacobs, B. and Aspland, H. (2001) 'Multicentre controlled trial of parenting groups for childhood antisocial behaviour in clinical practice.' *British Medical Journal 323*, 1–7.

Sells, S.P., Smith, T.E. and Sprenkle, D.H. (1995) 'Integrating qualitative and quantitative methods: A research model.' *Family Process 34*, 199–218.

Sheldon, B. (1995) *Cognitive Behavioural Therapy: Research, Practice and Philosophy*. London: Routledge.

Sheldon, B. (1998) 'Research and theory.' In K. Cigno and D. Bourn (eds) *Cognitive Behavioural Social Work in Practice*. Aldershot: Arena.

Shinn, M.R., Ramsey, E., Walker, H.M., Stieber, H. and O'Neill, R.E. (1987) 'Antisocial behaviour in school settings: Initial differences in an at-risk and normal population.' *Journal of Special Education 21*, 2, 69–84. Cited in Patterson, G.R., Reid, J.B. and Dishion, T.J. (1992) *Antisocial Boys*. Eugene, OR: Castalia Press.

Shorter, E. (1975) *The Making of the Modern Family*. Glasgow: Collins.

Sidman, M. (1989) *Coercion and Its Fallout*. Boston, MA: Authors Cooperative.

Simpson, A.E. and Stevenson-Hinde, J. (1985) 'Temperamental characteristics of three- to four-year-old boys and girls and child–family interactions.' *Journal of Child Psychology and Psychiatry 26*, 1, 43–53.

Skinner, B.F. (1953) *Science and Human Behavior*. New York: Macmillan.

Skinner, B.F. (1971) *Beyond Freedom and Dignity*. New York: Knopf.

Skinner, B.F. (1974) *About Behaviorism*. New York: Knopf.

Skinner B.F. (1989) 'The origins of cognitive thought.' *American Psychologist 44*, 13–18.

Slife, B.D. and Williams, R.N. (1995) *What's Behind the Research: Discovering Hidden Assumptions in the Behavioural Sciences*. London: Sage.

Stokes, T.F. and Baer, D.M. (1977) 'An implicit technology of generalization.' *Journal of Applied Behaviour Analysis 10*, 349–67.

Strauss, C.C. and Atkeson, B.M. (1984) 'Parenting: Training mothers as behaviour therapists for their children.' In E.A. Blechman (ed) *Behaviour Modification With Women*. London: Guilford Press.

Stumphauzer, J.S. (1976) 'Elimination of stealing by self-reinforcement of alternative behaviour and family contracting.' *Journal of Behaviour Therapy and Experimental Psychiatry 7*, 265–8.

Sturge, C. (1982) 'Reading retardation and antisocial behaviour.' *Journal of Child Psychology and Psychiatry 23*, 1, 21–31.

Sutton, C. (1992) 'Training parents to manage difficult children: A comparison of methods.' *Behavioural Psychotherapy 20*, 115–39.

Szatmari, P., Offord, D.R. and Boyle, M.H. (1989) 'Ontario child health study: Prevalence of attention deficit disorder with hyperactivity.' *Journal of Child Psychology and Psychiatry 30*, 2, 219–30.

Taylor, E. (1994) 'Syndromes of attention deficit and hyperactivity.' In M. Rutter, E. Taylor and L. Hersov (eds) *Child and Adolescent Psychiatry: Modern Approaches*. London: Blackwell.

Taylor, I. (1999) 'Functional assessment, functional analysis, and challenging behaviour.' In M. Keenan, K.J. Kerr and K. Dillenburger (eds) *Parents' Education as Autism Therapists*. London: Jessica Kingsley Publishers.

Taylor, I. and O'Reilly, M.F. (1997) 'Private events: A neglected and misunderstood concept in radical behaviourism.' In K. Dillenburger, M.F. O'Reilly and M. Keenan (eds) *Advances In Behaviour Analysis*. Dublin: University College Dublin Press.

Thomas, A., Chess, S. and Birch, H. (1968) *Temperament and Behavior Disorders in Children*. New York: New York University Press.

Thyer, B.A. (1987) 'Contingency analysis: Toward a unified theory of social work practice.' *Social Work 32*, 150–7.

Thyer, B.A. (1988) 'Social work as a behaviourist views it: A reply to Nagel.' *Social Work 33*, 371–2.

Thyer, B.A. (1996) 'Behavior analysis and social welfare policy.' In M.A. Mattaini and B.A. Thyer (eds) *Finding Solutions to Social Problems*. Washington, DC: American Psychological Association.

Thyer, B.A. and Hudson, W.W. (1987) 'Progress in behavioural social work: An introduction.' *Journal of Social Service Research 10*, 1–6. Cited in Gambrill, E. (1995) 'Behavioural social work: Past, present, and future.' *Research on Social Work Practice 5*, 4, 460–84.

Trinder, L. (1996) 'Social work research: The state of the art (or science).' *Child and Family Social Work 1*, 233–42.

Urquiza, A.J. and McNeil, C.B. (1996) 'Parent–child interaction therapy: An intensive dyadic intervention for physically abusive families.' *Child Maltreatment 1*, 2, 132–41.

Vikan, A. (1985) 'Psychiatric epidemiology in a sample of 1510 ten-year-old children – 1 prevalence.' *Journal of Child Psychology and Psychiatry 26*, 55–75.

Wahler, R.G. (1969) 'Oppositional children: A quest for parental reinforcement control.' *Journal of Applied Behaviour Analysis 2*, 159–70.

Wahler, R.G. (1975) 'Some structural aspects of deviant child behaviour.' *Journal of Applied Behaviour Analysis 8*, 27–42.

Wahler, R.G. (1980) 'The insular mother: Her problems in parent–child treatment.' *Journal of Applied Behaviour Analysis 13*, 207–19.

Wahler, R.G., Cartor, P.G., Fleischman, J. and Lambert, W. (1992) 'The impact of synthesis teaching and parent training with mothers of conduct-disordered children.' *Journal of Abnormal Child Psychology 21*, 4, 425–40.

Wahler, R.G. and Dumas, J.E. (1984) 'Changing the observational coding styles of insular and noninsular mothers: A step towards maintenance of parent training effects.' In R.E. Dangel and R.A. Polster (eds) *Parent Training: Foundations of Research and Practice.* New York: Guilford Press.

Wahler, R.G. and Dumas, J.E. (1986) 'Maintenance factors in coercive mother–child interactions: The compliance and predictability hypothesis'. *Journal of Applied Behaviour Analysis 19*, 13–22.

Wahler, R.G. and Fox, J.J. (1981) 'Setting events in applied behaviour analysis: Toward a conceptual and methodological expansion.' *Journal of Applied Behaviour Analysis 14*, 327–38.

Wahler, R.G. and Meginnis, K.L. (1997) 'Strengthening child compliance through positive parenting practices: What works?' *Journal of Clinical Child Psychology 26*, 4, 433–40.

Walshe, P. (1997) 'Bye-bye behaviour modification.' In K. Dillenburger, M.F. O'Reilly and M. Keenan (eds) *Advances in Behaviour Analysis.* Dublin: University College Dublin Press.

Watson, J.B. (1913) 'Psychology as the behaviourist views it.' *Psychological Review 20*, 158–77. Cited in W.M. Baum (1994) *Understanding Behaviorism: Science, Behavior and Culture.* New York: HarperCollins.

Webster-Stratton (1981) 'Modification of mothers' behaviours and attitudes through a videotape modelling group discussion programme.' *Behaviour Therapy 12*, 634–42.

Webster-Stratton, C. (1982a) 'Teaching mothers through videotape modelling to change their children's behavior.' *Journal of Pediatric Psychology 7*, 3, 279–94.

Webster-Stratton, C. (1982b) 'The long-term effects of a videotape modelling parent-training programme: Comparison of immediate and 1-year follow-up results.' *Behaviour Therapy 13*, 702–14.

Webster-Stratton, C. (1984) 'Randomised trial of two parent-training programmes for families with conduct-disordered children.' *Journal of Consulting and Clinical Psychology 52*, 4, 666–78.

Webster-Stratton, C. (1985a) 'Predictors of treatment outcome in parent training for conduct disordered children.' *Behaviour Therapy 16*, 223–43.

Webster-Stratton, C. (1985b) 'The effects of father involvement in parent training for conduct problem children.' *Journal of Child Psychology and Psychiatry 26*, 5, 801–810.

Webster-Stratton, C. (1989) 'Systematic comparison of consumer satisfaction of three cost-effective parent training programmes for conduct problem children.' *Behaviour Therapy 20*, 103–15.

Webster-Stratton, C. (1990) 'Stress: A potential disruptor of parent perceptions and family interactions.' *Journal of Clinical Child Psychology 19*, 4, 302–12.

Webster-Stratton, C. (1991) *The Dinosaur Curriculum for Young Children.* Seattle, WA: Seth Enterprises.

Webster-Stratton, C. (1992a) *The Parents, Teachers and Children Videotape Series.* Seattle, WA: Seth Enterprises.

Webster-Stratton, C. (1992b) *The Incredible Years: A Trouble-Shooting Guide for Parents of Children Aged 3–8 Years.* Toronto: Umbrella Press.

Webster-Stratton, C. (1994) 'Advancing videotape parent training: A comparison study.' *Journal of Consulting and Clinical Psychology 62*, 3, 583–93.

Webster-Stratton, C. (1998) 'Parent training with low-income families: Promoting parental engagement through a collaborative approach.' In J.R. Lutzker (ed) *Handbook of Child Abuse Research and Treatment.* New York: Plenum Press.

Webster-Stratton, C. (1999) *How to Promote Children's Social and Emotional Competence.* London: Sage.

Webster-Stratton, C. and Hammond, M. (1988) 'Maternal depression and its relationship to life stress, perceptions of child behaviour problems, parenting behaviours, and child conduct problems.' *Journal of Abnormal Child Psychology 16,* 299–315.

Webster-Stratton, C. and Hammond, M. (1990) 'Predictors of treatment outcome in parent training for families with conduct problem children.' *Behaviour Therapy 21,* 319–37.

Webster-Stratton, C. and Hammond, M. (1997) 'Treating children with early-onset conduct problems: A comparison of child and parent training interventions.' *Journal of Consulting and Clinical Psychology 65,* 1, 93–109.

Webster-Stratton, C. and Hammond, M. (1999) 'Marital conflict management skills, parenting style, and early-onset conduct problems: Processes and pathways.' *Journal of Child Psychology and Psychiatry 40,* 6, 917–27.

Webster-Stratton, C. and Herbert, M. (1994) *Troubled Families – Problem Children: Working with Parents, A Collaborative Process.* London: Wiley.

Webster-Stratton, C., Hollinsworth, T. and Kolpacoff, M. (1989) 'The long-term effectiveness and clinical significance of three cost-effective training programmes for families with conduct-problem children.' *Journal of Consulting and Clinical Psychology 57,* 4, 550–3.

Webster-Stratton, C., Reid, M.J. and Hammond, M. (2004a) 'Preventing child conduct problems, promoting child competence: A parent and teacher training partnership in Head Start.' *Journal of Clinical Child Psychology 30,* 3, 283–302.

Webster-Stratton, C., Reid, M.J. and Hammond, M. (2004b) 'Treating children with early-onset conduct problems: Intervention outcomes for parent, child and teacher training.' *Journal of Clinical Child and Adolescent Psychology 33,* 1, 105–24.

Wells, K.C., Griest, D.L. and Forehand, R. (1980) 'The use of a self-control package to enhance temporal generality of a parent training programme.' *Behaviour Research and Therapy 18,* 347–53.

Werle, M.A., Murphy, T.B. and Budd, K.S. (1993) 'Treating chronic food refusal in young children: Home-based parent training.' *Journal of Applied Behaviour Analysis 26,* 421–33.

West, D.J. (1982) *Delinquency: Its Roots, Careers and Prospects.* London: Heinemann.

Wiese, M.R. (1992) 'A critical review of parent training research.' *Psychology in the Schools 29,* 229–36.

Witkin, S.L. (1991) 'Empirical clinical practice: A critical analysis.' *Social Work 36,* 158–63.

Witkin, S.L. (1992) 'Empirical clinical practice or Witkin's revised views: Which is the issue?' *Social Work 37,* 465–9.

Witkin, S.L. and Gottschalk, S. (1988) 'Alternative criteria for theory evaluation.' *Social Service Review 62,* 211–24.

Wolff, S. (1977). 'Nondelinquent disturbances of conduct.' In M. Rutter and L. Hersov (eds) *Child Psychiatry: Modern Approaches.* London: Blackwell.

World Health Organisation (1992) *The ICD-10 Classification of Mental and Behavioural Disorders: Clinical Descriptions and Diagnostic Guidelines.* Geneva: World Health Organisation.

Worthen, B.R. (2000) 'Critical challenges that confront evaluation practitioners.' Paper presented at the International Conference on Evaluation for Practice, University of Huddersfield, UK, July.

Zeilberger, J., Sampen, S. and Sloane, H. (1968) 'Modification of a child's problem behaviours in the home with the mother as therapist.' *Journal of Applied Behaviour Analysis 1,* 47–53.

Subject index

Author index

chosen

THE STORY OF CHARLENE BARR

*sometimes the things we can't change
end up changing us...*

THE AUTHOR

David Barr is Charlene's brother, the oldest of six children in the family.

David currently teaches Religious Studies in
Glenlola Collegiate School in Bangor, Northern Ireland.
David went to Waringstown Primary School and Banbridge Academy,
completing a Bachelor of Arts in Ancient History and Politics
and a Post Graduate Masters of Divinity
before completing his PGCE teaching qualification
through Queens University, Belfast.

David lives in Belfast, is fanatical about Liverpool FC and loves Nandos.

ACKNOWLEDGEMENTS

I feel honoured that Charlene asked me to write this book. I trust and pray that
she would be pleased with my efforts.

I am indebted to all my family, Mum and Dad, Rebecca, Natalie, Bethany and
Serena for their comments and memories that helped me complete the book.

Thanks to Phil Alcorn, Alex Barr, Sarah Buchanan, Lorraine Cord, Rachel
Hanna, Diane McClelland, Audrey McCollum, and Emily Tickner for reading the
manuscript and giving me editing feedback.

I could never thank David Acheson of Tatch Design enough for all his efforts in
design and overall completion of this project from my writings.

Thank you John Rodgers and the Team at Tricord for all your help and guidance
to the family in storage and distribution of this book.

To all the many friends and well-wishers who encouraged Charlene
and loved her during her life.

Especially thanks to all our many friends in Uganda who inspired Charlene
and continue to inspire our family.

CONTENTS

To book a speaker
contact Janice Barr at 07709-806418
or info@charlenesproject.org.

More information is available at Charlene's Project website
www.charlenesproject.org

**All monies raised through the sale of this book
will be used in entirety to further the work of Charlene's Project.**

*"At the end of life we will not be judged by
how many diplomas we have received,
how much money we have made,
how many great things we have done.
We will be judged by;
"I was hungry, and you gave me something to eat,
I was naked and you clothed me.
I was homeless, and you took me in."*

– Mother Teresa

© David Barr 2015

This First Paperback Edition 2015
Designed by David Acheson, Tatch Design
Published by Charlene's Project.
Printed by GPS, Belfast
ISBN 978-0-9933011-0-0

Registered with the Charity Commission for N.I. NIC: 100589

INTRODUCTION

WHEN I FIRST BEGAN TO TYPE I did not know if this would be for a book or just a summary of our own reflections, as part of our coming to terms with what happened. As a result, a lot of the episodes that stand out and are recorded in this story may seem odd choices. My only defence is that they are recorded because they are special to us.

Charlene was a special girl. Her story would challenge any one of us, and if in this account it does not then that is a flaw in my writing, not in what has happened in and through her life.

In reflecting on how this tale would be told, I wrestled with the approach, more than the craft of writing itself. I didn't know how much I should share of the faith aspect of this journey: of Charlene's walk with Jesus, and His hand in writing all of her story through the painful times and also the joyous. We all wanted this story to go as far as possible to as many people as possible, knowing Charlene's story had touched many. Because of this I first wondered would it be wise to keep the Christian melody of Charlene's life to the backdrop – there, but not necessarily highlighted. Would that mean her story would be more accessible?

Quickly I saw what a lie that was. To do so would rob this story of the main character. This is not primarily a chronicle of the life of one girl, Charlene, but instead it is a story of God loving a lonely child, of keeping hold of her even when she rejected all love, of working through her and reaching many through a heart that loved Him. Charlene would be disgusted if the main reason she lived, the faith that drove her, was in any way belittled. She lived to glorify God and to negate that in her death would be a betrayal.

Another reason that cannot be ignored is that Charlene's life cannot be understood without considering the Christian story that permeates it and gives it meaning. The way Charlene, and each of us acted was in part due to our understanding of a God who loves each of us even when we do not deserve it and desires us to become part of a story much bigger than ourselves.

If you are reading this and do not believe in God, I ask you to understand this and bear with the story. True, perhaps Charlene's story could just be read as a heart-warming narrative of triumph against the odds devoid of her faith, but such stories, while beautiful, can be found elsewhere. Such a story could also run the risk of changing nothing within our hearts. In my understanding at least, such a story misses the point. Charlene understood herself to be serving God. I understand, as Charlene did, that our purpose in life is to love and be loved by a God who loved us enough to die for us when we least deserved it and following from that, to love others as God loves us. Such an understanding will underpin what follows.

David Barr
Charlene's brother

"Remember, dear brothers and sisters, that few of you were wise in the world's eyes or powerful or wealthy when God called you. Instead, God chose things the world considers foolish in order to shame those who think they are wise. And he chose things that are powerless to shame those who are powerful. God chose things despised by the world, things counted as nothing at all, and used them to bring to nothing what the world considers important. As a result, no one can ever boast in the presence of God."

– 1 Corinthians 1:26-29

"Be who God meant you to be and you will set the world on fire."

– Catherine of Siena

1
SHROUDED IN MEMORY

THE FAMILIAR SMELLS OF AFRICA waft through the windows and swirl around us in the bus. Smells of dust, of matoke cooking, of livestock and many of the other indescribable scents I associate only with Africa permeate the air. The sun beats down on the packed dirt roads and caresses my arm as it hangs outside of the bus. I can taste the hot dust on my tongue and feel the sting of the salt in my eyes as sweat runs in rivulets down my forehead. The bus rumbles down uneven roads, flinging us through every pothole and around every corner. However this is not the root of the unsettled feeling in my stomach. Instead it is the swirl of emotions churning through my gut.

The bus is small for our number; the remaining seven members of our family and a few close friends are crammed into every space available. It promises to be an emotional day, one tinged with rejoicing, but also filled with the pain of what should have been. My mind wanders to how I had imagined this day and my stomach knots. It is strange how you can hold hopes and dreams deep within your soul without realising it. As the day of the official opening approached, I realised I had always imagined that Charlene would be with us, with new lungs, healed in body, mind, soul and spirit. This would be the culmination of her story, where she would see her dream unfolding before her like a flower in bloom; we would look back and celebrate how the pieces had fallen together. This was the happy ending; all the suffering would be redeemed and everything would finally make sense. This was the dream we all held in one way or another: spoken by some, unspoken by others. The fact that the story has not finished as we had yearned is the cause of my heartache and the reason why, in some ways, I have dreaded this day.

Swatting distractedly at a mosquito, my wandering mind falls back further to the day, nine months previously, where the ending I had planned for the story became impossible from where I stood...

The day we said goodbye was a black day. Thick dread clouded our thoughts as we struggled to know how to cope with our hopes seemingly forever crushed. The previous few days had been a blur, with moments passing like a freight train, refusing to stick in our minds. Every part of us felt numb and in shock as the three days tumbled into one another. Dear friends who had travelled the road with Charlene had been there, and visitors passed through our home like ghosts. Every shared sentiment meant so much, but ultimately numbness and a feeling of unreality settled on us like a cloak; the days of mourning within the house passed in a grey haze.

We had visited Charlene many times over those days, where she lay in her bedroom, motionless, as if asleep. Memories would wind around us like snakes: of her last days in that room as she sucked desperately at the oxygen pumped to her mouth. Meanwhile, we longed for the day when the transplant call would save her from this living hell. Memories of her room in brighter days as she crouched over her latest jigsaw, meticulously sorting pieces and clicking the random mess of pieces that made no sense together, creating a masterpiece you could never have expected. This room now became a refuge, where we gathered to draw comfort from one another in our grief.

We prayed there and bathed in our memories, some brought joy, many brought pain. We laughed and we cried, just as we always had as a family. We clung to and took comfort from one another, united together in our grief. Our pain was raw, and our emotions blurred and ran together; laughter was never far from bitter tears. The day that we dreaded approached as unmercifully as winter.

On 30th October 2010 staff and pupils of Lurgan Junior High School were so very sorry to learn of the death of Charlene Barr, aged just twenty. Charlene was not only a past pupil of our school, but had become a friend, inspiration, and indeed a hero, to many of all the people who knew her.

I'm reminded as I write of a little girl's sparkling smile, a young woman's proud determination and such laugh-out-loud memories that she has left behind for us all!

(Extract from Lurgan Junior High School Magazine 2010-11)

Only flashes of memories from the day of goodbyes remain: Dad informing us that the police had arrived to escort the hearse because the crowd had swelled and surpassed all predictions at the church. The rain tumbling down like a mother's tears. Taking her little teddy bears out of the coffin knowing Charlene would want to see them given to children in Uganda. The final prayers as a family around Charlene before the lid closed on her frail frame. The journey in the hearse to the church we had attended together, never suspecting that our days as a complete family were ticking away.

When we did arrive there were people and cars everywhere, more than

I ever thought possible. The foyer of the church and every step on the stairs was crammed. On any other day, this would have been a source of wonder. That day it barely registered. Observations swept over us like a cold tide, with us unable to focus on anything but the task of getting to the front of the church without breaking down in the swirling storm of memories. Just get to the front of the church; just get to the front of the church...

Along with my Dad, a close family friend who had been so special to Charlene, and her primary school headmaster, I carried the coffin up the aisle. It was a long walk, and I fought to hold back the tears that pushed against my eyelids like a mighty current leaning against a dam. As we took one faltering step after another, it felt like we bore the weight of the world on our shoulders. My mind was vacant and I maintained a blank façade, until I heard a lady in the congregation saying, with empathy in her voice, "Aw, there's wee David carrying Charlene."

I started to crack, suddenly becoming aware that we carried my precious sister and that the time had come to say goodbye. The aisle stretched out indefinitely in front of us and I held my jaw tight as a vice as we stumbled along, blinking the tears out of my eyes. Stay strong; stay strong for your sisters. Please stay strong David. I longed to be with them now - far away from this time, this place.

When we finally reached the front of the church my father and I grasped frantically for the embrace of our family. Our family stood together in the front row of the church, desperately holding each other's hands as a drowning man would grip the hand of their rescuer, clinging to one another for support.

Gazing at the coffin before us, dark thoughts rose unbidden and sunk their teeth into my mind. I wore my sorrow openly on my face. All our cherished hopes and dreams had been cruelly dashed, and all the fears that had arisen in dark moments, which we had swept away to the recesses of our minds, now danced mockingly before us.

Little do I remember of that day, aside from the minister, speaking powerfully of the Jesus who Charlene lived for and in whom she found her meaning; his sermon culminated in a round of applause to that same Jesus. As the words seeped into our minds a ray of light shone through the darkness which had threatened to envelop us. Even in the shadow of death hope began to whisper anew. We remembered Charlene was not gone. She had simply gone to her true home for which she was created. Here on earth she had been waiting for her real life to begin...

Travelling on the road to Hidden Treasure School

The minibus grinds to a sharp halt as a herd of cows stumble across the road. Our driver blares the horn and an angry exchange erupts between him and the farmer as the thin cows slowly amble from one side of the road to the other. Their sharp horns weave from side to side as they wander, their hooves casting thick clouds of dust in the air with every tread.

The argument finishes and the cows move on; as the minibus picks up speed and resumes its bumpy progress, my mind drifts back towards the past…

It was a blur. All that dread, pain and loss condensed into a short service. Yet it was over so quickly and the service is a haze in my mind. Some isolated memories still bleed through the cracks in my memory of the moments after. We stood at the exit of the church in a line, shaking hands and greeting those who had been with us. Some people offered us words, brittle fragile things that broke as they were handed over. Others had no words. Many dear friends simply pulled us close and silently wept with us. The line never seemed to end. I was determined to stay strong for my sisters, to show no emotion; yet, on some occasions, with friends who saw through the veneer, I failed. I held the hand of Bethany beside me, and locked my jaw vice-like, willing myself, begging myself, to stay strong. Mum and Dad greeted and shook hands with so many; people were so kind to all of us. However, eventually the individual faces became a river flowing past us, as if we were stones at the bottom of a streambed.

The graveside sticks in my memory, with the cold rain spitting down upon us as if heaven itself wept. The rain ran down our necks like a brook. We clung to our umbrellas like shields against the painful reality of what we were seeing. As the coffin lowered and Charlene was laid to rest, it felt like everything was happening to someone else, anyone else. We shivered and whispered our last goodbyes to our cherished sister. Only later did we learn that, as Charlene's remains were put into the ground, the very next day, thousands of miles away spades and shovels would finally break ground on the land where the school - part of her legacy – would be built. As one chapter ends, another begins.

> "We each saw so many of our friends from far and near as we shook hands with the mourners at the door of the church and later as darkness fell at the little graveside in Waringstown, just below the church we had attended when Charlene had first joined our family all those years ago. It seemed as if everyone who knew Charlene over the years of her short life wanted to express their own sorrow to us as a family."
>
> Dickie

The day was hard, stinging our hearts as we longed for what could now never be. And yet it wasn't dreadful. Even in the midst of the gut-wrenching loss, hope shone. We were only to hear later that as the coffin had been carried into the church, a single dove flew, hovered and landed underneath its awnings. It remained throughout the service, staying in the shelter against the battering wind and rain, leaving only as the coffin passed beneath it on its way from the church. A dove - the symbol of peace, of hope, of the Spirit of God. Hope swallowed the darkness and triumphed, even on that day.

Such had been characteristic of Charlene's life, and indeed seemed to confirm the battle that had long been waged for Charlene's very soul; but I am getting ahead of myself....

My stomach lurches as we fly over a particularly deep pothole, dragging me from the succour of my memories. The thoughts still bring pain, however being here, on the way to the school my sister envisioned, brings some resonance to that day and shows her story is far from over. The journey starts only as the previous journey ends.

We crawl towards the school in the minibus, many of us exhausted from the work of the previous days. Each person on the bus is in differing states of mind. Some snores drift up the bus after the early rise, others chatter quietly. Still others sit silently, watching the African bushes encroaching towards us as the path narrows on the approach to the school. The atmosphere feels heavy. But as we drive up and see the sight awaiting us, all of our hearts swell within us.

"What would she think of this?" Phil, a close family friend laughs, a grin plastered across his face. We see the crowds from the community gathered together under a canopy they have erected, all beautifully and colourfully dressed in celebration. We see the crowds of children jumping up and down excitedly. We see them approach and run alongside the bus in their masses as we draw to a stop. All at once we are awake and aflame. Charlene's dream is here, birthed in sickness and pain, but blossoming in victory of life over death. As we scramble in anticipation from the bus, gripping eager outstretched arms and picking up bouncing excited children, holding them close to our hearts and smiling at their joyous faces, I know that Charlene herself is here, not buried in a patch of earth thousands of miles away in Ireland. In a wonderful, strange and mysterious way we are here with our sister. We didn't leave her behind when we made the painful trip to Uganda.

As I swing a grinning child onto my back my heart somersaults within me as I think of my sister. Charlene's life had been a struggle, a harrowing trial in multiple ways. It had been happy and filled with beauty on many occasions, but punctuated with physical, emotional and spiritual battles at so many junctures along the way. Her story was full of glorious mountains and devastating valleys. She was a child of God, loaded with contradictions, with a life full of blinding light and crushing darkness. Charlene's life was like all of our individual stories, loaded with all the emotions, experiences, joys and sorrows of life. A battle had been waged over her life, one that we had only seen glimpses of and will never know in full.

Ok I'm going to sort of start this journal again cause I sort of abandoned it all summer. I had a really good summer and enjoyed a fantastic trip to none other than Center Parcs and I even managed to stay well for the entire ten days, which was an added bonus. ☺ The rest of the summer was just spent with wee day trips here and there, which was just perfect and I didn't spend too much time in hospital!! Always a good thing.

Now we are into the autumn and things are back to normal. I am in hospital at the minute and to be honest today I am feeling quite fed up: fed up of waiting, fed up of always feeling tired and breathless and needing a stupid wheelchair to go anywhere. I know this whole transplant thing will happen in God's timing and I just have to be patient but it's hard. There's so much I want to do (Uganda++) and I HATE being physically restricted. Anyway I'll stop moaning now.

On the plus I am finally making small baby step improvements spiritually and making more time for God and to be honest I don't know why I didn't do it sooner cause it's pretty awesome and I love spending time reading my Bible now. God is great.

(Charlene's Journal – Last Entry)

Her story had led to this day of celebration in Uganda, and this was a cause of dizzying indescribable celebration. A community had been given hope and a future as a result of the faith and vision of a determined and courageous young girl. How had her life journey led to this? What brought Charlene from the neonatal intensive care unit of Royal Belfast Hospital for Sick Children to this small community deep in the heart of Uganda? How had this come to pass? Tales don't tell themselves, and as I stand surrounded by excited Ugandan children, my mind tumbles back to the stories my parents have told us of how our lives had first become entwined, to the story that had begun in the dark lonely days of her birth twenty years earlier...

Lurgan Mail headline after Charlene's death

2
BEGINNINGS

THE PHONE RINGS yanking Janice from her daydreams. Quickly she leans the brush against the wall and scrambles across the room towards the phone, frantic before it rings off. Fortunately the phone is on the table where she left it, and David and Rebecca have not incorporated it into one of their games. "Hello" she breathes quickly, lifting the phone to her ear.

"Hello Mrs Barr, this is social services, sorry to bother you," says the calm voice from the other end of the line. "We just wanted to ask you if you would consider a placement? We have a little girl who is very unwell; she has cystic fibrosis, you see. She has just passed her first birthday and up to now has spent her first year in hospital as she has been very sick and she has had no family to care for her. It's been hard for her, but we have reached a point now where we want to see how she will manage out of hospital and with your husband's medical background, you came to mind."

The voice continues. "We were wondering if you would be able to provide her with short term foster care. It will be good for her to get out of the ward but we have to be honest with you, she will be a lot of work. She needs physiotherapy three times a day to help relieve her illness and her medical condition is very precarious to say the least. It's obviously up to you, any thoughts?"

As the voice waits for an answer, Janice's eyes skim around the kitchen. She gazes at her two children and smiles. David and Rebecca are playing with blocks at her feet, building multi-coloured towers and then knocking them down with one sweep of their small hands, leaving bricks scattered across the floor, until they build another structure that teeters on the edge of collapse, awaiting its destruction. David is four, Rebecca is two and, while they get on well, they are still a handful.

Watching David dive across the floor for another brick to add to his wobbling skyscraper, she wonders for a second what this decision will do to the kids, what it will mean for them? Because already she knows what she is going to say; she has known from the moment she heard about the difficulties this little one has faced.

She takes a deep breath and dives blindly into the abyss. "Of course. I'll need to talk to Dickie first of all, but how could we say no? What is her name?" Janice asks, as David aims a sly swipe at Rebecca's tower.

"Her name is Charlene."

"Charlene," Janice says, tasting the name in her mouth. Rebecca's wails begin to echo around the room as David sneaks a look at her with guilt written across his face. "That's a nice name. What's her health like now?" Janice continues.

"She is better than she has been. She has had recurrent surgery to deal with problems from her cystic fibrosis; it's been hard on her. There have been repeated infections up to now, but she's well enough to have a trial outside of hospital and we've been looking for foster parents for a while."

"For a while?" Janice queries as she flashes David a look that promises trouble once she gets off the phone. David tentatively sets a brick he has taken from his sister back on her tower.

"Yes. We tried looking in the Belfast area for a while, as we thought it would be best to find short term foster carers closer to the hospital. However, we have not been able to find anyone, so we decided to widen the net. With your husband being a doctor, we thought to ask you."

As Janice thinks of this little girl, of how lonely it must have been in hospital, of the operations she has been through, her eyes flood with tears. Momentarily caught off guard she clutches the table beside her. As David and Rebecca squabble over another brick, she thinks of how they have always had parents to care for them. And she thinks of Charlene with no parent holding her hand on the way to the operating theatre and waiting desperately for her to come back. Empathy fills her afresh as if it has stabbed through her heart. Feeling her heart stir up within her, she knows she was never going to be able to say no.

"That's no problem," she says thickly, trying to disguise her sudden surge of emotion. "I'll give Dickie a ring at the surgery and then get back to you."

"That's no problem; then we can talk about the practicalities later. If you agree, we can arrange for you to come to the hospital for a preliminary meeting. Ring me when you have talked to your husband, Mrs Barr, and thank you."

"No; thank you," Janice says as she hangs up the phone. Her head is aflood with emotions tugging in every direction, and watching her children now laughing together as David tries to build their two structures together. She wonders how it will be for them to have another playmate; one who will demand so much of their time. But it will only be for a time, it is a short term placement after all. More than anything however, she wants to show this little one the love of a mother, for whatever length of time they have together. This was why they had wanted to foster in the first place.

As she dials the number to the surgery where her husband works, her swirl of emotions tugs her back towards the genesis of their dreams of serving God together....

"I can't believe you were late again Dickie," Janice cajoles gently as her eyes sparkle. It is 1981 and she and Dickie are engaged to be married. They had both gone to school in Dungannon but had not become close friends until they spent time together at Queen's University in Belfast. There, Janice had trained to be a Social Worker and Dickie studied Medicine; both had served together on the Christian Union executive committee. Now they were catching a few moments together in their hectic schedule, and true to form, her fiancé has turned up late.

Dickie stands sheepishly, his hands hanging awkwardly at his sides. Timidly, he pulls the chair at the table back and sits opposite Janice. "I'm sorry Jannie, I guess I just lost track of time. You know I'm not the most organised." He reaches tentatively for her hand across the table, and taking confidence from Janice not pulling away, he grasps it gently. "You're too good to me; I am a bit of a disaster."

"Yes you are," Janice replies, but she is laughing, and Dickie knows any danger has passed. Quickly they dissolve into conversation, leaning over the table and talking like conspirators, sharing snippets from their day. As final year approaches, their lives are becoming increasingly busy; any time they get to spend together is precious.

After ordering their meal, talk turns to their upcoming wedding; to any observer, it is clear, as they laugh together and tease each other that this young couple are very much in love. With the world at their feet, they have dreams, dreams their hearts share.

As the food arrives the talk again becomes serious. Slowly lifting a forkful of chicken to his mouth, Dickie raises an eyebrow and asks a question. "Janice I've been thinking, how do you see our first year of marriage? I mean, where would you like to be after one year?"

Swirling the water around in her glass Janice scrunches up her face, a look of confusion creeping across her face. "Where has this come from?"

"I don't know," Dickie says, shrugging his shoulders. "I've just been thinking again, and it's so hard to know what the next step is. I mean we both know where we want to go in the long run, but it's hard to know about the short term; the next step after we finally qualify, you know?"

"Yeah, I know what you mean," Janice muses. She stares thoughtfully into the distance before replying. "Well we both want to work overseas, we know that much."

"Yes," Dickie says, his eyes lighting up with passion. They both have constantly clung to dreams of working overseas in developing countries; these dreams were nurtured in their hearts long before they met. Now, as they pledged their futures to each other, it seemed their visions were confirmed; their dreams would soon come to fruition. "But how are we going to get there?"

"Well, the first step is finishing these placements and then, I guess, the obvious option is that you get a medical job somewhere in India, or maybe Africa. Once you have that, I can see what opportunities I could get to serve there."

"That's true," Dickie says, now with a wistful look in his eyes. "It's so exciting Jannie. I mean, we have dreamed so long, and now we are so close to it happening."

Janice looks down at the table for a second, her brow knitted. She struggles to articulate her thoughts at first, then manages, "Yeah Dickie, but have you ever thought we might be wrong?"

"What do you mean?" he replies, concern etched across his face.

"I mean, we are so sure this is where God is leading us, but what if we are wrong? What if He doesn't want us to go abroad?"

Dickie shakes his head emphatically. "No, why would God have given us this dream if we were not meant to fulfil it? Why bother stirring up our hearts for overseas work if He wants us to stay here? It just makes such perfect sense, and it's obvious our next step is to take a leap of faith and go overseas."

Janice looks up and a smile breaks across her face. "You're right; I just worry sometimes if we are called to stay here. But God wouldn't lay a dream in our heart if we weren't meant to fulfil it. So at the end of our first year together I would at least want visas sorted for wherever we are going!"

"Me too," Dickie laughs, his joy is infectious. "That's different from a lot of our friends who are getting married, Jannie! Some of them are talking of having two or three kids within a few years, can you imagine?"

Janice's eyes are wide and incredulous. "I know. It's funny. Not having kids doesn't bother me; maybe it should, but it doesn't." A long time before, both had agreed to never have children, feeling that having children would prevent them from carrying out the work they wanted to do.

"I know," Dickie says nodding. "I'll tell you what, it may be hard to know the very next step, but at least we know where we are going!"

"Indeed," Janice says raising her glass. "To the future!"

Dickie lifts his glass as a grin splits his face. "To the future!"

As the receptionist transfers her call through to her husband, Janice shakes her head at how naïve they had been and how their lives had unfolded. It had very quickly become clear that they were not meant to go overseas and their best laid plans were disrupted. The clear direction of their lives had grown obscured, with a fog descending over the bright horizon of their future. Not that the way things were was bad, far from it. It was just amusing to think how arrogantly confident they had been, and how God had brought them on a different journey than the one they had plotted out.

Dickie got a job as a General Practitioner in Lurgan and she had worked as a Hospital Social Worker for a time. Things had changed for her when what they had once planned would never happen had happened; she got pregnant.

How foolish they had been. Firstly David, then Rebecca came along; they realised what a joy children were, and it made her smile when she thought how they had been so sure they would never have children. When David was born she had stopped working, originally for a short time, but eventually the change became permanent. Some may scoff at her, but she felt she lacked nothing, and would not sacrifice her time with the children for the sake of another wage. Their time together was precious and passing fast; being at home with them meant that they had a catalogue of great memories and learning opportunities, with the world as their playground.

Now that they were not going overseas, they were living out the equally difficult task of serving God daily in the everyday, unglamorous things. This was a struggle, but every day they would pray together and try to think about how exactly they could serve God where they were. This had brought them to the idea of fostering.

On reflection, they both felt that they could open their home to short term foster placements. If her time in Social Services had taught Janice one thing, it was the need there was for carers. Her heart broke over some children she had tried to support; often she had felt powerless and impotent, finding them in deep despair, never having known love. After several long talks, they had decided to put themselves forward as short term carers, deciding that David and Rebecca were old enough for them to be able to care for another child on a temporary basis. As she was at home it was a realistic opportunity. Indeed, they had talked to David and Rebecca and, despite their limited understanding; they were enthusiastic about the idea of another sibling. David was especially enthusiastic about the possibility of gaining a brother with whom he could team up in arguments with his younger sister.

They had gone through extensive training and subsequently had been added to the foster carer list. The nervous wait began, not knowing what to expect along this path they had chosen to walk. They had a two week placement with a little boy aged two; any fears about how David and Rebecca would find it had proved unfounded, with all three laughing and playing games together. He had returned home and now, unexpectedly, on a day just like any other, this call from Social Services about Charlene had come.

Janice waits impatiently for her husband to get to the phone, drumming her fingers on the table. Her stomach knots with nerves as she thinks about what they were agreeing to. Can they care adequately for such an ill child? How will their children cope? Will they be good carers? No matter what happens, she wants to make sure this child feels safe and cared for while she is in their home. While she hasn't been able to serve God overseas like she once hoped, deep within she is sure that she can serve God by loving this

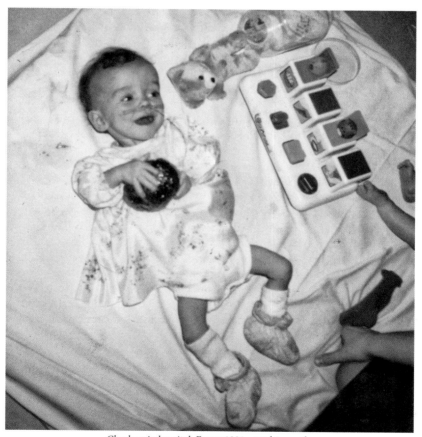

Charlene in hospital, Easter 1991 - aged 8 months

child. It is just a pity she will be only able to do that for a few short weeks before the placement will end.

"Hello?" Dickie's voice cracks from the phone.

His mind is tired from a busy day in the surgery as he listens to his wife's voice. She is ablaze with passion and fervour, and yet it takes Dickie a few seconds to grasp what she is trying to tell him. "She has cystic fibrosis?" he asks, rubbing the back of his neck with his other hand.

"Yes," comes the tinny voice down the line. "They say we would need to learn physiotherapy in order to treat her. I know it's a lot of work and taking care of a child who is so sick isn't something we talked about, but I really think we should do this. She has never lived out of hospital before."

Dickie bites his lip as he thinks. "Janice, I agree with you; I just worry that we aren't qualified to care for her. Of course we can adapt, and I can learn about the physio and treatment she needs, but it will be you at home caring for her during the day. You have to be sure about this."

"I am sure," Janice replies breathlessly. "And if we can help her at all Dickie, I think we should do it. Isn't it for a situation like this that we considered fostering?"

Hearing the excitement flooding through Janice's voice, immediately his fears are alleviated. From his wife's descriptions he can picture the child, and can imagine the series of operations she has had to undergo alone. Janice is right; situations like this are the reason they have gone into fostering.

Still, small waves of doubt lap at the edge of his mind, telling him he cannot do this. He knows Janice has complete confidence in his ability to care for Charlene, but fears and doubts plague him. What if he is unable to? Surely there are others more qualified who could care for her?

Ultimately, however, he knows that if he were to say no to helping such a child, he could never forgive himself.

"Have you talked to David and Rebecca?" he asks.

"Briefly, but you know what they will say anyway. They will love having a wee sister for a few weeks. They will spoil her rotten, though David might prefer having a little brother to wind Rebecca up with! We can talk to them later."

He takes a deep breath, then pushes any doubts to the back of his mind, and follows what his heart is telling him to do. "If you want to do this and think we can care for this wee girl Janice, then I'm with you. What's the next step?"

"I knew you'd agree with me Dickie!" He can hear the excitement in his wife's voice, and he can't help but be moved by her evident compassion for this child. "I'll phone the social worker back and we can arrange to go to the hospital, get some training and meet her. Would tomorrow suit you if we aimed for that?"

"Yes it would. I have to go here, there's a patient waiting. I love you Jannie."

"I love you too."

As the phone goes dead, Dickie just stands for a few seconds, wondering how their lives will change for the next few weeks. He turns to the door to again fall back into the flow of patients and he cannot help but grin, amazed at his wife's ability to excite and inspire him. His heart has been stirred up and he wants to give this child all the care and love he can. The time they will have together will be short, so he determines there and then to make the most of the next few weeks, no matter what comes.

3
STEPPING INTO THE UNKNOWN

AS THEY STEP INTO THE HOSPITAL Janice gives a squeeze to her daughter's hand. Rebecca paddles along happily, oblivious to the thoughts dancing through her mother's mind. Janice feels nerves and excitement battling for supremacy within her, and she does not know what to expect. As they enter the Royal Victoria Hospital in Belfast, she looks to her husband, walking beside her with David keeping step behind. His eyes are thoughtful as they make their way towards the children's cystic fibrosis ward, and she lets the silence breathe. She doesn't know what thoughts lie behind his calm face, but she draws strength from the fact that they will care for this child for a time together, come what may.

As the double doors swing shut behind them, a nurse steps forward from a nearby room, a smile lighting up her face. "Hello, how can I help you?" she says as she stands beside them. The electric light above casts an orange glow on the corridor ahead of them, and various cartoon characters gallop across painted walls. Bright colours blaze down from every wall and door, and in sharp contrast to the clinical monochrome corridors they have just left; this section of the hospital is homely, breathing life.

However, in the background she can hear the ominous sounds of machines beeping and gas flowing from a variety of machines, punctured by the occasional racking cough. The sounds provide a perpetual drone and a stark counterpoint to the deceptively homely exterior. Again Janice feels nerves cut through her, while at the same time her heart swells for the little girl for whom this hospital has been home all of her short life.

Dickie steps forward and extends his hand. "Hello, my name is Dickie Barr and this is my wife Janice. We are here to meet Charlene?"

Realisation dawns across the nurse's face like a sunrise, and she grasps Dickie's hand, shaking it, smiling. "It's good to meet you. The doctor is waiting for you in the office; I'll take you there now" She leads them up the corridor and David and Rebecca amble behind, eyes wide, drinking in the colourful displays. The nurse suddenly stops, turns and looks to the two of them, smiling. "How rude of me!" she says. "What are your names?"

David takes charge as Rebecca shelters behind Janice's leg, shy and unsure of the sudden attention. "I'm David and I'm four! This is my sister Rebecca," he says, gesturing in his sister's direction.

"Well it's good to meet you both," she says smiling gently. "Would you like to see some toys?" she says, pointing to a bright room off to the side.

Rebecca's shyness evaporates as she sees this room, and all nerves tumble away as they both scramble for the door, determined to explore and investigate every toy available to them. The nurse laughs as they leave, and turns to Janice and Dickie.

"They will be fine in there, I'll bring you to the doctor and then I'll keep an eye on them." With this she continues to walk up the corridor.

At the end of the corridor she stops at a door and knocks quietly. "Come in," a voice echoes, and Janice and Dickie step into the small office. The doctor rises smiling, extending her hand. "Ah, you must be Dr and Mrs Barr. It is a pleasure to meet you, please take a seat." Her voice is friendly and unthreatening and they are immediately set at ease, both shaking her hand and sitting down opposite her.

Without further ado, she shuffles through a series of paper in front of her and looks up, a kindly look on her face as she speaks. "So I suppose you want to know more about Charlene? Well, where to start? She was born just over a year ago, on the 18th July in Daisy Hill Hospital in Newry. It was immediately obvious to the midwives that there was a problem. She was struggling, and it became evident, on investigation, that her bowel was obstructed. She needed help and was transferred here for emergency surgery."

Janice realises her mouth is open, and she shuts it swallowing heavily as the doctor continues. "I assume you know the details of cystic fibrosis? It impacts the lungs, pancreas, intestine and liver amongst other things, so you can imagine how seriously it affects Charlene. It causes thick sticky mucus to form within her lungs for example, and manifests itself by causing breathing difficulties and frequent lung infections. It can cause poor growth and diarrhoea amongst other symptoms. Charlene unfortunately is a particularly bad case of cystic fibrosis and has had a lot to deal with."

She sighs, then continues as Janice struggles to process all this information. "How will I say this? Charlene has had a number of serious operations and many very serious chest infections; on a number of occasions we were not optimistic, but we had not banked on her spirit. Charlene is a fighter; that will become clear to you very quickly. She has survived against the odds. Her health has dipped dangerously several times, but every time she has rallied. The operations and infections have left their scars and marks on her, but she has defied every prediction made for her. She is a very impressive child," she finishes firmly, her lips a thin line. "She is very special to a lot of us here."

Any doubts that Janice had have long since fled in the face of the stream of words flowing around her now. She feels tears run like rivulets down her cheeks as she thinks of this child; she wants more than anything to see her now.

The Consultant's words break through, dispelling the thoughts in her mind. "Are you both sure you want to take Charlene into your home?"

The words flow from her mouth before she can think. "How could we not? Seriously, how could we not? We would be honoured to."

The doctor's gaze is unblinking and relentless, fixed on both of them. Then she blinks and it as if a spell is broken; a smile slowly grows across her face. She nods, as slow and deliberate as a glacier and speaks. "Yes, how could you not? How could you not?" Her voice tails off for a second, and then she shakes her head and continues.

Dickie's voice cuts through the moment like a knife, urgent and serious. "How can we care best for Charlene?"

The doctor looks up and continues. "Charlene is still ill, but she is stable and will benefit from being out of hospital and having a sense of normality. However, her long term prognosis is not good; to help her in her fight there will be a number of ways you need to care for her. She will need special medication as she is not absorbing her food. Also, she will need other medication for her breathing and various other ailments. As has been explained to you both, you will need to learn physiotherapy: several times a day you must gently clap on her back and try to loosen up the phlegm in her lungs so that she coughs it up. We can teach you how to do this, but it is time consuming for Charlene and for you."

"How else can we help her?" Dickie asks, dismissing mundane concerns such as time.

"She will have to be on frequent antibiotic doses and attend our clinics regularly so we can monitor her. She is on a lot of drugs and you will need to ensure she takes them. I cannot stress this enough; they are the only way of maintaining her health. There will also need to be regular hospital admissions for intravenous antibiotics directly into her bloodstream, to help her fight infection. As I have said, she is a particularly bad cystic case and needs all the support she can get".

Janice's eyes dart away as quickly as a frightened animal. The words are like an icy draft through her heart and she hears Dickie's voice as if far removed from her. She hears him ask about arrangements for Charlene coming home to them.

She hears how Charlene's needs are social as well as medical; although the doctors and nurses have cared dearly for Charlene in the past year, she has had no stable figure by her side. She hears of the love the medical staff has for her, and how a special couple called Pat and Terry have taken

Charlene into their hearts and visited her faithfully through the year. Despite this, it will be good for Charlene to experience family life for a while. As the story unfolds Dickie and Janice become aware from staff that little was known of Charlene's father and her mother had been to visit her a few times but infrequently. Sadly Charlene went through surgery and illness many times with no family beside her.

Images of what it would have been like for her own son and daughter in their first year, defenceless, dependent and all alone, flash across Janice's mind's eye. Although she fights it, images of them deathly ill with no parent to care for them, alone and abandoned to the world, fire through her; her heart is torn asunder for Charlene. Anguish comes on her as sudden as a summer storm, and her voice catches in her throat. Her heart as a mother goes out to this child for whom she already burns with compassion.

The ongoing conversations feel as if they are taking place in another world as Janice processes all she has heard this afternoon, until one phrase breaks through her emotional turmoil: "Would you like to meet Charlene?"

They both stand as Charlene is brought into the room and pads across the room towards them. She is small, so small, and is dressed in a beautiful pink dress. A smile splits her face as she looks at them, ambling around the floor and clutching her doll to her chest. Her brown hair has been brushed back, and her cheeks shine red and ruddy.

Dickie watches as Janice leans down and sits on the floor with her face alive, and says, "Hello Charlene, my name is Janice. How are you?" He smiles and feels warmth flood through him as Charlene giggles, holding the doll to her mouth, then ambles over to his wife's arms. Janice lifts her up into her arms, and she is radiant. Charlene babbles away, rocking her doll as she is held by Janice. It is clear that Charlene is a bubbly child; she is beautiful.

She reaches up, traces Janice's nose with her tiny hands and giggles again. She claps suddenly, then wriggles to be let down and Janice gently lowers her to the ground. As soon as she touches the ground, she fixes her eyes on Dickie and runs up, gripping his hand and swinging his arm backwards and forwards. Dickie lifts her carefully into his arms and gazes into her big brown eyes, like deep pools of water; he knows he loves her already. Time seems to stall as he rocks her gently; he looks up and sees his wife's face alight as she looks at him lovingly. He can hear David and Rebecca laughing and playing down the corridor, and he looks forward to introducing them to their new sister. As he holds her, for now, everything is right with the world.

One of the nurses coughs quietly then gently reaches for Charlene; Dickie passes her carefully back to her. "She is a great wee girl, isn't she?"

"Yes," he says emphatically. "She is. We will see you soon Charlene, we will be back in a few days to take you home." He waves to her, and she reaches up and grabs his finger, gurgling and giggling.

He knows in his heart of hearts that he would face and bear anything for this child. He wants Charlene to be part of their family, no matter how long she is with them.

A couple of days later Charlene wails in the back of the car and Rebecca quietly rocks her baby chair, while soothingly shushing her. David tries to hold her hand as she screams her lungs out, her face red as she weeps. Janice looks back, worry lining her face. "Have you tried her rattle David?"

When they had picked her up from the hospital a few hours earlier she had been bubbly as ever, not giving a backward look to where she had spent

August 10th 1991 - Charlene leaves hospital with her new family

the majority of her short life. It had been an emotional farewell for many of the nurses who had cared for her so faithfully, and as they had loaded her medication into the car it had been a pleasure to watch David and Rebecca fussing over her. They had been so excited through the last few days at the prospect of bringing Charlene home, and had taken turns to play with her while their parents sorted the last minute details at the hospital. Charlene had revelled in their excitement, laughing and giggling with the attention lavished upon her. They had driven off happily, firstly travelling to her new Grandma and Poppa in Bangor, who had held her and spoiled her with sweets. She had danced and ran about happily, but almost as soon as they left the house she began to bawl.

As Dickie focuses on the drive home, he stares into the darkness all around them and wonders what has caused her to cry suddenly. She seemed fine through the bright lights of Belfast until they had arrived on the motorway heading west towards their Lurgan home. What had changed?

As Charlene continues to screech, a thought hits him suddenly. "David, turn the light on," he shouts over Charlene's screams. David fumbles about in the darkness, then finds the switch and light fills the car. Instantly Charlene stops her wailing and flailing and settles back into her seat; she closes her eyes with a smile settling on her round face.

"Mum, she's stopped crying," Rebecca pipes up.

"I know that pet, thank you," Janice replies patiently and turns to her husband with eyebrows raised.

"It was just a thought," he responds. "I think she's afraid of the darkness Janice."

"Afraid of the darkness?" Janice ponders, her brow furrowed.

"Yes, think about it. She has been in hospital all her life. I bet she has never been in darkness before, she's used to being bathed in light all the time."

"You know what, you're probably right," Janice says quietly, staring straight ahead of her. She glances up momentarily to see Charlene asleep now in the light, clinging onto Rebecca's hand.

Charlene settles quickly into her new life, enjoying the games with her new brother and sister. The family adjust quickly to the new rhythms of their

Charlene playing in the garden

David with Charlene on her 2nd birthday

lives, with Charlene's need for regular medication and physiotherapy. During physiotherapy her frame racks with coughs as she violently expels the thick phlegm from her lungs. Her face is red with exertion as her blood vessels push to the surface of her skin. But then she will sit back at the end of her trial, wipe her brow, and run off to play happily with her new playmates. The Consultant is right, she truly is a fighter.

She has frequent trips to hospital and she has to stay in for some extended periods as her health dips. It is in those times that Janice feels a gap in her heart. At mealtimes, where she is not present, she feels that the family is not complete and realises that Charlene has swiftly become a part of all of them. She is so helpless and yet so ready to love, and she has found a way into all of their affections.

The trips up and down to the hospital become a part of their routine, and the Consultant is so good with all of them, not just fussing over Charlene, but David and Rebecca, too. During the appointments they play with the toys in the ward until Charlene is returned to them, striding forth confidently despite the line inserted into her arms so that antibiotics can be inserted more easily. She lets all the treatments and setbacks wash over her.

Days turn into weeks and weeks turn into months; what was short term fostering becomes a longer term arrangement. Charlene is treasured by both sets of grandparents, who lavish her with as much attention as their other grandchildren. Her Grandma and Poppa to her delight often bring her on visits to the lighthouse in Donaghadee. David and Rebecca devise game after game to play with her; she becomes an ever-present fixture in the family. David and Rebecca have moved into a room together so Charlene can have David's old room; she now sleeps with the light off and for now, everything is idyllic.

But behind the scenes paper work is shifting and meetings are held, as advice and professional opinions circulate unknown to anyone in the family; while attachments are forged within the house, far away a decision is recommended to move Charlene on to another short-term placement.

4
FIGHTING THE TIDE

AS JANICE CHOPS CARROTS in the kitchen, she glances up and gazes out the window into the garden; she cannot stop the grin that grows on her face. She can see David, Rebecca and Charlene having a series of races outside, and although David is trying hard to put some order into the proceedings, Rebecca and Charlene continue to charge around aimlessly. Charlene is running as fast as her short stumpy legs can carry her, determined to keep up with the other two. At the minute they have stopped while David formulates another game; as he haphazardly concocts the rules, Charlene dances, humming to herself and waving her dress around her as she spins. Returning to preparing dinner, Janice thanks God for her three children.

And they are her three children; already she sees Charlene as one of her own. Charlene running around without a care in the world, in spite of the illness stalking her like a black hound, has found a home deep within each of them. She is one of them now and as time continues to pass Janice dares to hope this placement will be a long one.

It has been a manic few months, full of trips to the hospital for check-ups. There is a set routine of treatment to adhere to during the day; she and Dickie take it in turns to practice the essential physiotherapy exercises. It is straining having to care for such a sick child, but she wouldn't change any of it for the world.

On top of all of this, Janice has felt the faint stirrings of another little one within her and she knows that child number four is on their way. She says faint stirrings, but as time goes on this one is jumping around more than David or Rebecca did during her past pregnancies. In fact, she has already cut out fizzy drinks as this seems to agitate the little one, sending it into jumps, kicks and punches of hyper excitement and hysteria. Janice is very excited about the future.

However, things have not been completely straightforward. Social Services have set up several meetings between Charlene and her birth mother, and these are the only times that Charlene has displayed discontentment, clearly confused by the situation. Janice has tried to explain to her what is happening, but for a child under two the situation is difficult to comprehend. Nevertheless, they have faithfully brought her to the appointments. In spite of this, on a number of occasions her birth mother has not turned up, leading to further distress and confusion for Charlene.

Social Services have laboured away in the background and Janice trusts they have Charlene's best interests at heart. As she pushes the thin slices of carrot to the side of the chopping board, she hears a shout from outside and sees Charlene waddling and jumping over a skipping rope David and Rebecca hold high for her. As she lands, she rolls in the grass and rises beaming and clapping, with a new grass stain to match her new dress. Janice rolls her eyes but laughs to herself. Life is good.

The phone rings, shattering her peaceful reflections; she sets the knife down and rushes to answer it. The voice she hears speak words that change everything.

"I'm scared Dickie," Janice says, her voice shaky as she looks out into the encroaching darkness outside. Night is falling fast and thick brooding shadows rise behind every tree, every hedge. The light from the day is a forgotten memory. "I was sure they had decided we would be a long term placement for Charlene."

"So had I," Dickie confessed. "But obviously not. What did they say exactly?"

"I can't remember exact details; it's a blur. They asked how things were, and then suddenly started to talk about moving Charlene somewhere else. They said she had complex medical needs and they felt she would benefit from being moved around different placements.

David, Rebecca and Charlene

31

I had no idea they were thinking of this Dickie!" she says, looking at her husband with anguish written across her gaze.

Dickie paces backwards and forwards across their bedroom as if on a lonely soldier's march, his head down and hands clasped behind his back. He speaks, his voice grave. "I know Jannie. I had thought with how things were they would extend the placement indefinitely, but they obviously feel her health is such that it is too much for one family to cope with."

Janice wheels around from her vigil at the window watching the creeping darkness, and her voice has an angry edge to it, passion bubbling through her words. "But that's the whole reason they asked us Dickie! Because of your medical background! And she has been stable with us. Surely if she is moved about from place to place it puts her health in jeopardy?" As she speaks, anger ebbs away only to be replaced by dread so thick she can taste it. Her eyes are haunted, and her voice is thick with doubt. "I'm so scared of losing her Dickie."

Dickie stops his pacing, and looks at his wife, compassion flows from his eyes as he walks over to her as her face crumples in on itself. He holds her close to him as her emotion bubbles up within her and flows down her face. "I love you Jannie, I love you so much. We will fight this for her sake, we will."

"I love her so much Dickie," Janice whispers quietly.

"I do too, my love. I do too," he murmurs quietly, holding her close. They hold each other for a time and slowly her tears subside.

"I think we should pray together," Dickie says, and they do. They wrestle with God over the child they believe He has entrusted to them. They continue to pray as the shadows lengthen and the darkness thickens outside. As they do, a peace beyond explanation begins to settle; it does not dispel or dismiss the fear and reality they face or deny the helplessness they feel. Instead it reminds them that they were never in control in the first place and allows them to hand the situation over to God.

As they finish praying, Dickie lifts their Bible reading notes and reads the passage they have for that day. As he reads, his voice rises in wonder. "It's from Exodus 23 Jannie. Listen to this! 'See, I am sending an angel before you to protect you on your journey and lead you safely to the place I have prepared for you.' That's a promise Janice, a promise."

"We could use an angel going ahead of us!" Janice replies. "This review meeting is tomorrow Dickie, that's when Charlene and our future will be decided."

"And we have to trust, we have to trust," Dickie says as he walks over to the window. Janice turns the light off behind him and now they can see the

Charlene as a flower girl at her cousin's wedding

stars, burning crisp and sharp in the sky. They are beautiful.

Sudden laughter rings through the darkness from David and Rebecca's room. As Janice flicks the light on again, she and Dickie share a knowing look and they head into their children's room. David, Rebecca and Charlene are sitting on the floor playing cards; they have lifted Charlene out of her cot and brought her to join them.

"Get to bed you three! Now!" Janice orders trying to be strict, but her smile contradicts her words.

"Can Charlene sleep in here tonight?" Rebecca asks.

"Yes!" Charlene says, rolling around on the floor in her red pyjamas.

"You three are wee monkeys!" Dickie laughs. "I'll tell you what, do you want to get your sleeping bags and sleep on our floor?"

"YES!" David says, jumping up and down, his small fist punching the air, before running to grab some pillows from their beds.

With all three chattering in the darkness by their bed, Janice and Dickie drift into the day that will determine the future, not just for Charlene, but for all of them.

Eight different people are crowded into the small living room, all practically on top of each other. Dickie clutches his mug of coffee tightly; warming his hands and watching the steam rise and dissipate around the room. The atmosphere is tense as different social workers and experts bandy about opinions and viewpoints on Charlene's future, while she plays in the other room with David and Rebecca. The same arguments have been repeatedly articulated, and it feels like they are just going around in circles. Janice and Dickie sit silently, answering any questions thrown their way, listening and praying as people they have just met decide their future.

"But surely her health will be endangered if she is moved elsewhere?" one voice argues.

"The assessment shows that that is not necessarily the case and in a situation like this, she should be moved elsewhere after every review. Her health is too much for one foster family to handle," volleys back another.

"How will that affect her socially?" queries one expert.

"She has only been here a short time; I doubt it will affect her much. The access visits with her mother are more important for her social development."

"But there have been numerous occasions where her mother has failed to attend; Charlene would benefit from the stability that the Barrs are providing," speaks up one social worker. She has been consistently arguing their corner and Dickie feels grateful every time she speaks up.

"Perhaps, but that won't be the case long term. Charlene cannot stay here long term," says another bluntly.

"Why not?" Janice blurts out, no longer able to restrain herself. She briefly looks embarrassed, then ploughs on regardless. "These few months have been incredible and we want to continue to care for her. We would love to have her on a long term basis."

"It's not possible, it's not normal procedure," says one man, his forehead furrowed.

For a moment no one speaks and tension hangs thickly in the air. Dickie gropes for words, but everything they have said has been shot down. What can he say? They already have an answer to everything. But then another social worker speaks. "But why not?" she reasons waving her arms as she speaks, accentuating her points. "First off, socially, Charlene needs stability, the very thing she has never had since birth. How can you expect her to develop normally if we constantly shift her from place to place? She can still attend access visits with her birth mother from here."

"Secondly, you have seen the recommendations and her health reports. Frankly, it would be dangerous and irresponsible to move her from here. Her health is stable and she has been able to regularly attend appointments. To move her would endanger this and, according to the doctors, her health is precarious. We can talk about this all we want, but our job is to put the needs of Charlene first." She pauses, looking them all in the eye one after the other. "Her interests are best served both socially and medically by remaining with the Barrs."

Her tone carries a note of finality with her and in the aftermath, there is silence. Dickie realises he has been holding his breath, so he lets a breath out. He looks at Janice and she is clutching her mug so tightly that her knuckles have turned white. Please let them listen, please let them listen.

Arguments are still bandied about but you sense slowly others changing their opinion. One by one, they confront the problems and soon the conclusion is that Charlene will remain where she is on a long-term basis.

That night, after they have kissed Charlene goodnight, they lie down in their bed and Janice's whisper slices through the darkness. "God did send an angel ahead of us. That social worker was our angel."

5
BECOMING A BARR

THE YEARS FLY BY, all too quickly, and the talk turns from long term fostering to adoption. Now it is unimaginable to Janice to think of life without Charlene; she is an integral part of the family, as much as the rest of her children. Natalie has joined them now and has added to the insanity within the house. She is everywhere, never low on energy, and together with Charlene, the younger two children leave a trail of destruction in their wake.

Charlene is still in and out of hospital frequently, yet she never complains. Together, the children grow older: day by day, week by week, month by month. To them, life is one big game with adventure after adventure: they visit the zoo together, pick raspberries together, working with their mother to make huge batches of jam. Many Sundays they take their bikes up to Castlewellan Forest Park and cycle around the lake. Their grandparents spoil them all and they often go to sleep over at both homes.

To everyone Charlene seems part of the family, but legally, that is not the case. After the uncertainty of repeated reviews and the constant fear that a decision made in an office far away will tear their family apart, they desire the permanence of adoption. Janice and Dickie have talked to all of their children, and all agree this is the route to go down to make Charlene an irrevocable member of their family, come what may.

"Mummy why can't they just do it now?" Charlene asks one day, looking sweetly up at Janice with her face crunched up in thought. "Why can't I be a Barr now?"

"Charlene you are a Barr now," Janice says picking her up and touching Charlene's forehead to her own. "It is just taking a while for the social workers to sort a few things out, but you have been a Barr ever since we chose you."

Charlene's forehead wrinkles and her eyes scrunch up as she thinks. "Why am I different from David, Rebecca and Natalie?" Her eyes seem sad as she tries to wrap her four year-old mind around a convoluted legal process that has been dragging on.

Janice laughs gently and says, "Oh Charlene," pulling her close and brushing her hair back from her forehead. She leans down and whispers in her ear. "You are special. All the others we had no choice with, but we chose you. You are very special to us; you make our family complete."

Charlene giggles abruptly and her eyes are bright as she leans down and pats Janice's tummy. Mischievously she says, "Not yet Mummy. Wait until

Charlene, Dickie and Natalie

they get here."

Janice laughs. They told them the news last week. She is pregnant with twins now; David is eight years old, meaning that they will have six children under the age of nine. "And it's David's fault these ones are on their way," Janice teases as she sets Charlene down. David had led his sisters in praying for twins for the last two years. Every night without fail they had prayed for twins, much to their parent's merriment. David had ulterior motives, wanting two brothers to even the odds and play football with, however the others just wanted little siblings to mother. Dickie and Janice had laughed at their innocence and prayers; they certainly weren't laughing now.

When they had broken the news to their children all four had immediately started to jump up and down in euphoria. "Is it twins?" David had blurted out, excitement etched across his face. "Yes," Dickie confessed, barely able to contain his joy. "YES!" Charlene shouted and dashed around the room giggling with Natalie following in her wake, unsure as to what was going on but determined to be involved nonetheless. "We're going to have two new brothers!" David yelled excitedly.

Aside from this good news, there was still the court case to consider and the date loomed large in their minds. They had fought against resistance from different social workers and been encouraged by the support from others. There were arguments over Charlene's welfare, the rights of her birth mother and her health. Additionally, in politically charged Northern Ireland, the fact that this was a cross-religion adoption was causing problems. Different reports had been prepared by many different professionals including her doctors. The future had looked murky over the past year, but they were determined to formalise what had already happened in their hearts long ago – Charlene becoming a Barr.

"Stop shaking your leg Dickie!" Janice snaps. His leg is shaking like a leaf, as it always does when he is nervous. He knows today should be a formality, but after such a long drawn out process he knows nothing is certain. They are sitting in the lobby of the Belfast High Court where the adoption should be finalised. "I'll try Janice, but I don't realise I'm doing it," he says as he rubs his hand across his head.

"Don't do that either!" Janice responds eyeing his hand on his head.

"Is my hair ok?" Rebecca asks, fiddling with the bow in her hair. They have taken all the children out of school for the day, as all of them want to be together as this struggle draws to an end.

"Yes, it's fine, stop worrying," David chimes in, even though he has no idea about what would constitute a good hairstyle. He is trying to read the book he has brought, and keeps getting frustrated by the constant hustle and bustle around him. As Natalie starts to skip from one side of the room to another while singing, he sighs and puts his book down.

Charlene is tugging on her dress and leaning in close to Janice. She has been uncharacteristically quiet all day and has not left her side once. Janice puts her arm around her daughter and gives her a squeeze. Charlene remains silent, chewing her lip. She looks up at Dickie, eyes concerned.

Dickie leans over and grasps one of Charlene's hands. "Charlene, tell us again what is going to happen today."

Charlene glances up and the hint of a smile appears at the corner of her mouth.

"Today is the day I become a Barr," Charlene says shyly.

"You already are Charlene, you know that?" Dickie says, squeezing her hand.

Big sister with Serena and Bethany

"Yeah, but today everyone will know," Charlene finishes proudly.

A voice echoes through the lobby. "Could Charlene and the Barr family please come forward?" Together they stand, with Charlene clutching her mother's hand for dear life, and Natalie holding Dickie's hand. David and Rebecca walk tentatively behind as they enter the courtroom.

The court case passes in a blur, and in contrast to the fear and trepidation in the build-up, the finale seems like an anti-climax; however, the result is not. Charlene steps from that court room as a Barr and the Barrs leave as a complete family of six. At least until the twin's due date later that year.

The memories fall from before my eyes like loosed shackles as I feel a tap on my shoulder. I turn and see a beaming friendly face before me. "Welcome David. My name is Isaac, I am the headmaster at Hidden Treasure," the man says, his eyes bright. He grips my hand, squeezing it tightly. "We prayed for your sister for so long, she was very special to us." The sadness on his face is genuine, and the din around us seems to momentarily grow quieter.

"Thank you Isaac," I say quietly, looking away for a second and drinking in the sight of the school before me. "This community was special to her too.

Thank you for your prayers."

"It is good to meet you, David. We would like to welcome you to Hidden Treasure," he says, holding his arm out to the canopy where the children all sit, poking each other and jumping around excitedly. Hearing the euphoric squeals of these children, whose lives have been changed, causes my mood to shift again; at the back of the canopy the choir is practicing.

"It is so good to have you here," Isaac continues smiling. I feel a little hand grasp for mine by my side and a small Ugandan boy is staring up at me, intertwining his fingers with mine. He is dressed in a shirt that is missing several buttons and is riddled with holes; his knees are scuffed, one of them bleeding. He does not wear any shoes and his shorts are dirty but his smile could light up the world.

As I say thank you again to Isaac, my new friend leads me off excitedly. As I try to speak to him he chatters away in Lugandan, and it is clear he does not know any English. He leads me over to the steps and motions for me to sit down. As soon as I sit, he jumps onto my knee and stares deep into my eyes. His big brown eyes remind me of my sister and again I miss her, I miss her so much. He leans in and closes his eyes, and as I wrap my arms around him and rock him gently I allow the flood of thoughts to entrap and engulf me again.

I have been remembering the stories my parents have told me of Charlene's past, of our family's past. For me the memories are fuzzy but raw; we have often talked of those times over the past year. We have retraced every moment of our time together, discussing the details again and again, as if fearful that if not articulated and relived, the memories will slip away like a breath on the wind. I have remembered their stories of the road to adoption.

That was not the end though; it was only the beginning of this tale and there was so much more to remember. The child begins to snore in the midday sun as I rock him quietly and I do not see the Ugandan skies. Instead, I see the videos we watched just weeks ago; the years fall away as precious memories play themselves out again and it is as if I am there once more.

6
MEMORIES

Growing up was always full of adventures, fun and games

BETHANY AND SERENA *have found a collection of old family videos from years ago and Dad sets up the old camera to play through the television. We see Charlene young again, pedalling and clinging to the swans at Bangor Marina, running races in the back garden, going down water slides in America. We watch her singing her heart out in her primary school choir, with the occasional gasp in between lines: a dark sign of the breathlessness to come. We see her attempting to skate board down our drive and watch her sitting on Granny's knee and on a children's train with Grandma. So many happy memories of us all playing together, running and shouting like madmen, causing us to question how Mum and Dad coped. We laugh, and miss her more than ever. So many memories…*

It is Christmas, always a time of celebration in our house. As soon as November hits, the countdown begins, and Charlene is always the one who campaigns most fervently to get the decorations up. Our house is one of those that goes completely over the top when it comes to Christmas. The holidays are spent with late nights of jigsaw puzzles, games and family time as decorations and lights hang from every window. My friend Jamie refers to our house as the Northern Lights, and when you come into the drive after school you can see why; in the encroaching darkness, every window is ablaze and welcoming.

The rule of thumb we established in our house, much to the protest and horror of Mum and Dad, was that the decorations had to be up by the 15th November, my birthday. Generally, our mission is achieved, tempered by the compromise of Mum pulling the curtains on the insanity until at least late November. Charlene, like all of us, loves Christmas.

It is Christmas Eve and we have decided to perform a Nativity for our long-suffering grandparents. Rebecca and I desperately try to keep order as the two-year old twins run in and out of the room and Natalie decides the angel she plays should perform a dance before anyone else is ready. We are dressed in a variety of ill-fitting dressing gowns, a varied assortment of tea towels attached to our heads by some of Dad's more colourful ties. Rebecca for the third time lifts Serena, one of the shepherds, outside the room, determined that shepherds should not tumble across the stage when Mary is visited by the angel.

The six year old Charlene stars, putting extraordinary emphasis into her role as shepherd and later (wearing a different tea-towel) as one of the Wise Men. When first seen by Mary and Joseph before the visit of angels, she exclaims, "Don't worry about finding a room, I sleep on the hill with my sheep." She leads Bethany and Serena, her fellow shepherds, around the room.

The visit of the angel to the shepherds is a revelation. "A baby is born, it's Jesus," Natalie shouts at the poor shepherds, while waving a wand she has added to her interpretation of the character.

Charlene begins to jump up and down in her green dressing gown, screaming "Hallelujah!" and causing one of the grandparents to fiddle with his hearing aid. She dances in the middle of the room shouting "Hallelujah," with such exuberance it's hard not to get excited. The twins mirror her every move, and being unable to master the word, "Hallelujah," just let out delighted squeals.

"We must go and find him. He will be in a manger," Charlene exclaims, as Bethany runs over to Rebecca's Mary, grabbing the Baby Jesus doll from her arms and carrying it over to Serena by its leg. After Rebecca corrects this variation in the story, Natalie decides the angel should also attend, jumping up and down shouting, "I'm coming too. Let's bring all the sheep." Grandma is on the sofa, shaking with silent laughter, tears running down her cheeks.

A later scene is just as interesting, as one of the wise men has fallen asleep in Mum's arms by this point. Charlene rocks the manger furiously, exclaiming, "It's Jesus! It's Jesus!" She is joined by Natalie and the newly awoken twins shouting with her. Rebecca and I stand bemused, before joining in. The script I had written lies abandoned on the floor under our feet. We finish with a rendition of 'Away in a Manger'. It is hopelessly out of tune, but no one cares. It is a great night; Charlene sings with all her heart, her eyes closed as she takes great gulps of breath, belting out her part. This is a performance which will not be easily forgotten.

To Santa,

I expect you're rather busy getting ready. David has a plan that next Thursday night we try to stay awake all night so we will be ready for you the next night. I hope it will work. I'm sure you're tired.

Loads of love,
Charlene xoxo

It is Christmas Eve and a mighty storm that has been brewing for days has broken with mighty winds raging furiously all around the house. We are in the living room eating Pringles and playing a family game which is fast descending towards anarchy. It is comforting being warm inside as the storm roars outside.

Suddenly the lights go out, and we are plunged into utter darkness. Serena starts to whimper and reaches for Mum, and Natalie mutters, "What happened Dad?"

"I don't believe this, it's Christmas Eve and we have no electricity. How are we going to have Christmas dinner?" Rebecca complains.

"Listen to the wind now," I pitch in. In the silence, the wind howls down the chimney and the rain lashes against the window as the dark silhouettes of tree branches loom ominously through the gloom outside. Charlene sits quietly in the darkness.

Dad and I are dispatched into the kitchen to find any light source we can; we return with a box of matches and a torch. Mum quickly works a miracle, finding candles and distributing them around the room. Once ignited, they transform the mood in the room. In the homely glow of the candles, we move closer together and munch on snacks while sharing stories and laughing at old memories. Charlene cuddles against Dad while the twins both drift towards sleep beside Mum. Rebecca, Charlene, Natalie and I play cards by candlelight for a time, before our parents finally send us to bed. We sleep in the same room in the darkness, scattered across the floor in various sleeping bags, drifting into another Christmas Day in each other's company, with new memories to cling to while we listen in comfort to the storm ebb and flow outside, as the candlelight shines through the darkness.

To the 8 Reindeer,

Thank you for leading Santa. You all have a big part to play. I'm sure you all get tired but then you fly anyway. My sister Natalie has little decorations of you and Santa and every time you see her she's making up stories with them.

Loads of love,
Charlene Barr
xoxo

It is 2000 and I grunt as Bethany and Serena jump on me to wake me. After a particularly intense landing on my stomach, I jerk up. We are all asleep in the same room on Christmas Eve, a tradition since the blackout two years previous. "What time is it girls?"

"Four, it's four!" they sing in unison, with their eyes shining like stars and huge grins plastered across their faces. Still dressed in their pyjamas, they dance across to Rebecca in her sleeping bag and repeat the same process. As Rebecca growls, Charlene screams from behind me, "Look out the window!" She bounces on the bed while peering into the darkness.

I stretch and yawn, moving to sit on the bed beside her. It is still in the depths of night outside and I know, without a shadow of a doubt, that Mum and Dad will not appreciate our four o'clock rise, especially considering their struggles to rouse any of us for something as mundane and periphery in our minds as school.

But the darkness is not what Charlene is excited about. The streetlights at the end of the road are hard to see, as a blizzard pulls flurries of snow twisting and winding through the air, the wind flinging it in handfuls upon the ground. We have to squint through the air, thick with snow, in order to see anything and the white ground sparkles with the shine from the Christmas lights that remained lit overnight. It looks like a white blanket has been rolled out before us and the snow continues to fall thickly.

Natalie, who has joined us by the window, screams, "It's snowing!" and

In the Rainbows

runs to inform Mum and Dad, who will be less than enthralled by this news at four o'clock in the morning. As expected, she returns forlorn. "They say we have to wait until half five!" she blasts scandalised. A collective moan shifts around the room; I, however would not mind another hour or two to sleep.

Charlene puts my hope to bed quickly, though. "Let's play cards!" she says. Within a matter of minutes the cards are dealt and we play for the next hour and a half, as the snow on the windowsill outside thickens.

At five thirty, the usual Christmas morning chaos unfolds with Mum and Dad reluctantly roused from their slumber. We wait for Grandma and Poppa to arrive before we open anything, and then have the usual fun seeing what is in our stockings. Dad takes picture after picture with his camera, just as he does every year.

As we eat a brief breakfast, we watch out the window as the dawn breaks over the winter wonderland outside. The blizzard has finished hurling snow upon us; however a light layer still falls. As the sun crawls above the horizon, brushing the tops of the trees, everything is tinged in a brilliant white. The bare trees outside are covered in a white coat and scratch at the belly of the clouds above. Hurriedly wrapped up against the elements, we venture outside to go to church. It quickly becomes evident the car is unusable: with snow massed around the wheels and the road an ice-rink. We decide to walk down, slipping and sliding as we go.

Natalie and I start off the madness. We rush to the top of the driveway and prepare a barrage of missiles for the rest of the family behind us. As they approach, a snowball is flung into the air in an arc that lands just at Charlene's feet. "Mum, look what they did. I'm getting you David Barr," Charlene yells.

Full scale war erupts as we progress slowly towards church, with shifting alliances forged and numerous betrayals. Our furious cries cut through the crisp morning air.

"STOP IT!" Mum's voice slices through the cold air like a hot knife and everything stops, apart from one solitary snowball sailing through the air and landing behind Natalie. Dad quietly lays one of his snowballs down on a wall we are passing, and we walk on in silence. A few snowballs are still flung from time to time, but after Charlene attempts to shove snow down Rebecca's back, we get another warning not to push our luck. Brushing ourselves down, we step through gently falling snowflakes into church.

On the treacherous walk home an uneasy truce rests in the air as we approach the gate. "Why don't we go for a walk in the field?" Dad asks. A field runs behind our house, and now it is a blanket of unspoilt snow, full of possibilities. "Yes!" Natalie screams and hops over the gate before slipping and falling unceremoniously on her face.

Before long we are in the field and all around us lies a sheet of white. Every step makes a crunch in the air and I look back, feeling guilty at the trail of our footsteps that have ruined the pure uncorrupted veneer of the snow. Serena opens her mouth wide as the snowflakes drift onto her tongue. I smile. I pick up a pile of snow and craft it into a ball. My hands are freezing, so I quickly choose my target, and fling the snowball at Charlene.

The snow breaks over her back and crumbles everywhere. She turns, with fury and rage in her eyes, and runs at me, picking up snow as she comes. "How dare you do that? I wasn't ready." With this signal, anarchy again descends on our company, with everyone joining in. This quickly becomes a 'boys against girls' contest, with Dad and me holding our own against the six girls. Charlene, still seething, flings snowballs all about me, but soon she calms and is swept up in the insanity of the game.

Exhausted and cold, we eventually cease hostilities with, at least from my perspective, a clear resounding victory to the men, and together build a snowman in the snow. Laughing, we walk back to the house, as soon our relatives will be arriving and Christmas dinner will be served. We walk back laughing, eight pairs of footprints twisting behind us in the snow.

To Mrs Claus,

It's properly a job feeding all the people in your house. My Mum knows what it's like feeding eight of us but you have so many more to feed. I'm sure you will miss Santa next Friday night, but don't worry we will all take our turn in feeding him.

Loads of love and care,
Charlene Barr
xoxo

7
ROLLING THROUGH THE YEARS

THE TWINS CONTINUE TO FLICK *through different scenes from our past caught on camera and we dissolve into fits of laughter at our actions, and indeed the clothes we wore. We tease each other as we watch, and remember Charlene and the fun we had together. There are so many scenes of Christmas; it had always been a special time of year to us, especially Charlene. We also recollect other scenes as we see them unfold before us...*

"Come on girls!" I shout. It is the holidays and we have decided to put on a show for Mum, Dad and the twins. Rebecca is already in the room; introducing the story, she is making up details as she goes along, bringing in fantastic elements as only a six year old can. Charlene steps into the room beside me, both of us dressed as clowns.

"What are you going to do to us?" I exclaim to Rebecca, truly believing I hold the aura of a great actor. "I'm going to hit you if you turn me into a frog," Charlene shouts, a line definitely not in the script. Rebecca casts a spell in this riveting story and I am turned into Pinocchio, Charlene into Mr Blobby (the only masks we have in the house). Then Natalie, a hyper two year old, arrives at full sprint in our midst, waving her wand at anything that moves. The script deteriorates from this point on.

A scene of madness has erupted as Rebecca runs around casting spells, trying to keep the story flowing while I am now bizarrely dressed as a pumpkin whilst Natalie spirals through the middle of the room in an impromptu dance routine. Dad tries to catch all the panoramic chaos on his new camera as Charlene rocks her little sister.

"Mummy, I want to be a Mummy," she says. Mum smiles, rocking Serena in her arms. Within minutes Charlene is back in the midst of the so-called story, refusing to follow the script and making up lines as she goes, causing Rebecca much frustration. Bethany sleeps soundly.

When I grow up I want to be a Mummy.

(Charlene's Noah's Ark Playgroup C.V.)

Games and competitions were always high on the agenda

"Charlene, your turn to serve," Rebecca yells. Charlene is seven, and we are playing volleyball in the garden: Rebecca, Charlene and Dad on one side and Natalie, Mum and myself on the other. Bethany and Serena, only just turned two, alternate teams depending on the score but mostly just watch, observing all the intense competition unfolding around them.

Charlene walks to the back of the court outlined with various shoes and jumpers, and then hammers her small fist into the back of the ball with all her might. It sails out and wide. "That's not fair, let me try again," she exclaims.

"I don't think so, it's my serve!" I yell, grabbing the ball and running to the back of the court. There is disagreement at this point and after intensive negotiations Charlene gets another serve, much to my frustration.

She steadies herself, looks at the ball, and again she whacks it; this time her serve sails true, dipping just over the net. Natalie knocks it up and Mum blasts it back, with Dad responding and smashing it straight into the mix on our side. This little interplay ends with Natalie tripping over one of the twins, lots of laughter and a pile of bodies lying in the grass in our garden.

Watching Charlene run around, no one sees her as any different from the rest of us, but in reality, she does struggle to keep up. Her lungs do not have the same capacity as ours, and though she fights to hide it, she can never run as fast or play for as long as the rest of us. She mucks in and is at the centre of everything, yet her illness does limit her. Unable to keep up, despite her desire to do so, she sometimes gets frustrated and storms off in games, enraged at her limitations.

She rarely lets her illness get to her and we play together oblivious to any thoughts of the future beyond what we will play next and how much of the summer holidays we have left before the dreaded return to school. Life is fun as we each have five other playmates around us. From Detective Club to Gladiators, we make up game after game. We lay out cushions in our living room, making boulders, which we must leap upon to avoid the lava and the monster, played by me, who swims around, trying to pull his victims to their firey demise. We have races and set up obstacle courses throughout the house and garden. Much of this is possible simply because Mum is so good to us, having left work when I was born, not knowing what was to come and how many would join me. She plays with us and spends time with us, trying to temper the more violent elements of our games; we are not lacking in good times.

That night, after the madness of volleyball, we crawl into the tent we have set up in our back garden. Charlene crawls in beside Rebecca and Natalie and under torchlight we play Uno, as the evening birdsong carries on the breeze outside. We play for an hour, then all lights are turned off as we prepare for sleep, stuffed into a tent much too small for eight, with feet ending up in a variety of places.

"We're all mad, who else would sleep in a tent in their own garden?" Mum laughs. All that waits for us in the next days are more games, more fun together. Charlene's health may hinder her, but it doesn't hold her back from anything we do together.

Charlene is a great character to have in the class. She will always greet you with a smile and enjoys a good joke. On the other hand she is hard-working and polite, always giving of her best. Her happy attitude to life makes her a joy to teach.

(Teacher's comments on Charlene's P4 report)

I stand in the queue, my heart beating like a drum. The sun beats down

Charlene in Mrs McCollum's class in Waringstown Primary School

on us and I can feel my shoulders fry in the heat. The line of people moves slowly up the steps, much too quickly for me, and I wait desperately for Charlene to back down and break.

We are visiting family in California and are at Hurricane Harbour, a sprawling water park with all the water attractions you could dream of, from wave pools to water slides to rapids. It has been a good day, and while Mum stays as far from the water as possible, the rest of us have been swimming down the circular river that winds around the park, jumping from one slide to another. Dominating the landscape is the intimidating 'Black Snake Summit', a tower with black tubes winding and twisting around it. Those slides look scary enough, but the crowning terror of this attraction is 'Venom Drop', a 75-foot free-fall with water cascading down a near vertical drop.

Talking in the car on the way to the park we all told tales of this infamous ride, with each tale growing in the telling: tales of serious injuries, of people losing swimming trunks, of peoples' backs leaving the ride due to the steepness and landing much further down. It had risen to nearly a mile high in our childish exaggerations and as we swam past it time and time again it loomed in our minds and dominated the landscape.

"That last ride was scary," Charlene shouts over the din as we swim through the rapids. She is eight years old and loves every minute in this water park. She has been attending swimming lessons for the last few years

Visiting family in California

and now it is paying off. Due to her more limited lung capacity she has always progressed more slowly than the rest of us, but she never let this get to her and just pushes herself harder.

"No it wasn't, I went down backwards," Natalie responds. This was probably true. Natalie, at six years old is showing no limits to her energy or daredevil nature. She swims past Charlene as Charlene splashes her with some water, with Natalie responding in kind. A full-scale water fight erupts involving all of us, until Dad intervenes with the threat of time on the sun loungers, out of the water.

A momentary calm descends as we drift until Venom Drop again looms over us, and we swim through its shadow. A chill hangs in the air until Dad airs the unspoken challenge. "So David, are you warmed up enough to go on Venom Drop?"

I do not want to go on Venom Drop. I have no intention of going on Venom Drop. Yet all my sisters are here, and I have few options if I am to preserve any male pride. So I grasp at the option that I am sure will save me. "I would go, but not by myself. What about you Dad?"

As Dad mumbles something about his back, I feel a wave of relief pass over me and congratulate myself on my quick thinking. Then Charlene speaks.

"I'll go," she says, carefully eyeing the tower beside us. We all gape at her, but she is serious. After a short argument where I argue she is too small to go on it, I am left between a rock and a hard place, and determined that my little sister cannot be seen to go on something I am afraid to, I muster a painted smile and we leave the winding river with Charlene aiming a final splash at Natalie.

The tower seems to grow ever taller and more terrifying as we approach and watch people, specks in the distance, getting on at the top and hear their screams before they emerge at the bottom seconds later, staggering unsteadily off. Fear grips me. I do not want to test out this ride.

My apprehension grows with every step, but I am determined not to show this to Charlene. She will back out at the last minute, and I will then do the big brotherly thing and escort her gallantly back to the family. But as we draw closer to the top she still chats away, obviously nervous, but still determined. I change tack, reminding her of some of the horror stories we have heard; she bites her lip as she takes another hesitant step up in the queue.

"Are you scared David?" she asks, looking me in the eye. I see flashes of fear in her eyes, and I feel guilty for scaring her. "Yes I am, but loads of people have gone on this and been fine. How will we be any different? Nothing could go wrong." Charlene nods unconvinced.

I look out over the water park. I can see everything from here, and the heights are dizzying. We have dried in the queue and with every step our bare feet roast as the sun beats down mercilessly on the ground. The people below look like ants swimming around and as I eye the main river thoroughfare that laces around the park I long to be back in with the rest of our family. But male pride is a powerful drug.

"Why do you want to go on this Charlene?" I ask turning. She looks so small compared to everyone else in the queue, and suddenly very vulnerable up here so far from the ground.

"Because you're going on it David. I want to go on all the rides and do everything you are doing. I'm still scared though."

"You know you don't have to? If you don't want to; I won't. I don't even want to go on this thing Charlene," I finally admit.

"No I think I want to. But will you go first?"

Charlene is braver than me, showing her typical determination and refusal to back down. This would be her greatest blessing and curse in later years in ways we could never fathom as we stood on a 75-foot tower in California captured in an instant of time. "Yes. I love you Charlene. If you change your mind, just go back down the steps," I say, accepting my fate and saying what I fear may be my final goodbyes as we step onto the boarding platform.

As I step forward I gaze down the throat of the slide: at the water cascading down into oblivion, at the ant-like people at the bottom of it, at the two inch sides which are the only protection against flying off, and I know beyond a shadow of a doubt that I do not want to go any further. Is this enjoyment? I look back at Charlene, standing there with her arms folded, so small, but so determined. She smiles at me, and I throw myself off the platform onto the slide.

Not all the myths are true. I keep my swimming trunks on to the relief of the rest of the paying customers and I suffer no serious injury, although I do bounce once or twice as I go down the slide, free-falling for a few seconds. However, within seconds, it is over in a rush of adrenaline; I pick myself up smiling and stagger out to wait.

I do not expect her to do it. I can just imagine her standing there, with oblivion yawning in front of her, gazing down into the maw of the beast. However Charlene, the small sick child who was not expected to make school, does not turn her back. She sits down and pushes herself off, emerging seconds later, laughing; she stands to join me, having conquered Venom Drop.

"Let's go again."

Career Ambition

I would love to be a children's nurse because I love little children.

(Charlene's Primary School Record of Achievement)

Charlene and Bethany

"We are completely insane." Mum says, matter of factly. Rebecca finishes spraying her hair, and fires the spray can to Charlene, who sets to work on her own hair, turning it a vivid red. She finishes, looks at Dad and smiles, saying, "Don't think you'll need this, you don't have any hair to spray."

"Oh very funny," Dad replies, smiling. "I'll just have to put

Charlene with family before the Liverpool match

this on instead," he continues, pulling on his Liverpool baseball cap. We are outside Anfield, and all eight of us are dressed from head to toe in Liverpool red, with an assortment of player names etched onto the back of our shirts, from Gerrard to Fowler. We are in the process of completing the image by turning our hair red with a spray we picked up earlier in the day. We will worry about any lasting damage later.

We have spent a week in Warrington in England, largely based around visiting coffee shops, treks into the country for football and touch rugby games, beautiful walks and then competitive board games in the evenings, which have led to many rows. The weather has been poor, and indeed, one day when we had planned a picnic, we ended up folding down the car seats and eating in the shelter of the car. This ended up being more fun than any picnic outside could ever have been. We have also managed to fit in a visit to the Liverpool museum, where the recently won 2001 Treble took pride of place, but today was the highlight we all looked forward to, the visit to Anfield for the Liverpool versus Spurs match.

We do look like we are mad, each of us with bright red hair adorned in an assortment of Liverpool clothes, and clinging to a myriad of scarves, flags and banners. We walk towards the stadium as if we are our own team, chattering away. "Stop singing," Natalie mutters, embarrassed, as Dad and I attempt a rendition of 'You'll Never Walk Alone'; Bethany laughing as she walks behind holding Mum's hand.

We make our ways through the ticket stiles and Mum does a quick head count, something that has always been necessary for us. "We are one down, who's not here?" she asks suddenly, frantic.

"Charlene, she's over there," Rebecca replies pointing ahead. Charlene is at the bottom of the steps leading up to the Kop, that most famous Stand, gazing wide-eyed around her. We surround her, and she looks up at Dad smiling. "Let's get up there; I want to see the stadium."

As soon as we emerge from the darkness of the steps and into the light with the pitch unfolding below, we all run to get pictures. From pitch side Charlene shouts for all of us, and we gather together for photo after photo.

As kick-off approaches we take our seats, nearly consuming a full row. The grainy tones of Gerry and the Pacemakers grind out over the loudspeakers and we stand. As the pre-match 'You'll Never Walk Alone' is belted out, Charlene, Bethany and Serena stand on their seats, holding a scarf above their heads and belting it out as loud as their lungs will allow. We are all out of tune, but this time Natalie is not embarrassed. Together, on the Kop Stand, we proclaim our love for Liverpool, and as Charlene's voice adds to the swell her voice resonates to the words.

When you walk through a storm,
Hold your head up high,
And don't be afraid of the dark.
At the end of a storm,
There's a golden sky,
And a sweet silver song of a lark.

Walk on through the wind,
Walk on through the rain,
Though your dreams be tossed and blown....

Walk On! Walk On! With hope in your heart,
And you'll never walk alone....

You'll never walk alone.

The hospital ward is familiar to us as we creep quietly along it. Bethany holds my hand as we walk and Natalie is leading us on, beckoning at us to hurry up. Grandma and Poppa walk with us, carrying filled plastic bags in their hands. We approach Charlene's room and Dad pokes his head around the corner. He smiles.

"SURPRISE!" we all yell as we leap around the corner. Charlene, who has been staring blankly at the television screen looks to us, and her face bursts into a smile. Her face looks drawn from her latest infection, but her eyes sparkle as we step into the room. We surround her bed and squeeze into every conceivable space, while the room erupts in chatter. Fitting ten people into a small hospital room is no mean feat.

Charlene has become ill again and after a steep decline, her frail body racked with coughing, she has had to be admitted into the Royal Hospital for another course of intravenous antibiotics. This is an all too frequent part of the rhythm of life for us; as always, our family feels incomplete when Charlene is not with us. However, during the times when Charlene has to be admitted, our lives revolve around the hospital. While we are at school, Mum will usually spend the day with her in Belfast; not a day will go past when she does not have a visit from at least some of us.

Today we are all hoarded around her bed, with Natalie and Serena lounging across the bottom of the mattress, Bethany balancing precariously on the edge of the sink, Rebecca kneeling on a suitcase and myself sitting on the window sill. Grandma, Poppa and Dad sit in the three seats we have borrowed from the corridor outside and Mum stands beside Charlene, stroking her forehead and talking quietly in the midst of the tumult of noise.

"I wasn't expecting all of you. What do you have?" she asks, and smiles as Mum produces a picnic from the bags we have carted up with us and lays them across the bed. Pringles, bags of sweets and chocolates are passed around the room as we chat together. Charlene sits in the bed surveying the scene and smiles. She still looks frail, and cannot eat much, but she does seem to be on the mend. The intravenous drugs are doing their work.

Charlene beams as she chats away. "How did the test go Rebecca? Did you see the Liverpool goals? What do you think of the murder on Coronation Street?" Starved of news, she asks a million questions, sharing her view on what she has seen on television, one of the few things she has to do as she passes the time while the drugs and extra physiotherapy do their work. She never complains, in spite of her pain. She is much too brave for that.

I smile as I hold an After Eight. Our family is close, and as I grow older, I have begun to reflect and realise how blessed and fortunate we are. These times in hospital, where Charlene has to go for prolonged trips two or three times a year, are hard, but we suffer them together. What affects one of us affects us all. What hurts one of us hurts us all. As I smile, surveying the scene around me and popping the chocolate in my mouth, I could have no clue how true this will prove to be.

By the time I'm an adult, I hope to have the following education…

Nursing and teaching so that I can run an orphanage abroad because I love looking after people, especially kids.

By the time I'm an adult I would like to be married with ten kids because I would love to have my own family.

(Charlene's Journal)

As I reflect on the videos, I feel the pain. This was our complete family and the dull ache of incompleteness yawns even more visibly. Those were good days. However two sceptres on the horizon cast a pall over our lives as we grew inevitably older and time marched on.

Firstly, Charlene's health was a constant issue as she grew. Our memories were punctuated by Charlene's frequent visits to the Royal Victoria Hospital. For weeks at a time when she grew ill, she would be confined to a hospital bed, with lines running through her arm and into her blood. Our lives revolved around her visits in those times and it was hard for her. Her health yo-yoed, with periods of good health interrupted by rapid descents into illness, which were more dangerous than we, her brother and sisters, ever realised at the time. Charlene and our parents shielded us from much of the worry, but she always rallied and we grew used to it, expecting her recovery as always. Her unbending spirit and determination was obvious to all. Periodic infections continued into her teenage years, and while we knew they would come, we always expected her to recover, taking for granted her healing and her fight.

This had been a constant shadow, but the second sceptre that began to rear its vile head over Charlene's life was a battle waged for her heart. When you are a child, you think like a child and rarely question your place in the world: who you are and why you are here. You drift by with little thought other than what adventure the next day holds, with your brothers and sisters as playmates and rivals in whatever you decide to do next. We all argued and teased each other:

it was part of the brother and sister dynamic. Charlene was in the thick of every game and every story, never questioning her place; she was a Barr long before a legal document said so. She knew this – she was one of us and we were a family.

However we cannot stay young forever. The flow of time can be cruel, it rules with an iron fist, and as we grow, childhood must be left behind forever. As Charlene grew older she began to question her place and the love she was freely given. Wounds, deep within her heart, festered and for so long we did not see, we did not realise. Gradually they emerged to wield devastating damage on Charlene's life and on each of us. The battle waging for her heart spilled out over all of us and we were all drawn in. This time of darkness must also be told.

8
DEATH OF INNOCENCE

THERE ARE PARTS OF THIS STORY *that are hard to write. In choosing to write of Charlene's life and love, the hardest decision was whether to include the painful details of this period in her life. We made the decision to record it for a number of reasons.*

First, she wanted us to. She asked me, as her brother, if I would write her account of this agonising time in her life to give hope to other adopted children. She wanted to do this when she was stronger post-transplant. Heartbreakingly, that was never to happen. So now this wish of Charlene's is manifested in the testimony of her life, her desire to give hope to others again fulfilled in ways of which none of us had dreamed.

Secondly, the triumph in Charlene's life cannot be seen without the darkness. Charlene was not perfect and to act as if she was does her a disservice. The miracle of her life is seen not just in the result of her life but also in how she triumphed over adversity: both physically and emotionally. She was more than a conqueror due to her wrestling with the darkness within. To tell her story without narrating this period would lessen her testimony and debase her journey. Light burns all the brighter when it burns out of darkness.

It is said that the first year is critical in the life of a child; the child emotionally bonds with the mother, shaped by her constant presence that protects them, nurses them, cares for them, responds to their cries and loves them. Charlene did not have that in her first year. Many good nurses cared for her with all of their hearts, and many prayed over her as she fought for breath. Likewise, one family, the Jardines, took Charlene to their hearts and visited her in hospital on many occasions but she did not have one figure, that one voice with whom she could bond. As a sick child, fighting to cling to life, she did not have a mother there in her first year. Spending it in hospital, often in ICU, Charlene made her own way in the world: independent but alone.

We all bear scars. Each of us carries fundamental flaws and weaknesses that come to light in our darkest times. A word spoken in anger, a relationship destroyed, an attitude unaddressed, each of these can reside in our core, unnoticed on the surface by others, but gnawing away at us and affecting us in subtle ways, or emerging years later in monstrous ways. Charlene was no different to any of us.

The lack of a mothering figure in her first year had a cataclysmic effect on her. When she was young, the scars were not evident and she joined our family, becoming an integral part of it with no problem. She was a bubbly little girl, very affectionate, who wanted to be a part of everything. She may have been sick physically, but in every other way, she was exactly the same as every other member of the family. We all knew this but Charlene did not.

"Happy birthday to you, happy birthday to Natalie, happy birthday to you!" we sing as Mum carries the cake over to the table. The eight candles crowning it lick the air and Serena's eyes widen; her mouth drops as she watches the chocolate cake draw closer. Grandma laughs as Bethany reads a joke from the cracker she has just pulled and an air of merriment hangs in the air. It is close to Christmas and the lights in the window sparkle on and off, as festive music echoes quietly in the background. Mum sets the cake down and Natalie blows at the candles, unsuccessfully at first, spitting more than blowing.

"Blow harder Natalie," Poppa says, his eyes dancing.

Charlene, sitting beside Natalie, leans in and blows with all her might, blowing out three of the candles. Natalie stops, brow furrowed and irritated. "Charlene, it's my cake, I get to blow them out."

"Well you're not doing a very good job are you? For flip sake, we're all waiting for you to hurry up and blow out the stupid candles, it's not that hard," Charlene mutters, and glares at Natalie with a sharp look that could slice through iron.

"Charlene, don't be rude. Sit back and apologise to Natalie," Mum says with a raised voice.

"Well sorr-rry!" Charlene says sarcastically, rolling her eyes and turning away from Natalie with folded arms.

"Charlene Barr, say sorry properly," Mum insists, as the situation worryingly starts to escalate. Recently, Charlene has started to act up a lot more and it bothers me. It has happened slowly, but seems most evident at birthdays. For whatever reason, when it comes to any of our birthdays, she always seems to cause problems and be sullen the whole day. Earlier in the year at Rebecca's birthday, she had ended up screaming at the twins and had to be sent to her room for the way she was acting. It angered me, especially her scaring the twins like that. We are all protective of the youngest of us, and as their big brother I am more protective than most.

"I said sorry, are you deaf?" Charlene spits back, eyes aflame. The tension is palpable in the air and what was a happy birthday atmosphere has been transformed in a matter of seconds into an icy stand-off, after a couple of careless words.

Dad intervenes. "Charlene, how dare you speak to your mother like that? What is wrong with you?"

"What's wrong with you? This is so stupid. I haven't done anything wrong." She turns to the rest of us, sitting watching the scene unfold before us. The candles burn on, unnoticed and the music still sings quietly in the background. The air hangs still. She catches my eye. "What are you staring at?"

"Wise up, Charlene. This is Natalie's birthday, don't mess it up for her. You're being a baby," I reply angrily. "What's your problem?"

Charlene bristles and I feel the heat from her enraged gaze. Her voice strikes out like a razor blade. "Keep out of this; this is none of your business. Who asked your opinion? Keep your fat nose out of it where it belongs." She is seething.

Mum stands up, furious. "Charlene, go to your room now. That is quite enough!"

Charlene turns to her in a flash and screams at her as rage bursts from every pore of her being, "Why? What have I done wrong? You're not throwing me out of a birthday party."

"Go to your room this instant Charlene; you have been rude to everyone. You can come out when you have calmed down."

"I'm calm now!" Charlene screams, flinging her arm wide and spilling her juice across the table, soaking a startled Rebecca.

"Room - NOW!" Mum shouts in response to Charlene. She gets up and stomps to her room, crying tears of rage as she goes and muttering words loaded with venom as she goes. She slams the door behind her.

We sit in silence for a few seconds. The candles still flicker as do the Christmas lights, but the world seems heavier than it did a scant five minutes ago. The twins look like they might cry, the spilled juice drips off the edge of the table and the festive music sings of Christmas being the happiest time of the year.

"So happy birthday Natalie! Aren't you going to blow out your candles?" Mum asks with a forced smile painted across her face. Natalie turns to the cake and blows: all the candles go out this time.

Evenings like this begin to repeat themselves, infrequently at first, but then more often as Charlene grows older, until they become a daily event: part of the rhythm of our lives. What is happening?

Under the surface, Charlene is finding it impossible to accept love. As she is moving towards adolescence, times are becoming more and more difficult as, slowly but surely, she begins to reject those around her and insists she is different, that she is unloved and is not one of the family. Her security eroded, she begins to treat the rest of us with contempt, lashing out with her tongue to wound in any way she can. As Charlene approaches her time in secondary school, the dark times in our family begin.

Dear Diary,

I'm so tired but I have had a good day. I went to school and then went up the town for lunch with Jordan. I came home and did some ironing because Mum hurt her back. But I was really rude to the twins today just cause they wouldn't help me tidy up. I'm really going to have to try and work at this.

Loads of love,
Charlene

(Charlene's Journal)

Every day it begins after school. Charlene lashes out over some perceived slight and refuses to respond to any conversation, sitting there sullenly, flinging out the occasional cutting barb at anyone who looks at her. Weeks go by where we cannot remember a single kind word she says to any of us.

Eventually Mum and Dad challenge her on her behaviour, which just seems to be what she is waiting for.

What steps will you take this week?
Think before I say something to my parents. I will not fight with anyone.

(Charlene's Journal)

"My loneliness is killing me," Natalie dances across the kitchen clutching a wooden spoon which she holds to her mouth like a microphone. She spins, flinging her arms in the air as she screams out the words. She is ten and sings at every opportunity she gets.

I grip my pen tighter, the algebra not coming easily to me. "Natalie, I swear, if you don't stop singing now you will never need to worry about your loneliness killing you, I'll do that particular job," I mutter frustrated. In response, Natalie sings louder.

Just as I turn to shout at her, a door flings open and bangs against the wall as Charlene strides into the room and stands with her hands on her hips and nostrils aflare. "Will you just shut up! You are so annoying and you can't sing anyway. So just shut up now or else I will do it for you."

Natalie stops spinning and glares at Charlene, defiantly singing the next line with an angry look in her eye. In a flash, Charlene storms across the room and grabs the wooden spoon from Natalie's hands and screams in her face, "I TOLD YOU TO SHUT YOUR FACE, ARE YOU DEAF?"

I push the chair back from the table and walk over to the two girls, worried now about where this is going. Rebecca enters the room behind me, attracted by the noise. "What's going on?" she says from the door, eyebrows raised.

"Did anyone ask your opinion?" Charlene fires back icily.

"I asked her opinion," Natalie says, her chin raised and eyes narrowed.

Suddenly, the wooden spoon is in Charlene's hands and raised as if to strike. In a heartbeat, without even realising what I am doing, I am holding her arm and preventing the strike. I feel her body shaking with rage as her eyes turn to me, burning with hatred and malice.

"GET YOUR HANDS OFF ME NOW, OR I SWEAR I WILL HURT YOU. YOU HAVE NO RIGHT TO DO THIS!" She is so small in stature, but her fury is visible and she seems to be filled with an intensity that is not her own. I am now enraged myself. How dare she threaten one of my other sisters?

"GIVE ME THAT SPOON NOW CHARLENE!" I let go of her arm but she holds the spoon away, so I lunge and snap it out of her hand. This inflames her further and she kicks me as I pass. It does not hurt, but I am galled and livid as I stand.

"Stop it, stop it!" Bethany is crying and cowering in the corner, terrified by what is going on, but the anger floods out of me.

"Don't be such a baby!" Charlene screams, cracking her voice like a whip, just as Mum enters the kitchen. As she surveys the scene, Serena sitting at the table staring stoically ahead and Bethany with tears running down her cheeks, she turns to Rebecca, "What's happened?"

"Charlene was going to hit Natalie," Rebecca responds in a murmur.

"That's a lie, it was him," she says pointing an accusatory finger at me. "Why do you always blame me? It's not my fault she's crying like a child."

"Give me the spoon now David. Go and do your work in your room." I walk past her, grab my work and go upstairs. I beckon to the twins as I leave and they come with me. We can hear the argument intensifying downstairs and the vitriol fired by Charlene becoming increasingly bitter. A thought crosses my mind: she is enjoying this. Somehow she enjoys this. As I look at the tear-stained faces of my youngest sisters, I feel a stab of rage. Why is she doing this to the family? How dare she?

A vicious war of words is waged back and forwards that night. For the fifth night in a row, we get little sleep.

What problems are you most worried about today?
My behaviour.

(Charlene's Journal)

The chair rocks backwards and forwards as she holds her daughter. Charlene is whimpering quietly into Janice's chest as Janice wraps her arms around her daughter enveloping her in love. She hushes Charlene, continually whispering soothing words into her ears, reassuring her it will be fine. "Don't cry; you don't need to cry."

It had been a long day. From the second she had risen, Charlene had raged against all her siblings and battles had been fought throughout the day, with little refuge possible for anyone in the family. Charlene had systematically targeted and flung spiteful and bitter words all around her, until she was condemned to her room. In the wreckage of the evening, when the damage was assessed, Janice had gone up to talk to her daughter. Although initially she had blamed everyone else but herself, she had changed her mood as if with the flick of a switch and, as tears flowed down her face like a waterfall, Janice's heart had broken. She lifted her in her arms and cradled her like a treasured doll as the rocking chair slid backwards and forwards across the floor.

"What's wrong Charlene? Why do you say the things you do?" Janice whispers quietly, worry lining her face and making her look much older than her years.

Charlene whimpers. "I don't know Mummy. I just feel as if nobody loves me."

Janice's visage threatens to break as tears well in her eyes and feelings of guilt rise within her. Is there something they have failed to show her? How could she think they do not love her? "Charlene that isn't true. We love you so much, all of us do. How could we not?" Janice whispers gently.

Charlene continues to cry, but the faint traces of a smile are playing on the edges of her lips. "I know, it's just sometimes I get confused."

Janice rocks her gently. "You are our daughter, Charlene and you were specially chosen by us. I love you wee pet."

Charlene pulls herself from the depths of her mother's embrace and smiles with a smile that would melt a heart of ice. "I love you too. I promise I won't do what I did today again."

They sit together for the next hour, with Charlene enveloped in her mother's arms and being affirmed in her love. They talk of love, of family, of identity until Charlene grows weary and asks to go to bed. As Janice lies in bed that night, she cannot help but smile wearily. "I really think there was progress tonight Dickie," she whispers across to her exhausted husband. "She listened and she seemed to get it. Tomorrow will be different, I know it."

That night she sleeps soundly.

The next day is no different from the one that preceded it. When Charlene is asked to clear the table, she rises like a viper, spitting venom at her parents. As the day unfolds, she repeats the patterns ingrained in her mind, and Janice stands bewildered, feeling lost and betrayed. Things should be different now.

As Charlene strikes out at Natalie in a routine exchange, Janice corrects her and then raises the spectre that has haunted her throughout the day. "Charlene, why? What about all we talked about last night?"

She does not know what she expects, maybe some remorse, maybe some reflection, but not this. As Charlene glares at her, a glint lights in her eyes and a smile crawls across her face. She cackles manically, then, biting each word off as if she relishes the taste on her tongue, she fires them like darts at her mother, laughing incredulously. "You actually believed all that? You stupid woman! Everything last night, didn't you know? It was all a game, and you swallowed all of it. It's all just a game I play!"

With these words, she turns and skips away, humming merrily to herself. With every step she takes, Janice's heart seems to shrivel and die just a little bit more.

9
SCREAM OF THE HEART

IT MENTALLY WEARS YOU DOWN. There are nights where the episodes start as soon as we get back from school. They rage for hours as Charlene screams in anger: apologising in one breath, then spitting it back a moment later. Often these times go on late into the night, while we have to drag ourselves up for school the next day: we have perfected the art of 'the mask', pretending everything is fine. No one can know how little sleep we are getting and how we fear going home. All the time we dread and know what is going to happen again later. Home, which has always been a sanctuary, is now a hell.

She threatens the twins with a hockey stick and often throws punches at us. One night, after a particularly long battle, we all slept on our parents' floor in sleeping bags scattered across the floor, exhausted until Charlene storms upstairs in a rage of anger that had fallen upon her and kicks me in the head where I lie. We begin to adjust our lives to match the predictable cycle of her rages.

There are other problems arising; Charlene begins to steal, sneaking into Bethany and Serena's room, taking all the money they had been saving. After lying about it for a long time, she finally confesses in waves of remorse. We have to start keeping our money in safer locations, never leave it sitting about. It is confusing being unable to trust your own sister.

Mum and Dad never stop showing and telling her of their love for her – she is the same, how can she not see this? Many times she does seem to accept it and an uneasy calm descends: things are again as they had been, as they should be. Please let it stay like this. Evil whispers lie into her ear and poison her mind, just as her physical illness saps her health; these lies eat at her like a canker and in an instant, she transforms before our eyes for no obvious reason. One second she is Charlene, the next she is not: hate flows from her eyes.

She tries to fight herself, oh she tries. Sometimes we can physically see the war waging behind her eyes, the shifting tides of her mind visible as the battle for her soul manifests itself. Fierce regret and bitter rage war across her face. Charlene tries and for days things are good, she knows and accepts the love around her. However, no matter how she tries, there are days when the scabs within are torn off and she bleeds afresh: her demons seize control of her. In those days, the wounds of our family bleed blood red. What affects one of us affects us all; such are the costs of love and they are terrible to pay.

Even in the midst of a tirade of rage, she sometimes stops still, realising what she is saying and tears fill her eyes. "I'm sorry Daddy, I don't mean it. Forgive me," she begs, with anguish spilled across her face. Then a shadow falls upon her again, casting her face in darkness and she says, "Come on, I said sorry, you have to forgive me now. So, can I watch the film now?"

Mum and Dad remain resolute in their discipline and the hate spills over again, as if a switch has been thrown and her words drip poison. "I HATE YOU! You have no right to do this, this is child abuse. I HATE YOU! YOU'RE TERRIBLE PARENTS AND I HATE YOU!"

It becomes harder to forgive. After a night of the vilest words spat at my parents and sisters, she would come to her senses in her room and write the most beautiful, heartfelt letters: asking for forgiveness and promising change. She would then slip them under Mum and Dad's door while they sleep, but within a matter of a day, she again vents poisonous words of hate, with an inevitability that becomes more and more grinding as time goes on. "What use is an apology if she does the same thing again and again?" I scrawl across my journal, ignoring the irony of the chronicles in that same journal of my repeated rebellions against the God I claim to follow. My heartfelt repentance was also followed grindingly by a habitual return to the same mistakes in a cycle of depressing inevitability.

At first, I believe Charlene is lying in those letters, fooling us and playing a game. This is true in part, but over time I come to realise that Charlene does mean every word, every word torn from the tortured depths of her despair and remorse, where a war rages within her that we can only see on the surface. On reflection, I begin to realise that Charlene is each of us writ large, showing clearly the terrible war that wages constantly over our hearts. Whom will we follow? What will we live for? She shows more visibly the cycle we all follow: of dedication and resolve to not carry out that betrayal ever again. As we set out, firm in our pledge, our treacherous hearts constantly betray us and we pathetically fall, again serving the things that destroy us with a crippling and crushing inevitability. Is there any answer to this cycle? That answer is there in the darkest times any of us can describe, but the cost continues to be paid.

26th June 2004

Dear Diary,

I have had a really bad day today as I was really nasty to everyone. I started off okay but when we went to PC World I saw this computer game that I wanted and when I asked Dad he said no and then I got really grumpy and nasty.

I heard them talking about holidays earlier too, and I am trying to promise myself that I will not mess up like I did last time. I then told them I was going to go for a cycle but Mum wouldn't allow me.

I really am a stupid person because I get myself into the silliest arguments. HELP!!!

Love always,
Charlene

(Charlene's Journal)

"What are you looking at?" Charlene shoots across the room at one of the twins, her voice a tight coil of fury. We have arrived back from school and are sitting around the table, ready to start our homework. Charlene has not been feeling well and so has been at home today. She is leaning against the radiator with a face like thunder, warning us of the storm ready to be unleashed if any of us raise her ire.

"Nothing," replies Serena, immediately casting her eyes downwards to her spellings.

"Well keep your eyes to yourself. I don't know why I even bother. What's so interesting over here anyway?"

"Leave her alone Charlene," Rebecca intervenes testily, trying to keep the peace. She is tired, Charlene having kept us up past two again the night before. This attempt at keeping the peace is a forlorn hope.

"Keep your nose out of this; it's none of your business. What has this got to do with you?" Charlene demands, immediately riled. "I'm sick of you sticking your nose in where it's not wanted."

"Wise up, Charlene," I interject, refusing to bite my too-quick tongue. "This is stupid." I know in my mind she is looking for a fight, that she seems to enjoy this and we should ignore her. However, I am finding this impossible at the minute and my frustration is continually on the verge of boiling up inside of me.

"Shut up, this is nothing to do with you. Why does everyone team up on me? You're all really annoying, why don't you just leave me alone?" she fires back, ice in her voice.

"I can't wait until you're at university and out of my way," Charlene spits at me, venom laced through her voice.

At that, Mum and Dad enter the room and the dynamic shifts, as Charlene pulls on another mask. Suddenly, all sweetness and light, her attitude transforms.

"Mum, did you see this? I saw a competition I could enter." She smiles sweetly, as if butter would not melt in her mouth; bile rises in my throat as a fist of anger shifts in my gut. She can shift roles effortlessly, hurling foul abuse at us and crying tears of rage one minute, but when the doorbell rings, she instantly becomes charming towards visitors. They pay special attention to poor, sick, innocent Charlene; if only they knew what she was really like! She often does the same with us: acting angelic with Mum and Dad, then sticking her claws in us when their backs are turned. It feels like we are trapped in a game of her own devising and I feel powerless to protect my sisters.

It strikes me then that I feel nothing for Charlene. If anything, I loathe her for what she is doing. I certainly do not feel an emotional love, when all she seems to do is take a twisted joy in hurting those around her. She seems to treat love as if it is a game, playing fast and loose with all of us: I hate her for it. I have seen the twins cry too many times and I have listened at night as Mum and Dad weep quietly, utterly exhausted. Too many times, we have had next to no sleep and then carefully fastened on our masks and gone into school with a painted smile as if everything is normal. How is any of this normal??!!

A painful question blasts rights to the core of my soul and weighs on my heart like an anchor that feels heavier with each breath I take. Don't I love my sister?

The voice on the phone chatters on incessantly. It is a close friend of Janice – one of the few people she confides in as to how bad things are and how much she is struggling. Her friend now shares what she is calling some 'home truths'.

Janice sits in the car park of Sprucefield, where she had earlier done some shopping in the lead up to Christmas. The car park is relatively quiet at this time of the morning as she holds the phone to her ear.

The voice stops for a breath, as if building up courage for what they are about to say. Janice feels dread coil in her gut. Then the voice continues. "Janice, you seriously need to consider giving Charlene up. Look at the pain she is inflicting on everyone. She is destroying your family and if you don't, the rest of your kids will end up resenting you."

She sits speechless, still holding the phone close to her ear. Her head shakes as if buffeted from winds on all sides; conflicting currents tug her heart and thoughts charge through her mind like an express train. "I have to go," she mutters, laying the phone in front of her and cutting the voice off mid flow.

She sits staring out at the everyday mundane goings on ahead of her: a magpie flies down and picks at scraps of an abandoned takeaway meal, a red car drives past her, a young couple walk close to her car holding hands, laughing at a shared memory. Although her eyes register these surface observations, she sees none of this. She is seeing very different images now.

She sees Charlene screaming, her eyes bubbling with poison as vile and venomous words drip from her lips. She sees her smile with malice as she slings a wicked barb at one of her sisters, reducing them to tears. She sees her rage across the room, leaving a trail of destruction in her wake.

She sees other faces too. She sees her husband crushed by the cruel words flung at him and David, his face an angry snarl defending his twin sisters. She sees Rebecca, giving up on being a peacemaker and growing increasingly withdrawn. She sees Natalie speaking to no one of her feelings, and contempt flying between her and Charlene. She sees Bethany crying, terrified of what she sees; Serena is stoic and unspeaking, her face blank. Now, she sees nothing as tears flow unobstructed down her face.

She wanted to help this child; that had been her dream. She had believed God had brought them all together. She loved her as her own, but Charlene had rejected her love and laughed mockingly in the face of it. How had it come to this? If this situation was truly God's plan, it would never have come to this, never! Where is God in all of this? Is He here? She slams her hands against the steering wheel in despair and the tears roll down her cheeks, unchecked.

Are her friend's words true? There seems to be no hope; she constantly worries about what this is doing to her family, who they are becoming. Deep down, she fears that the stark words her friend has spoken are indeed true. Will her other children resent her if they continue down this torturous, cruel road? She puts her face in her hands and weeps unashamedly. She weeps until she can weep no more and wrestles with God as she had years before

Family holiday

when she feared losing Charlene to another placement.

Time ceases to exist as she begs, cajoles and most of all, implores God for guidance. Are her friend's words guidance? Surely not? In spite of it all, the thought of giving up on Charlene sickens her to her core. As she prays, she feels a calm presence she cannot understand which reminds her of the love transplanted long ago into her heart. Then she knows that no matter what comes, her friend is wrong. She could no more give up on Charlene than she could her own heart. Never. Charlene is her daughter, even if she desires or chooses not to be. Nothing could change that. They chose this path, to be there for Charlene through all her illnesses. Charlene will never end her life the way she had spent her first year – alone.

But what would this road do to her family, to her other children? They had made the decision long ago. This dark path with traps everywhere, with fire raining down and attacks from every side. What will it do to them?

Wiping tears from her eyes, she picks up her Bible notes for the day and turns to the day's reading. As her eyes scan the page, her eyes then widen and threaten to flood with tears again and she whispers words of thanks to God above. He has handed her a promise. She reads aloud so her ears can hear the beautiful words.

"All your children shall be taught by the LORD,
And great will be the peace of your children."
Isaiah 54:13

As the words resonate through her head and heart, she looks to the heavens with tear-stained cheeks and smiles. "I'm holding you to this God!" she says. She feels as if a weight has been lifted from her shoulders. She feels as if she can see a light in the darkness, but knows the path ahead will not be easy. The cost will still be great. But she knows she is meant to walk it and has been called to walk it; she could never do anything otherwise.

As she hums a song of praise to God, with heart alight, she puts the car in gear and drives home.

10
WAR FOR THE SOUL

THEY SOUGHT SUPPORT FROM SOCIAL SERVICES long ago as they tried to figure out the best way forward for the whole family. Some coping strategies had been suggested and Charlene has started to occasionally stay at both grandparents' houses at weekends. Pat and Terry, the couple who had visited her often throughout her first year of life have also opened their home to her. They are all aware of the situation, but while at their homes, Charlene would be an angel, storing up her rage, which would be flung at her immediate family when she returns home.

Still, the fight continues within her. In her times of clarity, she would open up. "I need those times, Mummy. I need to get offside for a while to cope and I enjoy getting away. When I am home all the time I don't know what happens to me, I just don't know why I act the way I do. I can't help it. I try, I swear it," she says one day, face tortured and drawn. Her face crumbles in on itself as she starts to weep.

Janice pulls her close and lets her cry, shushing her gently. "I know Charlene, I know. We will keep working on this, but you must remember how your words and actions impact others."

She pulls her head back and looks at her, face earnest. "I will, I will Mum. Things are going to be different now, I swear it."

Despite this, they aren't. Not yet. Nevertheless, Janice believes they will be: someday. They have a promise.

As she pushes the hoover around Charlene's room, she shakes her head at the mess. The room is a disaster. She wonders again about the future. Charlene will soon finish Lurgan Junior High; she is approaching the end of her third year and the question of where she should go next looms large in Janice's mind.

She pushes the Hoover to the edge of Charlene's bed as she contemplates, mentally running through the options; she is pulled out of her reverie as the Hoover begins to choke on something. She turns it off and bends down to see what is causing the problem. As soon as she does, the smell hits her like a wave, assaulting her nostrils. She sees telltale crumbs leading like a trail under Charlene's bed, so she lifts the trail of the covers to see where they lead. Her heart stops and she gasps at what she sees.

Stacks of food lie in piles, stuffed beneath her bed again. This isn't the first time that Charlene has been hoarding and hiding food. Strewn amongst the hoard is her medication, with capsules and tablets scattered throughout the mess. Charlene has not been taking her treatments; this explained why her health had been dipping for a time. "Why? What is the sense in this?" Janice whispers, her mind in a tailspin. She fights the despair sinking its claws into her resolve, then fetches a pair of kitchen gloves, holds her breath and sets to work.

The conversation that night walks the familiar path, beginning with rage flung at everyone else and ending with bitter tears of remorse. Sitting in a crumpled heap on the floor, Charlene begs for help. And neither Janice nor Dickie know what to do. They pray with Charlene and the next morning they phone social services again. As her husband makes the call, Janice's stomach knots and she recites to herself the passage she read that day in the car, which has become like a comfort blanket, a fountain from which she continually drinks precious hope, however it does not make the painful realities of life any easier. She knows where they want to be, but how will they ever get there? The future looks bleak and unforgiving, threatening to squeeze all of the life out of all of them. They must live life one day at a time. Again, her thoughts spin like a compass seeking direction for the thought that dominates her mind: how are the rest of her children coping?

As I sit on my bed lost in darkness, the house is silent. I am still tense, half expecting to hear Charlene storming upstairs again; for now, it is quiet. In the still of night, there is no escape from the emotions churning and threatening to overwhelm me like a tsunami. Although at first I resist, due to my fear of what I will find, I begin to examine my own heart and the unspoken thoughts that swirl around me. My thoughts begin to flow, so I flick on the lamp beside my head and allow my hand to transcribe the scenes racing through my mind and before my eyes.

I would love to say I am faultless in all of this, but deep in my heart, I know I am not. My pen bites into the paper as I write. I write furiously, as if this will exorcise the storm brewing in my mind. It breaks me to see the pain she causes my parents, my sisters and especially the twins. As they are the youngest, I feel most protective of Bethany and Serena and ever since Charlene has threatened them with a hockey stick, albeit half-mockingly, I have become even more so. In my mind, Charlene can go for weeks without uttering a kind word; all we experience is her coldness. We have all reacted in different ways; some of the girls have closed themselves off, others live with a fixed smile, hiding what is beneath the surface. Rebecca responds with a patience that speaks of her grace. As for me, in honesty, I know I now cannot stand her, and there is little love lost between us. I feel nothing but rage.

I stop, breathing heavily and set the journal down. A shadow hugs the face of the moon, thickening the darkness outside. What is going on in Charlene's head? What is happening to our family? The atmosphere in our house shifts and changes with the wind, as if a war is being waged: different sides gaining then losing ground. It certainly feels like a war of attrition.

On top of my confusion, I feel guilt coiling around me like a snake as it sinks its jaws in deep and sucks all assurances from my world. Don't I love Charlene? What is wrong with me? Guilt is there with every breath, like a stone in your shoe that wears away at your skin with every step you take. Other questions emerge out of the haze in my mind. How does everyone else feel? If this is a war being fought over Charlene then surely we are all losing? What is love anyway?

The cloud passes from the face of the moon and a thread of a thought passes through my mind, which I claw at desperately: 1 Corinthians 13. That famous passage of love, read at every wedding I have ever been at. "Love is patient, love is kind. It does not envy, it does not boast, it is not proud." None of those phrases refer to an emotion, but to an action. Was love more than a feeling?

In those days I begin to learn a lesson I have tried to cling to since, a lesson our culture has forgotten long ago. It is the simple fact that love is a choice. Too much of the time media tells us that love is all to do with emotions, the glorious joining of two hearts, a joyous 'Hallelujah'. Similarly, we all know stories of people falling 'out of love'. In all of this love is portrayed as a matter of the heart, something which can come and go, mysterious like the wind. There is little we can do once it catches us except follow its urging no matter if it is right or wrong, and less we can do once it is mysteriously gone. People marry and divorce due to the fluctuating tugs of 'love', or so we believe.

That is a lie, or worse, a partial half-truth. Like most lies it contains a grain of truth, as obviously love will often involve emotion. But not always. Emotion is a by-product of love, not love itself. It runs deeper, love is a choice.

While Charlene is ripping my family to shreds, hurting my other sisters, and not saying a kind word for months, emotionally, if I am honest, I detest her. It tears me apart. Nevertheless there is a deeper truth to which I cling, more solid than my capricious emotions, which change hourly at the slightest provocation: no matter what she does or what she says, Charlene will always be my sister. I know I will always love her, because this love is not based on my emotional state. No matter what happens, I know we will always be there for her and care for her, because she is family. We will always love her, because love is a daily fight and struggle, a daily decision to say yes even when emotions churn, so much deeper than how you feel. But this kind of love is hard.

If God wrote me a letter about what He sees in me, it would say...

She tells lies a lot, can be mean and abusive. Loves me but doesn't really show it even though she reads her Bible and prays.

Try harder.

Lots of love,
God

(Charlene's Journal)

We sit in the car ready to head to church, after a gruelling day long struggle with Charlene. Our nerves are balanced precariously on a knife-edge as Charlene sits in the back alongside Rebecca and Natalie. She looks up and stares, a glint in her eye and her face scrunched up in anger.

"You all wouldn't care if I got run over by a f*****g bus," she spits, her voice wielded like a knife. At first we sit in stunned silence as her words wash over us, and then as one, we children dissolve into tears.

Church is not to be that night. We leave the car in tears, torn to shreds for a number of reasons. Firstly, the thought that Charlene could think that breaks our hearts. After everything that has happened, how could she say this? Secondly, guilt for our part in the arguments that have preceded the moment in the car sweeps over each of us. Thirdly, while this may seem small to some, Charlene has never sworn before. To hear your sister swear at you with such hatred in her voice is a watershed moment; it breaks each of us.

Charlene herself is instantly remorseful, seeing the pain her words have inflicted. She scrambles from the car, weeping as she follows us, apologising profusely. Even in her apologies, I know that this situation will replay itself in short course, like a CD stuck on perpetual repeat. Charlene is at war with herself, with half of her desperately wanting to love and be loved, whilst the other half bitterly and violently rejects any such love. However, the rest of us are caught in the crossfire.

A thought flashes through my mind as I sit down later. Church seems irrelevant now. Where is God in all of this? Whilst my family is being torn asunder, all we can hear is silence from above. I feel alone. What is the purpose of this? Why is this happening? Surely God could reach down and solve all of this in an instant and bring healing, ending the pain that is destroying those I love so dearly? A phrase from nowhere strikes me, derailing my thought processes.

Sometimes the most beautiful things have to be broken first.

Charlene spends the night screaming from her room, yelling vile things at Mum and Dad; I stand quietly in the kitchen. Today I do not feel rage, I just feel lost and helpless. All I want to do is help, but how?

Before I know what I am doing, I walk past Mum and Dad into Charlene's room. "What's wrong Charlene?" I ask from the doorway. Mum and Dad let me speak, standing silent as sentinels behind me. Charlene calms briefly, shaking her head as if emerging from a deep sleep. She looks at me. Her defiance falls away like a cracked mask. Sudden tears run down her cheeks as if a dam has burst and all of a sudden, she does not look fierce. She looks like a lost little girl, so desperately alone. She whimpers, in a voice so frail I have to move closer to hear it. "I'm afraid David. I have said such terrible things. I am afraid. I'm afraid you will send me away after what I've done."

My heart is moved, and without thinking, I reply with words that sound clichéd. Yet, they speak the deeper truth I have worked through in my head in the previous weeks and months. "Charlene, we all love you so much. You can never be sent away. Once a Barr, always a Barr."

Without waiting for a reply, I turn and leave the room, walking slowly to my bedroom. As I lie in my bed, I try to come to grips with the truth that flowed from my lips before I drift into the arms of my dreams. "Once a Barr, always a Barr." Where had that come from? It sounds so cheesy but I know it embodies truth; just like each one of us, nothing Charlene does will change her identity. She is our sister; this will always remain true, no matter what happens.

None of us will ever stop seeing her as our flesh and blood, our sister. In her mind she is different through birth, in ours, she is different only because she pushes everyone else away. Despite my personal feelings towards her when she hurts others I love dearly, she will never cease to be one of us. The bond that was made in a cold, stark courtroom has taken on a deeper, painful meaning in the years that have followed. That bond can never be broken.

Doubtless, there is immense pain in the midst of this onslaught. I don't know how Mum and Dad are navigating these dark times; this is costing all of my family a lot, but I know in that instant that we wouldn't have it any other way. Indeed, love covers a multitude of sins.

I grab my pen and quickly write down my thoughts before they evaporate like morning dew. "Never be fooled into thinking that unconditional love does not bear a terrible cost. But it is a cost worth paying."

I sleep more soundly that night than I have in a long time.

Lord please help me!

Love Charlene

(Charlene's Journal)

As Charlene sits on her knee, Janice can feel the stiffness and cold anger throughout her daughter's body. Despite this, Charlene remains rigidly on her knee, not wanting to leave the only safe place in this room that stares back at her with so many truths openly displayed on the walls. Charlene has kept these truths locked away deep within for years where she thought no one would ever see. Now they confront her and she sits sullen and rigid.

As she sits with Charlene, who refuses to fully accept any embrace she tries to give, Janice feels spurned and hurt. After talking for so long in this session, Charlene's innermost conflicts and struggles are bubbling to the surface, and Janice knows her daughter feels raw and vulnerable. Her carefully concealed wounds are exposed for all in this room to see. As Charlene sits unyielding, Janice breathes a prayer for a miracle, a breath of hope, anything.

It has been a long road. As part of the support provided by social services, they had contacted Dr McCune from the Child Psychiatry Unit, who had carried out a lot of work with the family for a number of months. His work had helped keep Janice sane as the promise she had been given grew in its emptiness as pain was piled on top of pain. His work had given her hope, although it had also been painful.

Some memories were still branded into her skull. She could still see one of the sessions where her family had sat together and talked of how they were feeling. Seeing the tears stream from her children's eyes as they discussed agonising words and images that were seared into their consciences had rent her asunder. She had sobbed as she heard Bethany and Serena, who were so innocent and quiet, speak for the first time of burdens they carried, of fears they held. All of them, including Charlene, poured out their hearts and wept together. She had hoped then that healing had finally come, but, as always, hope had evaporated like water from a lake in the desert and the next day brought a fresh wave of cruel abuse from Charlene.

Janice had begun to conclude in her heart that the battle was being lost. As the days flew past in repeating waves of wearying wars within their home, she had felt as if she was drowning. Moreover, the need for such professional help made her feel like a failure as a mother. She felt like she was grasping desperately for a rope in rolling, turbulent waters which threatened to overwhelm her. Nonetheless, the sessions with Dr McCune had brought a semblance of calm to them and she was grateful for this at least.

He had referred them to an organisation called Keys in England and suggested they go with Charlene for an assessment. She and Dickie had travelled over with her and, while there, therapists had observed Charlene and diagnosed her with Attachment Disorder. They explained that she would instinctively push anyone who got too close away, a result of her experience in her first year of life. She had not had one constant caregiver and though she had been cared for so well by so many of the staff in hospital, they could not compensate for the continual absence of a mother.

They had been backwards and forwards across to England and Sheila and Anne, the therapists, had carried out extensive work with Charlene. This was where they were now; Charlene had spent some time with Sheila and Anne earlier in the day and now Janice was summoned into the room to join them. Apprehension had speared at Janice's gut as she entered, unsure what to expect from Charlene, who strode dutifully to Janice and sat calmly on her knee. As soon as they sat, however, it was apparent how cold and rigid Charlene was. The tension was thick in the room, so thick you could taste it.

As Janice sits, her eyes roam around the room, taking in the strange patterns along the wall. A long roll of wallpaper has been stuck up with Blu-Tack and is wrapped around the room, clinging to the walls on all sides. Bricks have been drawn on this strip of wallpaper and at random intervals, she recognises Charlene's scrawl inside certain bricks.

Before she can squint her eyes to read them, Sheila's voice cuts through the tension like a hot knife through butter. "Charlene and I have been talking for a while before you arrived Janice," she says kindly. "Do you remember what we talked about Charlene?"

At first Charlene sits stoically and unrelenting, but as the silence thickens around her like a cloak, she spits a single word into the air. "Yes."

"Charlene, let's recap for the benefit of your mother," Sheila responds, eyes fixed on her. "You have built a wall around you that you think will keep you safe. You don't let anyone else get close to you; you told me this earlier didn't you?"

This time her reply comes more quickly and Janice can feel the tension and struggle in which Charlene is gripped. It scares her. "Yes," Charlene says.

"Your family have been trying to break through to you, trying so hard, but you won't let them. They have been using all sorts of tools to find a way through the wall, but they can't. Why is that Charlene?"

Charlene turns slowly towards Janice and looks her in the eyes. For a second she can see the torment behind her daughter's eyes, the struggle as two sides of her struggle for dominance. Charlene turns back to Sheila, and with her voice shaking now she murmurs, "Because I have all the strength. I built the wall, only I can take it down."

Janice feels the fight in her daughter. She reaches to pull her close but Charlene still resists, shrugging her off. She is fighting to release herself from the chains that bind her, but she is still putting up so many barriers around her. Why? What is the purpose of this session?

As if reading her thoughts, Sheila looks at her with compassion in her eyes. "We have spent some time today looking at this wall, Janice. We have put a roll of wallpaper all around this room with bricks drawn on, and before we brought you in, Charlene had been writing some of the things she has been doing to keep everyone else out inside these bricks."

As Sheila's words roll around her, Janice's eyes dart around the room like those of a frightened animal. As understanding of what these bricks represent wash over her, she squints and reads some of Charlene's scrawl. One brick directly ahead of her reads 'hoarding food', another to her right reads 'answering back', yet another reads 'trying to hurt brother and sisters'. There are more, so many more, so many bricks filled with defences Charlene has been constructing for years. Janice feels powerless. The walls with the bricks seem to constrict around them, and she feels as if the bricks are about to fall and crush all of them. She can't save her daughter. She prays again. "Please help Charlene," she whispers. "I can't. I just can't."

Sheila continues, her voice firm, like a rock to hold onto in a storm. "Charlene, it is too much to ask you to pull down these bricks all at once, but you must choose one, you must make a start. With every brick you take out the wall will get weaker. This is up to you now; which brick will you remove? What do you want to change?"

Her words hang in the air, which seems to thicken around them. Janice reaches tentatively for Charlene's shoulder, but again she is shrugged off. Charlene seems to shake from the battle raging within but she still does not speak. Nobody breaks the silence; it becomes suffocating and the accusing words written on the wall scream out from the bricks, mocking and cruel. Janice looks above her and mouths a prayer. "Please help her God. You promised. Please help her."

Charlene stops her struggle suddenly and all of the emotions swirling through Janice's mind grind to a halt as she waits for her words. Charlene turns to look at her again, blinking rapidly. She looks so tired, but as she stares into her mother's eyes she sighs as a thin smile slowly draws across her face. She then turns back to Sheila.

Charlene with Janice in Tollymore Forest Park

Her voice splits through the thick atmosphere like a thunderclap, dispelling the dark sceptres that had seemed to gather all around. "It's Mum," she croaks, her voice rough with emotion. "I want to change that brick." Her voice grows stronger as she speaks. "I want to trust Mum more and let her in. I want to trust that she loves me." As soon as she stops speaking she crumbles into her mother's arms, letting her hold her and soothe her. She seems utterly spent from the ordeal.

As her words still hang in the air, Janice hears a whistle ring through the room as the wallpaper strip of bricks tumbles down as one onto the floor, leaving the walls all around them white. The wallpaper of bricks with their painful mocking words lies unseen on the floor. The air is now still and Janice can feel peace, an undeniable presence in the air; she knows they are not alone and have never been alone ever in all of this. Something profound and deeper than she will ever understand has just happened.

Sheila looks at Janice holding her daughter, clears her throat and speaks. "Something really amazing has happened in this room just now." Slowly she walks to the door and leaves them alone; as Charlene silently clings to her mother, letting her hold her and love her while Janice whispers prayers of thanks.

11
TENTATIVE STEPS

CHANGE NEVER COMES QUICKLY; patterns are broken slowly, like a great granite face being slowly eroded down chip by chip. But every change begins somewhere.

New Year's Resolutions for 2005
Charlene
More respect
Better behaviour
Less selfish
Family Resolution
To be a family that impacts for God across the world

(Family Resolutions Book)

As part of their management and support, social services suggest periods of respite for Charlene and the family, so that she will have her own space to think things through. Charlene is close to finishing her three years at Lurgan Junior High School and one of the solutions they recommend is Armagh Royal School, where Charlene can board during the week and return home at weekends. While this seems hard for us, it is immediately clear that Charlene loves the idea of having her own space during the week.

She moves in during September 2005 and immediately sets to work decorating her room. She settles into Armagh Royal like a duck to water and, despite initial fears of her anger flaring up whilst at school, she is a model pupil and looks forward to returning home each weekend.

Time passes and though so much changes, so much stays the same. Charlene still wrestles with the beast inside of her and tries to conquer the darkness within. Like all of us, she fails as much as she succeeds. Some days she will erupt and the pain is as unbearable as it has always been.

Nevertheless, the time at Keys and Armagh Royal, where she processes so much emotion, changes her. It is often a case of two steps forward and one step back, but there is incremental progress for all of us. We begin to have weeks when things are good; Charlene's respite periods mean she is less likely to be overwhelmed by the riptide of conflicting emotions that swell around her when we are together. A sense of normalcy none of us dared hope for begins to settle around us.

27th June 2006

To Mum and Dad,

This is just a wee note to say I love you both loads and loads. As I sit here thinking about the past year I'm like WOW, I remember coming to view the school, then I blinked and here I am coming towards my GCSE year at RSA. I just wanted to say a big thank you for choosing this school, I have loved every minute of it. I owe you so much because if it wasn't for you two CRAZY people hanging in there for me and giving me another chance to be part of your WONDERFUL family, then I wouldn't be here today. Ever since I started boarding it has opened my eyes into just how much I take each and every one of you for granted, but now when I come home at weekends I realise how PRECIOUS you are.

Anyway I just want to say a HUGE thank you, not just for this past year but since you took me under your wings (little did you know what you had let yourself in for!). I really cannot wait until the summer playing out in the garden and just being together as a family, especially at Center Parcs (Pancake House!). I just want you to know that I am going to work SO hard at things during the summer because I really do not want to go back to the old ways (I'm 100% sure none of you want me to either).

Anyway I have babbled too much, but one more thing. I want you to know you are the BEST Mum and Dad in the world, and I could never imagine life without you. I LOVE everything about the way our family are, there is never a dull moment in the Barr house.

I love you so so much and please forgive me for all the stupid things I have said and done, I didn't mean any of it. I hope you both have a WONDERFUL summer even if it is BEDLAM! 4 weeks, 6 days until Center Parcs!

God bless and loads of love,
Charlene xx

(Letter written to Mum and Dad by Charlene)

One event that shows us how Charlene's heart is changing is the death of her beloved Grandma*. Over the years, Charlene seemed to encase herself in an ivory tower where nothing could touch her or hurt her. When loved ones, even her Granny**, who had been there for her died, Charlene remained stoic. That was before her time at Keys. This time it was different.

Grandma had always been so good to all of us, babysitting and being ever present at birthday parties, Christmas and family meals. Every day we got off the bus in Waringstown and walked to our Grandma and Poppa's house, where Grandma inevitably had a steaming bowl of Irish stew waiting for each of us. We laughed, joked and played with her. On Christmas Day, she would always sit at the kid's table with us and play our games; she was special and loved so much by all of us.

Through the hard times, Charlene had often gone to Granny's house and Grandma and Poppa's house for respite and their love for her had been instrumental in her healing. Grandma had given her a teddy, which she treasured and brought to her room at Armagh Royal where it took pride of place. They often joked together and teased one another, sharing a special bond.

In the summer of 2005, Grandma developed back pains. This was a surprise as she was rarely ill and ever fit as a fiddle, climbing a mountain with us that summer on a family holiday in County Fermanagh, with everyone else struggling to keep pace with her. She was diagnosed with stomach cancer and, despite a torturous course of chemotherapy, the cancer was too advanced and she passed away surrounded by the family in the winter of 2006.

Charlene is disconsolate. She weeps in memory of the unique bond she has lost. While Grandma lies in her coffin, she asks if she can place the beloved teddy beside her Grandma's earthly remains, something Poppa is more than happy for her to do.

It proves heart wrenching saying goodbye to a woman who has been such a huge part of all of our lives, but never before have we seen Charlene so distraught and broken by the loss of someone she loved. Yet, now she mourns, with natural grief, for a lost relationship that was undiluted by her stoic reluctance to love deeply. Watching her grieve shows us that she is changing and even in the midst of this painful time, hope blooms.

However there are still days that wind back the years. Still on family holidays, or on birthdays, the dragon can stir and rise up, and Charlene can inflict the most deadly wounds on all of us and on herself. Screams still can

---

Grandma and Poppa – Charlene's maternal grandparents
** *Granny – Charlene's paternal grandmother*

reverberate around the house, which summon the mocking ghosts we had hoped were gone forever. I wonder if things will ever truly change. Can a heart ever be completely healed? Looking at my own recurring mistakes, I struggle to believe it is possible.

Nonetheless, the final piece in the jigsaw comes from a place we never would have expected.

It is Christmas Day 2007 and we stand at the top of the stairs, trying not to fall over one another as Mum and Dad finish preparing the room we usually go into to open presents. As I yawn, I think it is unlikely we will be receiving presents this year.

Ever since Dad travelled to Uganda two years previously to do some HIV/AIDS prevention programmes in schools, that country had worked its way into our blood. Rebecca and I had travelled there the previous summer and fallen in love with the country and the people. From conversations over the dinner table, photos and stories shared, all the family had felt a burden grow for Uganda and we all became more dissatisfied with the commercial and self-obsessed world in which we were immersed.

This had led to the decision that this Christmas we would do without presents. We would not buy for each other and, instead of receiving anything from our parents, we had asked them to spend the money they would have spent on gifts for us on buying a goat or cow for a community in Uganda.

"Come on down," Dad's voice bellows from the room; there is an excited edge to it. We spiral down the stairs like a horde and pile into the room. Mum and Dad stand there, grinning from ear to ear and holding six envelopes with our names on them. They hand them out and we quickly tear them open, determined to satisfy our curiosity. As my eyes scan the page, confusion grips me at first as I try to decipher the words, then slowly understanding dawns on me and I stand open mouthed staring at my parents.

"What does this mean?" Serena queries.

"I don't understand," Natalie complains.

"Come on kids!" Dad exclaims. "Read it out Charlene." And she does.

Charlene Goat is booked for Uganda
Leaving Sunday 16th March
Returning Sunday 23rd March
Mum and Dad look forward to bringing their herd of goats
with them to Uganda
HAPPY CHRISTMAS OUR WEE GOAT

Rebecca stands with her mouth agog. "Does this mean we all are going to Uganda?"

"Yes, can you not read your letters?" Dad says smiling.

"Your handwriting is probably the problem Dickie," Mum interrupts, still beaming as she watches the idea grow on all of us.

A mixture of emotions churn within each of us as we realise what this means. Some are excited, others are nervous but mostly we are still incredulous.

"How can we afford this?" I ask aghast.

Mum glances at Dad for confirmation and after he nods, she starts to speak. "We were blessed.

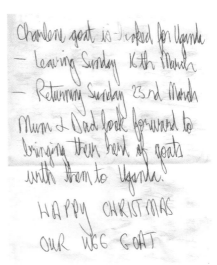

Charlene's Christmas Day 2007 letter informing her she was going to Uganda

This would never have been possible for us, we would never have had the money but good friends have anonymously given us the money to travel as a family. It would not be possible without them. They have blessed us incredibly."

Dad looks as if he could dance. "I've wanted to bring you all to Uganda with me for so long. I can't wait to introduce you to everyone there! Are you excited?"

We all start to chatter animatedly about the logistics of what the trip will look like. I am excited, and seeing my sisters' eyes bright at the thought enthuses me, but a knot of apprehension twists in my stomach too. How will Charlene react to all of this?

She stands quiet while everyone babbles to one another, like the calm eye at the centre of a furious hurricane. She reads and rereads her letter and her face is a mask. Then she looks up and smiles.

"It's fifty days until we go. I can't wait!"

One final reflection before moving on, if you will forgive me. This has been hard to chronicle for obvious reasons, least of all my own hard heart in these times. However many truths glimmer through the darkness of this difficult time I have been describing.

One deep truth that strikes me is that Charlene is exactly like each of us. In one moment, Charlene would throw words like daggers at those she claimed to love, hurting those who loved her in any way she could; in the next, she would write beautiful letters of apology. With the same tongue, she would spit curses and talk lovingly. Repeatedly, she would reject love and lash out at everyone around her, but then come back as if nothing had happened, not realising the emotional pain and cost she was inflicting on those who loved her most.

This is no different from our attitude towards God. Each of us, whether a believer or not, strikes out in rebellion against the God who loved us enough to die in our place by going our own way on our own terms. Often we later come back, expecting forgiveness and unaware of the pain we are causing the One who loves us. We do this again, and again, and do not realise the price this unconditional love bears.

Charlene would always be our sister, no matter how she hurt us. Equally, if we choose to follow Jesus, we will always be a son or daughter of the King, no matter how many times we strike out and go our own way because we are His.

However, love has a cost: a cost paid by Him. Grace – unearned, undeserved, unconditional love and complete forgiveness. It demands our everything in a response of love, while He bears all the rebellion we fling at Him as if we fire the very nails into His wrists. Mercy is not receiving what you deserve, grace is receiving what you do not deserve.

As the queue towards the flight moves onward, we all stand in silence, clinging to our hand luggage. Each of us has various thoughts swirling about in our heads, yet few of us vocalise them. Bethany and Serena are nervous, wondering how they will fit into the packed schedule Dad has planned. Natalie stands with her music flowing out of her speakers into her ears, but her rigid stance betrays her nerves. She is looking forward to the trip, but in some ways is not sure she wants to go. Time will tell.

Rebecca is humming away, looking forward to getting back to Uganda; she is excited about going back with her loved ones. Dad chatters quietly to an edgy Mum behind me, reassuring her and telling her this is the right thing to do, that God has provided. Charlene stands beside me, staring ahead, and I don't know what she is thinking. She carries in her travelling bag much of her medication. She is not speaking, just staring blankly ahead at the corridor leading to the plane. She has been so excited in the lead up to the trip, having written on her whiteboard how many days were remaining and letting us know the countdown on a day to day basis, yet here she stands, silent.

What is she thinking? Is she thinking of the pictures Dad has brought back from Uganda of the children she will soon see? Is she worried about how she will find things in this new climate with all her medication? Is she thinking about how God has been changing things for all of us? She stands silent, until the queue begins to move and we walk onto the plane to Uganda, where all of our lives will change forever.

If you could ask for one thing from the Lord, what would it be?
That he would let me go to Africa's orphanages if it is God's will.

(Charlene's Journal [2003])

Charlene's parents, Dickie and Janice celebrating their wedding anniversary in Uganda 2008

12
CRY OH BELOVED CONTINENT

AS I STAND AT THE FRONT I am very self-aware, noticing how sweaty my hands are and that I am shaking, very nervous before the sea of Ugandan faces. We are in a primary school just outside Kampala, the capital; hundreds of children sit quietly, listening to our every word. The crumbling building we are in is open on one side with a tin corrugated roof; I am thankful for the shelter as the sun beats down from above, baking anyone who steps outside. The generator roars in the background, providing power needed to run the projectors; the faint smell of petrol hangs in the air. We have suspended an old white sheet on the wall behind us to project on and I glance at it, seeing the title of the presentation: 'I'm Special, You're Special'.

I mumble through my introductions, feeling the weight of the children's eyes, but gradually relax as I go. The response to any question I ask is volunteered with a hundred hands and many of the answers make me smile, I am amazed at their honesty. All too soon, my section is over, and I hand over to Charlene and Natalie. Dad has asked all of us to play a part in the program and the two girls have prepared a role-play on friendship and peer pressure.

They stand quietly in their red T-shirts for a second. My brow furrows as I wonder if they are experiencing stage fright.

Then Charlene raises the mike to her mouth and launches herself, saying, "I'm so glad it's break time, that Maths was so hard."

"I couldn't get it at all, it was brutal!" Natalie responds, already playing her role well and with aplomb. I am not entirely sure that the Ugandan kids have heard the word brutal before in this context, but the two girls continue on, unperturbed.

"Well what were you doing at the weekend Natalie?" Charlene asks with confidence, clearly at home here in front of the Ugandan children. For a split second, an image of our younger selves performing Nativity plays flashes before me, then is gone.

"Well I went to see John, but his parents weren't at home. We talked for a long time, and we had a wee bit to drink - he had borrowed his parent's alcohol. We got drunk and well….well…," Natalie continues.

"Well what?"

"We had sex."

Charlene stands in silence, looking shocked. At this point, I don't know if this is part of their pre-prepared script or if she has forgotten her lines, but it works regardless.

Charlene in Uganda

Natalie continues, "It was great Charlene, you're missing out on so much. You should do it too, go on, don't be afraid, you would be stupid not to."

Charlene looks uncomfortable, "I don't know, should I?"

At this, they finish the drama and Charlene gives her mike to Rebecca, who talks with the kids about what decision Charlene should make and about peer pressure. As Rebecca speaks, Charlene and Natalie come back to sit down; she sits beside Mum and cuddles in. "You did well Charlene," Mum whispers and gives her a hug. Charlene smiles and the presentation continues.

The week flies by, with Dad having packed in a crowded schedule. We travel from school to school, both primary and secondary, delivering presentations and meeting a huge number of Ugandans. Wherever we go, we are humbled by the hospitality. Every time a presentation is finished, we are herded into the headmaster's office, where we are asked to sign the Visitors' Book, and are all offered soft drinks. Soft drinks or 'sodas' are not usually drunk in Uganda, they are an expensive luxury for the average person to buy.

They are sold in glass bottles, which are reused after they are finished. At first we refuse, knowing it is a sacrifice by the staff to offer us this when they have so little, yet every time they insist. Thinking of my own attitudes towards guests and indeed towards many things, I am humbled, and realise how we often fall short in the West.

Charlene loves her time there, especially her time with the children. Each time I look at her, she is holding a baby or playing a clapping game with a young child; her eyes dance as she laughs with them.

One thing Charlene, Mum and the girls love more than anything else are the bookmarks. Every night we stay up late making bookmarks out of card, writing Bible verses and decorating them with pictures. Every time I draw something, we play a game of guess what the picture is, as my artwork admittedly leaves a lot to be desired. At the end of every presentation, we give these out to each child along with sweets we have brought. From their reactions, you would have thought we had given them a note for 10,000 Ugandan shillings (about three pounds). Their eyes light up and they compare their bookmarks with their friends. As Dad and I load our speakers and other electrical equipment onto the roof of our minibus, I stop momentarily and look towards the rest of our family. As I watch my sisters, it is clear that all of them are falling in love with Uganda.

Lord Jesus,

I really do not know how to start this wee letter. As you know I have been nowhere near being a Christian and I am sorry. From this day I want to commit my life to you. I know I have always said that I'm a Christian, but over the last wee while I have felt like a 'Sunday morning Christian' and that isn't good enough, after all you're not a 'Sunday morning God' (thank goodness!). So from now on I am gonna live my life 120% for you. I know it'll be hard sometimes to stand up for what's right but I'm prepared to take whatever Satan throws at me. Thank you so much for all you have given to me, you are AWESOME. I ask please that you will help me whenever I get into bother and that you will forgive my failings.

All my love,
Charlene xxxxxxxxxxxxxxxxxxxxxxx

(Charlene's Journal)

The horns blare all around us as we sit in a traffic jam in Kampala. There is gridlock, with traffic converging on all sides into the street we sit on. Traffic laws seem optional here and I smile as I watch a minibus and taxi play chicken; both nose in front of a car whose driver is tooting his horn and shaking his fist angrily, while inching forward himself. Boda-bodas, the motorbikes that serve as taxis, weave in and out of the traffic, often taking considerable risks. It is mad out there.

The air is humid in the early evening and I can feel, even more than I can see, the storm swelling. The atmosphere feels electric and the hairs on my arm rise as it hangs outside the window of our minibus. It has been a day where the sun has beat down relentlessly, baking the dry earth, but now all the moisture that has been sapped into the atmosphere is gathering to return. Huge black clouds like hands, waiting to crash down on the earth below, gather above us and swallow the sun. The tension in the air is palpable.

Inside the bus some of us sleep and a few snores are heard from the back of the bus, where Rebecca is lounged across a row of seats, exhausted from the long day. The rest of us are singing loudly, with various competing tunes belting out of our mouths, rehearsing some of the songs we sing with the Ugandan kids. They tend to sing a lot better than we can ever attempt, and the most I can say for our cacophony is that it is a joyful noise.

Still the storm builds but does not break. We grind forwards in the traffic slowly, making any headway we can. Even though it is only early evening, outside is becoming black as night and the air is fast chilling. The clouds cover the entire horizon now and hang ominously as if ready to fall upon everything around us.

All at once they pour their grievances upon the earth. First one drop, then another. Then the air is thick with cold rain. They drum on our roof and bounce off the ground, turning dusty roads into muddy rivers. Still, the traffic slowly trawls forwards and we fall silent; it is hard to be heard above the din of the rain.

We continue to crawl through the traffic, listening to the onslaught of rain and watching as lightning splits the sky in two. The thunder rolls across the sky, as if a great battle is being fought far above our heads. The rain pours relentlessly, soaking everything I can see around me.

Suddenly Charlene pipes up from behind me. "Isn't the equipment on the roof?" We all sit in stunned silence for a second, hearing the heavy drops battering down on the roof above us as the thought seeps through our minds and the disaster dawns on us. It will be drenched!

Immediately Dad and I scramble for the door and heave it open. Dad pushes me up and I haul myself onto the slick roof, struggling to maintain a grip as I slip and slide. Cars behind us toot their horns as I hurriedly untie the sensitive sound equipment from the roof, where they have been exposed to the deluge for some time, and pass them down to Dad who hauls them into shelter. We do this as quickly as possible and I eventually swing myself back onto the bus.

I step onboard with my clothes stuck to my skin and rivulets of water rolling down me. I look at the equipment, and it is drenched as streams of water pour out of it. How will it ever work now? How could we have forgotten about it?

"This is a disaster," I mutter. The atmosphere feels deflated as we look at the equipment, wondering how we are going to do the rest of the week's programme without it. Suddenly Natalie giggles. "It is kind of funny though. How did no one remember the equipment?"

"And look at David. He looks like a drowned dog!" Charlene cackles, and suddenly we are all in stitches. Dad, who a moment ago had been standing sombre, now stands with a smile splitting his face as we laugh together. It is a situation where we have to either laugh or cry, and for now we choose the former.

Eventually Dad quietens us down. "I don't know what we will do if this equipment doesn't work but we will cope. Well done in remembering Charlene, it could have been a lot worse. I don't know how but it could have been! We will let it dry out tomorrow, and then Dave and I can test it at night. Let's pray now, to thank God for the day and also for a miracle with the equipment, because it will take a miracle!"

We bow our heads and close our eyes, blocking out the traffic and the lightning shattering the sky outside and we pray together, just as we have every night on the way home on the bus. Charlene opens the prayers. "God, thank you for our time here, and for our family. Thank you for all the people we have met. I know you can do anything God, any miracle, and I pray that somehow you will dry out the equipment and it will work good as new. Amen."

The next day when Dad and I test the equipment, it works as good as new.

What things do you want to thank God for?
The family He has given me. Showering me with His love even though I don't deserve any of it.

(Charlene's Journal)

The dust rises in clouds from the dirt-packed road as our group walk along it. Dickie leads the way chatting to Daniel, a local Ugandan pastor he is working with in the region of Luwero, north of the Ugandan capital Kampala. Janice walks beside them, listening to their conversation, but the rest of their family are skipping and singing as they follow behind, with a throng of Ugandan children keeping step, every footprint slamming into the dirt sending a cloud of dry dust into the air.

They are talking about the needs of the community when Daniel suddenly stops and looks back at the horde behind them. Their cries and laughs swirl around them like a storm. Daniel smiles and turns back towards the pair of them, and says, "Look at your children."

Dickie stops and watches. David is running around with a boy clinging desperately to his back, laughing as he is spun around and around and around. Rebecca is in the midst of a crowd leading them in song as they walk along. Charlene is tickling a little one who is dissolving in gales of laughter as they walk hand in hand. Natalie is chasing a number of children, weaving in and out of the throng. Bethany and Serena stick close together, each flanked by a number of Ugandan children latched to their arms. All of them are lost in the moment, playing and enjoying their time with the children they have met.

"You have done well Janice and Dickie," Daniel intones softly. "You have brought your children to Uganda when their hearts are still soft. Now they see."

Dickie looks at his wife and they smile to one another. They pray daily for their children and often through the painful years, it has felt like their prayers have gone unheeded but dawn has begun to break through, and they hope desperately that Daniel's words are true.

Daniel continues. "They see now. Uganda will claim some of your children, Janice and Dickie; their hearts have been broken for it."

The words hang in the air for a second and, although he does not know why, Dickie knows the words carry a deeper significance than he currently can comprehend. *'Claim their children...'*

As the crowd behind catch up with them, the moment is gone. A young girl reaches and grasps his hand, looking up expectantly. Dickie smiles and, with the rest of his family, he continues to walk down the dirt road.

The horn of the minibus toots and we know it is time to go. Charlene and Rebecca are sitting beside the bus surrounded by kids, all jumping around them and fighting for attention. I watch curious, as one small girl continually rubs at Charlene's arm with her fingers, with confusion written across her face. Slowly the girls rise and we scramble onto the bus, waving goodbye as we go and yelling 'God bless' in Lugandan.

As the bus drives off, we all immediately start to chatter and share stories of our latest experiences. "Charlene, why was that girl rubbing your arm like that?" I ask, imitating the action.

"Her name is Barbara, and I think she was rubbing it to see if my skin is black underneath the whiteness." We laugh; this makes sense, I have had the hair pulled on my arms multiple times for the same reasons.

Two of the children Charlene met in Uganda

I stare out the window and the familiar Ugandan sights roll past. Children are everywhere; they seem to emerge from every house, from every alley, from every hiding place, yelling 'Mzungu!' (white person) and jumping and waving as we pass. Many of them have nothing, dressed in filthy rags that hang in tatters on their thin shoulders. The homes are built of earthen brick, with reeds for roofing and an old sheet hanging over the one entranceway, serving as a doorway. It is pitch black inside the houses, with little natural light getting in and only one or two windows allowing the smoke from the fires inside to escape. There are no glass windows, no doors, there is no electricity, no fridges, no bedding and no electronic entertainment, the like of which we take for granted. Ugandan women stand outside: cooking, washing clothes in basins and taking care of their children. As we drive by they look up, smile, and wave.

Life is different here, with priorities varying and time operating at a very different pace. On one day, an event for a community where Mum and Dad are to speak is due to start at 1pm, but at 1pm barely fifteen people have arrived. Over the next three hours, people wander down at various times until over one hundred and fifty fill the small church. To many, 1pm means nothing, they know the event starts in the afternoon and that is when they come. Our family, with our notorious approach to timekeeping, feel quite at home.

"The people here are so beautiful," Natalie says. "I didn't think I would enjoy this but I don't want to go home. The people here are so welcoming, and I don't know… they seem to have more than we do in so many ways."

"Yeah they seem happier in some ways, I don't know how when they have so little," Bethany opines. It is true. We see great suffering and heart breaking situations; many people struggle to provide for their families from one day to the next. Yet, we also see close families, scenes of joy and situations of inexplicable happiness glimmering through the pain.

"How much have we lost in our culture?" I ask. "All we do is spend our time living for ourselves, with no thought beyond the moment as we entertain ourselves to death."

"You talk some rubbish," Charlene smiles with a twinkle in her eye. "But yeah, we do take so much for granted. I just wish we weren't rushing all the time, I would love to spend more time, like a week, with one community and really get to know the people."

I stare out the window again, remembering church on Sunday. It had been an incredible day, and I realised how little I knew God. I thought of how angry I get at God when anything goes wrong for me, treating God as if He exists for the sole purpose of making me happy. Yet here, where people have suffered injustices and tragedies that make me shake with anger, they do not blame God. So many worship and love Him with a purity and passion I envy, speaking of a God they know and trust deeply, who they worship with everything. They have seen God in the green pastures, but also in the valley of the shadow of death and they know He is there and loves them. They know that their lives are so much more than this brief touch of paint across life's tapestry. They know that this world is not their home.

I sigh, because I know I will forget. As soon as I go home, I will again fall in love with things around me that blind me from the truth; we are not created solely for this life or to live for ourselves. I will forget those whom I have met and I will forget that my lifestyle is built on the back of systematic injustices; I will allow my heart to become calloused and apathetic as I forget what real contentment is. Many of these people know God so much deeper than I do. I can see that they have such a deep relationship with God as they pray and sing to Him with such awe and such love. I realise so much of my worship is based on how I feel. Again, I am struck by how shallow a gauge emotions are.

I am roused from my reflections by raised voices from the back of the bus. Charlene and Natalie are fighting about something and, for a second, I am fearful of tempers fraying, of escalations like I have seen so many times before, Mum quickly intervenes, saying with powerful resolve in her voice "Charlene, Natalie stop it this instant. You have seen people who have nothing, and yet you argue about something like that? Do you realise how lucky you are with everything you have? Don't dare argue about something so petty!" I wonder if Charlene will react, but instead she looks out at the passing houses and is silent, drifting in her own thoughts.

The minibus grinds up a muddy lane with Ugandan homes all around us at either side. This is the moment my family has been most excited about. It is a project we have discovered through Ruth, a dear Ugandan friend; it is run by her family and is known as Jesus Cares. Ruth's parents have taken in a number of child-headed families, children who have lost their parents to AIDS and who now live alone, fending for themselves. This is a common problem in Uganda and today we are going to get to spend time with the families for a meal and games together.

We travel in the bus up dirt tracks riddled with potholes, often with overhanging branches that our bus driver has to hack away with a machete so we can get through. We collect the different families one by one. Many of them live in dwellings that are little better than huts, with six living in a house the size of a room in our house back home.

When we get back to the Jesus Cares Project Centre, we hear some of their stories. We listen to a family of five young girls, all HIV-positive whose parents have passed away from AIDS. The oldest of the girls, aged 12, cares for her younger sisters as head of the house. The project has allowed them to buy some pigs and hens; they sell the produce from them at the local market to support themselves. Periodically, the girls become very ill when they cannot get access to their medication.

We hear of one young girl born with deformities who was abandoned by her grandparents, who believing her disability to be a curse on the family placed her at the side of the road to die. Yet, her older sister continually carried her home, only for her to be brought back to the road again. Now thanks to the Jesus Cares project, she is being cared for.

We listen to a number of stories that shatter our hearts of stone as a river flows through and breaks apart mighty mountains. At first as I sit listening, I feel despair gnawing at my soul. What can we say to these people? What can we pampered white people ever bring into situations we can never understand?

I look over at Charlene. She sits with a young Ugandan boy on her knee and she is transfixed. She doesn't move; her eyes are wide and her mouth slightly open, drinking in every word as if it were life giving water. What transfixes her I wonder? Is it the realisation of how different her life could be

Two more children Charlene took to in Uganda

here? Of people who need medication as she does, but are unable to access it? Of children robbed of innocence and childhood, having to follow rules of an adult world to provide for their family? I do not know, but she hangs on every word she hears.

Again, I realise how wrong my first reaction has been. In spite of tragedy, these people all speak of a God they trust; who they believe loves them and provides for them. In comparison, I pay lip service to Him, but then sit wrapped in selfishness and obsessed with temporary fleeting pleasures. They have seen and believed that Jesus truly does care through this project.

After hearing the stories, we play games for hours and share a meal together cooked by Ruth's parents. We eat traditional Ugandan food, consisting of matoke, sweet potatoes, fried bananas, cassava, so-called Irish potatoes and a tiny piece of beef on the bone. We eat together with the families and then Mum goes out to the bus and lifts a number of cases we have brought from home, stuffed to the brim with clothes. One by one, she goes to each of the special families we have met and, with the help of the girls, distributes all the clothes. At home, in Ireland, we have wardrobes full of clothes we never wear. For many here, these gifts will be the only other items of clothes they own. The gratitude for something so small is humbling and puts us to shame. Who is blessing whom?

As we get back on the bus, I know that at least for now, our perspectives have shifted beyond recognition. I know from past experience that I will forget and my eyes will mist over again when I get back 'home', but how will it be for my sisters who are seeing this for the first time? Somehow, I know things have changed, I just don't know how yet.

He has removed our sins as far from us as the east is from the west.
Psalm 103:12

This tells us that God has forgiven our sins as far as the east is to the west.
When we stop and think about this is it pretty amazing that after all I have
done and all the hurt and pain I have caused that God is still willing to forgive
me, even though I mess up time and time again.

(Charlene's Journal)

13
DREAMS AND DEVASTATIONS

ONCE WE GET BACK HOME, things continue to be hard for a long time. Seeing the inane obsessions of the media and the pointlessness of investing our time in things that fill empty space but don't live past the day, we feel alienated. Natalie, who is sixteen, is heart-broken and frequently breaks down in tears; she wants to be back in Uganda. Rebecca yearns to go back also, wanting to nurse there now rather than wait until she gets through her degree. Gradually though, as if invisible chains growing around us tighten every day, we become inoculated to what we have seen and slip back into the path of least resistance and begin to forget.

However, part of us cannot forget and all of us have been changed by what we have seen. They say Africa gets in your blood and though this is true for all of us, it is especially so for Charlene. She makes numerous PowerPoint presentations of the photos and videos from our trip and prints out photographs, sticking them on her wall above her bed. She constantly talks about Uganda and I notice subtle changes in her behaviour. There are still days that sweep us right back to the worst of the darkest days, revealing the battle which is still raging for her heart. But the episodes are far rarer than before. I pray that I will learn to trust and let go of the lingering resentment I still hold, harboured away in the icy recesses of my soul.

As I am leaving home for Belfast on a particular day, Charlene shouts out after me, "I love you David." I stop still momentarily, "Love you too Charlene," I echo. I listen to the calm around the house, the peace settled upon it, and I whisper a prayer of thanks to God. I walk to the car smiling, knowing that the clouds are lifting after so long; the future holds hope and promise. We are becoming like the family of my childhood again and I know that each of us feels safe for the first time in years, not freezing at the slightest hint of a raised voice or dreading roars of rage every evening. I look forward to what the future will bring.

PRAYER REQUESTS

That I form a better relationship with God
My family – use them for Your work
God use me for whatever purpose
Become a woman after God's own heart
Give me the energy to do well in school and work for you
Less selfish and capitalist
My health – that I stay well
That I can maybe find a job
That I begin to find good Christian boys
That one day I will go on and get married

God is good!

(Charlene's Journal)

"So what about you Charlene?" We are sitting in Center Parcs on holiday in England in July and the sun is blazing gloriously in the sky above us. We are gathered around the table outside our villa, eating snacks and sipping on cold drinks, while sharing our plans and dreams for the future with one another. I say sharing but it has felt more like a grilling; seven people begin to bombard you with question after question.

"Why are we doing this again?" Bethany asks with one eyebrow raised.

"Because it is always too busy for us to do it at home normally," Dad replies matter-of-factly.

"Well, it's better than the 'Let's All Say What We Like About Dickie' game anyway!" Natalie mutters under her breath. Dad smiles and stares out over his glasses. "Actually yes, let's play that game."

"Stop it Dickie!" Mum says laughing. "So what about you Charlene, what are your plans for the future?"

Charlene is still chuckling at Dad, then goes into a coughing fit. For a few seconds, spasms and coughs rack her small frame until she regains control, red-faced. She shakes herself. These coughing fits have grown more common recently, but as usual, Charlene never complains. She is also wheezing more now, but I dismiss it as something she will rally from again, just as she always does. Charlene is a fighter; she will outlive the lot of us!

She has left behind the Royal Hospital now because she has turned eighteen, leaving behind the place where she fought off expected death in her first year and revisited several times a year since when her health demanded it. She had been well cared for there and none of us had anything but praise for those who tended to her. They had showed obvious affection for her and treated her not just as a list of ailments, but as a person. We were sorry to say goodbye.

She has now moved to the City Hospital's Adult Cystic Fibrosis unit, a move she did not find easy.

"I don't know," Charlene muses. "I really want to serve God, but what am I good at? I am never any good at exams or anything and I don't really know what I can do. Obviously if I could I would like to go on into Upper Sixth, but I am worried about my grades. After that, I really have no idea; maybe office work or something? What do you think?" she asked.

We talk and quiz her about a few things and Charlene weighs up the pros and cons of various options, until Mum asks a question that slices right to the core of the issue. "What's on your heart Charlene, what do you want to do more than anything else?"

Charlene scrunches up her face for a second and stares out towards the forest. All we can hear are the idyllic sounds of the forest – a duck quacking with her young, the wind blowing through the leaves, the splash of a fish coming near the surface of the river. A red squirrel scurries up the tree beside us, stopping half-way up and casting it's beady eyes on us, sizing us up. It continues on to a higher branch.

"I'd love to do something in Uganda, Mum, I really would. I just don't know what. I don't know what I can do there. I don't want to teach and I can't do nursing or medicine, but I would love to do something for the people there. And I would love to be a mummy." She smiles. Charlene has always been good with kids and wanted to be a mother for as long as I can remember. I know she will be a brilliant mother one day.

"The thought of mini-Charlenes running about fills me with fear though," Rebecca says and we all laugh.

"Do you think we will like each other's children?" Natalie asks, and the conversation quickly goes off on a tangent about the characteristics our children might have and who will be the cool uncle and aunt.

Eventually we get back on track and Dad looks at Charlene, smiling; "God has given you that dream Charlene, and I have no doubt He will use you in that. Who knows what the future will hold? Who knows where we will all be this time next year even? We must keep trusting in His perfect plan."

The squirrel runs back down the tree, holding a nut, though he goes by unnoticed as we all start chattering and joking about where each of us will be this time next year; we paint bright images of tomorrow.

Dear God,

I am sorry that I have been neglecting you recently. Beccs advised me to start writing my prayers down so here goes, I'll give it a try.

God you know all my wrongdoings and failings and I ask you for forgiveness in these areas. I thank you for everything and everyone You have given me. I am so undeserving and yet you gave me the most amazing family ever. Thanks.

Help me to stop worrying about exam results and realise that no matter what You have an amazing plan for me. Jesus thank you for everything. I ask that you will be with all my family and that you will keep them all safe.

Help me be a better servant for you. I ask that you also be with all the people in this world that are living in poverty and I ask that the leaders of countries like the UK and America will help.

Lord thank you so much for everything, I love you with all my heart. Please forgive my sins.

Charlene

(Charlene's Journal)

Charlene's dreams of Upper Sixth are not to be. Her health declines rapidly in the following months, and although she starts Upper Sixth, she grows more tired and unwell each day. Hospital trips seem to make little difference. She hates staying in hospital and finds the environment a lot tougher than she ever did during her time at the Royal Hospital. It is incredibly difficult to watch your sister slip deeper into illness before your eyes. Eventually Charlene is forced to accept that school will no longer be possible. Her formal education is over for now.

"I just don't know what I'm going to do with my life now. All my life is becoming is a series of trips to and from hospital," she says quietly one night when we are visiting her. She looks defeated and despondent. My heart twinges within me and I find no words; I know she finds it especially hard at the start of the week. At weekends, we are all together, whether at home or during visits to the ward, but on Monday morning, we all drift towards our normal everyday lives, with Rebecca and I going to university in Belfast, and Natalie, Bethany and Serena going to school. Charlene feels as if she is caught in a rut and left behind, wrapped in stupor and inertia, stalled on life's road due to her cruel affliction. I do not have the words.

"What use am I to God here? What am I going to be able to do? I don't even know if I will ever be able to have a normal job, things just seem to be getting worse. It's just really annoying." She sits with her eyes cast downwards, but then slowly she raises her head and smiles. "Not that I'm complaining, I get spoilt by you lot here, you bring me sweets every time you come. I'm going to end up a fat pie!"

We all laugh and Mum looks at Charlene with a look of pride on her face. "You're a brave girl, Charlene, and you are of use to God wherever you are. You want to serve Him and He knows that. We'll get you better in here and then see where we are."

"Yeah, I know I can be healed if He wants. I just cannot wait to get out of this oul' place," she says nodding at the ward door. Charlene has little love for the time spent here. She convulses suddenly, racked again by a coughing fit; all we can do is sit and wait for her to recover. Her face goes red as she heaves, low on oxygen, scrunched up as she coughs up the liquid thickening in her lungs. Mum reaches and holds her hand. All at once Charlene's face clears as the coughs pass and she smiles.

"So who are you playing this weekend in the hockey girls?"

How have you been healed from the pain of sin?

Having done many terrible things in the past I am at peace that I know now that God has completely forgiven me for it all.

(Charlene's Journal)

Normally Charlene's health went through peaks and troughs. Sometimes she got so sick and looked so frail that, if you didn't know her, you might see her and fear for her life. But then you wouldn't know Charlene. She always rallied. Always. She never complained and, even in the most horrible situations, when my heart broke for the pains she suffered, at the back of my mind I knew that she would recover. God, aided by the steely resolve with which He had gifted her, would preserve her.

In the lead up to winter, Charlene's health always declined. She had often contracted viruses and germs such as MRSA; her cystic fibrosis made her more susceptible to them. The winter of 2008 was no different, with her health worsening as the days grew shorter. However, this time she was not rallying. She had already foregone her hopes of finishing school, and even though I kept expecting her to begin to recover, it did not happen. Her times in hospital grew longer and closer together as we passed through December, into 2009. All of our lives started to revolve around that room in the City Hospital.

The wind captures the fallen leaves and lifts them up in a spiral, then deposits them in a small pile further down the street. The shadows lengthen and the rain spits down as we navigate the sodden footpath of Elmwood Avenue in the university area of Belfast. I pull my hood tighter against the bitter wind and walk faster.

"She'll be ok, won't she?" I glance at Rebecca, walking in step with me. She has a far-off look in her face as we walk. "Tell it to me straight Rebecca, I don't understand all this medical lingo that's tossed about. Why is she taking so long to get better this time?"

It's true. I have heard a lot of things about Charlene's bowel, about lines getting infected, pseudomonas, worries of a germ cepacia and diabetes, but I understand little of it. I just know things are more serious than normal and I feel powerless. In some ways, I have deliberately let the medical terms pass over my head, not wanting to face the fears which haunt my mind, wrapping my ignorance around me like a comforting protective blanket. I know Rebecca understands due to her nursing training and the look in her eyes chills my blood for an instant when she looks up. Dark thoughts swell, but quickly I dismiss them. As I await her response the wind blows soft, cold and lonely.

"It's not good David. She's sicker than she has been in a long time and she isn't responding to the usual treatments. I'm worried and I know Mum and Dad are too. We can't show the girls, though."

"She'll be ok, won't she? Things have been bad before, right?"

"I just don't know David." We walk in silence again as the fallen leaves crunch beneath our feet and are tossed around our ankles. This is now a ritual for both of us as, most days after lectures, either one or both of us will walk from class straight to the hospital to see Charlene. Often we will stop off at Starbucks to buy Charlene a coffee. Living in Belfast has its advantages for seeing her.

"What if this treatment she is on doesn't work?" I ask, puncturing the silence.

"We will wait to see if it works."

"But if it doesn't?" I insist.

Rebecca sighs. "Then she is in danger, as her lung capacity and ability to fight off infections isn't what it needs to be at the minute. You can see from her weight too, David; if any other infections come, she might not be able to resist them. Her body is spent from fighting off all these infections."

Silence falls around us again like a cloak and no matter how hard we wrap ourselves, the wind steals any warmth from our bones. Can things be this bad?

We chat idly as we cross the road and enter the hospital, glad to be somewhere warmer now. We squeeze into the cramped lift and exit onto Ward 8. Walking quietly now, in case Charlene is asleep, we peek around her door. She is lying there with an oxygen mask fused to her face in that twilight between the waking world and the world of sleep, with her eyelids flickering, but as soon as we enter, she stirs, shakes her head to clear the cobwebs and pushes herself up, smiling. Charlene pulls the oxygen mask from her head, and says laughing, "Well look who's here. Queen's hasn't chucked youse out yet, then?"

Seeing her spirits shine so brightly, I know the doctors and doomsayers will be proved wrong, like so many times before. Charlene will be okay. Charlene will always be okay. God will heal her.

Charlene in hospital

Jesus,

What can I say, You are so amazing. I love you with all my heart. I don't know where I'd be without you in my life. You make my life worthwhile. I am really sorry because I know I am covered in sin, please forgive me. I feel now that I am more on fire for you and I feel you living in me. Just help me please.

I also ask that the Western world will help the rest of your lovely world the way you meant it to be. You didn't want all this war and poverty in your world. I just ask for help for them.

Thanks for everything.

Charlene xoxoxoxo

(Charlene's Journal)

"I'm sorry, but we have to have this conversation now." The consultant sits staring at Dickie. He has been summoned to Charlene's room to talk about the latest developments and as soon as he steps into the room, he knows something serious hangs in the air. The consultant and head nurse are sitting in the room while Charlene lies on the bed with her back turned to everyone, awake but unspeaking. She looks as if she has shrunk somehow, drawn in on herself.

The consultant exudes a proper and professional air. She clutches Charlene's medical file in her hand, glancing down at it occasionally as she speaks, with information that is breaking his heart.

"Charlene's oxygen levels and lung function tests have deteriorated rapidly and are showing no signs of improvement; there is no other option now. Charlene needs a double lung transplant and we recommend that she is assessed for that."

Dickie sits, face vacant, and it feels like the oxygen has been sucked out of the room. Charlene has already been told this earlier in the day and lies with her back to the medical staff and to Dickie, unmoving. How can the world keep turning as news like this is delivered? He stares ahead, trying to take the information in. Concern for Charlene fills him. What is she thinking? She was not expecting this, not now, not here.

Being a doctor, he has always known that someday in the future Charlene might need to have a double lung transplant, but he did not expect it now. It was always a dark day far off in the future, he never envisioned Charlene facing this when she was eighteen. It feels like his legs have been jerked from beneath him, everything feels numb and unreal. How can this be? What thoughts are running through his daughter's mind as she lies there, looking so impossibly alone?

He knows the chances of a successful transplant are very small. Charlene's body is so wasted, she is so frail. She will need to get her body up to a certain weight before she can get onto the transplant list, as they will only try it if they believe the operation is viable. At the rate Charlene is declining, with her body being attacked on all sides by infection after infection, exhausted from keeping them at bay, how will she put on the necessary weight and be stable enough health-wise to qualify to go on the list? That does not even take into account how unlikely it is that a donor Charlene's size will become available...

"A transplant is something that we need Charlene to consider. Not everyone chooses to go that route, but we can talk about this later. For now we will hopefully see Charlene responding to this new treatment of antibiotics and then we can arrange an appointment with the transplant specialists in Newcastle, if that is the route Charlene wants to go down. There are of course risks associated with transplant. We can talk about those at a later juncture." The words were there, words that are so easy to say, but words that carry devastating implications. "Do you have any questions?"

Charlene does not move a muscle and silence emanates from her frame. There are so many questions now in his mind, exploding like popcorn kernels in a fire, breaking through the numbness and the shock. So many questions. If she does not go down this route, what is the prognosis? How soon can she be seen by the transplant team? Are there no other options? He does not yet know how much Charlene has understood; more than anything now, he wants time alone with his daughter, to talk to her, to hold her and to listen. The staff take their leave and shut the door behind them, leaving Dickie alone with Charlene who is lying there, staring out of her window into the blue sky outside.

Everything still seems to be running in slow motion. He gets up and walks over to stand beside Charlene; he knows from one look in her eyes that she understands exactly what this all means. She lies there with tears running silently down her cheeks. She knows the chances of getting well enough to go on the transplant list are small. She knows the chances of finding a suitable donor are smaller. She knows that the chances of surviving the operation are smaller again. The path ahead has darkened, as if entering the very valley of the shadow of death.

He grabs his daughter and pulls her close. "I love you so much Charlene and we will get through this. We will. God has a plan, even when things seem darkest. I love you."

He is holding Charlene's other hand so carefully and in his hand, hers seem to be swallowed up, her fingers stick-like. Her body is deteriorating and, unlike the rest of his family, his medical background means he has no veil of ignorance to protect him. He knows the full implications of the words that were passed moments before. "Do you have any questions Charlene? What are you thinking?"

Charlene swallows a lump in her throat and raises her chin, as a familiar defiance and steel solidifies in her eyes. So many times he has seen this determination and stubborn will fixed in the wrong way, destroying Charlene and those who love her most. Now this iron will is fixed against something else.

"I want to do this Dad. If there is no other way I will get better, I want to do this. I want to go the transplant route."

He squeezes her hand and finds his own cheeks are wet. He is so proud of his daughter. "We will take this one step at a time. We will get you on the transplant list first; we are all in this together, every step of the way. Soon you will have new lungs and these old ones that are causing you so much bother will be gone forever."

Charlene still cries quietly, but her heaving, silent sobs start to subside, seeming to be passed onto Dickie as he holds her. Soon she pulls herself from Dad's embrace, sits up and wipes her face. "You're right, sorry about moaning. I'll get my weight up first. We can use those tube feed things again."

She is referring to the tube feeds she has had to use in the past. They are a thick mix of blended nutrients in a milky fluid that hang in a bag by her bed, with a smell like sour milk rising from them. At nights, Charlene connects them to a tube leading directly into her stomach and, while she tries to sleep, they slowly pump this fluid into her stomach, trying to improve her weight by loading her tiny body with additional calories. Sometimes she wakes up to discover the tube has disconnected in the night, flooding her bed with the milky liquid and the smell permeating her body and bedclothes. Charlene has never liked them, finding they often make her feel sick and bloated. Up to now, she has always described them as horrendous and been adamant that she would not use them, but the nature of the game is changing.

He looks at his precious daughter. "Do you think you are up to going out Charlene?"

Family time

"Anything to get out of here. I just want to get away from here for a while." Charlene sighs.

"Okay, I will phone Mum and she and the others will be here in no time and we will all go to Nandos."

14
WRESTLING WITH DESPAIR

I GRIP THE PHONE and nothing seems to make sense. Dad's words seem to be in a different language, referring to someone else, not Charlene. Seconds before I had been casually sitting on the sofa with my housemates, screaming at the TV while playing Mario Kart and getting hit by red shell after red shell in the game. We were laughing and screaming at each other, and my highest priority scant seconds ago had been to beat Caz back into second place. Then my phone rang.

As soon as I heard the tone in Dad's voice I had withdrawn into my bedroom, where I now sit. Dad is trying to keep a calm voice, but I recognise that quiver in his voice. I realise that my knuckles, gripping the arm of the chair, have gone white. Half-formed fears race through my mind, like greyhounds released from a trap.

"Meet us at Nandos at six, we have something we need to talk about."

Nandos has become one of our favourite family haunts. Being a large family, numbers-wise, naturally, it has become a place where we eat together and talk about future plans. Our family has always had a weak spot for food, and as platters of chicken are shared between us, food disappears at record-breaking times, with each of us acting like a vulture. It is often literally 'stretch or starve', and I can almost imagine David Attenborough filming us while narrating about 'survival of the fittest'.

It is a place where we laugh, right the world's wrongs and just have fun being with one another. Charlene loves it and we have many memories of life and laughter there, yet I know this will not be one of those times.

"It's about Charlene isn't it? Is she ok?" I ask. I can hear the edge of desperation in my voice.

"We will explain when we are all together. See you at six, David. Love you."

The phone goes dead and I sit in my room in the stillness with my thoughts fallen in a jumble around my feet and I pray, listening for what God might say. I hear nothing.

We sit around the table together and Nandos is as I always remember it, seeming deceptively like a normal day. The desk at the front is a hub of activity, with chickens being cooked and served to various tables at a rapid rate. The serving staff move back and forward past us quickly, oblivious to the earth-shattering conversation passing over our table. We sit with our food half eaten, stopping mid-meal as we struggle to absorb the news. I have eaten well, but inside I feel empty.

Charlene has not eaten much, her portion sits untouched. Her shoulders are sagging and her face looks drawn. Her sunken eyes remind me afresh how ill she is. Gone is the vibrant young girl from the summer months; in her place is this sickly wraith. When did this happen?

"What do you mean a lung transplant, Dad? I don't understand. What will this mean?" Serena stammers.

"It means things are very serious, pet. Charlene's lungs are weak and she needs this operation, but first she has to get well enough to get on the transplant list. She needs to start responding to these drugs and soon; we also need to get her weight up, otherwise they will never accept her for transplant and they won't put her on the list. They won't do the operation unless they think it has a good chance of success. There are so few donors that they can't waste any lungs they get. If they were to do the operation now Charlene's body wouldn't be strong enough, so getting her well enough to get on the list is our first hurdle."

Charlene looks up. The world seems to hang on her shoulders as she says, "I'll take those feeds Dad, every night. They'll get my weight up. Sorry I can't finish this chicken though, I'm just not hungry tonight." Despair parades behind her eyes and she looks utterly defeated. Her voice sounds older than her eighteen years, jaded and tired around the edges. I am more scared than I have ever been before.

"Well is this good or bad? I mean it will be good when you get new lungs, won't it Charlene?" Bethany queries, worry lining her youthful face.

Dad answers for her. "Yes it will, but it's a long journey until then. As I said the first thing we do is get your weight up so you can make this list," he says looking at Charlene. She nods, staring at the table. It is obvious she has been floored by this news and it terrifies me seeing her so despondent. Charlene is never like this; an icy chill creeps up my spine as I see the fear in her frame.

"What about when we get her on the list? How long will it take for lungs to be found, Dickie?" Poppa asks, sitting across from me. Concern is also etched across his well-lined face.

"There's no guarantee, it depends. We would need to keep her weight above a certain level and wait for the call to come. It could be a day, a month, a year; it just depends when compatible lungs become available. We'll know more details later, but from what I can gather the transplant team is based in Newcastle and we'll need to go across to get Charlene assessed for suitability for transplant. Our priority is to get her well enough for all of that, and then we can think about what comes next."

"Yes, and once we do that and get you on that list, we will have a bag packed and ready to go," Mum says, reaching over and holding her hand. "We've got to be ready at any time. We'll need to work out what you are going to pack, Charlene," Mum continues, trying to encourage and rouse her from her despondency.

Questions tumble from everyone.

"So the next step is to get her well enough to get on this list?" Serena asks, her forehead lined with unspoken fears. "But Charlene, how are they going to do that, surely they have been trying to get you well for a while?"

Charlene stirs from her deep contemplation, as if emerging from the deep and unwrapping herself from layers designed to defend herself. "What you're asking me is what are they going to do differently?" Serena nods. "Well they talked to me earlier and they want me to spend even more time

Charlene did all she could – and more, despite her illness

in that flipping place than I do already, for all the good it will do. Apparently, it will mean that they are able to identify infections early so I'm kept well enough for this transplant. I'll hardly ever be home!" Charlene exclaims, before resuming her dull stare at the plate in front of her. Visibly she retreats into herself again.

Rebecca and Dad, the two medical professionals, look sombre and I know from their body language more than their words that this is not good. This will be a hard road to walk, one strewn with difficulties.

The air is thick around us. The bustle of Nandos seems a world away; I don't know what to say. I want to say something comforting, share a powerful Christian truth, an answer or antidote to this dark day, but I am so feebly lacking.

Mum breaks the silence. "This will be a path we will all walk together. It won't be easy for Charlene. The path will be hard, but I do believe God has His Hand on this, and we will take each step as it comes. The first thing we need to do is get you responding to this treatment and get your weight up Charlene, pet."

I have never seen Charlene so quiet. She looks defeated and I feel a stab of fear sinking claws deep into my soul. I know she needs to fight for this to work, but she is so demoralised. She had to leave school due to her illness, then was told she must have a double lung transplant. How does someone deal with that? While her other teenage friends are worrying about what hairstyles they will have, what they will do at the weekend, or what is the latest scandal in their favourite soap, she has been told she has to have a brutally risky operation or she will die. An oppressive atmosphere weighs upon all of us and our hearts break for our sister. What can we say?

Charlene blinks twice. Her forehead creases as she ponders; she looks about her. "Dad, I'm going to be in hospital a lot now, yeah?"

"Yes, why do you ask?" Dad replies.

"I'm just thinking, I may as well do something good with my time, right? It's so boring in there and it's just if I'm not going to be able to do anything else, I want to do something worthwhile. I want to do something with my life."

"You need to make sure you get well Charlene, focus on that first," Poppa says, disquiet in his eyes.

"No. I want something to do; I don't want to be thinking about this stupid transplant."

"What do you have in mind?" Mum asks.

"I don't know, I want to do something in Uganda. I was looking at the pictures again today and I miss there."

"What would you like to do Charlene?" Rebeccas weighs in.

"I don't know, I want to do something for those kids. There were so many kids everywhere we went; I just think how lucky we are and how little they have. Look, if I'd been born with this stupid thing over in Uganda, I'd be dead long ago. I just want them to have the opportunities I got."

Silence falls again, but this time it is not oppressive. The direction of the conversation has changed and we are mulling over our options. Rather than thinking about how Charlene will cope, we are now thinking how to help a community we do not yet know in Uganda, thousands of miles away. Charlene has shifted our focus from this terrible moment to a bigger picture we have forgotten in the storm.

Charlene looks up pensively. I can almost see the cogs turning in her brain. "Just thinking like... I had opportunities in school at Waringstown, Lurgan Junior High and Armagh Royal; they were all so good to me. I haven't been able to finish school and I guess there would be something cool about using that so that those Ugandan kids could have a school. I like that idea! I know what I am going to do. If I can't go to school, I am going to raise money to build a school in Uganda so that some of the children there can get an education" As if a light has gone on in the room, a smile crosses her face. It is the first time she has smiled tonight. I know Charlene's thoughts are now on the kids she fell in love with at Easter 2008.

"We have got to be careful Charlene, that would be a massive task and we need to focus on your health" Dad says with concern. But Charlene is resolute and slowly but surely she brings everyone round to her view of thinking. "I need to get working on this, this is so exciting" she says with a beam on her face so much in contrast to her demeanour of despondency just a short time earlier. "Only thing is, I have no clue how you would go about this all", she laughs starting a coughing fit again.

"Well I could make enquiries," Dad interjects. "We could talk to Fields of Life and see what they could do - if there are any communities that they know of that need a school. I could contact them tomorrow and start off the process."

"I'd like that, Dad," Charlene says with a far-off look in her eye. "And then after the school we could maybe build an orphanage and a..."

We all laugh. "Let's take this one step at a time, Charlene," Mum says chuckling. "Let Dad investigate this and we can see where we can go from here."

"Ok. How much do you reckon it would cost to build a school out there anyway?"

"Genuinely, I wouldn't have a clue. Maybe £50,000 or £100,000? I will find out," Dad responds thoughtfully.

Charlene shakes her head nonchalantly. "Well that won't be a problem. We'll have that by the end of the year!"

I stare at her aghast, eyes wide with disbelief. "From where Charlene? Let's see how much it costs and set a realistic target."

Her eyes light up and she looks at me laughing, "You just watch this space, and we'll see who is right!"

"You thinking a primary school then, Charlene?" Poppa interrupts.

Charlene turns, nodding enthusiastically. "Yes, for a start anyway. Oh Poppa, I wish you could have been with us, you would have loved the kids and they would have loved you. I remember them grabbing on to you and rubbing your skin frantically to see if you were black underneath! There were so many of them who had nothing, not even any real clothes and there we were in our red T-shirts. I wanted to help them but didn't know how; now I do." She stops for breath, and takes a quick sip from her Fanta. "I'd love to build a primary school first for the wee ones, and then see where we are."

She chatters away and Dad grabs a napkin, jotting down her ideas as they come. She seems more alive than she has been in weeks. Her hands weave through the air as she describes her vision, as if she is laying the bricks with her words. Her eyes sparkle like the first stars in a twilight sky. Her words tumble out quickly; as if afraid she will forget her ideas unless she articulates them now.

She does not look defeated anymore. She looks alive, as if filled with fresh breath. I have no doubt now that she will weather this storm and walk this road to its end because she is not just doing it for her, nor for us, but for the kids in Uganda who God has implanted in her heart. The sickness that seemed to hang over her like a cloak is now pushed to the background again. Her passion is infectious and soon we are all chattering away with ideas. Without vision the people perish. What happens with it?

"This is really exciting," Serena mutters through a mouthful of chicken. As we talk, the food that had been briefly ignored begins to disappear.

Thank you God, I think. Things make sense again and all the pieces seem to fit. Charlene has this vision and through her, God will build a school in Uganda. Then she will get her new lungs and go there to see the school God will build. It all makes perfect sense now.

"So, you'll be across with your new lungs at this new school before you know it Charlene." Rebecca says, mirroring my thinking.

"Oh, you just try and stop me," Charlene says eyes ablaze, taking another bite of her chicken.

God,

Have been meaning to do this for ages but just want to say thank you so much for everything. The life you have given me and the AMAZING family you have given me. Lord I pray that as we embark on this journey of transplant that we will feel your hand upon us.

God I don't understand why this is happening but I now realise that you are in control of it all and I gotta trust you. Lord the one thing I ask is that you grant the whole family the strength to get through it all.

Thanks, Amen.
Charlene xx

(Charlene's Journal)

15
ROAD TO REUNION

PLANS FOR THE SCHOOL begin to fit together very quickly. Charlene may be sick in hospital, but that doesn't limit her. Internet access on her laptop is her portal to the world outside, and she is unleashed on the cyber world, researching ideas for fundraising and emailing key contacts. At first, while the initial feelers are put out, she only shares her ideas with a few people, but she inundates them with emails. Dad is her able deputy, and contacts Fields of Life about available options, and by the end of the first week we have a provisional target in mind - £70,000 to build a primary school.

"I'm worried, Dad. Will she not lose heart if she doesn't raise this? I mean, that's an awful lot of money!" I ask him one night.

Without taking his eyes from the laptop, he shakes his head. "Oh ye of little faith. Watch this space David; you should hear all the fundraising ideas she is having. I think she could manage this."

Stephen Blevins, the Director of Fields of Life, meets Charlene and she pours her heart out before him. He explains that they have a number of options for a school as several communities have contacted them with hopes and longings for schools. We provisionally plan to go out in the summer to meet the communities and see if there is a place where Charlene's dreams can become a reality. As if it were pre-planned, the pieces fall into place.

Charlene blogging in hospital

This was my reading this morning after I heard about what was happening to you at the hospital. It's very appropriate!

Sometimes God allows us to become pressured – not to terrify us or cause us undue pain but to purify our character. It's interesting that God uses pressure in our lives this way. In the same manner, pressure is what makes a diamond pretty, precious, and priceless. Diamonds are treasured stones that many desire. God wants you and me to become His treasured stones that shine with His glory. He uses the pressures in our lives to create in us a thing of rare beauty that many desire. When we allow the stress of life to purify our nature, we permit God to work for good and His glory.

Dear Lord, sometimes my stress feels so heavy I think I can't go on. I have no breath or life left in me. But Your Word says that You make me lie down in green pastures. And Your goodness and love will follow after me. Oh, how Your Word refreshes my soul and renews my spirit. Be my strength; be my rest; be my ever-present help under pressure. With You, I can make it through. In Jesus' Name, Amen.

Loads of love xxxxxxxxxxxxx

(Email from Mum to Charlene)

With her heart captivated, the days at hospital do not seem as long to Charlene and slowly, her health starts to improve as she begins a long slog towards recovery. As she improves, it is clear that a question is building in her mind, but she does not articulate it to any of us at first. However, one day when we come to visit her it pours from her lips like water bursting forth from a dam.

"I'm well enough to go. I'm going back to Uganda in the summer with all of you. I want to see where the school we build will be." Her eyes are aflame with that same passion that was ignited in her one night in Nandos.

The room is silent at first as Charlene's heartfelt wish settles around us. Dad answers first, "I don't know Charlene. We have to think of your health and our target has to be getting you seen in Newcastle and beginning this whole process. Going to Uganda could jeopardise all of that."

Charlene immediately crosses her arms and stares with that familiar defiance. "I don't care," she says, each word spoken carefully and with bite. "I want to go; I want to see the place I'll be raising money for."

Mum looks uneasily at her and Poppa intervenes, "Charlene, you have to be careful. You will be able to do that when you get your new lungs; there will be plenty of time for that."

Charlene turns away, arms still folded as she looks out of her hospital window over the shining night lights of Belfast. "I'm not even arguing over this," she says, her voice now calm but still full of iron determination. "I'm going and that's that."

The conversation moves around in circles for a while and eventually Dad promises to investigate and see if there is any way it would be possible. Over the next few days, he fires emails to Uganda, to airlines and to doctors. A few nights later when we visit Charlene, he has some news for her.

"Charlene, I have looked into this. First off, this can only be an option if you maintain your health; you know that?"

"Yes, I will stay in here every hour of every day if it means I get out to Uganda again," she says with an excited air.

"Well I have emailed the airline for a start and they can get in-flight oxygen cylinders in case you need them."

"I won't."

Dad continues, ignoring her. "We can only consider this because of where we are staying in Kampala. The International Hospital is less than a mile from our accommodation in case you need to go there. I have been in contact with them and they are aware of the situation."

Charlene shakes her head, an incredulous look on her face. "This is so over the top, I'll be fine! But I can go right?"

"Well, I talked to the hospital staff here and they are heavily against it."

"And?"

"But they say it is your decision. They don't think it is wise and advise against it, but it is your call. What do you think? As your father, I agree that there is a risk, but your health is improving by the day and it is up to you. What do you think?"

"Well let me think about that one," Charlene says with sarcasm running through her voice. "Emmmm... of course!" A smile breaks through and lights up her face. "I'd go there today if I could, and there is no way anyone is keeping me away!" she says elatedly. "This calls for a celebration!"

Mum has been silent, but as she watches Charlene who looks like she wants to dance an impromptu jig on her hospital bed, she cannot help but laugh. "The hospital staff think we're mad Charlene, you do know that?"

"'Course we're mad. But it's more fun that way," Charlene exclaims, giggling as she says it. "Now, let's get these flights booked!"

Over the next few weeks, the embryonic plans take on more shape. Flights and accommodation are booked for July and a small team is assembled. Plans are laid down about what we will do when we get there. We decide to have a few folk carrying out Relationships and Sexuality Education programmes in schools with others in charge of distributing the clothes aid we bring to local communities. Others would lead Kids' Clubs during the day for the younger children with a few of the team tasked with constructing goal posts and swings at the schools we visit.

Whilst all this work is important, the jewel in the crown is to be the selection of Charlene's school. In the midst of the crammed schedule this is the day to which we look forward with anticipation.

As the trip draws closer, people kindly donate clothes and toys for the Ugandan families we will meet and Mum works diligently, often long into the night, sorting and packing the items into old suitcases. Dad arranges these for air freight to send on ahead of us, which allows a much greater volume of aid to be packed.

By the start of June, fifty-five suitcases are packed: filled to bursting point. Transport arrives to take them to the airport and we finally have our house, which had been a scene of chaos for weeks, back again. As the days tick closer to our departure we get more and more excited, but Charlene surpasses all of us in displaying anticipatory elation.

She is alive as she plans and talks of what she wants to do, ticking each day off as it passes and wishing time would pass quicker. Her excitement is infectious and our whole family eagerly awaits the return to Uganda, a place, where so many things changed for us.

I prepare to travel ahead of the rest, leaving on 8th June to travel to Rwanda and the Congo, where I will work with a few friends for a month and conduct some research. As I stuff clothes haphazardly into my bag a few hours before my flight is due to leave, I am excited. I'm excited about working in Rwanda and the Congo, but most of all I'm excited about travelling with my family again, especially so that I can witness Charlene's joy as she meets the community that she has set her heart upon helping.

Sadly life never plays out the way we want it. After a long period of relative stability, Charlene's health begins to decline again. She is still animated and euphoric about her trip back to the country she loves, but her physical health is slipping and she has returned to hospital. We all expect this to be a short relapse, but I can see the looks pass between Mum and Dad and I know they are questioning if this trip will be possible.

As I say goodbye to my family at the airport I wonder what will happen in the weeks before they are due to travel. Not knowing who I will see when July rolls around, I tighten the straps on my backpack, wave goodbye and step through the departure gate.

The sky is ablaze with light. Day has given up its' dying breath and night has fully come of age. There has been a power cut in the district of Kigali, Rwanda that I am living in with my friends. I can see the Milky Way painted across the canvas above me and the Southern Cross dancing above the horizon; as my eyes adjust, I see stars beyond stars: ones that I had not yet realised existed. They are like jewels scattered across the heavens and without the competition of city lights, I see the night sky like I never have before.

Nevertheless, my mind is not on the stars. I am trying to get a line from Rwanda to talk to my parents and currently the signal is weak. I walk around the house, hoping for improved reception as I hold the phone above my head like a mast. Near the gate, signal floods into it and I carefully dial the long number that will bridge the thousands of miles between Rwanda and Ireland, firing across two continents and crossing from one hemisphere to the other.

I have been in Rwanda for the last month working in a number of communities with a local organisation. Tomorrow, I will take the long ten hour bus ride from Kigali, Rwanda to Kampala, Uganda, where I will conduct research for my dissertation for two weeks. Then my family will arrive and we will investigate the potential site for Charlene's school together.

As my Dad's voice breaks through the shaky line, I realise how much I have missed them. I have loved my time here, but I am looking forward to being with everyone back in Uganda.

"David, how are you? How has the work been?"

We talk for a while and very quickly the conversation drifts around to their preparations for Uganda. We have been looking forward to this for so long.

"Charlene's very sick." From the periodic phone calls and texts, I knew she was still unwell, but I hadn't known she was as sick as Dad is describing. "She's still in hospital and hasn't been responding to the drugs in the way we had hoped."

"Will she be ok? Are things alright?"

"She'll be fine David, just keep praying." I know from the tone of his voice that things aren't as they should be, but the line is beginning to break up.

"Will she still be able to come here?" I ask, suddenly worried. How can we choose a school if Charlene, the vision-caster, is not here? This is her dream, her heart's desire.

"We will see. I know the line is getting bad, so from all of us, we love you so much. Phone us as soon as you get back to Kampala." I promise to do so and end the call.

I stand and stare again at the cosmos unfolded before me, but instead of wonder, I feel confusion squirm in my gut. God's power and majesty lie before me now, impossible to deny. Yet, how can someone so powerful not heal my sister? I feel useless here, miles away from the place I want to be.

Eyes fixed upon the heavens, I whisper my prayer. "Please let her come God, her heart is in Africa. Let her get well so my family can come together to the place where you want your school built. Keep her safe. Amen."

Back home, things are far more serious than I know. Dad does not want to worry me when I can do nothing. Charlene has deteriorated again and her dream of travelling to Uganda is becoming a pipe dream. For a long time, she ignores the truth staring her in the face as she talks confidently about what she will do in Uganda, as if she can push back this latest onslaught by ignoring it.

Regardless, one night, shortly before they are due to travel, the family sit in the hospital room in silence. Everyone knows what is coming.

"Have we decided where we all will be sleeping?" Charlene speaks into the silence, with a false empty chirpiness in her voice. She is trying to pre-empt the crushing inevitability she knows is coming. "Will I have a room of my own?"

There is still silence as Charlene jerks her gaze from face to face, an almost manic gaze in her eye. Eventually she lowers her head and stares down at the red hospital blanket, pulling it tight around her.

Dad clears his throat and speaks, as deep sadness clearly resonates through his voice. "Charlene, there is no way you can travel. We have kept holding out, but things have been going downhill for a while. You can't go this time."

Charlene's head snaps up and her eyes burn. "Yes, I will. I am going."

"You can't Charlene," Mum says gently. "It's not possible, it would be so dangerous. Your health has to come first and at the minute, you will have problems with the flight, let alone the heat and humidity in Uganda. If you went we would be saying goodbye to the transplant." Mum stops and approaches her, perching on the edge of the bed beside her. "I am so sorry."

"There are so many dangers; you would run the risk of becoming much more ill - or even worse. I'm so sorry," Dad continues.

Charlene leans into Mum and cries quietly, settling her head in Mum's arms. Bethany watches awkwardly, before walking over and laying her hand on Charlene's head. Serena joins her, standing at Charlene's side with concern knotted across her face.

She quickly gathers herself and the quiet sobs subside, until she raises her head and shakes herself. Now composed, she speaks with a steely resolve, "Well you are all just going to have to go and find this school for me. If I can't go, that's your job."

"No!" Mum immediately protests, shaking her head firmly. "I'm staying with you. The others will go, but I'm staying."

Charlene pushes herself upright and looks at Mum aghast. "There is no way! I will be so angry if you don't go, in fact I won't even talk to you. You have all those clothes to distribute and I need you to find this school for me. Let's be honest, you can't leave it up to Dickie over there, he'd probably end up lost and picking a school in Egypt or something!"

"Give me some credit!" Dad protests, and for the first time that night everyone smiles.

Mum does not though. Again, she shakes her head. "Charlene I am staying and that's final. I don't want to go if you're not there."

A contest of wills has emerged and neither Mum nor Charlene are backing down. "I don't want you here Mum, not when I need you in Uganda. Come on, you know I won't change my mind. You know how stubborn I am!"

Poppa has been sitting on the chair listening quietly up to now, but he chooses this time to intervene. "Janice, I will be here every day and her Aunt Lorraine will be visiting from America. You know the number of visitors she will have; if she wants you to go, you should go. I won't leave her side, she'll be sick of the sight of me!"

"Daddy, I can't go, not when she's sick," Mum says, her voice fragile.

Charlene reaches for Mum and it seems as if the roles have been reversed from earlier. "I want you to go Mum, I want you to go and send every picture you take to me. I'll be sitting here waiting for every report and I want you to find a school for me!"

The decision is not made that night; Mum and Dad wrestle with their decision every hour of the next few days, right up to the departure date. In the end though, Charlene is unrelenting and unwavering and, as usual, has her way. After a tearful goodbye, Mum, Dad, Rebecca, Natalie, Bethany and Serena leave to find a school for Charlene in Uganda.

From her hospital bed, Charlene takes on the role of blogging and keeping others informed of the team's progress. She also prays for the family and the rest of the team. Most of all, however, she waits to hear of the news from the community that the team will visit. Will this be the place where her vision is transformed into a tangible reality? Will the team discover the place she will one day visit with revitalised health and new lungs? Charlene follows the team's every move and prays, all the time fighting the unseen infection crawling through her and tightening its cruel clawed grip on her fast-weakening lungs.

Tuesday 14 July 2009

I am especially looking forward to seeing my family, and I'm not going to deny I have missed them. It has been a while and it will be good to see all of them again. I am gutted Charlene is not going to be well enough to come, but I know that she will get another chance, and before very long she will be in Uganda again, and the poor country won't know what hit it! She's a legend, and I am looking forward to seeing her when I get home. Continue to pray for her, especially as it must be hard for her not seeing me for so long (messing Charlene :-)). – David Barr

(David Blog Entry from Uganda)

16
SEARCH FOR HOPE

"EVERYONE COME HERE!" Dad shouts. Generally, we ignore Dad when he is sitting at his laptop; however, this time the excitement in his voice is palpable. Serena and Natalie drop their cards on the table and Bethany flings her book down on the chair beside her as we all scramble over to the laptop screen. Some of us sit on the back of Dad's chair, some on the arms as the rest stretch their heads around at awkward angles.

We are back from a busy day at a secondary school. Everyone has been lounging in the cool of the evening, unwinding back at our Ugandan base and Dad has been trying to connect to the internet for a while.

He has obviously got a connection because we can see image after image of Charlene flicking past the screen. She is smiling and dressed in an Ulster rugby top. I recognise the setting – it is Starbucks on Elmwood Avenue, just outside the hospital. In her photos, she is beaming beside a tall man; then I realise who it is and it clicks why Charlene is grinning from ear to ear.

Charlene has always loved watching rugby, although not necessarily for the sporting prowess on display. She has her favourites, none more so than Andrew Trimble, who plays wing for Ulster. This is who is beside her in each of these photos.

Dad is laughing and dialling a number. Suddenly, we hear Charlene's voice crackling on speaker phone. After filling her in on our news, she begins to tell her story.

"Right, I'm sitting in my bed typing away sending updates of what you lot are doing over in Uganda, and the physios come in and say we should go for a wee walk. I tell them to leave me alone, I'd rather not." In my mind's eye, I can see this scene and I imagine she may be understating this interchange. Charlene is well able to tell the physios or nurses exactly how she feels when she does not feel up to the hassle. "Eventually they persuade me, but I'm still in my pyjamas. So they get me changed. They all come with me though, so I know something is up."

"What happened Charlene?" Bethany asks excitedly.

"Well, when we get outside, the girls say we should go to Starbucks and, you know me, I'd never turn down one of those! So we get there, and I'm still none the wiser, but as soon as we get down I see all the physios there and they shout 'SURPRISE!' They had bought a cake and all for my birthday!"

"That was really kind of them Charlene," Mum responds.

"I know, but wait until you hear what happened next. Who comes striding into Starbucks, but Andrew flipping Trimble? I was mortified Mum, I wanted

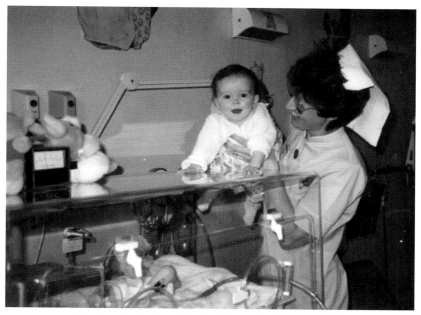

Charlene in the Royal Hospital during her first year of life

Charlene's second birthday

Charlene at Noah's Ark Playgroup

Coming out of Belfast High Court after the adoption

Charlene playing doctor

Charlene nursing either Bethany or Serena!

Natalie and Charlene get their feet wet in Donegal

Charlene as Snow White while Bethany and Serena dress as dwarfs

Charlene, Natalie, Rebecca and David on the train in Bangor

Charlene in her Waringstown Primary School uniform

At Center Parcs with Granny and Auntie Alex

Visiting family in California

Charlene in Uganda in 2008

Liverpool footballer Steven Gerrard sent a signed photograph to Charlene

Charlene abseiling down Belfast's BT Tower. She had sneaked out of hospital to do this – with an intravenous line in her arm

Charlene stepping out at her Armagh Royal School formal

Fundraising at Waringstown Primary School

Getting a lift from ex Irish rugby captains David Humphreys and Paddy Johns

Becoming an Honorary member of Lurgan College Hockey Team

Charlene fundraising with Santa at the Dolly Walk during December 2009

Charlene being surprised with a birthday visit from Irish rugby player Andrew Trimble

And getting a present of an Ulster rugby shirt

Christmas 2009. Our last Christmas Together

Center Parcs New Years Day 2010

*Borehole providing clean water
to Hidden Treasure*

*Janice and Dickie planting a mango tree
in Charlene's memory in 2011*

The same mango tree in 2013

Above: How Hidden Treasure School looked in 2009
Below: The change in Hidden Treasure thanks to Charlene and Charlene's Project

One of the school classrooms

The Barr family at Hidden Treasure School

Natalie, Bethany and Serena surounded by Hidden Treaure pupils

Cissy and her household with David and Rebecca

to die off. They had organised for him to come down and see me on my birthday, so he came and sat and had coffee with us. I didn't know what to say."

"I can imagine you chatted about how much you admired him for his sporting abilities," Wenford, a family friend and member of the team, chimes in.

"Aye, you keep out of this one Wendy!" Charlene retorts. "We talked away and he was lovely. I've added him on Facebook."

"I was so embarrassed but it was really kind of the physios and all. I will not be forgetting that in a hurry!"

"Ok, all together now," Dad shouts. "Let's sing happy birthday!" We all join in and sing happy birthday to her, our song crossing desert, savannah, sea and mountains to get to her ward. It is not at all in tune and the different parts are more likely a result of a lack of musical ability rather than any skilled harmonising, but when we pipe down Charlene is laughing.

"You lot are going to wake all of Africa! Love yous, now go and find me my school!"

"Love you Charlene, and don't you be dreaming of Andrew Trimble!" I yell. Charlene hangs up and we all laugh, then turn back to our card games and books.

Natalie and Charlene

Charlene, your big 19th! Soon you will be driving me around in that SWANKY Nissan Micra… and hopefully legally too! I miss you SOOOOO much and wish you were here. It isn't the same without you. But we will pick the site for your school, and Charlene you will help and bless so many with your school! You are such an inspiration to me and so brave! I just don't know how you cope, you never ever complain! I love you with all my heart and can't wait till you are in Uganda with me in the future! Love you,

Natalie xoxoxo
PS. Center Parcs here we come!

(Extracts from Charlene's birthday card left with her for her to open on her birthday)

To Charlene,

Happy birthday pet. All I can say is you make me the proudest sister ever. You are so special to me. The way you have handled your illness, especially the last few months has amazed me. Your outlook on it all is better than most people I know. I love you so so so so much. I'd be lost without you Charlene Barr. I am so grateful and know I and all the family are truly blessed that God chose and placed you with us.

Keep holding on to God pet. Sometimes life seems hard to understand, but it's him who holds the big jigsaw of the jumbled pieces we have here. I love you with all my heart. You inspire me wee Char. I love you so so so so so much.

Your big sis Becs xo

As the bus pulls into the small school they are investigating for Charlene, Rebecca's heart stops and her eyes drink in the sight before her. There are kids everywhere: many are dressed in tattered rags that hang off them and nearly all are barefoot. A few boys play football to the right of the bus, using a dried fig for a football, while the girls roll an old bicycle tyre with a stick, running after it as it rolls. They have no other toys.

As they clamber from the bus the dust rises from everywhere; Ugandan children run to embrace them. The dust stings Rebecca's eyes and she has to squint but she feels a surge of contentment as she lifts one little girl and holds her close. The child's big brown eyes, so like Charlene's, stare back at her and a smile dances across them. Rebecca laughs as another girl at her side tickles her; she jokingly chases her as the children scamper away squealing with joy and excitement.

She plays with the children as her parents stand by the bus, speaking to the teachers. We start to pass skipping ropes and frisbees out of the bus window and in a matter of seconds the children are playing delightedly with all their new toys. Some stare with puzzlement etched across their faces at the skipping ropes, so Rebecca sets the little girl down and calls Natalie over to help her swing the rope. Before long, a queue of curious children has formed and thrilled cries throng the air as some skip merrily and others fall laughing in the dust.

The tour of the school is brief and it breaks her heart. It is a small wooden structure consisting of three sections, but the separation of these 'sections' is facilitated by thin wooden partitions, half rotten. Gaps riddle the walls between the planks, allowing light to shine through and doubtless, the wind and rain when the rainy season comes. The structure is unstable and infested with termites, understandably threatening any long-term impact the school can have. Rows of backless wooden benches are strewn across the floor, where the children sit in long lines for lessons. There are no desks and because there is no equipment, spellings and sums are scoured into the wood at the front of the room. The teachers have to be inventive with their limited resources.

As her parents ask questions, the kids filter in and sit on the benches, squeezing tight together and watching the tour with delighted faces. Rebecca smiles down at them in an attempt to mask her hidden sorrow. She remembers her school years and how much she took for granted: the used file paper she cast away so readily, the shiny overhead projectors and the computer suites, the varied nutritious meals available at the school canteen. She compares that to this, thinking of how few of these children have eaten today and how they will have no food here at school or perhaps even at home when they return at the end of the day. As she reflects, Rebecca becomes more broken and struggles not to break down in front of the children, who are now swaying from side to side and singing.

She wishes Charlene were here. As she looks at the children in their makeshift clothes with so many disadvantages in their lives yet singing joyous songs of thanksgiving to God with eyes dancing, she knows she will remember and tell Charlene everything. "How can God allow poverty like this?" she had wondered, but she realises they can be the answer that God is providing. Suddenly, she knows that this is the place! Here Charlene's dreams can make such a difference to so many people.

The old termite invested wooden structure at Hidden Treasure in 2009

She reaches down and dances with a little girl, who is staring innocently up at her. Rebecca's smile is no longer fake, she feels wonderfully alive. She no longer sees a wooden shack riddled with termites, but a concrete structure with children dancing inside. It will be well supplied with resources, able to provide a meal for every pupil who comes. In her mind's eye, she sees Charlene dancing in front of this building with a circle of children around her, healed by her operation and able to visit the school she has dreamt of for so long.

"Bethany, what is the name of this school again?" she asks her sister, who is sitting by the wall, swamped by children scrambling to get into her arms.

Bethany looks up, laughing. "Hidden Treasure; its name is Hidden Treasure."

Rebecca nods and resumes her jig with the child before her. Hidden Treasure: this is the place where Charlene will see her dream come to life.

As the family steps back onto Irish soil, walking through the baggage reclaim, a figure steps out from behind a pillar, excitement radiating from her face. Charlene waves at us, her face beaming as Audrey, a family friend and Charlene's teacher in Primary School, catches up with her. They have come to welcome us home.

All the stress and fears of the last few weeks come crashing down on Mum and Dad and they run to her, showering her with kisses. Mum holds her close and she seems so small in her grasp. Dad picks her up carefully and hugs her, with his arms swallowing her up. Although she is nineteen, she still seems the size of child; so much of her energy is used up fighting the disease.

"How did you get in here, you wee monkey?" Mum cries, relief etched across her face. "This is baggage reclaim!"

"Oh, we managed to sneak through. I have my ways!" she laughs.

"You look healthier," Dad laughs. "We should go away more often!"

"I've got my weight up," Charlene says, pride shining from her. "I'm getting closer to the target, I'm nearly 40kg. We'll get on this transplant list yet!"

"She has been brilliant, Janice," Audrey says happily as she walks over and hugs each of us. "There was no way she wasn't coming to welcome you home, she has been counting the hours down! Welcome home everyone."

"I think this calls for a celebration, where is the nearest coffee shop?" Mum asks. Mixed emotions of relief and joy at holding her daughter again are clearly written across her face.

"Yes, somewhere where they have those lovely muffins!" Serena suggests, nodding frantically. "I slept through meal time on the plane."

Charlene reaches for Mum's hand and we walk out together again into the Irish drizzle.

We love you more than you know. Just wish you were with us – we're not complete without you. Love you so much,

Mum xx

Hey Shirly Whirly! Happy Birthday. I love you so so much and am really missing you with my whole heart. I really wish you were here. You are the biggest blessing our family has ever had! You are so brave and courageous and you make me look at myself and wonder where is my faith? I just wish I was more like you cause you are so close to God in your faith. Love you so much. Missing you,

Serena xoxo

(Extracts from Charlene's birthday card left with her for her to open on her birthday)

Charlene with Serena

17
NO BACKING DOWN

VERY SHORTLY AFTER WE RETURN, Dad and Charlene fly across to Newcastle for Charlene's transplant suitability assessment. This is where she will have her operation, when she eventually gets the call. We all wait expectantly at home for the call from Dad or Charlene that will tell us whether or not she will get on the list.

One wet day in August, Mum's phone rings. She runs towards the table, rummaging through mountains of paper as she tries to find it. "Has anyone seen my phone?" she shouts frantically, trying to find it before it rings off.

"Have you checked your bag?" Natalie says nonchalantly, without looking up from the computer. Mum reaches into the bag beside her and instantly locates it. "No," she acknowledges as she holds her phone to her ear.

Charlene's cheery voice pipes down from the other end. "Good news-ish Mum. Basically after all these tests I've been classified as suitable for this double lung thing as soon as I gain a bit more weight, they won't let me until then though. As soon as I hit the target weight, it will be time to wait for the phone call!"

"That's fantastic Charlene! What will that mean?" Mum asks.

"Well, once I finally get on this stupid list, we will have to have our bags packed ready to go. You'll have to help me choose some clothes! We will always need to be ready for a call because suitable lungs could come at any time and when it comes, we are going to have to rush to the airport and get a plane over to Newcastle straight away. I'll get my own private medical plane; it'll be like I'm famous!"

"We will get that bag sorted as soon as you are on the list. So the target is as it was; we need to get you to 40kg."

"Yep, so I will be on that list soon. They are going to fly out to take a look at me when I get close, so I will know for definite then."

"What happened when you heard you were suitable Charlene?" Mum asks.

"Well I asked them the obvious question: will I be able to go to Uganda when I get these new lungs," Charlene replies chirpily.

"Oh Charlene, I bet they didn't know what to make of you!" Mum laughs. "What did they say?"

"Well they laughed. They said no one has ever asked them a question like that before. Apparently there's risk of infection or something stupid like that, so they said no. Not that it matters. When we left I said to Dad, "That's what they think!" Once I get these lungs, no one is stopping me! Anyway, got to go. I'm not meant to be using a mobile in here and I don't want to get in trouble.

Dad is trying to get some sleep in the chair here; he will be snoring away in a second! Love you and see you soon," Charlene's voice breezes down the line.

"Love you Charlene," Mum replies, and she sets the phone down. We all look inquisitively at her and Mum smiles. "We're going to get there; if she gains weight, she is on the list."

"Well we need to keep praying then," Rebecca says, so we do just that as we join hands around the table. We move another step down the road to the day when Charlene will be healed.

Tuesday 18th August 2009

And so the dream begins.

Well have finally got around to starting this blog. It is here that I aim to keep you guys up to date with what is happening with my plans to build a school in Uganda and also my journey as I prepare for a lung transplant. I have recently completed a series of tests in Newcastle England to test my suitability for a double lung transplant and if everything goes according to plan I hope to be on the list within the next few months. God willing.

As many of you know I have been unwell for quite some time now and as a result had to leave school early. It was then that I came up with the idea of building a school in Uganda. I had been out previously and was due to go out during this summer however couldn't due to ill health. The need of the children shocked me and I saw that they were even being deprived of something as small as an education, something which in this country we take for granted and children complain about going to school. As a result I want to make a difference to a small number of children in Uganda by providing them with a chance to go to school. When the team were out in Uganda this summer I sent them with strict instructions to try and find me a primary school they thought could do with help. They found Hidden Treasure Primary, it is simply one little room made of sticks and mud where all of the children are taught together. I really do feel like this is the right school to be starting my project with and I pray to God that it will be the first school of many that the Charlene Project has helped to contribute towards. Thanks to everyone for your continued support and prayers.

Charlene

Throughout the next few weeks, Charlene's health fluctuates with many dips. Charlene continues to struggle on as the autumn leaves emerge in a mosaic of reds, browns and golds. A number of times her blood test show an increase in her white blood cell count, indicating that consistent infections are invading her body. She has to have her antibiotics changed yet again and administered intravenously. The problem is that she has become immune to so many of them because they have been administered so often, leading to a trial and error approach by the medical staff.

She has a portacath installed in early September: a thin plastic central line that will allow drugs to be passed intravenously, directly into her larger chest veins as her superficial veins are becoming more and more difficult to access. Her weight continues to hover at about 38kg in spite of numerous tube feeds, Domino's pizzas and home cooking brought up to her from Mum, and the last 2kg seem a hurdle too high. We are all concerned and fear that another infection could steal weeks of progress from her, pulling her weight down as it rages through her. Charlene continues to push for her target, determined and resolute as ever.

4th September 2009

Ok, so I am finally getting around to starting a journal. Something which I have been meaning to do for ages. The purpose of this journal is just for me to have somewhere that I can write down my thoughts and feelings of all that is going on in my life right now (which is a lot) whether it be about my ambition to build a school in Uganda (Hidden Treasure) or my journey as I prepare for a lung transplant. Sure I know it is still very early days but I really do believe and in a strange sort of way feel God telling me that it is going to happen. I know the road will be long, frustrating and bumpy but with the help of God and my AMAZING family I do believe that I will get to the end of the road.

Today I didn't do much else apart from sleep, so hoping tomorrow will be a better day and I will have more energy. It is so frustrating not to be able to do the things I did like eighteen months ago but such is life.

Anyway ciao for now!
Char

(Charlene's Journal)

Alongside this, Charlene is fundraising and publicising like there is no tomorrow. "I want to see this £70,000 raised by January," she announces brazenly.

"Charlene, you don't have a hope!" I scoff. "It will come, but you just need to be patient." I have been impressed by how generous people have been and how quickly the money is coming in, but £70,000 by January? Impossible!

Charlene smiles at me. "You don't believe it's possible? Watch this space, Davey Boy. That community needs that money for the school and it'll come sooner than you think."

More and more people do come alongside her to support her, organising various fundraisers from coffee mornings to sponsored walks. Alongside this, UTV approaches Charlene for an interview; this terrifies her, even though it is clear to the rest of us that she is a natural. She fires out blog entries onto the web, setting targets for money raised and getting excited as more and more people join with her efforts to bring the funds together. This encourages her massively, giving her struggle to reach her target weight renewed impetus.

Monday 21st September 2009

GMTV Interview

Well just got out of hospital there this afternoon to complete my IV antibiotics at home. The good news is that my weight has reached the 39.8kg mark so the 40kg necessary for Friday's appointment is within reach.

Jane and Nicola from GMTV interviewed me this afternoon about the school and my fundraising I was dead nervous but the girls were great and put me right at ease (even if one of them was a Man U supporter!!!!) It goes out tomorrow at 6.35am, 7.05am and 8.05am (how inconsiderate, they clearly are not aware that Miss Barr does NOT do mornings).

On the publicity front had a phone call from Sunday Life and they coming tomorrow to do an article. Who knows, next I'll have my own reality TV show!

Hope with all this publicity I get more of the funds needed.

All My Love
Char

In late September, the big day arrives and the consultants arrive from Newcastle. Charlene is apprehensive about the feedback they will give her at the end of the day. Has all her work paid off, or will she be rejected for the transplant list?

As the consultants assess and observe Charlene throughout the long day, they are encouraging and friendly. Mum spends the day by Charlene's side, knowing that their conclusion will massively impact her in the days and weeks to come.

At the end of the day, the consultants sit down and tell her the good news that if she continues to progress with the weight gain, she will be on the list by the end of the week. Charlene is overjoyed and immediately rushes to her computer to share her news with the world.

Friday 25th September 2009

Good News

So today was the big day where I would find out whether or not I would be put on the waiting list for a lung transplant. So as Mum and I walked into the room I was rather apprehensive as to what was going to be said particularly as I was working so hard to reach the necessary 40kg. So off I went and stepped on the scales and the final number was 39.3kg/6st 3 lb. Apparently the average weight for my height 148cm /4ft 8.5in is 45kg-55kg.

So basically the consultant from Freeman Hospital, Newcastle said that there were a couple of things to consider.

Initially there had been a query over my liver as it was a bit enlarged. However after exploring this they were not too concerned. Phew!

Next was getting the right mix of antibiotics that would work best for me afterwards if I was to receive a transplant. So the microbiologists in Newcastle have found a couple of good mixes and have just to find the BEST one that will work.

At the assessment back in August they had to check my blood type and it turns out that I am O+ so as this is the most common it will work in my favour if I am to be listed.

So at this stage I was feeling pretty ok about the situation as they had not said anything that made me feel like it wasn't going ahead. However they then proceeded to tell me that there are antibodies in my blood that would mean that 20% of organ donors would be a no go. At this point I was not sure where the whole thing was.

Then after giving me a quick summary the consultant told me that if I continued to progress with my weight gain they were happy enough and I would be placed on the list by... THE END OF NEXT WEEK.

Will keep you updated.

Up to now, we have all focused on just getting Charlene on the list. We have prayed and longed for a day which is fast coming. Yet, as one challenge is surpassed, another waiting game comes into play; now we must be ready for a call at any time of the day. Mum is the first contact alongside Charlene, Dad is second and I am third. Whenever the call comes, one of us must rush Charlene to the airport to catch the small plane that will carry her to the hospital; then the final leg of this journey will begin. We must be ready at all times.

Now every time the phone rings, our hearts soar. Every time it vibrates, we hope; but it is never Newcastle. Still we wait for that day when our fears will end and our hope will find fulfilment.

In October, Charlene's health dips drastically. She complains of chest pains, runs a high temperature and suffers from bouts of vomiting. Although she resists hospital at first we have little choice but to readmit her. It becomes clear that something is seriously wrong and the doctors struggle to diagnose the exact cause of her steep decline. For the first time, thoughts I never wanted to have, and had never yet considered, begin to form in my mind.

Charlene in hospital encouraged about one of her first donations towards building the school

18
DANCE WITH DEATH

"DAVE, ARE YOU OK?" I see concern on Chloe's face and I know I must look like a mess. My hands are sweaty and I can hear my blood pounding through my skull like a torrent; I know I am not thinking completely clearly. I feel as if I am in the midst of a hurricane and all I know is that I do not want to be here. I want to be two hundred metres from here at the City Hospital.

It is a Monday evening, deep in October. Charlene has been in hospital for a few days now and, though I first wrote this off as another routine yo-yo in her health, the medic-speak filtering out of the ward scares me. I can see fear growing in my parents eyes a similar fear to a rabbit caught in the headlights of an incoming truck, and I am starting to realise that words like 'infected line', 'clot' and 'abscess' mean a great deal more than I know.

Charlene spends a few days in the confines of her room in Ward 8; the news coming out is not positive. The medical staff are still unsure of the exact diagnosis of this new affliction despite a rigorous series of tests. She is exhausted. Mum has been with her all day and, having finished work, Dad is on his way to the hospital, but I am not there.

Instead, I am at Queen's Christian Union (CU) in the Students' Union. It is a three minute walk from the hospital and from the back door of this building, you can see the place where Charlene is confined, looming over the street. It sits unfeeling in the skyline like a block, with yellow veins running up its sides as if carrying its lifeblood. In the darkness, it seems to crouch, morbid and staring blindly outwards. I hate the place.

It is a Mission Agency Night at CU, so the theme of Mission is central to the evening. The different organisations that host this particular night had asked if they could interview a few people from CU on their mission experiences and how mission abroad impacts mission at home. I had been approached for an interview, having been in Uganda, Rwanda and the Congo in the summer. An interview would cause me to break out in a cold sweat at the best of times; I am always nervous before anything like this and struggle to know what to say when conversation turns to what happened in Africa this summer and what we had seen. How do you describe the indescribable? How do you share emotions you cannot even name? Ever since I was asked to do this, I have been dreading it.

Standing before Chloe, one of the CU committee members this year, the dread choking thickly through my veins is no longer to do with a five-minute interview. I don't fully understand what is making Charlene so sick at the minute, but I know from talking to Rebecca earlier that things are serious and fears that lie unspoken, locked away at the back of my mind, are threatening to break out.

"My sister's sick Chloe, really sick. And I don't know what to say for this interview thing. I haven't had time to think about it." Rebecca has gone in to find a seat, I feel suddenly alone and vulnerable.

"Is she ok? Are you sure you want to do this Dave?" Chloe asks. I nod. Even in the midst of everything, I know this is important; there is a connection between Charlene's fight for her new lungs and Africa, and in my limited way, I need to share some of our experiences from the summer.

"Do you want to pray?" Again, I nod and Chloe walks with me to a corridor away from the hustle and bustle of those arriving. We stand beside a window and I can see the incessant drizzle outside, the depressing, constant fall. It is dark and as cars pass outside, they send up spray from their tyres. I don't know what I am going to say.

Chloe prays and as she does, some of the worries in my head recede. The unspoken fears I have for Charlene are pushed back behind a door in my mind and locked away, for now. I know I am not shaking as much and, for the first time in a few hours, I stop staring at my fears. Instead, I bring them before a God who is bigger than any scenario I can conjure up. You are in control, aren't you God? You can save Charlene, can't you?

"Mrs Barr, I'm sorry to be the bearer of bad news, but you are going to have to face up to this." The consultant stands in the corridor, with steam rising in wisps off the coffee she is holding. Mum has left Charlene's room to try to speak to the consultant, catching her as she is about to enter her office. As she listens to the words, her breath is stolen away.

"Things are very serious as I'm sure your husband has explained to you. Charlene is in a very precarious situation and even if we can resolve this problem I don't expect her to be with us at Christmas."

Dead air. What can be said?

"Now if you'll excuse me, I have to go." The consultant turns and walks away, with each high-heeled footstep punctuating her statements. The world should stop, but it keeps turning. Mum turns, puts her hand on the handle and prays. "Please save my daughter," she whispers before she enters to resume her watch at Charlene's side.

As my legs swing backwards and forwards below me, I try to figure out what I am going to say, but my mind is still on my sister, not on what I will say in front of four hundred people. Rebecca leans forward and whispers, "I love you David, I'm praying," and then I know it is time for me to speak briefly. I walk to the front of the room and survey the sea of faces, but I do not feel so alone. Rebecca has spoken to a few people and some key friends scattered around the room know the situation; I know they are praying for Charlene right now and I feel more at peace.

The interview flashes by quickly. The only part where I struggle is when I talk of Olive, because I am reminded of things that I have forgotten. I tell them about meeting some widowed women in Rwanda; one girl called Olive told us that she lay on the floor of her home with her family in 1994, during the genocide, when she was 5 years old and listened as men outside discussed whether to raid and butcher everyone in the house now or wait until later. This girl's story could only be told because they chose to pass over the house. She ran. Her family experienced horrendous hardships that none of us in that room could begin to wrap our minds around. During the genocide, her mother was raped by seven different men in one night; she contracted HIV.

While speaking about this I stop for a second with my voice suddenly rough with emotion, grasping feebly for words as I remember. "Instinctively, when hearing of such things our hearts break, as they were created to do. And, if I'm honest, I lash out at God in anger, asking how He dares to let such things occur to His children, to those He claims to love, but I have so much to learn. I realise that God loves and aches for these people more than I ever could. He mourns and detests the actions of mindless hate as well as the apathy and blindness we in the West often choose to wallow in; He is with them. I am humbled by the faith that people like Olive and her mother show and I am ashamed when I listen to them sing of God's provision and love. They know Him more than I have yet dreamt."

I remember their songs of pure praise, with tears running down their cheeks, as they sang of a God they knew intimately in good times and times of devastating darkness. I know afresh that I do not know God in the same way, that my faith is so shallow and based around my wants, like a screaming spoilt and needy child. As I speak, I remember to again trust God with Charlene. He is there beside her, He is broken by her pain; He is beside her on every step of this journey, wherever it leads. He loves her even more than we do because He created her as His own, for a purpose that I do not know the end of yet. We need to trust him with the big picture. My problem is letting go.

As I stumble back to my seat, I am both glad that it is over, but also that I did it. Charlene's sickness, mission and the situation in Africa seem to be entwined and in fusion in more ways than I can yet grasp.

The lift moves grindingly slowly. I will it to move faster, but as Rebecca and

I stand, the red numbers above our heads still crawl at a snail's pace towards '8'. I am afraid of what I will find when we get there.

After the meeting was over, Rebecca and I went outside for some fresh air with Phil, a friend of ours. A number of people were going to a coffee shop and had asked if we would join them, but a series of texts answered that question for us. The texts were grim and to the point; the electronic letters unforgiving and emotionless, spelling out the cold reality for us - Charlene's situation was fast worsening. We ran the short distance to the hospital to join our family there, having no idea what to expect.

As we enter Charlene's claustrophobic room, I feel the knife of fear twist in my gut. Charlene is as sick as I have ever seen her. She is lying on the bed, white as a ghost with her face sunken. Tubes wind their way into the line going direct into the veins in her arm, pumping a concoction of chemicals into her blood and an oxygen mask that wraps right around her head is fastened to her. She lies wraith-like and you can see from the way she is shaking her head with her eyes clenched that she is in torment. Charlene is never a person to complain about her daily pain, but tonight she is in agony, screaming and writhing in pain. The fact that she is not attempting to disguise this as she normally does fills me with dread.

All the family are here. Bethany and Serena grip the metal railing by her bed and their knuckles are white. Natalie stands on the other side of the bed; she is ghostly pale and her eyes are full of fear. "Dad?" Rebecca asks, voice trembling.

Dad takes Rebecca and me aside, out of Charlene's hearing and gently explains; "They still aren't completely sure, but she has been diagnosed with a clot in her lung and an abscess. It's very serious." This means little to me, but it means something to Dad and to Rebecca. In front of Charlene, they will never show it, but I can see they are distraught.

The peace I grasped earlier has fled. The door of unnamed fears I had locked away flings wide open and black thoughts flood my mind. For the first time, I fear Charlene may leave us and it terrifies me. Scant hours ago we had been worrying about a multitude of mundane things that won't live past today, now we are faced with the reality that we could lose Charlene. I feel cold. This cannot be. Not when we seemed to be getting so close to transplant.

We talk to Charlene and try to cheer her up, but she is in severe pain. Wired up to a drip, she lies there, unable to speak with the oxygen mask attached to her face. Our fears go unspoken, but we are all sore afraid, terrified of the same thing. We feel powerless. All we can do is stand with her and pray, stand so she knows she is not alone in her desperate wrestle with death itself.

We talk a lot that night as we are in and out of her hospital side room;

Mum and Dad are unable to answer the twins' questions about whether Charlene will be ok. Dread grips Rebecca and I as we text prayer requests around to many of our friends, asking for prayer. I feel powerless. Waves of panic lap at the edge of my consciousness and it occurs to me that I had never before realised how much we take for granted the health and wellbeing of those we love, nor how limited and impotent we feel when they are in danger. The inertia gnaws at us, the waiting and wanting to help but being unable to do so.

The hours drag on; Mum and Dad know the girls need to get home so they can get to school the next morning. "One of us should stay tonight," Mum says looking down at Charlene, who is sleeping for now. Mum's face is pale and drawn; it is easy to see the toll this is taking on her, she has had little sleep over the last few days.

"I'll stay tonight," Rebecca volunteers.

"No, you have a nine o'clock class. I don't have anything until eleven; I'm doing an Arts subject! I'll stay tonight." After a short discussion we agree, on the proviso that I call if Charlene deteriorates in any way. "We will have our phones on all night David, let us know if there is any change," Dad whispers as he leaves, kissing Charlene on the cheek.

"I will. Love you Dad," I reply.

Charlene is still asleep and the only sound in the room is the oxygen firing through the mask and into her lungs. Outside, the city lights shine in the rain and I can see distant cars move down the Lisburn Road, their headlights striking out against the darkness. I think of how I have driven that road many times, preoccupied with my own selfish desires, without thinking of the suffering and death dances that are occurring in the hospital I drive past. Now I know.

I make up a bed in the green chair at Charlene's feet, and watch my sister. She sleeps fitfully and again I'm struck by her weakness, but also by her bravery as she has fought against overwhelming odds. I wonder how much longer she can keep going. I try to sleep, but every time I close my eyes, my mind is filled with dark thoughts that spiral through my head, one after the other, like a slide show on a loop. The thoughts circle in my head like vultures, picking at my hope like it is a rotting corpse. Never before have I felt so helpless. I want to do something, anything to take away her pain, but I cannot.

Charlene coughs violently again, roused from her slumber. Her coughs rack and convulse her body, making her face red and strained; it sounds like she is coughing up her very lungs. She is covered in sweat. I sit wide-eyed and all I can do is listen and pray that the gasps will not be her last. She finally stops and, with ragged breaths, turns to try to sleep again.

I am so afraid that she will suddenly be overcome in her valiant struggle and stop breathing. I look around the room for a buzzer if it comes to this and having located it, resume my watch of the night. I am agitated, afraid we will lose her; I cannot imagine this. Yet, she keeps breathing, drawing in the oxygen that floods her mouth and nostrils, every breath like a prayer to God.

I wish I had an answer. Any of us will take her pain upon ourselves, but we cannot. There is a gap between us that can never be bridged. We can do nothing to change the situation and it is devastating. All I can do is sit and watch with her, praying she will be strengthened in her fight. As a brother who instinctively wants to protect his younger sisters, I feel like I am failing Charlene. I cannot imagine what it is like for Mum and Dad.

Monday 19st October 2009

Really ill

Dickie writing. Charlene has had a really difficult day. Has been very ill - antibiotics changed again, other medication added in and minor surgical procedure scheduled for tomorrow. Please remember her and if you pray, please pray for her. Thank you.

The night crawls by and the early hours of the morning are lonely ones. I set my phone alarm for every half hour to check that the oxygen mask is on correctly, that Charlene is still breathing regularly, and I try to sleep. As she drifts between sleep and the waking world, occasionally spluttering and heaving as a coughing fit falls upon her, I watch and pray. As Charlene continues her fight, I begin to understand how much we take for granted and the extent to which every breath is a gift from God.

In the quiet of the dark and listless hours between dusk and dawn, that seem to never end, I think back to days I had pushed to the back of my mind: those days of pain in our home, where Charlene's heart was fought over and all of us were scarred. I think of how I hated her actions and that, for so long, I had held resentment towards her within my heart. I feel regret that I allowed this to build and reside within me, harbouring bitterness, twisting around and choking my heart like thorns. I do not know when, but things have changed forever: my own cold, calloused heart has been healed.

I know that I truly love Charlene from the depths of my heart and my anger towards her is gone. As I watch her taking laboured breaths, praying desperately for her safety as a drowning man grasps for a lifeline, I know that God has wrought a deep change within my divided heart. I love Charlene, not just in the deep true way I discovered long ago, but also in emotion, word and deed.

Dawn breaks through, shepherding the darkness away towards the western sky. Morning comes, as does Mum. "How is she?" Mum asks quietly as she enters, not wanting to wake Charlene. I wonder how much sleep Mum got.

"She's ok Mum, she has slept a good bit. She's tired."

"You'd better go David, you'll be late for your lectures," Mum prompts. I smile, muttering about how that will be expected anyway and walk over to my sister. I lean in and kiss her gently on the cheek, whispering in her ear, "I love you so much Charlene." She sleeps on, deep in dreams, but her eyelids flicker at my whisper.

As I leave, Mum sits on the chair that became my watchtower and awaits Charlene's awakening.

Tuesday 20th October 2009

Improvement and Thanks

Dickie again:
We are in so much a better place tonight than last night. Yesterday was very, very difficult but today Charlene has picked up the baton and fought and battled back against all the odds. The central line has been successfully removed and Charlene has a little bit more energy today and tons more fight than we could ever have hoped for. There is clearly a long way to go, and we have been going two steps forward and two steps back, but things are again pointing and moving in the right direction - a real answer to the prayers of so many. Thank you to everyone who has been praying for and thinking of Charlene.

Sorry we have not been able to answer all the texts and messages, but your love and support means just so much to Charlene and all the other Barrs.

God is always good. God bless.

This cycle repeats itself through the next few days, with Mum or Dad mostly taking it in turns to watch and pray over Charlene every night. Rebecca and I relieve them when they allow us, but this is rare. Natalie, Bethany and

Even when I walk through the darkest valley, I will not be afraid, for you are close beside me. Your rod and your staff protect and comfort me. Psalm 23:4

Serena are up in the hospital room late into the nights, but despite their protestations, Mum and Dad insist they go home every night to be well rested for school. The night watches are long, especially for our parents; we do not know as we watch beside her if Charlene will greet us the next morning.

Incredibly, and defying the ominous predictions, Charlene rallies and is soon sitting up, chattering away. "Charlene, put that oxygen mask back on," Dad says, attempting to be stern one night we are all gathered in her room together. He can't help but smile though, flooded with relief that his daughter has been returned to him.

"This old thing is so annoying; I can't talk when it's on. I'd be mortified if anyone saw me with it, it makes me look like a robot!" she says, before eventually acquiescing to Dad's request. She is smiling again and, although she is still clearly weak and tired, she seems to be on the road toward recovery.

"It might be a good thing if you're not talking Charlene; it's the only way to shut you up!" Natalie says with a grin on her face.

"Well at least we are getting out of October. I swear, October is always my bad month!" Charlene exclaims, smiling.

As laughter fills the room, we are all aware how close we have come to disaster. We have reached the eleventh hour, but have been granted more precious time. It seems clear to me that Charlene has been preserved, that God has His Hand upon her until the appointed time; He is keeping her safe until those lungs come. Then it will all make sense and all of this suffering will be redeemed. As she stands in Uganda, opening the school that would never have been built were it not for her illness, the school that God planted in a heart that had been assaulted and tormented for so long, then it will all make sense and the story will be at an end. I see her standing cutting the tape at Hidden Treasure, with her new lungs breathing in the Ugandan air that she has loved from the moment she stepped off that plane in 2008: she will be healed.

Thursday 22nd October 2009

I'm Back

Just a quick update to say that I am beginning to improve. I think I can honestly say that this last week was probably one of the worst I have ever experienced. Sure there is still a long way to go but put it like this I'm already pestering the docs to let me home so that can only be a good thing!!

Thanks so much to everyone who is praying for me and the family, Facebooking us and texting us. Mum and Dad have been sitting with me most days and I always love when they read out all of the texts they have received Thanks so much folks they really do help.

On the fundraising side of things we have hit the £10,000 mark so keep it coming folks. Thank you so much.

Thanks Again
Char

19
WINTER DAYS

THE NEXT FEW WEEKS are a swirl of business for Charlene as she blogs and works incessantly at raising the profile for her dream, determined to raise the money necessary. She works tirelessly, almost with tunnel vision, as if she believes her time is short, and even when she is back in hospital her laptop serves as her window to the outside world as she communicates non-stop via Facebook and email.

Her problem with the abscess and clot in her lungs means Charlene is now off the transplant list again. Any time she is off the list, as she is now, her drive to get back onto it is remarkable.

Mum, Poppa, Bethany and Serena arrive one evening to see her in hospital and she is sitting upright in her bed, bent over her laptop, hammering away at the keyboard. As Mum and the twins enter the room, her eyes light up and she says, "Look at this, I finally got the new blog entry typed up."

"How are you Charlene?" Serena asks as she sits down at the end of her bed, but Charlene waves away her questions. "I'm fine, I'm fine, quit your worrying! You got any news from Hidden Treasure?" These are always Charlene's first words, even when she is clearly not fine. Her eyes are set on a different sight than her immediate health and both her focus to get back on the transplant list and the drive to raise the money for Hidden Treasure spur her onwards. She refuses to take her eye off the goal and nothing is going to get in her way!

"No," Mum replies. "But your father did get a call from BBC and they want to interview you about the school if you are up to it next week."

Charlene bites her lip. "Can you or Dad not do it? I really don't like this stuff; I have no clue what to say!"

Charlene has already been interviewed by UTV earlier in the year and the story of a girl awaiting a life-saving double lung transplant, while fundraising for a school in Uganda, is one that is arousing interest.

"Charlene you were excellent," Poppa exclaims. "Your Grandma would have been so proud of you. You go down there and speak from your heart, that's all you need to do."

Charlene nods. "Well if it gets more money in for those kids to go to school, then I'll do it. I'm going to end up embarrassing myself though!" she chatters happily. "Here take a look at the blog."

Charlene never craved attention, strongly disliking appearing on camera or TV to 'promote' the project, though she knew the benefits of doing so, and dutifully did her part – however it was her story intersecting with 'their' story in Uganda which really made people sit up and take notice.

How often have we heard appeals about Africa, or seen terrible images on our TV screens, and remained unmoved to react? The fact that Charlene suffered so much herself, yet still turned her attentions onto the needs of others separated this story from others.

(Charlene's Project Newsletter)

Charlene sits beside the Christmas tree and stares nervously at the camera. "Is this where you want me to sit?"

Tara Mills smiles and says, "Yes, that's perfect. You will be great Charlene, just talk about how you are raising money for the school in Uganda. Whenever you're ready," she prompts encouragingly.

Charlene swallows and starts to speak. As soon as she does, her nerves seem to fall off her like shackles as her words flow from deep inside. "Well, I started the blog in August and from there it started taking off. People have donated money online and different people have done fundraisers as well."

"The kids were walking miles to school in bare feet and ragged clothes; they were leaving their houses, which were just wooden shacks, at six or seven o'clock in the morning. They'd be at school until about four or five every day and wouldn't even get lunch, then they'd have the journey home, yet they were so excited to be at school and to be learning. I came up with the idea of building a school in Uganda because I thought if my education couldn't continue then it would be better to help others go to school."

The flow of words dries up as Charlene stops and stares expectantly at the camera; she has said her piece. The camera man steps back and nods, satisfied. "Was that ok?" Charlene asks anxiously.

"Yes Charlene, well done," Tara reassures her. "You did really, really well. I just have a few questions for our information, if that's ok?"

"Yeah sure, fire away."

"So I know you are waiting for the transplant, but are you actually on the transplant list at the minute?" Tara queries, pen and notepad in hand.

"Yes and no. I need to be a certain weight before they will consider me for transplant, you see. At the minute, I'm not there as I lost weight when I was sick recently, but when I am up to 40kg again I'll go back on the list and whenever lungs that match my size become available, I have to be ready."

"The difficulty is that not enough people are signed up to donate organs," Dad chimes in. "So it's just waiting until suitable ones becomes available."

"Thank you. Charlene we will go and take a look at the footage and put it together into a report," Tara says, slipping her pen into her pocket. "You are a very brave girl and it has been lovely to meet you. Have you got any fundraisers coming up soon?"

Charlene nods her head excitedly. "Yeah, we do actually. We are having a walk for all the women on Saturday; we are calling it the 'Dolly Walk'. Everyone collects sponsorship and on the night they start at the church and walk the same distance the children in Uganda have to walk to get water every day. I want to use the money to build a well for the community, you see."

"That sounds brilliant Charlene. So will you be waiting for everyone to get back with a cup of tea in your hand?" Tara says smiling.

"Not on your life, I'm going to do some of this walking myself!" Charlene retorts.

"We'll see if your health is up to it, Charlene," Dad says, urging caution, but he knows that if Charlene wants to walk on Saturday, she will walk. When she sets her mind on something, Charlene's dogged determination

Charlene doing her Dolly Walk December 2009

usually means she gets what she has set her mind on. It is this spirit that is the outpost of all of our hopes for Charlene getting her transplant.

That Saturday, in the bitter cold outside, Charlene, although very weak and ill, manages to walk 100m down the road, achieving her target.

Thursday 10th December 2009

Busy Busy Busy

Sorry I'm only getting around to blogging now but things have been hectic.

I am now out of hospital five weeks today and my dream of avoiding being in before Christmas is beginning to look more like a reality. Now that I have been doing so well I am enjoying more trips out which I am really enjoying and I am definitely getting into the Christmas spirit. I had my CT scan today however I will not get the results until Friday when I have the clinic appointment with the transplant team from Newcastle. Please pray that the abscess will have significantly decreased in size/disappeared as this will be the main factor on whether I make it back onto the list or not.

Project wise things are going fantastically well with the total now over £31,000. The Dolly Walk is coming up this Saturday night and so I am looking forward to that. I have been busy getting it out there as I can and was lucky enough to have the lovely Tara Mills from BBC Newsline come down and film me for a piece (terrifying!!!!) and then on Monday morning I set off nice and early (well 10am :)) for an interview on U105 with Pamela Ballentine which was an experience lol - actually seeing inside a radio studio was pretty cool. I will try and get both interviews up on the website.

So all and all things are going well. Thanks so much to everyone who is continuing to support the project and I promise I will do an update sometime over the weekend after the Dolly Walk.

Char
xx

Charlene being interviewed in the UTV studio by Pamela Ballentine

Family holidays have always been special to us. So many times, as we eat together around the dinner table, our conversations will wander towards memories of crazy things we have done as a family on holiday. Charlene loves them as much as any of us, and if there was a holiday destination we had more good memories of than any other it was our trips to Center Parcs. A trip has been booked for December, but the only question as December creeps past is whether Charlene's health will be stable enough to allow us to go.

We have always talked about going to Center Parcs in the winter, but have never done so, mainly due to the prices. However, one day in a fit of the head staggers, Mum and Dad finally book a week long trip there, with us planning to leave on Boxing Day and come back a few days into the New Year of 2010. I have a nagging suspicion rooting in my mind like a weed as to why my parents have done this - perhaps they wonder whether we will have many more holidays together as a complete family - but I refuse to give voice to this traitorous thought.

In the run up to Christmas, Charlene's health dips again and she continues on her antibiotics. With Christmas fast approaching, doubts about whether the trip will be possible begin to surface. However, any time we raise this concern, Charlene refuses to hear any of it, sticking her chin out defiantly with a determined look in her eye, insisting, "We are going to Center Parcs, you just try and stop me. Make sure you have those bags packed, ready to go!"

We all half-heartedly pack our bags for going, unsure as to whether or not we will be unpacking them again in a few days when the trip falls through. Every day we talk with Charlene about the trip and try to prepare her in case it is not possible. But Charlene is dogged in reaching her goal.

Ultimately, just before Christmas, her health improves, seemingly by sheer force of will alone. On Christmas Day, we sit around the table and talk. We are all tired after a good meal, although Charlene, on a large number of her tube feeds every night to get her weight up, is not hungry.

"What exams does Santa do?" Natalie asks, her red hat from her cracker resting precariously on her head.

"This is going to be rubbish," Serena interjects. "Pass the Shloer down here please could you Bethany?"

"His HO-HO-HO Levels! I crack myself up!" Natalie exclaims, ignoring Serena. "Anybody else got any others?"

"That's an old one," Auntie Alex says, chuckling to herself.

"I told you it would be terrible," mutters Serena under her breath.

Dad intervenes. "Okay girls, one second. Charlene, do you feel up to going? The hospital phoned and said they really wouldn't advise it and we want to do what's best for you so that we can get you back on this transplant list again." His concerned demeanour is somewhat negated by the pink hat that keeps sliding down his forehead.

"Of course I'm going! I don't care what they say, they can go and take a hike," Charlene spurts out. "The way I look at it is I want to live my life to the max and take the chances I get. I don't know how long I am going to have to wait until I get these lungs and I am not going to sit around wrapped in cotton wool, doing nothing until it happens. Of course we're going."

"Are you sure Charlene?" Rebecca insists. "You know how you are feeling and you can't afford to put yourself at risk."

"There's no way I'm not going, they have a Starbucks and all there. If I feel sick, I can go and sit in there until I feel a bit better sure." She reaches for another cracker. "Now who wants to see if they can get a better joke than Natalie?"

I shake my head and smile. Charlene catches my eye and offers me the other end of the cracker. As I reach over, her bravery strikes me all over again. No matter what faces her, Charlene never complains, never feels sorry for herself and refuses to show how sick she is. Her spirit is remarkable and puts my own to shame. It is this spirit that God has given her, tempered in the fire of both her war against her creeping illness and her struggle to accept love, that will drive her to get this school built and to get new lungs; I have no doubt. We pull the cracker.

"Ha ha, I win!" Charlene says. "You need a hat to hide your bald patch, though."

I instinctively raise my hands. "I do not have a bald patch!" Then I smile. It is good to have everyone together for Christmas, like so many times before. So many good memories of Christmas together, with so many more to come I am sure.

As we all laugh Mum raises her voice over the din, commanding our attention, "Well we will all have a good time together in Center Parcs then. Merry Christmas everyone. Charlene, we need to pray that you will be sitting here at this table for Christmas dinner this time next year with new lungs."

"Yeah, and with the school built. Listen everyone, why was Santa's little helper depressed?"

"Not another one," groans Bethany.

"Because he had low elf-esteem! Because he's an elf, you see?" Charlene cackles before ending up in a coughing fit.

As the madness continues to hold sway over the table, I know this is going to be a good holiday.

20
ON THE BRINK OF A YEAR

"THAT LAKE IS COMPLETELY FROZEN; do you think there are fish at the bottom?" Bethany asks. We are standing by the lake in Center Parcs, where a multitude of pedalos, canoes and windsurfers usually skim across the surface. As children, we explored all the nooks and crannies of the lake by pedalo, arguing at length over who would have the honour of steering.

Today there are no boats on the lake as winter rules supreme. The lake is as glass, frozen solid by the deep freeze that has descended and pulled the country tight into her embrace. The biting cold is showing no signs of loosening its grip. The ice is thick and mirror-like, perfectly reflecting back the azure sky above. All that can be seen are a few ducks who continue to brave the elements, slipping and sliding over the ice beside a small pool in the centre of the lake; only this shrinking oasis has escaped winter's touch thus far.

"I don't know," I reply. "But I bet you could cross that lake by foot and have no problem. That ice is thick."

"Okay, I dare you then, see if you can cross it without breaking it," Natalie challenges. Immediately I feel my male pride at stake, but before I can accept her wager, Mum steps in between us.

"Don't you dare be so stupid? That would be so dangerous and such a bad example to your sisters. No one is going out on that ice; I can't believe you were considering it David. I'm really disappointed in you."

"I wasn't actually going to do it!" I protest indignantly.

"Yeah right!" Rebecca mutters under her breath behind me.

The ducks waddle towards us, occasionally tumbling on their beaks as they traverse the precarious ice. Charlene pulls the old loaf she has brought out of her bag and waves it above her head. "Let's feed them, they must be starving!"

She passes out mouldy slices of bread to everyone and we break off pieces and toss them towards the ducks. It is obvious they are hungry as they dive and race each other for each morsel that falls on the iron ground. Natalie and I are the first to see the potential in this, tossing bread at the feet of Bethany and Serena, who screech and leap backwards as ducks lunge towards them. This quickly develops into a game with a lot of jumping, dodging and creative placement of bread around others, while the ducks scramble about gobbling up bread wherever they find it. Eventually we are all exhausted from laughing, warm trails of mirth running down our frozen cheeks.

Charlene is red faced and ruddy, both from the cold and the laughing. "Do you reckon we could lead them into the outdoor pool?" The pool lies just behind us; its tendrils of steam rising like fingers from the bubbling surface, climbing and dissipating in the semi-arctic atmosphere. "Let's try it."

Charlene lays a trail for the ducks, who follow dutifully, swallowing up each piece laid down. She looks like the Pied Piper with the trail of ducks following her every move, but much as she tries, she cannot entice her followers to plunge into the steaming swimming pool.

"That's enough everyone," Mum proclaims, restoring some semblance of order. "Let's get back to the villa and we can all have coffee."

"What about hot chocolate?" asks Serena as her eyes widen.

"I'll make you some hot chocolate when we get back," Rebecca reassures her as we carefully start to make the trek through the treacherous pathways back to the villa. Dad quickly calls guest services and they send a van to collect Charlene. She is able to get out and about, but any excessive effort, even walking somewhere, exhausts and weakens her. There is a jarring difference between the girl I see now and the playmate who tirelessly played games in the garden with me as a child. The memories of how she used to run around with us, surging through obstacle courses we made in the garden and cycling and exploring little country lanes in the long idyllic summer months seem to belong to a lost world that has been stolen from us. But I know this is just a symptom of her weakening lungs and look forward with renewed vigour to the long-awaited transplant call.

As the van approaches, Charlene swings around and looks at Mum and Dad. She is breathing heavily and sweat glistens on her brow; she is tired even from the short time we have spent beside the lake. Her eyes sparkle though, and her spirit shines out of them, defying the frail physical frame in which she resides. "So can we come down to the lake tomorrow night for the New Year's Eve fireworks?"

"It will depend on how you are Charlene, it's forecast to be very cold," Dad warns cautiously.

"It will be fine; I'm not missing the fireworks! I'm not going to be a muppet and sit in my bed on New Year's Eve!" she insists as the van grinds to a halt beside her. "I'm away on, I'll see you all back at the villa. I'll stick the kettle on and I might even make a start on your hot chocolate, Serena!" She steps onto the van and shuts the door behind her, waving to us as the van drives on, Charlene disappearing up the road ahead of us.

On holidays, we have always spent time playing cards and board games in the evenings and this trip is no exception. We play games such as Whist and Sevens, as well as board games such as The Big Taboo and Articulate. Our family is competitive, especially when teams divide down gender lines; Dad and I on one side, Mum and the girls on the other. The Big Taboo is an especially infamous game due to the arguments caused by alleged cheating (or different interpretations of the rules, depending on who you ask), leading Mum once to exclaim to Dad in the heat of a Pictionary round, "The only good thing about this marriage is the kids!" We spend a lot of the long bitter evenings in our villa, playing games and sipping on hot spiced apple juice.

It is clear now how ill Charlene is. She can no longer stay up late and has to go to bed earlier in the evening, getting physically exhausted very quickly and sleeping a lot more. She finds any sort of exertion draining and any mild exercise leaves her looking spent and drawn. Nonetheless, she never complains and continues to act as if all is well, refusing to acknowledge her illness, as if she can defeat it by pretending it does not exist. Her indomitable spirit continues to shine through everything she does.

We have brought Charlene's tube feeds with us and every evening Dad sets up the feed pump driver beside her bed; she picks up the long clear tubes that wind like ghostly snakes across the floor and plugs them into the plastic peg tube that has been secured in her stomach by operation. Over the course of the night, they slowly and relentlessly pump the calorie rich fluid directly into her stomach, filling her. They are doing their job well, slowly increasing her weight, though it is not easy for Charlene. She is often very sick in the mornings as a result of the feeds, throwing up and losing much of the calories she has gained over the course of night. However, although she hates being linked to oxygen and her feeds at night, she remains determined to get her weight up by hook or by crook in order to be well enough when the long-awaited call comes, and no sacrifice is too much.

The medication she is on has been building over the last few months, and recently she has been diagnosed with diabetes on top of everything else, meaning she has to inject insulin daily - an injection she adds to the other she has to take daily to thin her blood and prevent lung clots forming again. The cocktail of drugs she is on boggles the imagination and in the mornings she sits up groggily while Dad prepares her different intravenous medications; she dutifully holds her nose and gives them to herself one by one via her intravenous line.

It is truly a God-send that Dad is a doctor as he can help her in her preparations and make sure she is taking exactly what is needed. He is also able to assess any problems. One night at Center Parcs, it becomes clear that Charlene is having an adverse reaction to one of the new drugs as a red rash snakes up her legs and begins to lace her body in small red spots; Dad is able to identify the drug and discontinue it temporarily.

Looking at Charlene it is clear how much she has sacrificed through her life. Her body bears numerous scars from her lifelong struggle to halt the creeping, merciless progress of the disease that is rotting her body from within. It is so clear that her spirit, full of life and fire, is inhabiting a shell. Her face has become bloated from the steroids she is taking. Her neck bears scars from previous surgeries where plastic tubes have been inserted into her veins so that powerful antibiotics can be run straight into her blood stream when necessary. Her right arm has a line directly attached running straight into her chest veins for ease of access, and she has it wrapped in white bandage to hide it from prying eyes. Her chest bears several scars where doctors have operated, an especially prominent scar cuts straight across her abdomen from surgery in her first year of life. It also holds the peg that has been installed for her tube feeds. All of this has been necessary, and Charlene would have had it no other way; without these things she would have lost her fight long ago. However, this does not negate the cost. Her body is ravaged, and the sickness shows no mercy.

Yet, Charlene stands. She does not fall and she does not let any of this define her. I marvel at her. Charlene is a young woman and having five sisters, I am acutely aware of the burden society inflicts on girls and the cruel and poisonous lies that are whispered into their minds about what they should look like. For Charlene, wraith-like and painted with scars across her body, it is hard. She dreams of falling in love, getting married and most of all, having her own children, as any young girl would. But she never complains about how her body is being torn apart in an effort to slow the grinding hunger of her cystic fibrosis. Never once does she feel sorry for herself, for she has her eyes set on a different goal.

She wears these burdens lightly, and her identity is based not in her disease or her misfortune, but in something deeper. For so long she struggled to find who she was, but things have changed and her identity is based in the God she desires to serve, in her love for Uganda and the love of her family.

Never does she complain and, as a result, it is often easy to forget how sick she is. However, it is becoming impossible to ignore. While we carry on as normal in Center Parcs with games and numerous trips to Starbucks, where Charlene loves to sip on her lattes, over all of this hangs the pall of her mortality and the steady decline of her health.

I know Mum and Dad are becoming aware that unless the call comes soon, everything we do could be a last. It could be a last holiday, last trip, last meal together, last game, last anything. She needs this transplant. Fear begins

I praise you because I am fearfully and wonderfully made; your works are wonderful, I know that full well. – Psalm 139:14

Fearfully and wonderfully made just screams out to me that God made each and every one of us so perfectly. What He made was wonderful. Also the term fearfully to me means that we should fear God in a healthy way and the works that He does because the end result is always perfect and finished as He intended.

God sorry for complaining about the body you have given me and always trying to change it. Lord I just ask that you will help me see myself the way that you see me and also accept that I am built like this for your sole purpose.

Amen

(Charlene's Journal)

to stalk me as I dwell on this and that fear robs joy from every moment.

Regardless, Charlene refuses to dwell on her limitations. We go bowling early one morning and she rouses herself and comes, refusing to use the bowling ramps, picking up a ball much too heavy for her and flinging it with all her energy down the alley. We go to play badminton and, although she is unable to play, she comes and orders a coffee and sits and watches from the side, critiquing our technique. We go to the swimming pool and, while Charlene can't go swimming due to the line in her arm, she reads at the side of the pool and talks to Mum who sits with her. We spend more and more time doing things together.

New Year's Eve rolls around and the temperature drops like a stone as the night advances, ripping away any heat still clinging to the ground. Thick clouds crawl across the skyline and devour the mountaintops in the distance. At first we do not plan to go out to the fireworks but Charlene insists, furious at the suggestion that we will just sit in this night. Eventually Mum and Dad relent, we call the van to bring Charlene down to the lakeside decking and we leave the villa to meet her there.

"It is absolutely baltic!" Charlene exclaims, her breath clouding in mist before her. All of us are wrapped in layer upon layer of clothing to protect us from the bitter cold around us. We have arrived early, a novelty for us,

Center Parcs December 2009

and have managed to get standing space right beside the lake stretching out before us; half an hour of 2009 remains.

Normally on New Year's Eve , the members of our family are scattered all over Northern Ireland, visiting friends at various house parties. New Year isn't a time we usually spend together; in fact this is going to be the first time we have been together for it in years. Invariably, New Year would be hyped up and then is a let-down as the party string falls from the lampshades and the warbling sounds of Auld-Lang-Syne fade. Every year it is a good night with friends, but nothing special. This New Year, spent together as a family, is going to be different.

"It was forecast to be cold," Rebecca reminds us. A red scarf is wrapped tightly around her neck, and her blue coat is pulled close. "These fireworks had better be worth it! At least it's dark enough we will be able to see them."

It is a dark night; no stars or moon can be seen and the clouds loom thick and black above us. The lights on the decking shine especially brightly into the darkness. The trees around the lake reach and scratch towards the sky above, shrouded in cloud. The lake is still frozen solid and shines like an iridescent mirror, reflecting back any light that falls upon it. The surface of the lake is flawless and, as I follow it with my eyes away from the light, it becomes like a black mirror, a hole that goes on forever. It is beautiful.

Dad clears his throat. "So any New Year resolutions? How about being nice to Daddy all year?"

"Wise up old man," Natalie jokes, mock punching him in the arm.

"Well for you Rebecca, it's got to be to stop your flirting with every boy you meet. We saw you with that lifeguard earlier!" I tease. We all laugh, including Rebecca. This is patently untrue; Rebecca does anything but flirt and it is a running joke in the house.

"Seriously though," Dad interjects. "I have one for Natalie and the twins."

"It's going to be the hockey, I bet you a fiver it's the hockey," Serena mutters to Bethany under her breath. Bethany rolls her eyes.

"It's for you to win the Kate Russell this year," Dad says wistfully, a far off look in his eye, confirming Serena's suspicions. The Kate Russell is an All-Ireland schools hockey tournament and Dad has long dreamt of watching his daughters play for a victorious Lurgan College team.

"Yeah that's right Richard," Mum snorts. "Let's not worry about Natalie's A-Levels or Bethany and Serena's GCSEs next year. Their New Year resolution should be about hockey!"

"You are obsessed," Bethany says laughing, but Charlene raises her arm and interrupts us. "Actually that's a great target. I'm going to come to every game to watch yous, and I want to see yous go all the way this year. I'm going to be your Number One fan, that's one of my resolutions. Don't let me down!" she says beaming. *

We quieten down as more and more people arrive behind us and the seconds tick closer and closer to 2010, a year where everything must change one way or another.

"What other resolutions do you have, Charlene?" Mum asks quietly. The air around us seems to have stilled and grown heavier, as if holding its breath, listening. The encroaching darkness hangs back and everything seems weightier, more significant all of a sudden. It is as if time itself has slowed for a second more, before it takes the plunge into the New Year.

Charlene breathes and her words mist and drift away as she speaks them. "I have two others. First is to get this school started; we need to get the money in and I want the building started. I want to see those kids in that new school building as soon as possible. You think of where they are going

---

Charlene was made an Honorary Member of the Lurgan College team and supported her sisters and the College faithfully, even insisting on attending a Schools Cup game in County Donegal just ten days before she died. Natalie, Bethany and Serena along with the whole Lurgan College team made it their challenge to win the Ulster and the All Ireland Kate Russell Trophy after she died. This they achieved in 2011. Charlene would have been so proud. (see photograph on Page 138).

to school at the minute, it's not on; especially when you look at all the money we waste in our country. I want to get that well put in soon, too."

"Second is the lungs, obviously; the sooner the better. I'm sick of going in and out of hospital and all these stupid drugs and feeds. That's a big target for me."

"Those are good targets Charlene, and they are targets for all of us too," Mum confirms quietly. "We're in this together."

As Mum finishes and the moment passes, time seems to restart again, resuming its steady flow as a silence settles over our conversation. Fifteen minutes remain until the new decade and, as if it had been waiting to hear our New Year's resolutions, the first sprinklings of snow fall lightly from above. Within a matter of seconds, it comes thickly, bringing obvious delight to each of us. The snowflakes spiral down from the clouds far above us, dancing along on gentle breaths of the wind, landing silently all around us. The mirror-like illusion of the lake is shattered as thick blankets of snow fall on it, blurring the distinction between land and water. Snow is everywhere, creating a real winter wonderland. It couldn't be more magical, like a scene from a Christmas card.

"Let me take a few pictures," Dad shouts over our excited chatter, whipping out his ever-present camera.

"Dad!" Charlene moans. "You might as well get that thing fixed to your hands; you never stop taking pictures with it."

"Everyone get together for a picture. Smile!" he says, holding it out in front of him and fiddling with the flash.

We take it in turns taking pictures and posing together as the snow dusts us with a thin white layer. Every picture captures a point in time, a memory that will never be lost.

"Look at David; he looks like he's got dandruff!" Natalie screeches, pointing.

"Stay still then," I retort, shaking my head and sending the snow flying off me and onto her. Before the snowball fight can develop, Mum wisely intervenes, reminding us about the other people around us.

Music starts to pipe out through the tinny speakers behind us, with Westlife's voice screeching out through the snow. They are Charlene's favourite band and she is immediately singing along. "I believe in angels," she belts out, with Natalie creatively harmonising alongside her.

"Seriously girls, they are terrible," I complain. "They are everything that is wrong with modern music. They don't write their own stuff and are glorified karaoke. They just stand there and every single song ends in the same key change." This line of argument fails spectacularly, as Mum joins in with the singing and the girls' voices growing all the louder, drowning me out. Dad laughs and leans in, the snow gathering on the rim of his glasses. "Don't bother David; it's a battle you'll never win. If only they played a bit of Charlie Landsborough!" I smile shaking my head. "I don't know which would be worse!"

The countdown begins, with the snow whirling through the air around us, conducting its own silent dance. We join in with the shouts all around us. "TEN, NINE, EIGHT, SEVEN, SIX, FIVE, FOUR, THREE, TWO, ONE…… HAPPY NEW YEAR!" As the clock strikes midnight, the fireworks begin over the lake, splitting the sky, while the music of Queen booms out through the air.

"Tonight I'm gonna have myself a real good time, I feel alive. And the world, I'll turn it inside out yeah," we belt out, joining in with the words of 'Don't Stop Me Now', and making up our own words when we get to bits we don't know. We sing as best we can, but generally make a mess of it as we laugh in the snow.

We laugh together as a family, enjoying one another's company and relishing seeing Charlene giggling in the snow; fears for the future forgotten for a moment. For now, all is good with the world.

"This time next year Charlene," Rebecca whispers as the music fades and the snow continues to curl around us. "This time next year, everything will be different. You will have those new lungs."

"2010 will be our year," Charlene nods firmly. "I'm twenty this year and I'll get new lungs for my birthday!" In this moment of magic we all believe this and wait expectantly, enraptured by the hope so dear to us - the fulfilment of this story where Charlene will be healed of this affliction. We know this will be the year where our reality will change forever.

"Let's get back to the villa before the roads are impassable," Mum suggests. "We can sit down and have some mulled wine."

"Can we play cards when we get back?" Bethany asks, while Serena nods beside her. Serena looks like a snowman in her white coat, with snow bunched on her shoulders and her nose red and cheeks rosy from the cold.

"I don't see why not," Mum agrees. "We need to make sure the boys are beaten tonight, girls!"

We head back to our villa and drink mulled wine, talking of our dreams for the year ahead while snow falls heavily in the dark outside, coating the world in a thick blanket. It is truly a blessed New Year and as our hearts fill with the spoken and unspoken promises and wishes for the year to come, we cling to them like a man on a precipice, hanging desperately to a rope. Buoyed by Charlene's resolutions, we dare to hope that 2010 will be the year where everything changes.

21
SWINGS AND ROUNDABOUTS

Wednesday 20th January 2010

A Quick Hello

I am indeed back in hospital for a little while but cannot really complain as I enjoyed a lovely 2.5 months out of the place :) My best record in well over a year. Unfortunately I had to come back in as after just a week off IV antibiotics my lungs decided they didn't want to play that game anymore and enjoyed the way the IVs made them feel. I was quite hopeful when I came off them but unfortunately my chest declined rapidly without them which is a bit disappointing but I guess it just means I'm going to have to stay on IV antibiotics until I get my transplant. Also in that week that I was unwell I lost a load of weight so I have been working on that and am as determined as ever to reach that 40kg.

I do have to say that the time I enjoyed out of hospital was fantastic and I had the BEST Christmas ever with my family, even managing to get to Center Parcs which right up until we were due to go was looking doubtful but I managed it and had a fabulous time.

The school project is just going from strength to strength with the total at around £62,000. Seriously a MASSIVE thank you to each and every one of you out there. When I was starting this project I could never have imagined it would come together like this. God truly works miracles. I am seriously so excited and have a mental picture of all these little children walking into a proper building of a school for the first time ever and it's thanks to the generosity of you guys.

Ok it's probably time I headed to bed but as I leave you tonight I ask that you please remember the people of Haiti. These people had nothing to start with and their country has just been turned upside down by such disaster. Please pray that they will continue to find more survivors. Thank you and goodnight.

Love Charlene

OVER THE NEXT FEW MONTHS, the drugs and feeds continue to do their job, maintaining Charlene's weight. We constantly pray that she not only gets back onto that transplant list but stays on it. While she got back on the list at the end of December after recovering from the lung clot and abscess, the question dominating all our minds is whether she can keep her weight at the required level. Many times, it seems precarious, especially as Charlene's health dips, sometimes knocking weeks off her progress in a flash. Yet, she refuses to give in and in the face of heavy odds she again gets to and maintains her weight at 40kg.

"It's in!" I'm woken from my sleep on the sofa by Charlene's voice echoing around the house. I hear her moving rapidly down the hall, shouting excitedly for Mum, "Mum, come here now! Everyone, come here now! It's in!" I shake my head to clear it of cobwebs and as the last wisps of sleep leave my fuzzy mind, I wonder why Charlene is so agitated. She shouldn't be yelling like that, it can't be good for her. I get up and amble toward the kitchen where Charlene has returned, and where she is now looking as if she is fit to burst in front of the computer screen, her eyes transfixed on a figure in the corner of the webpage she is on.

She has just got home from another stay in hospital and is ecstatic to be back sleeping in her own bed and in the thick of things again. It has been frustrating for her to go back into hospital after such a comparatively long time out and the constant change in antibiotics is taxing on her, as infections constantly try to break through her battered defences.

But it is clear as we arrive in to see what the fuss is about that Charlene's mind is far from the worries about her illness. She is in a fit of euphoria and looks like she could dance across the room, like she used to be able to do when she was a child. It seems as if months have been unwound and she has been momentarily released from the cruel vice grip of the cystic as she calls us towards the web page she has open. As soon as I see, I understand.

"We've done it! £70,000, we have enough to build the school! We have the money!" She has her own web page open, where she has been tracking every penny pledged towards the school she has staked her heart upon, and it is clear that the total has crawled just past the £70,000 mark that she has been fixated upon for so long. As the realisation dawns on the rest of us, we start to chatter excitedly.

"Charlene, that's brilliant."

"I'm so proud of you!"

"I don't believe it."

Charlene turns around and eyeballs me triumphantly. "I told you we would get £70,000 by January, and you didn't believe me. I told you God would supply. You should believe me next time."

I laugh. Her joy is gloriously, beautifully infectious. She has been truly vindicated on this one. "I was wrong and I'm glad for once. Charlene, that is epic. I don't believe it."

"Believe it!" she says, looking ready to do a jig at any second. Bethany and Serena walk over and hug their big sister. "People have been so good; I'm going to have to thank people. First I need to phone Dad though," Charlene says, returning the twin's hug.

It is incredible. We know from Dad's communications with Fields of Life that once the target was reached, the building could start - as long as there weren't any hiccups. Charlene's dream is becoming reality quicker than I dared hope.

At home

"We will need to thank God together" Mum reminds us. "What's next Charlene?"

"Well, we need to set a new target for a start. It's not over; we need to talk about other ideas. Like I said, we have to finish raising the money for that well; it's a joke how far they have to walk every day for water."

"You're not one to rest on your laurels are you Charlene?" Rebecca says, laughing.

"We can't have people thinking it's over, can we?" she says, her face jubilant and glowing with precious life. "I'm going to phone Dad and then I'm thanking people on my blog."

As she begins to bustle about, I can do nothing but feel grateful. This story is progressing so much better than I hoped and I know that the cystic cannot and will not win. We have God on our side and, in the words of Charlene's favourite verse that she is now quoting left, right and centre: "...if God is for us, who can be against us"?

Monday 25th January 2010

I Can't believe I'm Posting This!!!!!

Ok I'm not going to waffle (probably the first time ever :)) but what I do want to say is never in a MILLION years could I have seen myself writing this post in January 2010. Let me just tell you a little of how this came about. As you know my health has deteriorated greatly over the last eighteen months or so. April/May 2009 was a particularly bad time and the whole transplant issue had just been brought up (something I personally really was not expecting). So anyway one evening Mum, Dad, Poppa, David and the girls came and took me out to Nandos at Victoria Square (seriously in the Barr household food makes everything better!!!) and basically the topic came up of building a school in Uganda for the kids out there that don't have the luxury of going to school. Well let me tell you I went back to the City Hospital that night and could not sleep at all I was that excited about the plans.

July 2009: I was unable to go to Uganda with the rest of the family and instead spent a lovely summer in the City Hospital. This is where they found the school Hidden Treasure and between Facebook, emails and telephone calls between us we knew that this was the right school to build. I mean just take a look at the classroom.

So I then started this blog at the end of August with a view to keep people up to date with my progress health wise but also with the fundraising efforts and the building of Hidden Treasure Primary School.

So at present I am just home from hospital today after a ten day stay and am feeling really good. Thanks to everyone on this blog as it is thanks to you that I am feeling as good as I am because I come home to the news that....

Charlene's Project has raised the necessary £70,000. I actually do not know what to say apart from a MASSIVE thank you to every single one of you for your prayers, donations and support. I could never in all my life have imagined that we would have the money in in the space of just five months. Isn't God great? Thank You. Thank You. Thank You.

So what now? Well we have been in talks with Fields of Life who are ready to start building right away. However we have been advised that it is best for the school to have a well so that the children and community can have an outlet for water and also teachers' accommodation so we have moved the goal posts and are now aiming for £100,000 to meet these extra requirements and I know we can do it.

Thanks again to absolutely EVERYBODY.

God Bless. As the Ugandans would say God is good all the time, all the time God is good.

Progress is never simple and the road we walk has its ups and downs. After getting this fantastic news, almost as if she had pushed herself to reach this point, Charlene's health begins to slip back and much of her progress over the weeks before is undone. She has to return to hospital and although at first she stabilises and returns home quickly, it is not long before she is readmitted. Any time she tries to come off the antibiotics her health immediately drops, so she has to remain on them perpetually now. Her weight hangs below the required watermark again and for now she is again off the list until she can push herself over the 40kg mark again.

On top of this, there are some complications in Uganda with the ownership of the land, so the building is frustratingly delayed. While this is difficult for Charlene, it also galvanises her and, as if in inverse correlation, as her health dips she works all the harder, pushing to reach her targets. She writes, she blogs, she emails and every penny that arrives brings her joy. Her ideas have started to branch beyond a school now, with her daring to give voice to other dreams she holds for the future. No one can ever accuse Charlene of a lack of faith!

My health remains precarious to say the least so the challenge now is to be well enough and fit enough to travel to England for the surgery, should a donor be found. This I know is a tall order!

But I am aware that all of this is totally in God's Hands, and I trust Him for all that is ahead.

(Extract from Charlene's Letter to Waringstown Primary School)

However, Charlene's time in hospital is starting to wear her down. She hates the hospital and shows it while there. Fortunately, any time she is well enough we are able to take her out for the night, so we often arrive together and take her out for a meal or a coffee: anything to get her out of what she is now viewing as her prison cell! Mum and Dad are up daily; Rebecca and I call in on our way back from lectures. Charlene is finding it hard, yet every time we arrive in her room we are greeted with the same response.

"How are you Charlene?"

"I'm fine," she always says, swatting the question away. "How are you? What's the craic at Queen's?"

The more time goes on, the more it becomes clear that the real Charlene is shining through and will never be confined or limited by the shell of a body she is inhabiting. We continue to pray and wait for the healing miracle.

Sunday 28th February 2010

Back In

Just a quick blog to let you know that I have been back in hospital for the last week. Just generally feeling rubbish and my weight down to 35.9 kg. However I was able to get home for the night so that is always a positive. Don't really know when I will get out, however they are talking of keeping me here until I put a sufficient amount of weight on so that I can get on the list. As much as I don't like that idea part of me is telling me to go with the idea because at the minute we are sitting in limbo with my weight not going anywhere. So if it was to move things forward I might just do it for a while. Anyway I will keep you all up to date anyway and thanks again everyone for your continuing support and prayers.

Char
xx

As the trees blossom and birdsong returns to Irish skies, Charlene is able to get out more frequently at weekends, even if only to be home for a day. It is good to be together on a Saturday and we look forward to these days, where we usually end up playing some insanely competitive game. Even with this to look forward to though, Charlene's times out of hospital are becoming harder for her as well.

"Mum I don't want to go out in this. I don't want people to see me," Charlene's voice cracks as she looks in Janice's eyes.

Charlene is sitting in the wheelchair she has been given by the hospital for her transport. She sits sunken into it, despondent and distraught; her head bowed slightly, as if a great weight has settled on her. Her eyes look to the floor and she looks so tired, so sick of the weaknesses of her body, a body that is simply unable to match her heart and spirit.

Charlene's strength has continued to weaken and she is now unable to do the things once taken for granted. Walking for any extended period of time exhausts her and causes her to gasp for air. Adjusting to the new limitations of her body and her fast fading lungs is not easy and she is struggling to adapt to this new normal.

"Charlene, no one will care," Janice says encouragingly, but there is a sorrowful edge to her voice. Her heart breaks for her daughter. While all the rest of her children can run about everywhere, going to school or university with no limitations, Charlene has had to give up on her aim of finishing school and step by step many of her vital functions are being robbed from her. "It will be good to get out of the house. We will go and get a cup of coffee and talk about the next step in Uganda."

Even this is failing to rouse Charlene. "I just hate people looking at me as if there's something wrong with me. I hate what they must be thinking. I don't want anyone feeling sorry for me."

Janice bends down and leans forward on her knees, raising Charlene's head up with one hand and resting her other hand on her knee. Her legs are so small, stick-like due to the effects of her cursed disease. Janice looks Charlene in the eye. "What's wrong sweet heart?"

Charlene sighs. "It's just annoying. Everything keeps getting worse. I never thought I'd end up in a wheelchair, I remember running about playing football. Now I can't even walk anywhere, it's so stupid!"

Janice reaches for Charlene's petite hand and grasps it. It seems like yesterday she watched her kids play endless games for hours on end. Charlene would inevitably be in the thick of things, a bit slower and more easily tired perhaps, but never missing an opportunity to do whatever the others were doing. Now things are so painfully different. She squeezes Charlene's hand. "It's just for a time. Soon things will be different and you can forget about this wheelchair."

Charlene scowls. "I can't get these flipping lungs soon enough. Then I'm going to run a marathon or something."

Janice smiles. "Will you come for coffee then? I'm meeting Dickie and otherwise I'm just going to have to listen to him go on about hockey the whole time. You can't leave me alone to that!"

She laughs, then her face clouds over again. "Yeah, it's just hard. I know I shouldn't care what people think, but I do. I know it's stupid. I just can't bear them looking at me."

Janice knows there must be so many frustrations carried within Charlene's heart that she never speaks of. She knows it must be hard for a nineteen year old girl to watch her classmates from school go off to jobs or university, while she is confined to a hospital bed or wheelchair, barely able to walk anymore. To feel stuck in limbo: watching a sandglass with the grains fast trickling through, while waiting desperately for a call that never comes.

Yet, she is so proud of her daughter who refuses to let this be her identity, never dwelling on the situation she is in. Charlene Barr is not the girl with cystic fibrosis; that is not what defines her. Instead, she is the girl whose greatest desire is to serve the God she loves and to build a school for the children in Uganda with whom she has fallen in love.

"If anyone stares at you, I'll give them a clip round the ear Charlene. Are you ready to come? Otherwise Dickie will be sitting there talking away to himself. You ready?" she says rising, still holding Charlene's hand.

Charlene looks up and her expression brightens, as if someone has lit a candle inside of her. "Yeah, I'll ram into them with this wheelchair as well then. Let's go, I think I'm up to a latte."

What expectations are you holding on to that need to be given over to God?

My life plan (marriage, children, career)

(Charlene's Journal)

22
FIGHTING REALITY

STUCK INSIDE HOSPITAL FOR WEEKS AT A TIME, Charlene copes best when she has a target set before her. She ends up booking a week away for the family during Easter at Center Parcs as a surprise and something to aim for. For a time it is uncertain if Charlene will be well enough or if we will have to cancel the trip, but true to form Charlene's health picks up at the last minute and we head off for a week at Easter. There is one proviso however. Charlene must carry oxygen with her, being on constant oxygen at night and carrying cylinders on the back of her wheelchair during the day, with the oxygen tube plugged in just below her nose. When she is out and about without it she has started to struggle recently. But this compromise is one she is willing to accept if it means we can get away for a family holiday.

The sun beats down on us that week, a complete contrast to our last visit in the depths of winter. We pack T-shirts and shorts and for a change actually get to wear them. Whereas usually our times at Center Parcs are a hive of activity, running from one activity to the other, this time is different. Instead we spend a lot of time together in Starbucks or by the lake, talking. We go for walks and cycles, taking it in turns to push Charlene in her wheel chair. It is a joy to see the squirrels and rabbits scampering through the deep forest, anticipating the fast approaching summer.

It is a strange trip. I remember Charlene racing ahead on her pink bike down the paths hugged by trees, or swinging her racquet wildly in tennis. I remember her spiralling down the water slides and playing football in the shade of the trees. That was not long ago. In Center Parcs it strikes all of us how fast her free-fall is becoming. Even when we were here at New Year, four months before, she had been able to walk, albeit needing a van to travel from place to place. Now she is in a wheelchair, and constantly attached to the oxygen cylinders. We need this transplant soon, as all the drugs in the world are not slowing the onslaught being inflicted on her by the disease burrowed within.

We enjoy our time together, spending a long time talking of Uganda and our hopes and fears for the future. But we know Charlene will need to go into hospital as soon as she gets back, and we wonder what her weight will be. She continues on her tube feeds while we are on holiday and eats as much as she can stomach, desperate to put a suitable amount of weight on so she can return to the list.

As soon as we return home Charlene returns to hospital. But this time there is good news. While her health is poor, her weight has been maintained, and the doctors decide that she can go back onto the transplant list. The flip side of this however is that she must remain in hospital so they can ensure her health remains stable. While she resents this, getting back on the list fills her with renewed hope for what will come in the months ahead. The wait for the call that will change everything forever drags on.

Tuesday 20th April 2010

A New Chapter Begins

Ok so as you guys know I have been working to get my weight up to the necessary 39kg so that I could be placed on the transplant list. Well yesterday was weight day and I am pleased to say my weight is 39.7kg (I know I'm a wee fatty but aw well) I know this probably sounds strange but I am actually thrilled, I know this probably doesn't say a lot for my faith in God but there was a lot of time between September (when I was first placed on the list for all of... a week) and then with the stupid abscess and me losing a load of weight I honestly doubted whether or not I would actually get to this stage, because for months and months the weight just wasn't going on. Although I was sick when I was away I only lost like 0.4kg which was really good (probably all the good food at Center Parcs) so if anyone from the NHS is reading this Center Parcs trips are fantastic forms of treatment lol :).

As of now although I am still in hospital I am on the list and the only thing we are waiting on now is THE CALL which really could come at anytime, which means for once in our lives the Barrs will have to be organised and ready to go once the phone rings.

I swear God truly works miracles. To consider that I have gone from having a lung abscess (which is pretty serious) to being placed on the transplant list all in the space of 6 months is pretty amazing and something tells me He is not done working miracles just yet.

God Bless you all and thank you for your continued prayers.
Char
xx

"David, how are you?" Charlene's voice crackles down the line as I walk bent double against the wind and rain down Elmwood Avenue. After the sunny weather at Easter the weather has returned to its usual cheery self. Walking quickly to get to shelter and somewhere warm, I chat to my sister.

"I'm not bad, how are you? Was late for class again this morning, I could blame you after our wee family trip to Tony Roma's last night, but it more likely was watching 24 with Phil, Tim and Richard until 3am that may have caused me problems," I joke.

"Jack Bauer still alive and well? I don't know how he keeps going!"

"Aw Charlene, he isn't too bad. The character is based on me you know, though they had to tone him down and make him look slightly weaker in the TV series to make him more believable," I respond, struggling to maintain a straight face.

"You talk the biggest pile of rubbish, you know that?" Charlene scoffs down the phone. "I'll tell you one thing though, knowing you I bet you haven't eaten yet today, have you?"

"Well, I had a cup of coffee at lunchtime? Does that count?"

"I swear David Barr, you need a good woman to take care of you, you're worse than Dickie! Rebecca just got here and we ordered pizza. I've already ordered you one, so I don't want to hear any arguing. Meet the guy in the foyer and bring it up for us ok?" Charlene's voice drifts from the phone.

I laugh. I often get a call about pizza from Charlene as I sit in my room working or when returning home from lectures. Charlene loves her pizza, specifically 'Dominos' and collects their vouchers like there will be no tomorrow. She frequently places an order by phone, and either struggles down to the foyer to collect it, or asks one of us to pick it up for her when she is feeling unwell.

"Sure, I'm on my way. You're a legend Shirley Whirly!" pulling out the nickname we sometimes tease her with.

"Don't dare call me that or you'll be out on your ear when you get here," she screeches down the phone. "Love you!"

"Love you too, see you soon." I hang up and resume my struggle against the wind, treading the familiar steps across the Lisburn Road and up towards the City Hospital. People stagger past with their umbrellas blown inside out and the wind is building towards a gale. It will be good to get inside.

The Dominos deliveryman is already there when I arrive and I apologise and pay him. I notice he is looking at me strangely but think nothing of it, thanking him and heading merrily towards ward 8.

When I enter the room Charlene is already propped up on her bed, eyeing the pizzas expectantly. Rebecca is sitting on the green chair in the corner where I sat months before watching the long hours drift by while praying desperately Charlene would reach morning alive. Rebecca has her nursing notes spread out before her and is working away. I remember she had a half day and so must have spent her afternoon here.

Charlene's face is red and puffy now from the steroids pumped into her system to build her up, but her mirth shines through as she looks at me. "What did he say?"

"What did who say?"

"The pizza man?"

"Nothing, why?"

"Cause I was really embarrassed. He phoned to ask where we were, and I told him where to meet you. And I wasn't thinking and I accidently said, "Love you," at the end of the call. There was no way I was going down after that; I'd never have been able to look him in the eye! He would have thought I was rare!"

"It was hilarious," Rebecca glances up grinning, reaching for her pizza.

I hand it to her and pass Charlene the small one she has ordered. "He did look at me strangely, now you mention it," I say, starting to work on my own pizza. "I hope he didn't think it was me who called him, that would be pretty awkward. Though I would hope he could distinguish our voices! Anyway how are you girls?"

We chat over shared pizza, enjoying each other's company. Sharing pizza with Charlene in the hospital is something we all do. She loves doing it, even if she can rarely finish it due to her illness. However the craic we have always belies the circumstances and the cold clinical surroundings where we eat together.

"You sure you don't want to come?" Charlene teases, looking exactly like a cheeky monkey must look. "Rebecca and I were talking, and we'd be happy to buy you a ticket."

"There is no way you will get me within one hundred miles of that concert," I mutter in between slices of pizza. Charlene and the rest of the girls are heading to a Westlife concert at the Odyssey tomorrow night, and have been excitedly counting the days for weeks. "Westlife are the bane of modern music and are…"

"Yeah, yeah, yeah, I reckon you're just jealous," Charlene mocks.

"Yeah right!" I reply indignantly. "Name one original song they have done?"

"Flying Without Wings," Rebecca offers.

"Well aside from that?"

"Fool Again," Charlene chimes in.

Rebecca with Charlene at Center Parcs

"Ok so there are one or two. But seriously, they are poor, and…."

"Whatever David," Charlene interjects laughing. "Are you not impressed I'm getting Dad to go?"

"I worry about that man! Although man may be too strong a word…" I respond and we all laugh together. Charlene is really excited about the concert, although she will have to go in her wheelchair with Dad as her carer. However there is no way she will allow something like that to limit her experience.

As we are chatting Mum, Dad, Poppa, Bethany and Serena arrive and descend like vultures and within a matter of seconds any remaining pizza is demolished. It is good to be together, and I am reminded how blessed we are as a family. We are together in all of this, unless it involves a detour to a Westlife concert!

Friday 7th May 2010

A Quick Update

Just a wee quick update to let you know where things are at. I am still in hospital – 8 weeks and counting! :) But things are pretty stable and I am still on that list which is good. They aren't too keen to send me home cause me being me likes to try and do too much when she goes home and shall we say maybe pushes the limits a little bit, and they are worried that if I go home for good I will just deteriorate and end up back at square one which I so don't want to happen. Whereas being in hospital I am forced to sit here and do nothing. I don't like to admit this but I do kind of see their point. So we reached a compromise and I'm going to stay here as long as I get home one or two nights a week and then maybe we can look at being home long term. So pretty much I get out for good behaviour lol.

This week has been a good week with me weighing in at 42kg (can we say OBESE!!!!) and then on Tuesday night I was allowed to get out for the evening to go and see my boys (Westlife) I even took Dad along but secretly I think he really enjoyed it (though he would never admit that :)) It was a brilliant night and I must say Shane just gets better looking every time! Also my inflammatory markers in my blood went from being like 200 to 42 in the space of a few days which is really good. So that pleased us all. Let's hope it stays there!!

Got home overnight last night and slept in my own wee bed for the first time in weeks. AMAZING. So I'm looking forward to my next wee outing home. To be honest it's what keeps me going. This morning we had our first Newcastle scare. Mum, Dad, David, Poppa and I went out for coffee and didn't Mum's phone go off with a withheld number? Sure enough it was Newcastle, so there was Dad and me looking at each other trying to piece together what they were saying to Mum on the phone. Turns out they needed a blood sample from me and that was it. To be honest that's ok cause at least it means they are working at my stuff over there and keeping me in mind, and anyway it wouldn't have suited me anyway – I was out enjoying coffee thank you very much! :)

On Hidden Treasure front things are going really well and we are now up to about £94,000 which is awesome but keep it coming people cause I have an orphanage to build afterwards! Also Dad was talking to the folks at Fields of Life yesterday and they are going to start building within the fortnight how awesome is that. God is just amazing and I am so excited to see the things that are achieved through this wee school and all the little kids that will hopefully get the chance to get to school thanks to all you guys. Thank you all so much. You are all legends. God Bless you all.

Char

Her Westlife ticket

23
DOUBT

IT IS PAINFUL TO WATCH Charlene continue to decline. Whereas before she found it humiliating to go out in the wheelchair she does not even question it anymore. Brief weeks ago she carried oxygen cylinders as a precaution, but now she needs to have them on and pumping oxygen to her nostrils any time she is out. They are now vital to her, the air around her no longer holding enough to support her weakening, heaving lungs. On one occasion when we are out she forgets to turn it on, and all too quickly begins to gasp for air. Her face turns a deep shade of blue, deprived of oxygen. We are momentarily frozen with shock, until Dad discovers the problem. Within seconds of the turn of a knob Charlene is her usual self, joking away as colour returns to her cheeks. It is clear how desperately she needs these lungs now. But still the call does not come.

Oh my goodness I am actually the worst journal keeper EVER! The last two weeks have been ok, at the start I was feeling rather rough and started being sick (which is never good) and I was just exhausted. Got my antibiotics changed and am now starting to feel a huge improvement, praise God!!!

Things at the minute are going well, I'm still locked up but feeling good and my weight is back up to 41kg. As long as I get regular trips out I think I can stick it out another while longer, but can't wait for that call to come. God is working miracles with the school in Uganda and I think they are going to start building very very soon and there also may be an orphanage in the pipeline. How cool is our God?

(Charlene's Journal)

There are still delays in Uganda, as the administration details on land ownership drag on and slow down the process. But Charlene still works tirelessly. Her heart for God is evident to any who speak to her. However, like many who serve God, she can never see it in herself.

"I just worry that I am not any use to God. What do I ever do for Him?" she asks me earnestly one day in hospital. The doubt eats and oozes through her voice. "I find it hard to concentrate reading the Bible and I rarely do it. I'm not a very good Christian," she sighs resignedly.

I don't know what to say. Racked by my own doubts as to my usefulness to God I can identify with her insecurities, yet seeing how clearly God has His Hand upon Charlene, using her vision to inspire people here and in Uganda, the conversation seems surreal. I think about where she has come from, and the battles she has had for her heart and with her body. I think of how her attitude has been transformed and how she has channelled her horrendous circumstances into a way to serve others. She has never allowed herself to be a slave to her situation. It is evident that God is using Charlene. It is clear her faith is strong. Her expectations of God daily put my jaded doubter's heart to shame. How could she doubt her own use to the God who loves her so dearly?

"Charlene, it's not your fault that your energy is low." She is perpetually tired now, and the effort of reading her Bible is difficult. "And our faith isn't based on what we do or how we feel. It's about accepting that we are fallen and cannot do it by ourselves, and then accepting God's love and sacrifice for us. You are saved and loved by Him Charlene, and your life shows the outcome of that. Look what's happening in Africa through you: but that doesn't make Him love you any more, He has always loved you. It's just in you being so willing to love and follow Him that He has shared His vision with you. He trusts you with it."

She sighs, and murmurs, "I don't know. All I do is lie in this bed all day, what use am I?" Charlene periodically talks about this, her doubts about herself and her doubts that God could use her, misgivings about ourselves we all experience. Only we can see the blackness in our own hearts, and to be honest it is hard to know, to really believe, that God sees their depths - all the darkness and twisted motives that dominate, the truth of who we really are that we show no one else and even refuse to face up to ourselves - He sees this and loves us anyway.

"Charlene, look at the work you are doing in Africa, and all the people the Project is impacting, both here and in Africa. You can be an example here too in the hospital."

"Hmm, maybe," she replies, lost in her thoughts. "You better go, you'll be late again."

"Ok, well let's pray first. Would you like to pray Charlene?" Charlene shakes her head. She doesn't often like to pray out loud, and although I sometimes push her to do it, she stands firm, preferring to keep her requests private, reflecting her nature.

I assent, and we close our eyes, but not before I cast an eye over her lying there, so vulnerable and frail in the hospital bed, with a host of tubes fastened to her arm and nose as she breathes heavily and frequently. The fear of losing her suddenly washes over me like a mighty wave, but I push down my deepest fears and refuse to entertain them for now. Instead, I pray. "God, please heal Charlene, keep her safe. Heal her so that she can be released from hospital as soon as possible, so she can be home again. Heal her and keep her safe. Let her know your love for her and how you have a plan for her because of what you have done. Keep her safe and use both of us today. Keep her safe. Amen."

Well isn't this going good, two days in a row ☺ Didn't do much today cause I was feeling tired and stuff so I just took it easy, although my lovely Mummy brought me a Starbucks and stayed with me for a good wee while this morning. Oh how I love when these guys come to visit, it's just too quiet in here. Cannot wait to rejoin the hustle and bustle of Barr life. I'm feeling a bit better this evening and have just had a pizza for tea. I am totally aiming to get home this week, don't think I can take being locked up here much longer. Dave came to visit me with another Starbucks (I'm really going to be climbing the walls!!!).

As of last night I'm really trying to make time for just God and I. I know I have no excuse as I have all the time in the world but I just find it so hard to concentrate ☹ Anyway I'm going to go now and make some toast or something. So hungry ☺

Laters!

(Charlene's Journal)

Charlene still refuses to succumb to her limitations or to feel sorry for herself. She also manages to scramble to peaks of comparative good health from time to time, and in those times it is as if the clock has been turned back months. She laughs and breathes freely without her oxygen mask: in June, she comes home after fourteen long weeks in hospital.

Monday 7th June 2010

Long Overdue Post

Sorry I am only updating this blog now but I have been quite busy lol. I got home from hospital on Wednesday and seriously with the amount of stuff I gathered after a long 14 weeks I nearly needed a removal van. Things have been going really well since I got home and I have just enjoyed sitting out in the back garden sunning myself :) (long may it continue). I was kind of worried coming home because before I would only last a couple of days and I would be back in hospital again but this time I have been out nearly a week and am still feeling great and even have the energy to go out for wee cups of coffee and even a driving lesson. Yeah I know they told me to take it easy when I got home but when did I ever listen to sensible advice? :)

We are still waiting for the beginning of the school build but hopefully this will happen soon. This week we had Barbara over from Uganda and it was lovely to have her over as I haven't seen her in two years and it was nice just to experience a wee bit of Uganda again.

The Barr house is now getting into full competition mode with the World Cup only days away. We have all picked teams to support out of a hat (we are very competitive) so strangely I am really looking forward to the World Cup starting. Just as long as England go out in the early stages! :)

Charlene never ceases to surprise us. At the end of June she takes the main stage at Summer Madness in the King's Hall, sharing her vision and what she is trying to achieve, encouraging young people there to sign up to the donor register. Although she has to bring her oxygen on stage, she refuses to bring her wheelchair, and even though she is terrified beforehand, physically shaking with fear, she speaks from her heart and challenges everyone there. We are so proud of her.

Dear Charlene,

Thank you for your update. You won't know me but I am an old friend of your Mum and Dad from university days. Your Dad and I lived in the same house for three years and shared the same room for one! I met him at the City Hospital on Thursday.

Your faith is great and in this life and the next one your reward will equal that faith. Part of the reward will be to see the blessing you have brought to other lives – the people who know you personally, others in your own country – like me and my family – whom you don't know – and then others in far off countries like Uganda who will give thanks for all you have done for them. In our weakness we accomplish much more for God than we ever realise, for God is only willing to use people who know they are weak – so that he gets all the glory and praise. AND God is getting a huge amount of glory through your faith in him and desire to help others.

Just as you are touching more lives than you realise, so also there are many more people thinking and praying for you than you will ever know. I and my wife Rosie and daughter Ellen are some of them.

Charlene, it is an honour and privilege to know you – even if it's only from a distance. We look forward to getting good news about you and Hidden Treasure School in the future.

Yours sincerely,
(Rev) David Cupples
Enniskillen

(Email to Charlene from Rev David Cupples)

As the World Cup rolls down we are all enthralled, watching every game we can, and competing against each other after drawing different teams out of a hat. Everything morphs into a competition in our house! Charlene unfortunately draws France who tumble out of the competition in a blaze of self-destructive glory and strike action. All action in our house grinds to a stop every time a game begins as we sit glued to the television. The days tumble into one another.

Still her health twists and turns, and she is forced to return to hospital from time to time.

Ok so I need to do better at writing here. I'm useless!! Today I'm sitting in about 24 degrees of sunshine. It's glorious. Went home yesterday for a lovely BBQ, don't really want to be stuck back in here now ☹ As I sit here with my iPod on shuffle the song 'Trust in the Lord' has just come on. Very apt as I suppose I really need to improve on that. I need to trust that me being in and out of hospital all the time is in God's plan for me no matter what the outcome of this whole situation is. To be honest, and I know this is wrong, but it is hard, and I pray every night that my faith in God will grow. I am so hoping though that the call for transplant comes soon cause health wise I'm in a really good place and I have a pretty packed out summer with so much I want to do. Only I suppose it's all in God's timing ☺ And that is pretty cool.

(Charlene's Journal)

Charlene is able to spend a lot of time at home during the summer and as the summer days drift by, summers past replay in my mind: when we ran together, carelessly living in the moment as only children can, without thinking beyond the next game we would play or our next adventure. Yet, time ticks mercilessly by like sand falling through your fingers, and the tighter you grasp the quicker it falls. This summer while we sit outside and play football like we used to, Charlene no longer joins in. Instead she sits in her wheelchair watching us with oxygen flowing through the tubes wrapped around her. Time is cruel to those she holds in her thrall.

Again, we decide to go to Center Parcs for a family holiday in August. From the instant it is booked Charlene sets her sights upon it, writing the number of days left up on the Whiteboard in her room and letting us know daily how much time remains. Having a target always helps Charlene, and she agrees without complaint to go into hospital prior to the trip so she will be able to travel.

Anytime we suggest caution to Charlene -to not push herself, to spend more time in safety in hospital, that maybe we shouldn't be going to places like Center Parcs - she sits up straight as if a fire has been lit inside her and angrily exclaims that she wants to live life as much as she can. She has lost so much and she just doesn't want to lose any more. She argues that she would rather have a shorter life where she gets to do everything she wants to do than one where she lives a bit longer, but wrapped in cotton wool. In her eyes, there is no guarantee this call will ever come.

So we prepare to get the boat over to England, all eight of us making sure we are free for this time together. Although it is unspoken, each of us knows that unless the miracle comes, this will likely be the last time we make the familiar trek to Center Parcs together. So each of us cancels other commitments, gets time off and prepares for another and perhaps final trip into the forests of England.

24
WAITING ON A MIRACLE

SUCH IS THE STATE OF CHARLENE'S HEALTH that we take two cars with us on the trip, one with all of us and our luggage, and another car full to bursting with Charlene's wheelchair, oxygen, medication and other vital regalia she has to carry.

I drive the car with Charlene's medication, and as oxygen cylinders rumble against each other as I join a roundabout I turn the wheel and talk to Bethany beside me. "You think how much stuff she needs, it's crazy Bethany. When did this happen?"

"What do you mean?" she asks, turning to look at me, confusion on her face.

"Well I'm thinking back even to six months ago when we came here, she didn't need half this stuff. Each month that goes by she needs more and more medication, more and more oxygen, more and more support. You never really notice it in the day to day getting worse, until you suddenly stop and think."

"Yeah," Bethany says, with a wistful look in her eye. "Do you remember her trying to lead the ducks into the swimming pool? The snowball fights?"

"I do. I also remember your scream when you thought the ducks were going for you and Serena."

"That was mean," she says smiling.

It is strange, but even in the face of the cumulating evidence of how sick Charlene is, in the daily madness of life you never really notice how serious things are getting. It only dawns on you when you stop and remember days forever gone.

"Do you ever think we are naïve?" I wonder aloud.

"All of us you mean?" Bethany asks.

I fumble with my words for an explanation. "Yes. I mean here we are with a full car of medication she needs for a week-long trip, but we don't see this as disaster. We just see it as a pain for Charlene, a terrible one, but one that will be done away with when she gets her transplant. Are we being stupid?"

"I don't know." There is silence in the car. The country road we are driving along is quiet, and the mountains in the distance scrape the sky. Deep dark loughs hang in valleys below us, an early morning mist shrouding their mysterious secrets from any wandering eyes.

Bethany's voice cracks through the silence that had gathered like a clear pool all around us, but her voice is a whisper. "Have you ever thought she might not get the transplant?"

Again, thoughts I fight to keep buried flood into my mind's eye unbidden.

But I answer as firmly as I can, gripping the steering wheel tight. "Yes Bethany pet, I have. But we have to trust. One way or another Charlene will be healed." I swallow, looking in my rear view mirror and seeing the wheelchair sticking up from the back seat. "Bethany, would you be mad at God if things don't happen as we hope?"

"No, I don't think so," she answers. Her voice is quiet but strong. "He loves her and wants what's best for her even more than we do."

"Yes and there's a bigger picture than we can ever see. I love you Bethany."

"I love you too David. But let's not talk about this. The call could even come today."

I nod, and it is true. The overnight travel bag is ready as always, easily accessible in the other car if it is needed. I know Mum will have her phone near at hand as always.

As the tyres gobble up the miles before them I am glad we are away together again. Who knows when anything could be the last time? None of us are guaranteed a single moment.

Ok so it's been a while since I journaled ☹ But to be honest I'm struggling right now, spiritually mainly. I just can't seem to focus, sit down and read my Bible. I know it's so stupid, here's me who has all the time in the world and I can't make time to sit down with God ☹ I'm seriously such a failure, I mean I pray but to be honest that's about it. So my target is to make time each day for some God/Char time cause right now I feel like crying and I hate it. I mean I ask God for this, that and the other and yet I can't give Him anything in return. SHAMEFUL+++!

Other than that things are going good. I am just loving being out and with my family. I am seriously the luckiest girl alive with the people I have around me. THANK YOU GOD!

I'm still waiting on 'the call' but to be honest you come to accept that it's all in God's timing and I just gotta learn to be patient as I know it's gonna happen when He wants and His timing is perfect. Night for now.

Char xxx

(Charlene's Journal)

Being the only boy I am as always given the short straw of sleeping on the sofa. Fortunately in this villa there is a pull-out bed, so every night I pull out the sofa, set up the bed and sleep. Charlene is in a room just off the living room where I sleep, and all night long the ventilator runs. It is wired to give a high-pitched warning signal if there is ever a dip in the oxygen intake, alerting everyone if the user is no longer breathing, but this one frequently gives off a series of false alarms, requiring someone to reset it. During the night Charlene's ventilator goes off innumerable times and from my position on the shore of my dreams I hear Dad getting up time and time again to check the apparatus and Charlene's wellbeing.

In my twilight reflections I wrestle with the obvious. Charlene is perilously close to death, we all know this now whether we accept it or not. Very few people know the true seriousness of Charlene's illness, partly because they only see her when she is well enough to be up and about, but also because Charlene refuses to ever show the depths of her illness, underplaying it and putting a brave face on, even to us. It can be frustrating. Often she has been so ill it has scared us, yet when she recovers she writes in her blog about a 'bad wee spell'. She is master of the understatement!

As the ventilator wails again in the depths of night, I stir and shake my head to clear it of dark dreams. As I hear Dad amble to Charlene's room, checking her and resetting the system I sigh heavily. Often when people assume she is well, she is miles from it. The number of times she has been gravely ill yet insists on going out of the house on her wheelchair for some fresh air, and when she meets someone she throws on her winning smile and reports that she is well, despite the fact that as soon as they have passed by she needs to get back home as she feels so ill and exhausted. Charlene is brave, braver than anyone I have ever met.

We have a good time in Center Parcs, although in the mornings Charlene is no longer able to get up, lying on. We spend a lot of time in and around the villa, playing games and talking together. Although it is more restful than the times we were here as children where everything was lived "a mile a minute", just being together now is good. Now we savour every moment together, and I find myself wishing I had appreciated what I had long before.

When it comes time to leave, we pack the car and push Charlene to the car park. "Are you glad we came Charlene?" Mum asks.

"You bet I am. It's better than rotting away in an oul' hospital bed! It was good craic, and sure we even beat the boys at the games."

"You will all need to keep hold of that memory girls, it won't happen again," I jest.

"I think they made it up personally," Dad chimes in.

We all stand together around Charlene in her wheelchair. The call has not come this week. We know it has been good to get a break, but when we get back into the cars and drive home, we will be back within the whirlpool, with Charlene in and out of hospital, on her IVs and getting progressively worse while praying for the saving rope of the call from Newcastle to grasp onto as she tumbles towards the black vortex.

"What next Charlene?" Dad asks as we stand together.

"I just want to hear the news that the land is bought and see the building of this school started so we can look at what happens next. I just want to see that."

"And I just want to get this call, it's taking so long." She sits with her shoulders slumped. The silence feels oppressive. But slowly Charlene rouses herself, casting off any self-pity or fear, and as she gazes around and smiles it as if she has grown taller in her seat. "But would you worry, all you can do is keep waiting. At least I'm on the list," she says breezily. And this is so important to her, just to be on the list, knowing that at any time, on any day, her phone can ring and everything will be different forever.

"I want those lungs," she continues. "Because I want to go out to see that school. I want that more than anything in the world."

"I think we should pray together now," Mum says quietly, almost at a whisper. The air is still around us, and no one else is in the car park. "To ask Him for these things. Next time we are at Center Parcs Charlene will have new lungs."

We all nod, and gather close together around Charlene in her wheelchair. Bethany and Serena join hands, then Serena reaches for Dad's hand, and one by one we all join hands in a circle. We join together and bow our heads in that car park as the wind blows through the rustling leaves in the tall trees overlooking our wee family.

One by one we pour our hearts out before God, begging Him for the construction of the school to begin. Pleading for the call to come. Imploring Him for healing. But most of all we pray that we know Him and for the strength to serve Him better. We ask for the faith we so often lack, and we pray for wee Charlene, as she sits on her wheelchair with oxygen flooding her nostrils, that she will be able soon to walk again, to breathe clean air again.

Then we open our eyes, get into the cars, and drive back home ready to face whatever will come.

Well haven't I been a naughty girl! Sorry I haven't written in a few days, I have been so exhausted. Anyway I'm still locked up (hopefully not for much longer!!!). I'm hoping now that my antibiotics have been changed (again!!!) things will start to improve and then I can get home. Didn't do much all day yesterday but then Mum, Dad, Poppa, Bethany and Serena came and we had an amazing meal at Tony Roma's ☺

Today I literally slept all day, my energy levels are so bad which I find so frustrating. The girls had hockey and when that was done the gang came to visit me with Domino's pizza (at this rate I'll be obese). I am just so thankful for the family God has given me, the fact that they are all riding this journey with me just astounds me, I mean it must be so hard for them being on the outside looking in and yet they never complain! Thank you God for such a wonderful family ☺

I haven't been great at my quiet time the last few nights which I feel awful about, I just feel so wiped out. I know that is no excuse so I'm gonna try and improve cause right now I feel like the worst Christian ever. Please God help me with this. Anyway, that is all for now, I'm going to head to bed (wish it was my own though ☹ *).*

(Charlene's Journal)

"That's her I bet," Dad says laughing. It is half one in the morning and Dad has just received an email from Uganda confirming that the land has finally been bought and the construction can begin. On reading it he immediately fired a text through to Charlene in hospital, expecting her to pick it up in the morning. But he underestimated Charlene.

Within half a minute of sending the message the phone is ringing, and we all hear Charlene's excited screeches on the other end of the line. She has been waiting patiently for this news for weeks, and her prayers have been answered. In hospital the school has been her outlet, her driving goal, especially as her health refuses to remain stable. Checking her email and Facebook obsessively for news, she has been waiting desperately for this email, as a man lost in the desert longs for water.

"So you were checking your emails again when you got the text? I thought you would be asleep, I didn't think you'd get it until tomorrow!" Dad laughs, the lamp light reflecting off his glasses. We can hear Charlene's voice from the other side of the room, so it is clear to all of us that she is ecstatic.

"An orphanage? Ok Charlene, well let's get this school up first!" Dad cautions, but a grin is splashed across his face. "Get some sleep! Mum will be in first thing, and we will all head out tomorrow night to celebrate."

Charlene continues to babble on the phone and Dad nods, agreeing.

"Yes, I will see if Nandos is free. It's where the dream started after all! Now get some sleep, love you Charlene." Dad hangs up, and his smile swallows all of his face. His eyes are dancing. "She's excited. And she wants to go to Nandos tomorrow night. Oh you should have heard her! God is good."

One of our prayers has been answered, and we continue to wait expectantly for the answer to our second prayer.

Friday 27th August 2010

BIG BIG News!!!!!!

Ok I definitely without a shadow of a doubt think this is up there with possibly one of the best posts I have written. The land has been purchased and all the legal things have been handed over to Hidden Treasure so they will be able to start building really soon. I am actually so excited.

I'm back in hospital and at half one last night (yes I'm quite the night owl, pity the same can't be said for during the day though!) I got a text through from Dad to say he had just received news from Uganda to say everything had been signed over and they are now ready to plan the actual building of the school. Needless to say I was on top of the world.

Now that we are at the next step please just pray that the building of the school goes smoothly and the children of Hidden Treasure will get their new school soon. Thanks again everyone for your love, support and prayers for this project. I could never have believed that when we had the dream in the pipeline of embracing all of this that things would actually take off. How AMAZING is God ♥

It is so difficult to watch Charlene. Her appetite has shrunk and her face is puffy and bloated from the steroids pumped into her system. She has regressed from the thin oxygen tube that snaked up to her nose, now often needing a full mouthpiece that wraps its black straps around her head, engulfing her mouth and nose, and loudly pumping life-giving oxygen into her ragged, spent lungs.

Janice sits beside her bed and gazes at her. The weeks are running together, and it has somehow become October. Charlene still has her good days, when she defies the state her fragile form is in and winds back the months, but they are becoming more infrequent. Still her eyes are fixed on Uganda.

Now Charlene lies on her hospital bed, half asleep. She is sleeping so much and is often listless, any activity sapping her energy. She looks like a straw doll lying on that bed, brought to the edge of her resistance.

How can things be like this? Will you not heal her? Where are you in all of this? Janice's prayers ricochet off the roof as if stopped by the concrete floors above her. Where is the hope in all of this? Dark clouds of despair gather on the horizon of her soul, and cruel thoughts poise on the edge of her consciousness, eager to leap forward and suffocate any remaining hope.

Words sit curled up in her mouth. "Charlene, do you ever get angry that you have cystic?" she blurts out, no longer able to let the words go unspoken. The words taste bitter as they spill from her mouth but she can no longer help herself. Charlene holds so many of her thoughts close to her heart, never giving voice to them. What is she really thinking?

Charlene opens her eyes as if woken from a slumber. She turns to her mother and looks at her, gripping her in the deep pools of her eyes. She reaches up and unstraps the oxygen mask, setting it on the bed beside her as it continues to fling out oxygen to no one. This time Charlene does not hold her thoughts close to her heart. This time she gives voice to them.

Her voice is frail, but firm, spoken with iron will and firm conviction as her eyes widen, wider than the sky. "No of course I don't Mum. Because if I didn't have cystic fibrosis I wouldn't be in this family, I wouldn't know Jesus and I wouldn't be building a school in Uganda." Her words seem to reverberate around the room. They were formed through years of struggle, of pain and tragedy, but they bear testament to a deeper truth, a reality deeper than this surface hospital room could ever contain. The knowledge that they are all caught in a bigger story than they can ever comprehend licks at the shores of Janice's mind.

Charlene sits back again, reattaches her oxygen mask, and breathes deeply. She reaches for Janice's hand and holds it, drifting back towards sleep. Every word she has spoken is true, and it is clear she can see what they, caught up in the day to day struggle, forget all too easily, just as they forgot so easily the truths revealed to them in Uganda.

God has a plan, and He will protect Charlene, whatever happens. Each painful step, as her heart was fought over and as her body falls apart, she has never been alone. She has been held close and been made into something beautiful. And Janice knows the story is not over.

> *What are some specific thoughts to consider when insecurities creep into your mind?*
>
> *That God made you the way you are for a special purpose.*
>
> (Charlene's Journal)

As October drifts by, and again the nights come earlier; as the leaves tumble from the trees and as we slope towards winter, Charlene continues to fight and wait for the call. Her spirits dip, so Mum and Dad decide to give her a target to aim for, and so they use Mum's beloved Tesco tokens to book a few days at half-term in the Culloden. It seems an exercise in futility, being unlikely that Charlene will be well enough, but it gives her a target, and the news invigorates her.

In Uganda the materials are purchased and the work teams recruited. Basil and Wenford, two trustees in Charlene's Project, book flights and prepare to fly out to oversee the start of the work. They are frequent visitors to Charlene, and she excitedly gives them a list of things she wants them to check. Thoughts of Uganda cheer her immensely.

We know an end is coming as all the threads begin to draw together, we just do not know yet what end it will be.

Sunday 17th October 2010

Long overdue post

I'm sorry I am getting so bad at this blogging business :(but things have been kind of busy around here as I have been in hospital for the last two and a half weeks. Thankfully I am getting home tomorrow. Things have been kind of tough this time as I have been struggling with a stupid cough and my oxygen SATs are being pretty stubborn and refuse to go past 85 which isn't great but

I'm managing and cannot wait to get home and say hello to the world again. I already have loads planned for when I get out so it's going to be hard to remind myself to take it easy lol.

Things are starting to get VERY exciting with Hidden Treasure School. All the land has pretty much been handed over and purchased and this week Basil and Wenford are heading out to Uganda to meet Eugene and hopefully get the school building started. I'm actually so excited if a little jealous cause I really want to go out there so bad but both men have told me there is no room in any of the suitcases so think I'll just have to stay put.

Please pray for the guys as they head out this Thursday that they will have a safe and successful trip and that the ball will start rolling to get the building started.

Thanks again for all your love and prayers.

Charlene

Charlene lies on the sofa in the kitchen, her chest rising and falling rapidly as she draws in the pumped oxygen that has become her lifeblood. Janice sits on the sofa beside her, looking down at her precious daughter, while Dickie leans forward from the other sofa, hands clasped and peering over his glasses and straining to hear Charlene's every word.

It is Sunday and we are due to head to the Culloden on Wednesday. Charlene has been allowed home from hospital for the day and we have lit the fire in the living room so we can all sit together, and probably watch a DVD as the evening progresses. But for now Charlene has asked to speak to her parents alone, so they have moved back into the kitchen for a time.

Janice knows some things are on Charlene's mind. All day she has been uncharacteristically quiet. True she is very tired, but from the lines on Charlene's forehead and her nervous tapping on the table during lunch, she knows Charlene has something on her heart, something bothering her. So it is no surprise when she asks quietly if she can speak to them. Now they sit together in the kitchen, far enough away not to hear the idle chatter from the other children in the living room. Here the only sound heard is the life-giving oxygen pumping into Charlene's lungs, relentless and constant.

Charlene pulls her mask to the side, still allowing the gas to flow unobstructed into her nostrils, and breaks the silence. She speaks, and her eyes are screwed up as she pours out the thoughts that have been welling up inside her for weeks. "Mum, Dad, I've been thinking about some things and I wanted to talk with you about them. I've just been thinking, in case I don't make it, you know?"

Janice reaches for Charlene's hand and grips it. Her fears rise up and grasp for her heart, but she speaks out, denying them a foothold now, for Charlene's sake. "But you will make it Charlene, you will." Doubts have long since bubbled through Janice's consciousness, but she knows Charlene still believes and needs their support through all of this. "What's on your mind though sweetheart?"

"I know I will, but it's just if," Charlene responds. She pauses for a second, with the sound of the oxygen filling the silence. Then she dives in deep, with all the pent up thoughts and fears that have filled her mind in the long lonely hours of the night and her times in the hospital ward welling up and bursting from her heart. She speaks quickly, expelling her worries from deep within, as if to articulate them will be a relief. "Mum, Dad, if I don't make it, will I go to heaven?"

A smile lights up Janice's face as she laughs incredulously. "Charlene Barr! You tell me that one. How do you get in to heaven?"

Charlene smiles in spite of herself, and answers, "You trust in Jesus and follow Him."

Janice shrugs her shoulders as Dad smiles at his daughter. "Well?"

Charlene laughs and some of her worries seem to tumble from her shoulders as she is reminded of the truth she knows. "Well that's that one sorted anyway!"

Almost immediately however a shadow falls upon her face and the smile in her eyes evaporates. Her eyes fill and she looks to the ground, no longer willing to look Janice or Dickie in the eye. For a minute she says nothing, until Janice squeezes her hand, unsure how to help Charlene with what is weighing her down.

Charlene looks up, and with anguish written across her face spits out the question that has haunted her. With her voice laced with regret she asks, "Why did you keep me Mum and Dad? Why did you keep me after all the crap I put you through?"

Janice reels for a second and her heart breaks within her. How long have these thoughts haunted Charlene? For how long have her demons whispered lies and stolen peace and joy from her, filling her mind with doubts? "What crap?" she asks.

Charlene snorts and looks her straight in the eye. "You know full well what I mean." Her eyes are pools that threaten to spill over at any moment.

Everyone who donated money received a personal 'Thank You' from Charlene

Janice responds without thinking, words flowing from her lips without forethought, words tempered and forged through the journey they have been on together. "Charlene, all of that is gone. Completely gone forever. We don't remember it; it is forgotten, gone forever."

Charlene interrupts the flow, still adamant, regret hanging from her every word, "But I haven't forgotten. I just can't forget Mum."

"Oh Charlene, we love you so much," Dickie says, emotion flooding his voice.

The life-giving words continue to flow from Janice like a fountain, from a healing well deep within her. It is as if the words are given to her. "You must forget Charlene, because it is all forgiven and forgotten. We have forgotten. Your brother and sisters have forgotten. God has forgotten. You must forget. God has taken all of our sins, all the worst things we have done, and destroyed them forever so they can no longer hurt us. They can only hurt us if we refuse to let go."

She continues. "He has taken our sins from us as far as the east is from the west. He has thrown them, forgotten forever, to the bottom of the ocean floor. All that crap you're talking about, it is all forgotten forever Charlene. God has removed it completely and you are free from it. You must forget it because it is only you who remembers it now, and you cannot allow it to hurt you anymore. God has worked a miracle in all of our lives Charlene, and He loves you so much."

As these words pass over Charlene it as if they bring her succour, and as if the sounds themselves give healing. She sits up straighter and the shadow on her face passes, and the weight that was so long burdening her is lifted. Janice knows in that moment that this is part of Charlene's true healing, that this is her daughter coming to know a peace that passes all understanding. Any lies that have been poisoning her mind are dispelled for now, and Charlene nods, accepting the answer.

"Ok. Just one more thing that has been bothering me though. You know how hard I have been finding it to read my Bible and stuff; I'm just so tired all the time. And I just feel like a rubbish Christian. What have I ever done with my life for God?" Charlene sighs. "I just feel like I have done nothing with my life," she mumbles resignedly.

Dickie answers this one. "Charlene, first off, God loves us and it is not dependant on what we do. But you have done something with your life. Look at Uganda! Because of your life and what you have done with it, kids who would never be able to go to school are going to be able to get an education. You have done so much with your life."

Charlene shakes her head, a frown on her face. "Yeah but I just find it hard sometimes." A spasm of sorrow crosses her face and she looks at Janice. "Mum you know what I mean. If I don't make it I'll never get to do all the things I wanted. If I don't make it I will never get married, and I will never have kids. I wanted to beat you, I wanted to have more kids than you have, and now that might never happen."

Janice's heart breaks within her, and all she wants to do is reach down, hold her daughter and weep with her, weep until the tears stop flowing like a river. Her pain coils within her like a snake, because she knows Charlene is exposing her heart, revealing what she has kept hidden, and Janice knows that as the days slide by this dream will probably never be. It destroys her to see Charlene distraught and disheartened like this. But she cannot show her, she must encourage her. She must be strong for her precious child now.

So instead she shifts herself closer and puts her arm tentatively around Charlene's weak, frail shoulders. And from a well deep within herself, in spite of how she feels, she laughs. At first she fears it will sound hollow, but as she gives it breath Janice feels stronger and her laugh fills with life, defying the shadow death threatens to cast over all of them. It has been defeated long ago.

"Charlene, you want kids?" she says, smiling and defying the tears that threaten to overflow at any moment. "You will have so many, way more than I ever had or could even dream of. If you don't make it, think of the number of children you will have through this school! Think of meeting them for the first time, then playing with and praising God with them forever in heaven! Because of this school you will have more children than I could ever even count!"

Charlene looks at her thoughtfully for a second, and then a smile slowly breaks across her face, like the sun emerging through a hazy cloud. "Yeah, I guess you're right." Just like that, she snaps back into her normal chirpy self. "But that's enough of that; here I am going on as if it's the end of the world! I don't want to talk about this anymore; this call could come at any minute!"

Dickie stands and offers her his hand. "Do you want to come into the others by the fire?"

"Aye why not? As long as you can carry this stupid oxygen thing, it's impossible to carry," Charlene replies, her face transformed from mere seconds ago.

"Of course," he says, picking it up with his other hand. Together they walk towards the living room where the others chat lightly as the fire blazes from the hearth, flames dancing across the coal. And as Janice watches she sees a spring in Charlene's step that was not there earlier. While they may still wait for physical healing, she knows that a much deeper healing has been at work, and she has seen a glimpse of this miracle. Humming a tune to herself she follows them in to join her family.

It is the day we are meant to go to the Culloden and Charlene remains ill. We have resigned to cancel the trip and are preparing to go to the hospital for the day. Booking the trip has served its purpose, giving Charlene something to aim towards, to give her a focus, even if the actual holiday is not to be.

Janice's phone rings, and when she answers it Charlene's voice is charged and bubbly. "They say I can go Mum, they say I can go. I'm getting out of this place one way or another; can you come and get me?"

She can do nothing else but laugh. "Charlene you are incredible."

"Shut up, no I'm not," Charlene replies awkwardly. "Can you bring a bag of clothes for me? And I'm sorry but you are going to have to help me pack up my room when you get here."

"That's no problem Charlene. And yes you are incredible. We are on our way," she says as she hangs up.

She looks at the rest of her family, all drained from the coming and going to hospital, from the worry and fear. Everyone get your bags packed and into the car, and as soon as Dickie gets home, we are going to the Culloden."

25
BEAUTY IN BROKENNESS

THE BLUE BUS PULLS IN before the archaic architecture of the Culloden Hotel. As we crawl up the stately drive, the floodlights by the road shine into the gathering darkness, refusing to be consumed and lighting up the estate in an ethereal glow. We pull right to the door of the Culloden to get as close as possible for Charlene, who is sitting in the middle row with her oxygen tank slouched beside her. The entrance to the hotel yawns before us, with stately stonework adorning the porch. The lights reflect of the ornate exterior, evoking a friendly ambience, while casting some corners in shadow, hinting at mysteries and places to explore.

We all clamber from the car, hauling our bags as we go. The rain pelts down around us, water flinging itself to the ground with reckless abandon. We are temporarily parked at the entrance way, blocking the roundabout that encroaches toward the porch until we can get Charlene in from the driving rain. Everyone runs for the welcoming glow of the lobby, while Mum pulls out and assembles Charlene's wheelchair. Dad and I help lift Charlene into the wheelchair, keeping hold of her oxygen tank, and move towards the doorway. Together we lift her up the steps, leaving behind the cold, unforgiving squall and entering the warm, friendly lobby, where a fire burns in the corner.

"This is amazing," Serena whispers, gazing around wide-eyed at the antique furniture and chandeliers, while shaking herself dry beside the fire. Even though she has only been outside for a few seconds, steam rises from her as the drops of water on her sodden jacket evaporate into the air.

"Let's go check out this art exhibition over there," Bethany suggests to the rest of us, referring to a sign pointing to a side room where an art exhibition is on display.

"Art?! Who cares about art? What are you on Bethany? I want to get up to the room and play cards!" Natalie scoffs.

"I think they are giving away free Shloer at it," Bethany observes drily. There is a scuffle of feet as we all pile in to see the art.

After feigning interest and showing our cultural ignorance while sipping on long stem glasses of wine and Shloer, we head for the gold doors which open up to reveal a lift plated in mirrors. We all get in, squeezing tightly to fit all our luggage and the wheelchair in the compact space.

As the lift slowly rises, Poppa chuckles, "Well isn't this fancy? I could get used to this!"

"I can't believe we come here on Tesco tokens, and take all the free drinks,"

Rebecca shakes her head incredulously.

"We'll end up being chucked out if we're not careful. The doorman was giving us some look as we came in, we looked like a bunch of country bumpkins coming in with all our bags," Charlene says smiling. It is good to see her smile. It has been so hard for her in the last few weeks, and although she has continued to put a brave face on things, the constant attrition of her weakened body has worn at her both physically and emotionally. For now she is laughing and it is clear to see she is glad to be out of hospital for a while.

The travel has tired Charlene out, so Dickie brings her to the room and gets her settled while the others head into the other room to play cards. The rooms are majestic and grand, with beds you can sink into, lavish wall hangings and views over all of the grassland and walkways outside where the rain still beats down relentlessly. Dickie pushes her into the room and rests her chair beside a window while he prepares her bed. She looks out, through the rain pelting down outside.

"Dad?" she calls weakly. "What are they doing walking from there?"

Dickie strides over to join her by the window, blurry with the droplets running down the window like tears on a child's face. They have a good view of the driveway up to the Culloden, and a strange sight greets them. A long bus is parked half-way up the winding drive to the entrance, and tripping out of the bus is a throng of young people dressed beautifully for a formal. As soon as they get out of the shelter of the bus they stumble along in the rain emptying from above, with water ripping through intricate hairstyles and down the back of starched collars. The driveway is slick with a slippery sheen, and the girls are hitching their dresses up and running as fast as their high heels can carry them, while the rivulets running down their faces paint swirling patterns in their make-up.

"It must be a school formal, but that is harsh on them facing that weather. I don't know why the bus hasn't parked beside the door. It would have saved them from being in the rain."

"Hmm," Charlene muses. "They look so beautiful." She sits in silence, watching the couples running together down below, with many of the guys chivalrously holding their jackets above their date's heads to shield them from the rain. She looks like a child again, so much smaller than a twenty year old should be. "I sometimes wish I could go to a formal again. I loved the one I went to when I was in Lower Sixth," she says wistfully, her voice quivering. Charlene is suddenly engulfed in coughing again as another fit descends on her, and tears run down her face from the exertion. His heart breaks for his daughter, and he helps her up and carefully lays her down on her bed. While she drifts towards sleep he draws up and prepares her many intravenous drugs.

He administers them to her carefully, holding her stick-like arm in his hand gently. Her veins are deep and blue, snake-like, writing up her arm. She is pale and listless as she lies there, and after he finishes her treatment he lets her sleep. He hopes she will sleep the night.

Don't be concerned about the outward beauty that depends on fancy hairstyles, expensive jewellery, or beautiful clothes. You should be known for the beauty that comes from within, the unfading beauty of a gentle and quiet spirit, which is so precious to God. 1 Peter 3: 3-4

(Underlined in Charlene's Bible)

While Charlene sleeps we play cards for a while in the other room, and then start to play some of the board games we have brought, leading to the predictable schisms forming down gender lines as time goes on and accusations of cheating and unfairness are flung through the air. After a while we take a break in the aftermath of another win for the men, and sit sipping on

the complementary tea and coffee.

"Let's play Ten of a Kind now," Natalie suggests. Ten of a Kind is a game we had bought a number of years ago and one that had led to more arguments than any other game we play.

Poppa laughs, shaking his head. "If it goes anything like the last few games, we will end up waking the whole hotel. We might end up sleeping in the car yet."

"It's those two who should sleep in the car," Natalie grunts, eyes narrowed at Dad and I. "There is no way they won that last game."

"I'd be happy to play Ten of a Kind," Dad responds placidly, pointedly ignoring Natalie's bait. "The question is can you girls take being beaten again, without resorting to cheating. I think it would be better if you all lie down for a while first, as judging by your anger in the last game you are all a bit irrational and tired. It might be better if you all had a nap first," he continues, casually stirring the pot.

"You are so annoying," Serena rails, half furious, half amused.

"Let's be fair Dad," I say, feigning impartiality. "Let's make the teams more fair by mixing them up, as at the minute they really aren't much of a challenge for us."

"You are so patronising David Barr," Rebecca fumes, glaring at me. We continue to wind each other for a few minutes as the game is set up.

"Would Charlene be up for playing?" Bethany asks, her voice rising above the din. "She loves this game, and I think she'd be annoyed if we played it without her."

The tumult of noise stops and Dad looks at her. "I'll check pet, but she's asleep and I don't think she will be up for it. But I'll go and see now. Natalie will you finish setting up?" he asks, rising from his seat.

As he leaves we finish setting up, but we are subdued now. It has been good tonight, but it hasn't felt as it should. It is obvious that someone is missing. Without Charlene joining in the screams of protest and allegations of cheating, frantically screaming out answers when it is her team's turn, or trying to sneak her counter on a square or two, it hasn't been as it should be. And we all know that she won't be up to the games tonight, not with her as laid low as she is now. If a call came now, would it even matter? Would she even be able to get on the plane?

When I stop to think it is clear that Charlene has been on an ever tightening spiral downwards for months. Looking back to how she was a month ago, then two months ago, then three, it is obvious things are worsening, and dangerously so. But at the back of my mind I have seen her rebound so many times from the edge and claw her way back from the precipice time and time again, that I still cling to the belief that she will be ok. Somehow, she will be ok.

The door cracks open as Dad pushes Charlene into the room in her wheelchair. "I can't believe you were going to play without me," she says scowling. Looking at the fire burning in her eyes I know she will never be beaten. There are things this disease can never take from her.

Still the clouds fling their wrath towards the ground below. Janice can hear the heavy rain drops crashing against the window outside, and she pulls the blanket tighter around her. She has just got into bed and Dickie is getting ready for bed. Janice knows she will struggle to sleep with so many thoughts dancing through her mind. From the bed beside her Charlene's ventilator heaves as her chest rises and falls, Charlene taking short sharp gasps, and she wonders how much longer Charlene will be able to fight. She would give anything to fight for her, to take her sufferings, but all she can do is to love her with everything she has.

As the deluge continues, she wonders momentarily was it a good idea to bring her out of hospital, but as quickly as it comes the thought is dismissed. She does not know how long they have left as a family together, so every memory crafted is now precious beyond measure. All illusions of the importance of wealth and prestige have been stripped bare and seen for the cruel and fickle thieves and imposters they are. Without a shadow of doubt the only things that matter are the relationships and ties that bind them to each other.

She knows Charlene hates the hospital and wants to take every opportunity she can to be out of there. She would far rather reach her end spending herself in adventure and in the arms of her family than slowly fade away in a sterile hospital ward. Janice knows she will continue to respect Charlene's wishes in this area. Charlene had also begged her parents if her fight were ever to become hopeless that she be brought home. Lying down to try to sleep Janice hopes and prays that the day their fight becomes hopeless is far, far away.

She smiles as Dickie and her recall the day they have had, of how Charlene wound up the guys in the game, and screamed answers out enthusiastically on the girls' turn, the fires of competition blazing from her eyes. They talk back over the night, of the free Shloer and...

Janice suddenly sits bolt upright in the bed, panic etched across her face. "What's wrong Janice?" Dickie murmurs sleepily, yawning as he gets into bed beside Janice.

"Dickie, did you ever go back to move the car?" she exclaims frantically, staring at the red numbers on the clock beside them which read 2:30.

His face blanches and he scrambles out of bed, pulling his clothes back on haphazardly and grasping for the keys.

"You mean it had been out there for six hours?" Natalie cackles, clearly delighted as we all discussed the antics of the previous night.

"What did the doormen say when you got down last night Dickie?" Poppa asks, "Were they angry?"

"More relieved if I'm honest. I arrived down and instantly they asked was it my car. I explained that Charlene had been unwell and after I got her in and settled we all completely forgot about the car. They were just happy to see it moved."

"And that's not the best bit!" Charlene shrieks, nearly dancing in her chair. "Go on Dad, tell them what happened."

"Well the car completely blocked the driveway, so no vehicle could get close. They had no idea whose it was, so there was little they could do but wait. Remember that formal group I told you about? Turns out they had to park halfway up the driveway and get out in the rain because that was the closest they could get to the hotel with our car blocking the way!"

Natalie looks embarrassed as Rebecca puts her hand to her mouth. "That's awful! The poor girls!"

"And guys to be fair," adds Serena.

"But there's more!" Charlene says, clearly bursting to see our reaction when we hear what she heard as soon as she had been woken up.

"Well this bit is really bad," Dad ventures sheepishly. "They couldn't identify the car you see, and they were worried because it was parked just outside the lobby. So they phoned the police and reported it as an abandoned vehicle."

"What?" Natalie demands, eyes wide.

"Yeah, they were worried it might be a bomb," Dad confesses. "But the police cross checked it and it came up that we were guests who were staying in the hotel. But by that point the reception staff were gone so the doormen had no way to contact us. At least until I arrived later."

"That's terrible," Rebecca shakes her head slowly.

"No, it's brilliant!" Charlene says cackling. "We come here on TESCO tokens and we end up having the police called on us! Only our family."

Poppa laughs. "I'm sure it's not something that happens every day at the Culloden!"

"That is so embarrassing," Bethany says, but she is smiling. Life is never boring with our family, and together again, we reminisce about past awkward situations we have been in together. We have walked a road together, and we will continue to do so, no matter where it will lead.

I put my foot down and accelerate, passing the slow moving traffic to my left. It has been a long day of lectures this Friday, and I am rushing to rejoin my family for dinner at the Cultra Inn beside the hotel. While the girls have been off for half term, the hectic Teaching PGCE course ticks obliviously on, fast approaching the first eleven week placement. I feel a twinge of fear, not knowing yet where I will be placed. This time next week I will be finishing lectures and getting ready for my last weekend before the madness starts.

I pull into a car parking space, and sprint to the restaurant where my family have saved me a seat. It has been a good three days, and we are going to eat together one final time before heading for home. It promises to be a mad weekend: the twins have coursework due to hand in and Mum and Dad have a lot of work they need to do that has built up over the past few weeks. We hope Charlene will be able to stay out of hospital for a while, but if the same trends continue, she may have to go back in next week.

Everyone is huddled around a circular table when I arrive, and the air is filled with chatter. Charlene has pulled her wheelchair in close alongside Mum and Dad, and everyone's eyes are gliding quizzingly through a menu.

"Hey David, good day? Take a look at the Early Bird menu, they have an offer on," Mum suggests as I sit down.

We place our orders and the conversation flows freely. To pass the time until our food arrives we play a game, starting at the letter 'A' and going around the table naming countries beginning with that letter until someone fails. Then we continue through the alphabet.

"Are we on C now?" Bethany asks. "My turn then, China."

"Columbia," Serena fires back instantly.

"That was my one, emmmm….. Canada!" Rebecca yells.

"Chile," Mum exclaims.

It's Poppa's turn now. "Columbia," he says confidently.

"It's already been said," Serena chirps smiling.

"Has it? Well I'll go Cuba then."

"California" Natalie says excitedly.

"Not a country!" we all chorus as one.

We love to play this game, and keep going, taking our turns one by one until the food arrives. Charlene is in the thick of all the action, joking away. It is easy to see she is making an effort, as she looks tired and drawn. The oxygen tube runs into her nose all the time, pouring the breath of life into her. But just as she refused to miss out on any action as a bubbly three year old, she will not contemplate missing any now. She may not be well enough to eat, but she still orders a latte and sips on it now. She will never allow this disease to rule her.

Charlene is jubilant, having received pictures that morning sent from Basil and Wenford in Uganda, showing pictures of the assembled team of builders shaking hands and preparing to begin work on clearing the land of trees and undergrowth. The work is due to begin any day now. On seeing the pictures Charlene had squealed like an excited child, finally seeing her dream coming into reality. Her prayers are being answered.

After the meal we don't leave immediately, continuing to sit and talk.

I whip out my phone to take a few pictures. "Charlene, can I get one of you?" I ask, pointing the camera in her direction.

"Wait!" she protests frantically, yanking the oxygen tube from her face. "I don't want a photo with this thing on," she explains defiantly as she fumbles with the oxygen hanging by her side.

I steady the camera, taking a second while I fiddle with the settings, and already Charlene is panting without the oxygen sustaining her, but she does not put the tube back in. She will not until I get her picture. I quickly snap the picture, and she slips the tube back into place, inhaling deeply.

"Here Charlene, want to see?" She grabs the phone and looks, then hands it back and nods, satisfied.

When we arrive home we haul our bags inside and knackered, all begin to make treks for bed. Recently Charlene has been sleeping on a carefully made bed in the kitchen as getting down to her own bed has been too much of an effort, exhausting her further. To get up and dressed from her bed in the morning has often been too much for Charlene, so she has preferred to sleep in the kitchen where she can doze all day and still be in the thick of the action unfolding around her.

But tonight in the busyness Charlene interrupts the preparations. "No," she croaks. "I want to sleep in my own bed. I haven't slept there in a long time, and tonight I want to sleep in my own room."

Dad pushes Charlene carefully towards her room, and prepares her bed. He helps her gently from her wheelchair, and Charlene shuffles towards her bed, clutching his hand for support and bent double like an elderly woman. I carry her ventilator from the car back into her room and Dad prepares her medication as normal. She is quickly linked up to all the equipment and Natalie carries her in a glass of water. As she lies back in her bed, utterly spent and bone weary, a smile cracks across her thin face and the years and sickness seem to roll off her.

"I love yous."

We all say our "good nights", as the ventilator rumbles relentlessly on.

26
PRECIOUS BREATHS

CLICK, CLICK, DELETE, CLICK. My essay is making slow progress. Where will I be on placement? How will it go? Have I enough sources in my essay? Why is my laptop so useless? What are the girls watching? What do I have to do this week? Thoughts cascade through my head one after the other, mundane every day thoughts, many of them of little significance but they would soon be etched into my mind forever because of what is about to unfold. I work away at the essay, distracted by the sitcom my sisters are watching in the background.

It is a normal Saturday and I am still getting back into a working mind frame after the good times at the Culloden. I know the relief Charlene gets from those trips, and I am sure we will plan something for Christmas so she has a horizon to again focus on.

It is a strange day in some respects in that it is one of the rare occasions our entire family is at home. With Rebecca on nursing placements, myself on the PGCE course, and Natalie, Bethany and Serena often at hockey at the weekends, it is rare this is the case. Yet today we are all together at home; Poppa, Mum, Dad, Rebecca, Natalie, Bethany, Serena and I. We have eaten together earlier in the evening, talking and joking away, with Charlene barely awake but listening on the sofa, as much a part of proceedings as anyone else. It is a familiar scene, and nothing feels special, nothing feels strange.

After eating the girls had headed into the other room to watch a TV show they had recorded, while I reluctantly returned to my essay with coffee cup in hand, racking my brains for a way to say something that had been said many times before in much better ways than I ever could. As I stare blankly at the screen before me my thoughts coalesce on the day so far. It is clear that Charlene is caught in the grip of a difficult day.

As normal, Bethany, Serena and Natalie had headed out to play hockey in the morning, with the ever enthusiastic Dad and Mum to cheer them on. Charlene had awoken with the hustle and bustle as they prepared to leave and asked if she could be brought into her usual daytime spot on the sofa in the kitchen, so Mum had prepared her spot and carried her in carefully, propping her up gently in a sitting position and making sure the oxygen was flowing. While the others headed to hockey, following the old Saturday morning routine like clockwork, Rebecca had stayed to finish packing shoeboxes which she had been filling with the help of some friends for kids in Romania. I worked at my assignment, with a Monday deadline looming. All morning long we regularly checked Charlene was comfortable and had water, as she drifted in and out of sleep.

At one point when Rebecca had come to check on her, she had slowly opened her eyes, and weakly beckoned to Rebecca to come closer. Rebecca bent down, struggling to reconcile this emaciated figure with the vibrant girl she had played weddings with when they were younger, and Charlene's frail voice cracked in Rebecca's ear. "Can you check, is the oxygen on?"

Rebecca's heart had spiked then as she saw Charlene grappling more for breath now, her face paler than usual, but when she checked the ventilator all had been well. After double-checking all the connections she fixed Charlene's position, and this had seemed to give her a measure of relief as she tumbled straight back into the comforting arms of sleep.

We continued to watch her carefully, but Charlene spent most of the morning asleep. This wasn't unusual, as recently when she dipped badly she spent her mornings withdrawn and continually fatigued, usually recovering substantially and becoming perkier towards the end of the day as the medication did its work.

However as the day wears on Charlene doesn't perk up. Even when the hockey fanatics return, she doesn't sit up as she usually does, remaining listless and stoic on the sofa and letting the noise and conversation wash against her like waves beating against an ancient cliff-face.

Dickie looks at Charlene and shakes his head. She looks worse than he has seen her in a long while, and her body looks a shell of the girl who had held his hand and bravely chosen to fight this battle for transplant. He remembers how her voice shook as she made her choice, and his heart swells with pride. Thinking of how Charlene had claimed her victory already in turning her back on the darkness that had flooded her soul and poisoned her mind for so long, and accepted the open unquestioning hand of love and acceptance that was offered to her, he is overwhelmed.

But her suffering is agonising to watch now and it breaks his heart. He suspects the end may not be far away now, and the thought causes his blood to run cold. He fears a long, painful drawn-out battle that lasts weeks and causes Charlene such torment, but he hopes and prays that this will not be the case. He gasps a prayer. If you have to take her home, let it be painless. But please don't take her home.

Dickie bends to the ventilator and checks it, but it is working fine, pumping out oxygen at the same stable rate as it has done for weeks. That is not where the problem lies.

He watches her, her chest heaving as she sucks in air rapidly as if she has just run a marathon. He reaches down and checks the oxygen has free access through her nose, then gently kisses her cheek.

"I love you Charlene," he whispers. She stirs slightly, then grows still, like a leaf touched by the wind.

I haven't typed anything new in a while, and the thoughts spiralling through my skull are nothing to do with the ideological approaches to the teaching of Religious Education, so I set the laptop aside for a second. I try to watch the programme the girls are watching but the images merge and my mind meanders down a dozen different paths. Charlene is still in the other room on the sofa, where Dad is working and Poppa is sitting down with a cup of tea before he heads for home.

If someone withdrawn from Charlene's situation, who sees her infrequently, perhaps once or twice a year, were to walk in and see how the disease has reduced her they would be horrified. They would see that Charlene is gaunt and emancipated, although bloated in the face due to the steroids she is dosed on and that her complexion is pale due to lack of oxygen. The drone of the ventilator would burrow into the observer's skull. They would watch her sleep most hours of the day on the sofa on her makeshift bed, and even when she temporarily woke they would see that she was listless and groggy.

Compared to her state eighteen months before the transformation is cruelly stark. Although sick then, she put up the illusion to everyone that she was the epitome of health - never complaining, always vibrant, but this past year has dealt cruel successive blows, as if premeditated to knock her off her feet completely. Charlene had first to accept the need for a wheelchair, then the need to be on oxygen constantly. She is unrecognisable from the chirpy girl eighteen months before. An infrequent outside observer would notice these things.

"I'm going to go and get a drink," Rebecca says, getting up and stirring me from my morbid thoughts. I pick up my laptop. Looking at it I realise I'm going to need to restructure the entire section I have just finished. I shake my head to clear it of the clouded thoughts, and begin to type.

As Rebecca leaves the living room she can hear Mum hanging the washing from the Culloden on the radiators upstairs. It is cold today, and that will be the only way to get any kind of warmth into those clothes to dry them. Rebecca hears the ventilator continuing to do its work as she walks down the hall towards the kitchen, but it barely registers so familiar has the sound become. Poppa is still sipping on his tea at the kitchen table, staring sadly at Charlene who is still asleep.

"Where's Dad, Poppa?" Rebecca asks.

"He headed down to Charlene's room darling, I think he's calling the consultant," he replies.

Rebecca nods and walks to the fridge and pours herself a glass of Diet Coke. Her throat feels parched, and she sips from the cool glass as she tiptoes quietly over to Charlene, careful not to waken her. Charlene is still panting for breath, and it is obvious that today has not been a good day. Usually she improves as the hours tick past, but not today. Lines of worry lace across Rebecca's forehead. Will Charlene be ok?

Watching her, she thinks of how things have changed. Charlene's decline has been slow and incremental, and watching day to day and up-close, you don't notice the small changes. Everyone in the family knows Charlene is desperately sick, but watching her now Rebecca feels like she has been kicked in the gut as she realises how long Charlene has been close to death, and how lucky they have been to have her with them for so long. A year ago, at the time of the lung abscess, they should have lost her. But they didn't, and Rebecca realises that they have all grown complacent.

Rebecca bites her lip. To her the drone of the ventilator has become background noise, Charlene's gaunt look a temporary pain for her until she has her transplant, her wheelchair a fleeting inconvenience for the same reason. Surely all these things must pass? It is all part of the plan, part of the journey. All would be redeemed. God is surely bringing her as close as possible to the abyss so that the miracle will be all the more incredible. That makes sense doesn't it? Doesn't it?

As Rebecca watches, Charlene stirs. Rebecca reaches down and strokes her hair that has stuck to her forehead.

"Would you like anything Charlene?" Rebecca asks so gently. Her compassionate heart and motherly instinct, honed by her nursing training, longs to relieve her sister's suffering in any way she can.

Charlene's eyes jerk open and she stares at Rebecca as if from a far off distance. She tries to speak but her voice catches in her throat. So she points at the glass in Rebecca's hand.

"Of course Charlene," and Rebecca lifts the glass to Charlene's mouth. Charlene reaches up and lifts the mask from her mouth just enough to leave space for the glass, and as Rebecca holds it she takes a massive gulp, letting the cool liquid flow over her parched lips. It is clear she is thirsty again, but Rebecca worries about keeping her mask off for too long.

Getting up, Rebecca fixes her oxygen mask and squeezes Charlene's doll-like hand. "I'll get you a straw now Charlene, it will be easier for you to drink."

As he paces around the room, Dickie's heart is filled with sorrow as he talks on the phone to the consultant. "I'm phoning because I want to talk about a few things. Charlene has got a lot worse in the last twenty four hours and

Janice and I are even worried about moving her at present. She isn't in a lot of pain currently, but I wanted to enquire about a syringe driver for pain relief if things continue, as I don't want her to be in any discomfort."

He does not want to make this call, but he has no choice. His words drop like lead weights because he knows that with this conversation he is finally facing the inevitable truth that he has tried to ignore for the last few weeks, the monstrous elephant in the room, that Charlene is no longer well enough for transplant. Everyone has waited so long for that phone call, but it has not come to pass, and now it is too late.

He knows that many of the others still hope. They have seen Charlene get indescribably sick so many times, and be confronted with devastating predictions from doctors, yet every time she has pulled back from the brink, as if guided by a hand behind the scenes. He knows that as a family they have believed for a long time that she was being prepared and protected for transplant, although from conversations with the older ones he knows that privately their faith in this has begun to waver due to her frequent declines in health. Yet every time in the past Charlene has rallied, and Dickie knows that to many in the family they have no reason to believe this time will be any different. But he knows. He sees the subtle change in her colour and knows she is no longer taking in enough oxygen.

As the consultant cycles through the available options, Dickie is afraid. Should he talk to the younger ones? They have not talked together about if the unthinkable should ever transpire. They should have this conversation soon, because he does not know what hopes and fears, what dreams and nightmares, the youngest are wrestling with. Perhaps later today.

Upstairs Janice is trying to fit all the wet clothes from the washing machine onto the radiators. It has been quite a good week, and it has been good to see Charlene having such a good time. If the call is not to come, she wants Charlene to be as happy as she can when she is well enough. And one thing Charlene seems adamant about now is that she remains in the kitchen.

When she arrived back from the hockey she had asked Charlene if she wanted to head to her bed, but she had feebly shaken her head before going back to sleep. Even listless and withdrawn, she wants to be on the sofa beside the kitchen table rather than in her bed. To her this means that she can still be involved in the general bedlam of mealtimes, even though she no longer feels up to eating. Charlene wants to be part of the family, not an invalid imprisoned in her room.

Shaking out a wet towel, Janice knows she is glad Charlene is in the kitchen with them. It is the hub of the house. Janice knows that she has set up the bed in the kitchen for the rest of the family as well as for Charlene, as family mealtimes would never be complete without her. Everyone in the house wishes to be together more now than ever, so much more so as Charlene has grown more and more ill.

She is so proud of her daughter and hopes so desperately that she will pick up from this dip, that there are many more days of being together still to come. She loves the golden times of bringing her for coffee, relieving her of the doldrums of the hospital ward. She loves the laughs they have together as they try to match-make all the other children in the house. But she knows those times are ending, and it crushes her. From talking to her husband quietly earlier, far from the ears of her children, she knows that Charlene may be past the point of no return, no longer well enough for the transplant and the weight of the world seems to fall on her.

Stopping for a second from her work, she prays. God, if you must take her, let her pass into your arms peacefully. Please.

No words are coming. I simply cannot concentrate on this essay, and all my thoughts keep spiralling down to one common point, my sick sister. I can no longer fight my black doubts as to whether she will be healed now, but when I doubt I feel guilt, wondering if I lack faith. So I choose to cling anew to the hope that has sustained all of us. She will be healed. This is just another dip before she again rallies, the darkness before the dawn, that will make her ultimate healing all the more miraculous, whether supernaturally or by transplant. It all makes sense in our heads, as it does in Charlene, at least when she speaks of it.

But I know that Charlene has been healed long ago of her real ailment, the toxic anger that ate at her heart and the poison that seeped through her mind. Healing has already come. Still, doubts as to if she will ever be physically healed streak through my head like lightning flashes lighting up the horizons of my thoughts. As my darkest dreads assault me anew I fight them off desperately and try to concentrate on my essay, but all I can focus on is the flashing line hungrily awaiting my typed words.

I shake my head and let the dam open, allowing my mind to be flooded with more mundane thoughts. In these moments I worry and think about things like what my placement will be like, what I will take to Belfast when I raid the fridge later, and what I will do in the next few days with friends. In mere seconds, my universe will shift forever on its axis and all my paltry concerns will be cast down. In a few moments my priorities will shift and my petty fears and self-obsession will assume their rightful place. But not yet. In these few minutes all is normal. There is no warning. There is no special feeling. The world just holds back for one more breath before it changes everything for us forever.

Rebecca returns to Charlene with a straw in the glass, and sits on the sofa beside her. Is it her imagination, or has Charlene grown paler in the minute it has taken to find a straw? Regardless, as soon as Charlene sees the drink she again carefully raises her mask and while Rebecca holds the glass she gulps down the Diet Coke. After a few mouthfuls she leans back and slides the mask down over her mouth again, allowing the oxygen to stream into her lungs. She closes her eyes.

But a few moments later she is struggling again. Charlene seems to be having more difficulty breathing, now gasping desperately at the oxygen flooding around her, struggling to take enough in. Rebecca's blood freezes and her heart stops as the machine beside her begins to give out a terrible high-pitched beeping like a harbinger of doom, the dreaded signal that not enough oxygen is being taken in. No. Please no. She jerks upright and looks around her with desolation strewn across her face. Poppa has set down his tea and is white, his face frozen and a shadow of fear hanging over him. Rebecca breathes deeply and yells at the top of her voice, her voice shrill and infused with raw fear.

"Mum! Dad!"

27
SAYING GOODBYE

ONE SECOND DICKIE IS ON THE PHONE to the consultant, the next he is rushing through the kitchen, his steps seeming all too slow. He hears the beep and Rebecca's screams and rushes to his daughter.

Janice charges down the stairs, her heartbeat reverberating through her skull. Her thoughts are sluggish, but she knows that she wants to be downstairs now. Not in a second, but now. There are so many steps. Her blood runs cold within her veins and her darkest fears, that she had hidden away for so long, claw and tear at her mind.

At the bottom of the stairs, just a few steps away, the living room door is flung open and she sees David, Natalie, Bethany and Serena fire out as if from the barrel of a gun.

We all move as one. There is desperation in Rebecca's voice, terror and dread layered through it. All of us in that room move in the same instant. At one moment I am sitting with an unfinished essay on my knee, the next I am standing in the kitchen with my precious, precious family. Everyone is there, and the ventilator machine is giving off a high-pitched warning beep. I don't try to work out what this might mean, I just know that Charlene is sprawled with her back against the arm of the sofa, gasping for air, and her eyes are wide and transfixed on something in the garden outside. She is struggling to breathe.

With no conscious thought, all of us are suddenly around her as she lies on the sofa, some standing, some kneeling; some holding her hands, some laying hands on her, we all cling to her. All of us, including Poppa, crowd around her where she lies. Charlene is now drained of any colour and is taking rapid shallow breaths, with wide eyes and her mouth open.

We crowd around Charlene, and we all know this is the end. But there is no wailing, no anguished cries. Of course there are tears: red hot, they slip down our faces like rivers, but they are silent. Without speaking to one another, we each know that we do not want to scare her. Dad so gently slips the now useless mask from her face, and for the first time in Charlene's life she is not fighting against what is coming. Instead she remains transfixed on something ahead of her, something through the window in the garden outside. I sit at her feet with my hands on her withered legs, with all of us crouching around her and speaking tenderly to her.

"We love you so so much Charlene."

"Think of the kids in Uganda, think of how God has used you Charlene."

"We will see you soon Charlene, we will see you so soon. This is not the end."

"You are loved by so many Charlene, both here and in Uganda."

"I love you so much Charlene, you are so special to all of us."

"Charlene we are here, and we will stay here. You are beautiful Charlene."

"I am so proud of you Charlene. I am so so proud."

"I love you pet"

Eight different voices speak to Charlene, speaking truth to her, telling her how much we love her, and talking of the school in Uganda that is being built because of her. Time seems to hold as we look at her and love her.

We have always feared if Charlene were to pass from us, that she will fight at the end and it will be very painful for her. But Charlene, for the first time in her life, does not fight. The fighter is surrendering as she steps into her real home, shrugging off the shackles of these shadow lands and discovering what she has been being prepared for her whole life. While we whisper to her, she gazes with eyes wide out the window before her into the garden, and her eyes do not flinch no matter what we say. Her mouth is open wide, and there is no fear in her big, brown eyes. If anything there is awe, there is wonder.

None of us turn to see what she is looking at. Who knows what we would see, perhaps nothing human eyes can perceive while they are glazed and drowning in the trappings of this life and things that do not live past today. Our eyes are fixed on Charlene as time freezes with us all around her telling her of our love for her. But Charlene is gripped by something else she can see. I don't know how much she hears us, as this world fades into shadow around her and the dawn breaks on her true home. What are her eyes fixed on? Are they fixed on her Saviour who has been with her always, every painful faltering step of the way, always leading her on hand in hand, and now beckoning her to Him?

Charlene fixes her eyes beyond us and gazes with no fear, but with wonder, and we tell her of our love for her, our precious Charlene. We hold her and we walk her home. Finally she closes her eyes, her head lolled to one side, and she looks as if she has simply fallen asleep. She has left us. She looks more peaceful now than she has in over a year. She is spent utterly living for things that are eternal.

I struggle to remember details as our reality twists and ripples. We rise and stand beside her, grouped in a semicircle. I do not know who moves first, but all of us younger ones begin to move back to where we had come from, retracing our steps as if rewinding a tape. Our movements become a blur and we are standing together in the living room where we used to jump from sofa to sofa and perform in plays we had hastily written. And each of us feel like children now. One of us is missing. We stand there, and the hammer of reality still does not fall on us, not yet.

Poppa, Mum and Dad enter the room and we stand there together. And finally, inevitably, Dad speaks, and the hammer falls. "Charlene has gone home," Dad says, his voice breaking. At that the wails from the depths of our souls claw from our throats, as grief washes over us like a flood. "No, no, please God no." "Why?" "How can it be?" We all come together; all hold each other, clinging to one another desperately as a shipwrecked man will cling to a rock in a storm. I hold Bethany as she weeps into my shoulder and I weep with her, our sorrow pouring out of us, yet each drawing comfort from the other. Mum draws Serena close and Dad holds Rebecca, while Poppa pulls Natalie into his embrace. We lose track of time. We sob openly and unashamedly, basking in the anguish and pain as realisation settles upon us like snow upon a mountain top.

Details of that night are disjointed in my mind. Phone calls are made and people come, close family friends and visitors. The phone rings. There are knocks on the door. The phone rings again. We sit and talk, but we are not really present. Not really. We do not disturb her for a long while. We all sit and converse in the kitchen where she lies on the sofa with her eyes closed while people arrive, and it is natural in a way that is impossible to describe. She has lain there so much in past weeks so she would miss no family time or action, and there is something natural about staying with her in the room now and welcoming people in with us as we sit around the table. Charlene looks as if she is in a deep slumber. We mourn and grieve together, and she is not disturbed or moved for a long time.

Then the undertakers come and take her away for a time, but bring her back home within a matter of hours. We want her to be home tonight. The thought of drifting into the darkness of sleep when she is not home with us is unthinkable. They bring her back, dressed in her favourite wee dress, and she lies as if in deep rest in a wooden box, which we lay upon her bed so she can sleep.

That night, Dad's phone rings again and I answer it. Rebecca and I have agreed earlier that we will take all calls, trying to help in any way we can. This call stands out from the others. "Hello David, it's Stephen Blevins here. I am so sorry; I have just heard what happened." Stephen is familiar to all of us, having been involved with Fields of Life when Charlene first approached them about building a school in Uganda. Hearing him speak I am reminded of the legacy Charlene's life will leave. It is good to hear from him.

"David, I just have this picture of Charlene in my head, ever since I heard the news and I wanted to share it with you," Stephen's voice echoes in my ear. "It's a picture I have of Charlene in heaven now, running through fields, with new lungs and able to breathe fully and cleanly like she has never been able to do here on earth. And I was just thinking that as children in Uganda get the opportunity to go to school because of how Charlene lived, as they find Jesus at the school, grow up and pass on to heaven, she will be playing and singing with them there forever."

After everyone else has left that night, I share this with my family. It strikes a chord with all of us. She has always wanted her own family, her own children, and now she has that, with the Ugandan children who will come to know Jesus at her school; her children, and now she is in heaven worshipping forever with a multitude of African children and among African voices. She is home.

We go into her room before we go to bed and stand around her, holding hands in a tight semicircle and praying. Things have not happened as we hoped, a truth that causes great pain. But as we pray, it is as if a ray of warm sunlight falls on our shaking hearts, basking us in its' warm, whispering glow. It does not take away the pain, far from it. But it speaks to our hearts, and reminds us in our agony that this is not the end of the story. We will see her again.

We know she is in no more pain; that her struggles are at an end. Cystic fibrosis has not beaten her, she stood up to it all the way, and she has now been released to a place beyond its reach where it can never claw at her ever again. We prayed for healing for so long, and it has been answered in a more permanent way than any operation could ever have done. Any new lungs would also have shrivelled over time, as the cystic could never be purged from this weak frame she carried here. It would slowly have eroded away at her other organs, never satisfied in its hunger.

We never wanted to lose her, but the ones in pain are ourselves who are left behind, not her. She is freed from this human shell, running and breathing like she has never been able to before. She has been healed in a way we still cannot grasp with our eyes shrouded by the temporary trappings of this world. God has answered our prayers and given her a new body and new lungs, ones that will never weaken, never be assaulted again. He healed her heart on earth; He has healed her body in heaven.

For I am already being poured out like a drink offering, and the time for my departure is near. I have fought the good fight, I have finished the race, I have kept the faith. Now there is in store for me the crown of righteousness, which the Lord, the righteous Judge, will award to me on that day – and not only to me, but also to all who have longed for his appearing.

2 Timothy 4: 6-7

28
THE DARK NIGHT OF THE SOUL

GRIEF IS NOT EASY TO DESCRIBE. It comes in waves, overwhelming your heart and threatening never to let go, then ebbing and receding before it again comes from nowhere like a tsunami. The next few days, weeks, months and year pass in flashes and time seems to run together, making it difficult to distinguish clear moments. Some episodes however do flash out, like lightning on the horizon of a dark storm cloud…

Basil and Wenford phone us on Sunday, the day after Charlene's passing, and describe how they broke the news to the church community in Maya, where Hidden Treasure School is sited. They describe with heavy hearts how the community wept openly, and prayed for our family. This community who have never met Charlene are devastated to hear of her death. The church body fasted and prayed for Charlene in the past, and their love for her is humbling. We are encouraged and so thankful for the prayers of our Ugandan brothers and sisters.

Flashes remain in my mind from the day of the funeral. Around the kitchen table where so many memories of Charlene laughing and the family eating together stick out, Rebecca, with voice shaking and cracking, reads a passage that had comforted since Charlene's passing, one that embodied and said better than we ever could what Charlene's life signified:

> *Remember, dear brothers and sisters, that few of you were wise in the world's eyes or powerful or wealthy when God called you. Instead, God chose things the world considers foolish in order to shame those who think they are wise. And he chose things that are powerless to shame those who are powerful. God chose things despised by the world, things counted as nothing at all, and used them to bring to nothing what the world considers important.*

I Corinthians 1:26-27

This passage resonated with the realities of Charlene's life, of how a sick child, left alone after her birth, had achieved so much more than many who have all the advantages she was denied. God chose her and loved her, using her to subvert the natural orders of this world and show that those we see as the least can open our eyes to the deeper realities we blind ourselves to.

The funeral is a blur, with moments scuttling past us as we sit like sentinels staring blankly at the coffin at the front of the church. But the songs and the passages on that day remind us of what we can never ever forget. We sing songs Charlene loved and they confirm the deeper truth we so often struggled to see.

One of these songs was crafted from the words of the 23rd Psalm:

And though I walk the darkest path
I will not fear the evil one
For You are with me and Your rod and staff
Are the comfort I need to know.

And I will trust in You alone
And I will trust in You alone
For Your endless mercy follows me
Your goodness will lead me home.

Charlene had sung this often, and today the words speak truth deep into our present experience. God does not promise that following Him will lead to our pain disappearing. But He does promise that in good times and bad, in light and darkness, in glorious mountain tops and deepest valleys of gut wrenching pain, we are not alone, and He holds all of us in His Hand. The ending of our stories find fulfilment in His.

Janice stands in the line as the crowd passes by like snowflakes in a blizzard. Faces are as a blur to her as peaks and troughs of emotion surge over her and chip at her resolve. As she grips hands with the fellow grievers who pass by, her smile is sometimes forced and painted whilst in the grip of painful loss, and other times happy and natural as the knowledge that Charlene is truly home pushes itself to the fore.

As Janice shakes the hand of one woman a bell of faint recognition rings in the back of her mind. The woman before her is smiling sadly, her eyes lined with sadness. Another woman stands beside her with arm outstretched. "Janice, we are both so sorry," one ventures.

"Thank you so much for coming," Janice manages. She stops for a second, gripping the hand before her, then asks the question eating at her mind, "I know your faces."

The first woman smiles. "My name is Christine and this is Barbara," she replies. "We were nurses back in the Royal Victoria Hospital where Charlene spent her first year."

The pieces fall into place, and Janice finds herself pulling them close. "Yes,

yes I remember. Thank you, both of you, you were so good to her," is all she can manage as her words threaten to choke in her throat as the debris of her memories fall upon her again.

As she pulls back, Barbara looks at her and her eyes sparkle. With emotion dripping from every word she says, "It was a beautiful service Janice, it was incredible for us to see what she became. God really used her."

Christine is nodding. "We prayed for her every night Janice, did you know that? Every night as she was so sick in her first year, we prayed over her cot."

Again Janice feels the faint touches of awe as she is reminded anew that they have been playing roles in a story bigger and more beautiful than they will ever be able to comprehend. "Your prayers were answered. Those prayers were so key. God heard them, and everything today has come to pass in part because of your prayers."

As the faces continue to move by this conversation sticks with her, and she remembers again the many prayers in despair, and how Charlene's life had been redeemed and transformed in rejoicing. Her death was not a lost fight, the war had been won years before, and each prayer had been vital to that fight. The rest of that awful day no longer seems so awful to Janice as she clings to that truth as a mother clutches her new-born.

The day after her earthly shell passes into the earth, spades break the earth in Uganda and the construction of her school begins. As her body lies beside the remains of her beloved Grandma, just across from her Granny's grave, the school rises quickly and is soon completed. The original fundraising target for the school was £70,000, an amount I scoffed at in disbelief, doubting it could ever be raised. Charlene didn't scoff. The amount of money raised when Charlene leaves this temporary land is nearly £120,000.

More and more money flows in as people give generously in the aftermath of Charlene's leaving, and her legacy lives on, flowing outward from Maya in Uganda. In addition to the well for the community which is completed a month after her death, teacher's accommodation is built for the teachers working at Hidden Treasure. And we know Charlene has many more dreams, leaving fresh visions and challenges in her journals that will keep us occupied for years to come. Her story has not ended.

The weeks and months that follow are hard, harder than any of us could ever have imagined. Knowing where she is and how God has used her life to craft a beautiful picture does not make our loss any easier to bear. We still feel incomplete. We stumble through the next few months, operating on a day by day survival basis. Some days things seem easier, as if we are starting to heal. Other days it is as if the scab has been ripped off and we bleed afresh and it as if we are back beside her as she passes from our world to the next.

Painting done at Hidden Treasure by Wendy, one of Charlene's Primary School teachers

The project continues to raise money and gather followers and supporters. The work in Uganda has not suddenly stopped – indeed the school has risen from the ground with exceptional speed and craftsmanship. The children are being taught in their new school and clean water is available in the community for the first time ever, but there are still many vulnerable children and community needs that Charlene would want us to impact. Charlene's Project will continue to make a difference in the community.

(Charlene's Project Newsletter)

The nights are hardest. Many nights I lie unable to sleep, my heart heavy in my chest and choked with sorrow so thick I feel it will smother me. When sleep mercifully pulls me into her embrace I sometimes dream that we are together again. The sun blazes down on us as we run together and I laugh as I chase

Charlene around and around in game after game. I feel happy again. But when I wake the great weight that has been lifted from my mind comes crushing down again as reality takes me and refuses to release her grip.

Other nights I wake in a cold sweat with horrifying dreams of losing other members of my family. On those nights I lie with my fear choking me and drowning in the endless agony of silence, desperately begging God not to steal any of my family from me, until dawn's rays spill through my curtain to pool on the floor and another day begins.

Christmas crawls slowly by with all its painful memories of the Nativity plays, the snowball fights and the blackouts. A thick layer of snow falls, reminding us of New Year the year before, and our hopes then for the year to come. January slides by, then February, March. Times are hard, but we are supported by one another and by good friends who are by our side constantly. We are overwhelmed by the kindness of friends and of strangers, by food brought to our house, by letters and cards written, by friends who sit with us and listen when we are at our lowest, by prayers from those around us.

We sit and remember, laughing and crying over memories, piecing together Charlene's life and discerning the impact it has wrought on us forevermore. We remember her spirit. We remember her fight. We remember her bad times. We remember her good times. And in all of this we talk, pouring out our joys, pains, regrets and precious memories into a pool, healing together and drawing comfort from what has gone before and what will come in the future.

Some days I am afraid I will forget; that memories now sharp will dull with time, that they will gather dust and fade with the relentless tide of time washing over them. I am scared that I will forget aspects of her face, the way she smiled, the way her eyes would crease as she laughed. Some days I retreat more and more into the deceptive refuge of my crystallised memories.

Many days I feel a pain and numbness descend on me, like a barbed wire twisting around my chest, compounded by a complete inability to do anything to relieve the weight building on my shoulders. My sisters are the same and I worry about them. So often I leave my thoughts unspoken to be the false idol of strength for them. We all struggle in our own ways, sometimes opening up to each other but sometimes nursing our mortal wounds in private.

It is hard. In an instant we have lost a sister, a daughter, an integral part of our identity and our worlds will never be the same again. 'Normal' is gone forever, and a new 'normal' begins. Even though Charlene's decline was slow, her death seemed to come so suddenly and none of us had really been prepared. We learn how to adjust together.

It is the little things. When we are out together as a family it is noticeable that someone is missing. There is now a seat free in the car. When describing my family to strangers I catch myself saying I have five sisters, and have to start again. The girls do not hear her yells anymore at hockey games. A chair sits empty at the dinner table.

But we are truly not alone. God is faithful in all of this, and while we grieve we grieve knowing we will see her again. God's promises in His Word speak to our hearts, and we remember that through her life, through her illness, and through her death, so many people have been blessed, so many hearts touched. We are truly caught up in a greater, more beautiful story than we could ever comprehend.

> *And I am convinced that nothing can ever separate us from God's love. Neither death nor life, neither angels or demons, neither our fears for today nor our worries about tomorrow – not even the powers of hell can separate us from God's love. No power in the sky above or in the earth below – indeed, nothing in all creation will ever be able to separate us from the love of God that is revealed in Christ Jesus our Lord.*

Romans 8:38-39

We visit her final resting place at key times, praying and remembering. We are encouraged by the inscription on a nearby gravestone, bearing the words, "Until the dawn comes and the shadows flee away." We cling to the beautiful words from Revelation describing the end of time which cause us to tear up every time we read them aloud:

> *I heard a loud shout from the throne, saying, "Look, God's home is now among his people! He will live with them, and they will be his people. God himself will be with them. He will wipe every tear form their eyes, and there will be no more death or sorrow or crying or pain. All these things are gone forever.*

Revelation 21:3-4

Charlene is nominated for the Spirit of Northern Ireland Awards, a ceremony we attend together in May. It is an incredible night, hearing inspiring stories of individuals who have sacrificed so much and served others in such staggering ways. There Charlene's story is also told, and we are humbled when she wins the overall award. As my family stands together on the stage we are nearly overcome. Her legacy lives on.

Pictured with The Priests, the family accept the Spirit of NI Award on behalf of Charlene

An inspiration to many, an angel of blessing to all,
Beautiful and tender-hearted, a girl who heeded her Master's call,
You poured yourself out despite your pain,
The difference you made was huge not small.

You found jewels in the dark and passed them on in heartfelt compassion,
You gave away love like it was going out of fashion,
Just like Jesus, you were his hands and feet,
A bright star twinkling and flashing.

In your short life you accomplished so much more than some three times your age,
With the broken, hurting and poor you did so wilfully engage,
Unlocking burdens through Jesus,
Seeking to free many from their pain filled cage.

You've gone to your reward now, sweet, godly Charlene,
Safe with Jesus, totally healed,
Skipping about in pastures green,
May others from your legacy crown,
Jesus as King and by his blood be made clean.

(Poem by Joanne Peden)

242

29
THE JOURNEY HOME

AS THE SUMMER APPROACHES we book flights to Uganda, to visit and work in the school Charlene has built. The official opening is scheduled for then, a time we had once hoped would be the occasion when Charlene, fresh from transplant, would again embark for Uganda. This has of course not come to pass, and as a result our thoughts are mixed as we prepare to head in August. Some close family friends who have walked the road with us come along on our trip.

We arrive and it is hard. On the plane there is no need for oxygen tanks for a small determined girl. There is no need for us to carry a wheelchair. There is no return for a brave fighter to the same bed she slept in three years previously as her life was transformed by the seeds planted in her heart.

Times are still good however. We visit our driver's family one day, getting a picture printed for him with his family, a small gift which means the world to him. We practice singing songs for our visit to the church on Sunday, with some eventually deciding to mouth silently in the back row when the time comes. And we look forward to meeting the community again, awaiting the day of the official opening with a strange mix of longing and dread.

And so we return to where this story started. With us travelling on a small bus, the sweat dripping down our faces as we approach the school for the official opening, filled with a mix of joy at seeing Charlene's legacy, but also trepidation and grief with the knowledge that she is no longer with us to see it. But as the bus carefully crawls up the dirt path towards the school, and the strong brick building built to replace the wooden shack rises before us, a concrete testament to what Charlene has achieved, all of our hearts swell within us and the agony evaporates.

It is a carnival atmosphere, with the community dressed in their best, gathered under a canopy that has been set up for the day to provide shelter from the beating sun. Crowds of children, some dressed in their Hidden Treasure uniforms, scramble and run alongside the bus as it parks, jumping, waving and laughing. Their joy is infectious, and we realise today is not a day of mourning. It is a day of rejoicing, and Charlene would be disgusted with us if it were ever any other way. We pile out of the bus all at once, and lift smiling, happy children into our arms, holding them close and laughing with them, as if they were Charlene's children. And as we dance and shake hand after hand, moving towards the heart of the community gathered in the shade of the new school building, we know the truth. Charlene is here and always will be in so

Time together before the official opening with all the pupils

many ways. And her story is not over. Because she is part of a bigger story, one that will never end. She is a part of God's story and His work on this desperate and lost planet.

Janice stands with her arm near shaken off as hand after eager hand is flung in her direction, and she cannot restrain the smile lighting up her face like a beacon. It is a blessing to see the pupils at Hidden Treasure scamper across the ground before the new building, and a joy to see the community come together in celebration. So much of her also longs for her daughter by her side. Charlene who never believed she could be used by God and always underestimated herself. She wishes Charlene could see the clear evidence of God's hand over her life - that she could be here.

She feels a gentle tug at her sleeve and looks down to see an eager face looking up at her. She is a young girl, scarcely more than eight. As she stands there she sways from side to side. By her hip she holds a baby who must only be around 6 months old. The baby stares up also, eyes drinking in the sights around her.

As Janice bends down and shakes the young girl's hand, the girl seems tentative. "I am Janice; it is lovely to meet you. Is that your sister you are taking care of?" The young girl's eyes dart around her, and she bites her lip nervously, but eventually the young girl plucks up her courage and looks deep into Janice's eyes.

"It is a pleasure to meet you Mrs. Janice," she murmurs shyly. "I wanted you to meet my little sister. We named her after your child. My sister's name is Charlene."

All the hustle and bustle, the laughter and the music, the sights, sounds and smells around her fade away for now. For this beautiful moment all that Janice can register are these beautiful children before her. As Janice looks deep into the brown eyes of the little baby named Charlene, cradled in her sister's protective arms, she thinks of her own Charlene. In those deep brown pools Janice can see her own daughter's eyes, and images flash through her mind one after the other. She sees Charlene waddling into the hospital office the first time they met. She sees her sprinting after her brother and sisters in the garden, determination lining every fibre of her small frame. She sees her in her little red dress the day of the adoption. She sees her on her first day of school, so proud and so excited. She sees her in her hospital bed with the whole family around her, as they share pizza and laughter together, trading stories.

Her heart constricts with sorrow that Charlene cannot be here, but instantly it swells with joy as she knows Charlene is here in spirit. As the wide eyes of the Charlene before her drink in everything she sees, gurgling excitedly, she knows part of Charlene will forever be here in Uganda.

Swallowing her tears Janice reaches out. "You are both absolutely beautiful.

Cutting the cake at the opening

Thank you for introducing me to Charlene; you are such a good big sister. Can I hold her?"

The speeches are beautiful and there are a number of choirs who come and sing and dance in celebration, including the school choir. All the community eat a meal that has been prepared for the day and the school children devour it quickly. A cake is brought out, and after our parents cut it my sisters distribute it among the crowds.

Later Mum and Dad move towards the entrance of the school, where a bright red ribbon is coiled over the steps up to the stone building. Mum is given a pair of scissors and as crowds cheer she cuts the ribbon and it falls to the ground, parting and allowing the crowds behind Mum and Dad to flow up the steps behind them.

A plaque is unveiled outside the school, bearing an inscription dedicated to Charlene:

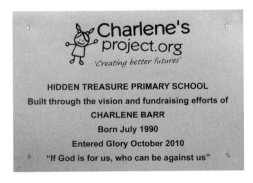

One of the moments chosen to mark the day and commemorate Charlene is the planting of two mango trees. They are to be planted in front of the main entrance to the school, with the plan being that they would grow as the school grew, and the sweet mangos that grow from it each year will symbolise the fruit from Charlene's service to God. Truly a testament to Jesus' words, "Truly, truly, I say to you, unless a grain of wheat falls into the earth and dies, it remains alone; but if it dies, it bears much fruit." Charlene's death, both to her past pains and her physical death, have brought true life, both to her, and to so many others, more than she ever knew in this life.

Mum and Dad plant one of these trees. It is bedlam, with children crowding around from all sides as they plant it. As with many memories this moment is poignant.

It is a bittersweet moment as Janice drops the sapling into the ground and scoops soil around it. All she can see are hundreds of feet around her as everyone clamours for a view. She takes a moment to stare at the soil scattered across her fingers and the seedling valiantly fighting to push its head out of the ground, and from the corner of her eye a pair of shoes catches her gaze. Standing beside her now as she plants this tree in memory of her daughter is a small Ugandan child. The child is gazing down at her with big brown eyes, just like Charlene's. The child smiles timidly, drinking in the sight of Charlene's mother and the small tree she has planted that pushes stubbornly through the soil. The child is wearing a pair of Charlene's shoes. All of Charlene's clothes have been brought out and distributed to the community she loved. Now Janice can see Charlene's shoes, adorning the feet of a Ugandan pupil at the school God has built through Charlene.

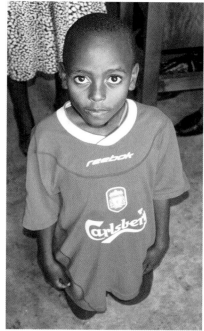

Rispus receives Charlene's Liverpool jersey

As she stands with tears prickling her eyes, she can see that many of the pupils are wearing clothes that had once belonged to Charlene. This is just as she would have wanted it. Truly, Charlene is present in Uganda that day, in deeper ways than we can ever comprehend.

We finish the day with celebrations, with singing and dancing until night begins to fall. We hear Ugandan songs and teach Irish ones. We try to learn Ugandan dances much to the mirth of our Ugandan teachers.

Over the next few days we work hard and are blessed.

Friendships are made at Hidden Treasure, forged through the events of the past and tempered in the ten days we spend together. We are blessed in so many ways and grow to further love the community where part of Charlene will always reside. Our fates have been tied from long ago in ways we will never understand until we one day see the bigger tapestry. We are stunned when we hear stories of how long they have prayed for the building of the school, and how little they knew that as they prayed God was raising up a small child thousands of miles away to answer their prayers.

I knew you before I formed you in your mother's womb. Before you were
born I set you apart and appointed you as my spokesperson to the world.
Jeremiah 1:5

(Underlined in Charlene's Bible)

It is hard to say goodbye, but we know we will be back. As we get onto the bus I look back towards the school God has raised up through a little child who had seemed small in the eyes of the world. Left at birth and inflicted with a disease that ate away at her, He had chosen her specifically, worked within her heart, walked hand in hand with her and used her to bless a community and answer prayers prayed thousands of miles away in Uganda. Back home had only been half the story. Here was the other half. As I take the last step onto the bus to travel back to our lodgings to pack, I look at the mural painted on the wall of the school. The painted smiling faces on it stare out at us as we leave, bearing Charlene's favourite verse below it, and now we know those verses' truth deeply. If God is for us, who can be against us?

"For I know the plans I have for you," declares the LORD, "plans to prosper
you and not to harm you, plans to give you hope and a future." – Jeremiah
29:11

This verse is amazing, it assures us that God knows the plans that He has
for each and every one of us individually and that we have to trust Him.
He also assures us in this verse that the plans He has for us are plans for
good and not for disaster. This can be hard, especially when something bad
happens, it is so easy to blame God. What we instead must do is seek God's
strength to get us through those tough times and He will see you through.
Course things don't always happen the way WE want and God takes us
a completely different route than we wanted to go in our lives. How often
though has that happened and when you look back we see that our own
original plan totally wouldn't have worked and yet the path God took you
down was the best thing ever. We just need to learn to trust Him.

(Charlene's Journal)

Some days are still hard. I wish I could have written another ending, the one we all toiled and hoped for. Some days the pain is fresh and dark emotions threaten to swallow you up and never relent their vice-like grip on your heart.

But for every one of those days there are many days where we see a small glimpse of the bigger picture, of the thing of beauty he has created from Charlene's life. And drawing comfort from one another, we look to the future and remember the deep truth that this story is not over. Charlene lived her life as part of God's story, and because of that her story will never end. We will see her once again. And when that day comes, this story will have been but the introductory line, in the opening paragraph, of the prologue to a beautiful story in the library of awe-inspiring stories God has redeemed and woven into a masterpiece.

The rest of that story is still to be written, and Charlene lives on long beyond her years trapped on the surface of an unforgiving planet. Her challenge lives on. But we all know that soon we will see her again and all to the glory of the God who walked with her every step of the way. If God is for us, who can ever, ever be against us?

There are many rooms in my Father's home, and I am going to prepare a place for you. If this were not so, I would tell you plainly. When everything is ready, I will come and get you, so that you will always be with me where I am. And you know where I am going and how to get there. John 14:2-4

(Underlined in Charlene's Bible)

PERSONAL REFLECTIONS

I HAVE THOUGHT A LOT ABOUT CHARLENE since she passed into the real world. We all have. I have said already nearly all that I plan to say but I want to reflect on some of my personal thoughts that have tumbled out of my mind even as I have written; I hope you allow me these final reflections. Forgive any of my clumsy turns of phrase and lines of thinking if you can. As I review all that I have written the conclusions that tumble onto the page before me are Christian ones. I believe the real story here is about God and His love rather than Charlene.

As I have thought a lot about my sister, about her life, about her adoption, about her love four key things shine through more than any others as I have written.

1 Charlene's adoption resonates with my understanding of God's love for us. Charlene was chosen by my family and became flesh and blood to us, a child of my parents and a sister to all of us. The formal adoption was a mere piece of paper; she had become one of us long before, just as we become sons and daughters of God when we accept Jesus' sacrifice. Even in our darkest days, when the relationship was costing everything and inflicting terrible scars upon Charlene and all of us, she was still our sister, and Mum and Dad's daughter. Charlene would always be a Barr, always be one of us, no matter what she did, as the relationship did not depend on her or on her behaviour or her ability to measure up to a certain standard. She was adopted into our family on a permanent basis.

The same is true with respect to our relationship with God. He loves us more than we can ever comprehend. If we choose to follow Him and accept His sacrifice we are adopted once and for all, we become sons and daughters of God. And this relationship is not dependant on our ability to measure up and appear worthy of it, it is pure grace: pure extravagant, costly and painful love from God. As in Charlene's favourite passage in Romans, nothing can separate us from the love of God through Christ.

Charlene's struggle to accept love is very similar to the struggle within each one of us. Within us, if we are Christians, a war is waged, with part of us wanting to live selflessly, do good and to follow God with an undivided heart. Yet equally entwined around our hearts like a snake rages a side of us we hope no-one else ever sees. A side that thinks only of self, that would walk over everyone, that desires all that is dark within the world, a side of us that is in love with the things that would totally destroy us. Light and darkness cast in opposition. Charlene knew that battle more than most, but we all know it if we are honest with ourselves.

Romans 7 captures this perfectly and could have been penned by Charlene herself.

So the trouble is not with the law, for it is spiritual and good. The trouble is with me, for I am all too human, a slave to sin. I don't really understand myself, for I want to do what is right, but I don't do it. Instead, I do what I hate. But if I know that what I am doing is wrong, this shows that I agree that the law is good. So I am not the one doing wrong; it is sin living in me that does it.

And I know that nothing good lives in me, that is, in my sinful nature. I want to do what is right, but I can't. I want to do what is good, but I don't. I don't want to do what is wrong, but I do it anyway. But if I do what I don't want to do, I am not really the one doing wrong; it is sin living in me that does it.

I have discovered this principle of life—that when I want to do what is right, I inevitably do what is wrong. I love God's law with all my heart. But there is another power within me that is at war with my mind. This power makes me a slave to the sin that is still within me. Oh, what a miserable person I am! Who will free me from this life that is dominated by sin and death? Thank God! The answer is in Jesus Christ our Lord. So you see how it is: In my mind I really want to obey God's law, but because of my sinful nature I am a slave to sin.

Romans 9:7-25

Charlene's story echoes this wonderful story of redemption. Those who accept what God has done for them and follow Him are adopted into His family, as sons and daughters of God. Even in that situation however, we lash out, one second praising Him, the next cursing Him and those He has created with the very same lips. We are schizophrenic, inconsistent and hypocritical. But most of all we are all too human, tragically fallen.

But there is a glorious answer. The cost of unconditional love is borne by God not by us. But that does not negate the cost or the pain our fickleness inflicts on the One who came to save us.

Charlene, eventually, accepted love, and was transformed by it and through her others were transformed also. We must equally learn to accept God's love and realise the freedom that comes from the relationship not being dependant on our efforts, as the cost has already been paid. We must equally be sobered, being aware of the pain we inflict on God who bears all the cost out of His love for us so that we will never have to pay that penalty of our hard hearts.

2   Even possibly more importantly, Charlene's story only makes sense as part of a bigger story. If Charlene's story ended in her death it would have been transient, tragic and bittersweet. Incredible and beautiful yes, but still ultimately tragic. After all that had been done through her and her valiant fight against all the odds, she was ultimately defeated by the disease that ate at her, and her life was brought to a premature end, with her fading from life forever.

However, Charlene believed this was not the end. Charlene's story did not end with her death, because she is part of a bigger story, one we can all be a part of if we so choose. Charlene chose not to live for wealth, prestige or her own glory, transient lies that dull our soul's eyes and whisper cruel false promises of meaning and satisfaction. Instead, she chose to be a part of the work God is doing on this earth. She chose to be a willing participant in His rescue and redemption of all people, calling all people into a restoration of their purpose in existing – to be in relationship with their Creator.

This story goes on long after any of us pass from this temporary land to where our real lives await us. We can choose to live for ourselves in stories that may shine for a time, but ultimately end tragically. Or instead our story can be written within His story that goes on forever and will never end. We can choose to stop trying to write our own story, and let Him mould our story into His story. Charlene gloriously chose the latter, and because of that we will see her again. We are all caught up in a story, this is not something we can avoid. The question however is what story do we find ourselves in?

Live a life filled with love for others, following the example of Christ, who loved you and gave himself as a sacrifice to take away your sins. And God was pleased, because that sacrifice was like sweet perfume to him. Ephesians 5:2

(Underlined in Charlene's Bible)

3   It is so hard to see the bigger picture when we are caught up in the hurricane of life. It is only in retrospect we can look back and see where everything begins to fit together in Charlene's life. It seems clear to me in reflection that Charlene was chosen at birth, even arguably before birth, and every step, from her struggle to accept love to her battle against her illness, she was shaped and prepared for the work she would do in Uganda, helping and saving people who had prayed faithfully for years for such a thing.

At the time we saw none of this. As Charlene hurt those I loved I did not know why. As Charlene lay sick with the disease that would drive her to build a school in Uganda I raged at God. But I could not see the bigger canvas. Just as you cannot appreciate a masterpiece when you stand an inch away, I could not see the bigger narrative, the bigger picture when I was up close.

As each day melts into another we do not have the time or indeed the desire to stop and think of where we are going, and where all of our lives fit into the bigger picture. What type of story are we in? In the midst of life's pain, tragedy and madness this can be a hard question to answer.

Many times in the story of Charlene's brief sojourner on this side of eternity, if you had no knowledge of what was to come, you may have wanted to stop living it, to stop reading it. It was too painful, too agonising. Why were these things happening? To what purpose? The story appeared to make no sense.

However in the present we can rarely tell where our stories are going when we are caught in their midst. It is only as we take a step back and allow God to craft the story, trusting Him, that the story makes sense, perhaps only when we arrive on the other side of the veil. Because none of our stories are our own and they only make sense in light of God's big story.

This tale has been a journey and I know it is not at an end. Charlene had such big plans, her legacy remains here and in Uganda, not least of all in her challenge and impact on all of us.

4 Finally, Charlene's life presents a challenge to all of us. I wish I remembered every day how blessed I am to have another day to live, having so many advantages Charlene never had. But I would be lying if I were to say I remembered. Instead my gaze turns ever more depressingly inward and to the bright lights of the world around me.

But when I am hit by a memory and clarity falls like a bucket of cold water over me, I realise that life is so pathetically short. The question we all should ask ourselves is; what are we doing with it? What are we living for? Charlene made her choice and it is one we all face daily. Will we choose our immediate pleasures and temporary satisfactions in an attempt to titillate ourselves and stave off boredom and pain? Or will we instead choose to walk the often painful road and strive to live for things that will outlast us, spending ourselves in service to our Creator and others?

If you try to hang on to your life you will lose it.
But if you give up your life for my sake, you will find it.

Matthew 16:25

It is a daily choice and one I struggle with, more often than not choosing David Barr over Jesus Christ. But every day presents new mercies: a new opportunity and a new question. What then shall you live for? And who then shall you serve?

As I have said Charlene's journey continues. Charlene had big dreams, and God's plans extend far beyond her.

*... if God is for us, who can be against us? **

Romans 8:31

---

* This was Charlene's favourite Bible verse

EPILOGUE

OVER TWO HUNDRED AND FIFTY UGANDAN CHILDREN
now attend Hidden Treasure Primary School in Maya just
outside Kampala. Many of these children are now sponsored
by supporters here at home in Ireland, who encourage them by
writing letters to them. The sponsorship money allows the school
to run and provides food for the children, as well as providing
help to the families and community in Maya as a whole. A
second school, Kahara Primary School, in Western Uganda has
become the second school supported through Charlene's Project.
Like Hidden Treasure the community there now has clean water
through a bore hole that has been sunk near the school. Teams
are visiting regularly from Ireland and now from USA delivering
educational, sports and humanitarian programmes. Relationships
continue to be developed. Charlene had written down many
hopes and dreams in her journals about what she planned to do
in Uganda and beyond. Through Charlene's Project her family
and friends are committed to continue the work that Charlene
had started.

The seeds that this young girl planted during her light walk across
the face of this planet are already producing a wonderful harvest.
Praise be to God.

For more information on the ongoing work of Charlene's Project
see **www.charlenesproject.org** and
www.facebook.com/charlenesproject

*"I have one life and one chance to make it count for something...
My faith demands that I do whatever I can, wherever I am,
whenever I can, for as long as I can with whatever I have
to try to make a difference."*

– Jimmy Carter

Thank you for reading Chosen –
I hope you have been encouraged by Charlene's story.

More information is available at Charlene's Project website at
www.charlenesproject.org

If you would like to support Charlene's Project
in any way or if you would like to book a speaker
contact Janice Barr at 07709-806418
or info@charlenesproject.org

Charlene's Project is Registered with the
Charity Commission for N.I. NIC: 100589.